I Have Found God

Complete Works

VOLUME I

COMPLETE WORKS
OF
ELIZABETH OF THE TRINITY

Centenary Edition
(1880–1980)
in three volumes

I
Major Spiritual Writings

II
Letters From Carmel

III
Diary—Personal Notes
Letters of Her Youth—Poems

Edition produced, presented, and annotated
by Conrad De Meester, Carmelite

Elizabeth of the Trinity
Carmelite

I Have Found God

Complete Works
VOLUME I

General Introduction
Major Spiritual Writings

Translated by Sister Aletheia Kane, O.C.D.

ICS Publications
Institute of Carmelite Studies
Washington, D.C.

I HAVE FOUND GOD, COMPLETE WORKS I—MAJOR SPIRITUAL WRITINGS
is a translation of Elisabeth de la Trinité,
J'ai trouvé Dieu, Oeuvres Complètes, Tome 1 / A
(Les Éditions du Cerf, 1980)
Copyright © by Washington Province of
Discalced Carmelites, Inc. 1984, 2014

ICS Publications
2131 Lincoln Road NE
Washington, DC 20002-1199
www.iscpublications.org

Typeset and printed in the U.S.A.

Photos used with permission of Dijon Carmel (Dijon-Flavignerot)

Library of Congress Cataloging-in-Publication Data

Elisabeth de la Trinité, soeur, 1880–1906.
   Complete works of Elizabeth of the Trinity.

   Elisabeth de la Trinité, soeur, 1880–1906.
   Complete works of Elizabeth of the Trinity.

   Includes bibliographical references.
   Contents: v. 1 General Introduction. Major spiritual writings.
   1. Spiritual life—Catholic authors—Collected works.
   I. Title.
   BX2350.A1E45 1984   271'.971'0024   84-3748
   ISBN-10   0-935216-01-4 (v. 1)
   ISBN-13   978-0-935216-01-1

TABLE OF CONTENTS

Foreword 1
Biographical Sketch 7

GENERAL INTRODUCTION

Prophet of God 21
Elizabeth's Thought on Her Posthumous Mission 28
    A Visible Mediation   30

The "Circular" and the "Souvenirs" 32
    The *Circular*   32.
    The Preparation of the *Souvenirs*   34
    The Contribution of the *Souvenirs*   36
    The Diffusion of the *Souvenirs*   40

A "Doctrinal" and "Spiritual" Approach
to the "Complete" Works 41
    The Collection of the Writings in
      View of the Beatification   41
    Père Philipon's Book   42
    Evaluation   44
    Towards the "Complete Works"   48

The Autographs and Their Origin 50
    Inventory   50
    Letters Preserved and Letters Lost   51
    The Writing of Letters in Carmel   53
    The Poverty of the Paper   55

The Dating of the Letters 57
    Reference Points   58
    Her Writing   60

Our Options for Establishing the Text.................... 63
    Spelling Errors   64
    The Punctuation   66
    The Capital Letters   67
    Other Conventions   68

Elizabeth and the Influences to Which She Was Exposed... 68
    Père Vallée   69
    Elizabeth's Originality   71
    Testimony   72

MAJOR SPIRITUAL WRITINGS

I Heaven In Faith

Introduction... 85
Text... 94

II The Greatness of Our Vocation

Introduction... 121
Text... 124

III Last Retreat

Introduction... 131
Text... 141

IV Let Yourself Be Loved

Introduction... 175
Text... 179

Prayer: "O My God, Trinity Whom I Adore"................ 183
Annotations.. 184

ABBREVIATIONS

ACD   Archives of the Carmel of Dijon.

AL   *Elisabeth ou l'Amour est là*, by C. De Meester (cf. Foreword).

Ang   *The Book of the Visions and Instructions of Blessed Angela di Foligno*, DDB, 1895, third ed.

CE   Composition Exercises, of Elizabeth of the Trinity, in PAT

Circ   *Obituary Circular of Elizabeth of the Trinity* (1906).

Exc   Excursions in the Jura, of Elizabeth of the Trinity, in PAT.

GV   *The Greatness of Our Vocation*, Major Spiritual Writing II.

HA   *Histoire d'une Ame* (Story of a Soul), of Thérèse of Lisieux.

HF   *Heaven in Faith*, Major Spiritual Writing I.

D   *Diary.*

L   *Letters.*

LF   *The Living Flame of Love*, by St. John of the Cross, in *Life and Works* . . .,Paris, Oudin, 1892, third ed., Volume IV.

LL   *Let Yourself Be Loved*, Major Spiritual Writing IV.

LR   *Last Retreat*, Major Spiritual Writing III.

P   *Poems.*

PA   Procès apostolique (Apostolic Process) followed by the number of the paragraph in the Summarium of the cause of beatification of Elizabeth.

PAT *Elisabeth de la Trinité. Paroles, annotations personnelles et premiers témoins oculaires* (cf. Foreword).

PN   *Personal Notes.*

PO   Procès de l'Ordinaire (Bishop's Process). (Cf. PA).

PS   Philipon Survey, in PAT.

RB   Récit biographique (Biographical account), in PAT.

Ru   *Rusbrock l'Admirable* (Oeuvres choisies), Paris, Perrin, 1902.

S   *Soeur Elisabeth de la Trinité. Souvenirs*, Carmel of Dijon, first edition of 1909.

SC   *Spiritual Canticle*, by St. John of the Cross (cf. LF).

SRD *Semaine religieuse de Dijon* (revue).

The number which follows the abbreviation refers, for Elizabeth's writings, to the paragraph numbers of this *Complete Works*; but, for the other books, to the *page*, except for PA and PO (cf. *supra*).

ACKNOWLEDGEMENT

It is with pleasure that I acknowledge my indebtedness to all those who have helped me in any way in the preparation of this volume:

to Fr. Conrad de Meester, O.C.D.,
for his brotherly encouragement;

to Fr. Adrian J. Cooney, O.C.D.,
for his careful work in reading and editing the manuscript;

and to my sisters of Lafayette Carmel
who made helpful suggestions and came to my aid.

Sr. Aletheia Kane, O.C.D.

Foreword

We joyfully present to our Christian brothers and sisters the writings of Elizabeth of the Trinity, which appear here for the first time in their entirety.

Doubtless history will be surprised when it verifies that three-quarters of a century was necessary since the death of this great contemplative on November 9, 1906, for the integral publication of her works to be realized. Her desire to remain "hidden in God" has been well served by the vicissitudes of time!

And it was only pure Chance—a word which since then I gladly write with a capital letter—which led us to consider this edition, happily favored by the coincidence of the centenary of Elizabeth's birth on July 18, 1880.

Certainly Elizabeth of the Trinity is already known, perhaps more so abroad than in France. Since 1909 the *Souvenirs*, her first biography written by her prioress, has experienced a wide diffusion and has been translated many times. One of her prayers *O My God, Trinity Whom I Adore* is loved and recited almost everywhere in the world. Large extracts from her writings have been published, and Elizabeth has already taken her place among the classic authors of the Experience of God.

But this edition, of which the greater part of the texts has never been published, and which has benefited from ample information, has the good fortune to present to us Elizabeth's whole personality. Alongside her most sublime features, her lofty praises of the divine Mystery, we hear the rich harmonies of her other keyboard, her whole humanity. The somewhat blurred halo which surrounded Elizabeth like that of a medieval saint gradually comes into focus.

This winner of the first prize in piano at the Conservatory of Dijon loves to listen to the music of silence, but in her enthusiasm she also loves to communicate its message.

1

Is what she says about her joy in finding God the only reason so many letters from her short life have been kept? Surely there are also other reasons: her inexhaustible human tenderness and her warmth of heart which led each correspondent to believe that he was "the most loved." Those first animated notes to her grandparents, to her father whom she will soon lose, to her mother, already reveal the child's vivacity and sincerity. Later, enchanted by all that is beautiful and noble, by everything that has a certain music, the young girl will feel both dwelt in and possessed by a mysterious Presence which claims her; and this occurred even on trips, at dances or during her piano recitals. Won long ago by Jesus, she experiences his word "more cutting than a two-edged sword" (Heb 4:12).

Her *Diary* and her *Poems* reveal a divided heart as she faced the future. Should she obey the love and demands of her family or answer the call to union and contemplation in the monastery only two hundred meters from her home? Before becoming a Carmelite, Sabeth Catez knew suffering and growth. Already at eighteen she gives herself fully to the present moment and the concrete situation, cost what it may, and through it all she radiates among her wide circle of friends the presence of God which fills her.

It is a great gift from God for Elizabeth, and somewhat unexpected, when after a long delay she can finally devote herself entirely to Jesus and his Church in the Carmel of Dijon. There she will live silently and lovingly as a happy Carmelite. Irresistibly drawn by her faith in the presence of Love within her and by the quest for continual prayer, she sings the praises of the Father, the Word and the Spirit; and she opens herself unconditionally to their life in her. She ardently longs to become for Christ "another humanity in which He can renew His whole Mystery" (PN 15), including conformity on the Cross and participation in his saving work in the world. This officer's daughter loves her "Master" and her sisters so resolutely, so ardently, that this intensity will mature and consume her in less than six years.

Elizabeth's Message Is Not To Be Limited

If she likes to listen, she also likes to express herself! Her letters—that crowd of witnesses!—allow us to follow the flight of
this loving and energetic spirit up to the last days.

The preparation of this edition has convinced us that, thanks
to a much more abundant documentation than we had before,
we can avoid limiting Elizabeth's message in the future. Certainly,
we must emphasize her special graces of recollection and prayer,
of listening to and understanding the word of God. That is her
charism which won for her the love of contemplatives, priests,
and theologians. But now the scope of this charism expands
wide enough to encompass in its light the smallest events of our
daily life, the least encounters with our neighbor, which, like so
many sacraments, reveal God's presence and demonstrate how
we are to give ourselves to Love at each moment. The charism of
Elizabeth of the Trinity goes so far as to show us that the contemplation of the Word is prolonged in the concrete act of the
gift of self. Finally, what makes her so close to us is that she had
to seek God in faith, in a life more hidden and more monoto-
nous than our own. And what makes her so different from us is
not at all that she was the object of so many graces from God but
that she was so terribly logical in her faith in Love present, Love
inviting her.

We must place Elizabeth of the Trinity among those who
have lived fully their faith "as if they had seen the Invisible"
(Heb 11:27) and who have tasted the joy of his Shadow; place
her, in any case, among the anawim! She accepted the rich gifts
with which she was endowed by nature and all the graces that
God lavished upon her with the simplicity of a child who knows
it is deeply loved by its father, overflows with gratitude, and
realizes what its response must be. Clear as light, she radiated
these gifts with an overflowing spontaneity as easily during a
dance as she would later among her sisters of Carmel and in her
letters to numerous lay correspondents. If some have given the
impression of a speculative Elizabeth of the Trinity, a theologian, today let her find her natural place among the simple,
among the poor to whom the Good News was destined first of all

and whose faith is perhaps their only wealth. In the measure
that this spiritual daughter of St. Paul and St. John of the Cross
drew near to God, the simplicity of her gaze of faith guided her
more and more. Her "Master" was not the God of the Philoso-
phers, but He of whom she said when she was dying, using the
key words of John the Evangelist: "I am going to Light, to Love,
to Life"—the answer to our most existential thirsts.

In a noisy world, Elizabeth of the Trinity invites us to create a
silence within us so that we may not live on the margin of the
essential, of the fully human, of the fully divine. She shows us to
what a happy plenitude faith in Love, Who dwells in the inmost
depths of our being, can lead us—wherever we are, whoever we
are or have been.

Our Edition

The concern to make the numerous writings of Elizabeth accessible to all brought up the problem of their presentation. It was
necessary to divide the whole into easily handled volumes. But
should it begin in chronological order with the first writings,
that is, with the letters of her childhood—(however appealing
they might be)? Or with the poetry of the young girl, which has
no properly poetic value but which, read from another point of
view, is revealed as an authentic cry of the heart?

It seemed advisable to us not to listen first to the child Elizabeth. She has to attain to a certain maturity on the level of expression—all the more so as her formal education was very incomplete—before she can fully communicate her experience to
us. Later, profit can be found in discovering the growth of the life
of God in the young musician's soul. (The chronological indications that mark the texts allow for reading the documents in the
order in which they were written if one should wish to do so.)

We were hoping (and the Foreword of Volume III bears witness to this) to content ourselves with two volumes, but the demands of criticism, of history, and of spiritual exegesis caused
the size of our General Introduction and the annotations to
grow beyond our desires. Our editor judged that it was better to
divide the first volume into two separate books that would be

easier to handle as works of meditation. Also a lower price would allow separate purchases at intervals.

Volume I contains, after a Biographical Sketch and the General Introduction, the four *Major Spiritual Writings* composed by Elizabeth at the end of her life.

Volume II assembles all the *Letters* written *from Carmel*. There is also an index of names, as well as biblical and other references for the whole of the *Complete Works*. (This is the place where it will be the most useful.)

Volume III groups together the *Diary*, the *Personal Notes* written during the course of her life, the *Letters of her Youth* (1882–1901), and all her *Poems*.

On the margin of this edition, but closely linked to it, we will soon publish two other works. The first is entitled *Elizabeth of the Trinity: Sayings, Personal Annotations and the First Eyewitness Testimonies*; it is in a sense a dossier on Elizabeth containing all the papers necessary for the understanding and study of this great mystic. The second, entitled *Elizabeth, or Love is There*, does not claim to be a reading guide to the *Complete Works*, but simply a spiritual commentary and a companion on the way. Having traveled Elizabeth's itinerary many times, we will draw attention to the most important stages and to some noteworthy points of view.

These editions will surely arouse new discoveries, great and small, relating to Elizabeth's life and writings. With a view to improving our work, we invite the reader to share them with the Carmelites of Dijon at their new home in Flavignerot.*

We entrust this integral work on Elizabeth to every friend who is seeking God. It was no little labor but the happiness of the friendship which brought about this edition was doubled by our joy in meeting a prophet of the presence of God, one of the race of saints! We sense in her the Fire of the Spirit. May a spark from this Fire fly into the hearts of many of our brothers and sisters who read this book.

Conrad De Meester, O.C.D.

*Address: Carmelites of Dijon, Flavignerot, 21160, Marsannay-la-Côte. The Monastery is 13 km. southwest of Dijon (near Corcelles-les-Monts). One can visit Sister Elizabeth's cell, which has been transferred there, as well as a small museum where many souvenirs are preserved.

At the end of this foreword I would like to express my deepest
thanks to:

Mother Marie-Lucie, Mother Marie-Michelle, and all my sisters of Dijon Carmel for their entire confidence and their
friendly, joyous, and prayerful hospitality;

Jacques and Jeanne Lonchampt whose friendship made our
long and intense collaboration a lifelong memory;

my brother, Bernard Bro, O.P., who greatly encouraged me;

my sisters of the Oudenaarde Carmel and the Secular Institute
of Notre Dame du Carmel (Ghent) for their invaluable material and spiritual help;

my superiors and religious brothers of Kortrijk who gave me the
necessary leisure and whom I thank in the person of Raymond Hoornaert, mentioning in particular his photographic work for these editions;

all those who willingly answered my requests for information
and whom I will cite further on (cf. p. 79);

Mgr. Albert Decourtray, Bishop of Dijon, for all the interest he
showed in this edition;

his collaborators, priests, religious and lay people whom I met
and of whom I can name here only Pierre Chevignard,
Peter Fletcher, and that unforgettable brother, André
Jouffroy, Chaplain of Carmel.

Together let us thank the Lord for having given to his Church
the always young Elizabeth Catez who became ever more "of the
Trinity"!

C.D.M.

Biographical Sketch

Up to Her Entrance in Carmel

Roots

On Sunday morning, July 18, 1880, Elizabeth was born at the military camp of Avor in the district of Farges-en-Septaine (Cher), France, where her father, Captain Joseph Catez, of the 8th Squadron of the Equipment and Maintenance Corps, was stationed.

The birth was a difficult one. The two physicians present had already warned the captain that he would lose his first child. The mother suffered greatly for thirty-six hours. But at the end of the Eucharist that Captain Chaboisseau was celebrating for their intentions, little Elizabeth arrived in this world. The child was in good health, "very beautiful, very lively," Mme. Catez would recall. On July 22nd, the feast of St. Mary Magadalene (which would delight the future contemplative), she was baptized.

The parents were no longer young. Joseph Catez was born May 29, 1832, in Aire-sur-la-Lys (Pas-de-Calais), the fourth of seven children of André Cattez [sic] and Fideline Hoel. They were poor; the father was a simple farmhand who could neither read nor write. He died at the age of forty-six when Joseph was eight. The mother died in 1876 at the age of seventy-five.

Joseph, his expression clear and candid, had to make his way in life with the energy and perseverance that will characterize his daughter. At twenty-one he enlisted in the army as a volunteer. For almost nine years he participated in the Algerian campaign, and later in the War of 1870 in which he was taken a prisoner in Sedan. Made a lieutenant in 1872 and captain in 1875, he was stationed at Lunel (Hérault) when he married on September 3, 1879, Marie Rolland, daughter of the retired

Commandant Raymond Rolland of the 7th Regiment of Hussards, who at that time was living in Saint Hilaire (Aude).

Elizabeth's place of origin on her father's side was the Northern region of France. Her mother's family came from the Southern region and from Lorraine. Her grandfather Rolland was born in Pexiora (Aude) in 1811; he entered as a volunteer in the army and in 1842 married Josephine Klein of Lunéville where he was then stationed. It was there that Marie, their only daughter, was born on August 30, 1846. After retiring, M. Rolland settled again as an inspector in his native region.

Marie was a sensitive girl, gifted with an amiability that would win her many friends. Her first fiancé died during the War of 1870. It was a long and deep sorrow. Her diary, part of which remains, shows that she then devoted herself to a serious Christian life, entertained perhaps for a time the idea of a religious vocation, and also suffered periodically from an anguished conscience—rather Jansenistic, say some witnesses.

"A Real Devil"

The Catez remained at the camp of Avor about nine months. Little Elizabeth heard the sound of the bugles, saw the soldiers and the horses. It was there that her father was named Chevalier of the Legion of Honor.

From May 10, 1881, Captain Catez' company was stationed at Auxonne (Côte-d'Or). In a series of letters Mme. Catez speaks of her Elizabeth, the little Burgundian of twenty-one months, "She is a real devil; she is crawling and needs a fresh pair of pants every day." She is also "a big chatterbox"! Such are the earliest reports of the future saint. But there are some which have a more mystical quality. "She went up at the Offertory and kissed the Crucifix; she was throwing kisses to it before she got there." "She not only prays" for her sick grandmother "but she is teaching her doll how to pray; she has just very devoutly made her kneel." We see Elizabeth with her famous Jeanette in photos of this period as a little girl who knows what she wants!

Dijon

A little while after the death of his wife on May 9, 1882, grandfather Rolland came to live with the Catez family. A new change of garrison brought them to Dijon around November 1, 1882. They moved into the Billiet villa on Rue Lamartine near the railroad station at the edge of the countryside. Their friends, the Guémards, were their neighbors. There Marguerite was born on February 20, 1883.

As much as Guite was gentle, so much was Sabeth, the little captain, unruly! But she had a good heart and loved her parents very much. Guite recalled her sister's childhood: she was "very lively, even quick-tempered; she went into rages that were quite terrible; she was a real little devil." Her ardor and her sensitivity did not yet know how to orientate themselves. Her mother speaks of her "furious eyes." Her little friend of a few years later, Marie-Louise Hallo, also the daughter of a military man, recalls her "flashing eyes." But then it was in the context of fervor and warmth.

In the Catez family harmony reigned. Note this phrase from a letter (April 28, 1885) of Mme. Catez to her "good Joseph," perhaps already suffering from heart trouble, who was travelling in the North: "Do not forget my advice; take care of yourself; do not drink too much beer or smoke too many cigars; take care of your health and think of us." Five imperatives in two lines! The wife, who could easily expatiate in her letters also knew how to summarize. Do we perhaps detect between these lines the anxious and domineering temperament of Mme. Catez (the same temperament which can be discerned in Elizabeth's *Diary*) and the lively and sociable side of the Captain, joined to his sense of duty and loyalty?

The letter continues: "The little ones are more or less well-behaved; Elizabeth often thinks and speaks of you; she is counting the days," as witness the few words she wrote to her "little papa" (L 2 and 3). On June 2, 1885, Captain Catez retired.

Rue Prieur

If up to now little Sabeth had known the tears of rage and those
of repentance when she had annoyed her mother—tears which
sprang only from the eyes—soon she would know her first true
sorrows and the tears that well up from the heart.

On January 24, 1887, Raymond Rolland died. He was so
skilled, they tell us, in "the art of being a grandfather". Eight
months later Elizabeth suffered a new grief, and how much
more painful! On Sunday morning, October 2, M. Catez, who
had already had several heart attacks, died rather suddenly.

The three funeral orations do not have much significance.
More revealing is the fact that the official organ of the diocese,
the *Semaine religieuse* of Dijon did not hesitate to give the full
text of Captain Chézelle's speech on this "excellent Christian"
who, according to the writer, was "a very close friend of the
Archpriest of the cathedral" although M. Catez had not lived in
Dijon for very long. *Le Bien public* printed Captain Lafour-
cade's speech.

As her pension was now reduced, Mme. Catez had to leave
the house on Rue Lamartine. She moved with her daughters
and a young domestic servant into the second floor of a house,
which no longer exists, on Rue Prieur-de-la-Côte-d'Or, on the
other side of town.[1] From her window the little Elizabeth could
see an unfamiliar building in a garden: Carmel.

The sudden disappearance of two loved ones and the uproot-
ing from Rue Lamartine must have left the child with a keen
sense of the fragility of life, and must have bound her even closer
to her mother and Guite. The "trio" (this will be her expression
later) were very close but not closed in on themselves. There
were faithful friends, new relationships with those who lived
near their house on Rue Prieur, and annual trips to visit relatives and friends. There was no lack of horizons for the little
Sabeth who, in Dijon, lived near the big Park and the countryside.

Without being rich, Mme. Catez was sufficiently well off to
assure the education of her children. Around the age of seven,
Elizabeth received her first private lessons in French from Mlle.

Grémaux. Probably in order to prepare her for a career as a piano teacher, her mother enrolled her in the Conservatory of Dijon when she was eight. The usual subjects were studied at infrequent intervals, but music held by far the first place: there was the work at the Conservatory; there were courses in common and private lessons, then at home long hours of daily practice.

The death of her father might have tempered the vivacity of the child but, despite that, life resumed its normal course. And so did the "rages." Indeed, Mlle. Grémaux recalled the "iron will" of her little pupil and her already striking recollection in church (for it was Elizabeth's nature always to go to the depths of things), but that should not cause us to disregard her faults. Guite recalled that her sister's rages were sometimes so violent "that they threatened to send her as a boarder to the Good Shepherd [a house of correction that was nearby], and they prepared her little bag."

But Sabeth was also very upright, and when she realized that one must not be a burden to others, she quickly took herself in hand. Witnesses say that her first confession, at the age of seven, visibly engaged her in the struggle against her caprices.

And then, there were so many beautiful qualities in this lovable, generous, and straight-forward heart! Letters 4 and 5 witness, not without a mischievous tone, to her good resolutions and in particular to her efforts not "to get angry." There we also read this sentence of a little girl of nine-and-a-half: " . . . since I hope that I will soon have the happiness of making my first communion, I will be even better behaved for I will pray to God to make me better still" (L 5).

"I Am Not Hungry, Jesus Has Fed Me"

Sixteen months separated her from that day. Elizabeth fervently applied herself to the catechism lessons, which, however, did not prevent her from being sentenced one day by the vicar to kneel with a little friend in the middle of the walk.

What took place in her heart on that April 19, 1891? During Mass and thanksgiving tears of joy flowed down her cheeks. As she left Saint-Michel's she said to Marie-Louise Hallo: "I am not hungry; Jesus has fed me. . . ."

We can guess the intensity of the first encounter with the Body
of Christ from a poem of her youth (P 47) written on the seventh
anniversary of this communion — one of those poems written
only for herself in Jesus' presence as part of her intimate diary.[2]
On the evening of her first communion, in her beautiful white
dress, she went to visit the Mother Prioress of Carmel. Marie of
Jesus explained to her the significance of her Hebrew name:
Elizabeth, that is, the "House of God." The little girl was, and
remained, profoundly impressed by it. That morning she had
felt so strongly that God dwelt within her!

On June 8, 1891, she was confirmed in the Church of Notre
Dame.

Witnesses unanimously emphasize her very noticeable progress in making a gift of herself after her first communion. Gift to
whom? To Jesus: she understood the love that he shows us in his
suffering and death, in his eucharistic presence among men.
Jesus animated her in her inmost depths. Often, when she received communion, tears of joy covered her face. With all her
energy she learned to forget herself for Jesus, for others. Her fits
of anger were lived through and conquered within. She felt won
over by Jesus. She loved to pray.

Around the age of thirteen, her confessor helped her to get
through a painful phase of scruples. The catechesis of that time
surrounded the approach to God with meticulous prescriptions;
the danger of sin threatened on all sides and the just Judge did
not overlook anything!

At fourteen, one day after having received the Body of Christ,
Sabeth Catez felt irresistibly impelled to consecrate her whole life
to him and to make a vow of perpetual virginity. A little later, the
project of the religious life which she had nourished since she was
seven took shape in this word which was spoken to her interiorly:
"Carmel."

Elizabeth-of-the-Big-Feet

But let us not consider only the interior physiognomy of her
whom Canon Angles, a close family friend, remembers as "always at the head of the group." The young girl of fourteen will

herself complete her image in a composition exercise that Mlle. Forey, her new teacher, gave her:

> To draw one's physical and moral portrait is a delicate subject to deal with, but taking my courage in both hands I set to work and begin!
> Without pride I think I can say that my overall appearance is not displeasing. I am a brunette and, they say, rather tall for my age. I have sparkling black eyes and my thick eyebrows give me a severe look. The rest of my person is insignificant. My "dainty" feet could win for me the nickname of Elizabeth of the Big Feet, like Queen Bertha! And there you have my physical portrait!
> As for my moral portrait, I would say that I have a rather good character. I am cheerful and, I must confess, somewhat scatterbrained. I have a good heart. I am by nature a coquette. "One should be a little!" they say. I am not lazy: I know "work makes us happy." Without being a model of patience, I usually know how to control myself. I do not hold grudges. So much for my moral portrait. I have my defects and, alas, few good qualities! I hope to acquire them!
> Well, at last this tedious task is finished and am I glad!"[3]

There are, however, two big lacunae in this charming exercise without complexes. First of all, not a word about her musical talent. She had already won her first prize at piano when she was thirteen; she participated in the concerts the Conservatory organized in town, which were reported in the papers. *Le Progrès de la Côte-d'Or*, for example, wrote on August 8, 1893:

> Mlle. Catez, first prize at the piano, of M. Diétrich's class, received unanimous applause after the *Capriccio Brillant* of Mendelssohn. It was a pleasure to see this young child scarcely thirteen years old come to the piano; she is already a distinguished pianist with an excellent touch, a beautiful tone, and a real musical feeling. A debut like this permits us to base great hopes on this child.

In Letter 7 Elizabeth relates with dignity how the Prize of Excellence was unjustly taken away from her in 1894.

A second and greater lacuna: not a word about what is the flame of this life, the soul of her soul—her love for Jesus. If, obviously, she cannot speak of it in a homework exercise, she will do so freely in the intimate journal of her poems, as in the following few verses that are almost contemporary with the exercise just cited:

> Jesus, my soul desires You,
> I want to be your bride soon.
> With You I want to suffer—
> And to find You, die. (P 4)

"For My Heart is Always with Him"

A mysterious Presence already accompanied her. Few of those close to her realized that her rich vitality was orientated towards another Life: within, without, beyond. A nostalgia for Jesus, for Carmel, for Heaven, filled this young girl of fifteen and sixteen. Then, at seventeen, she discovered the earthly perspectives that this love implied; she accepted her concrete situation and all that caused suffering to her young heart, already animated by a very contemplative desire for oblation, as witnesses, for example, Poem 43.

After her first prize in piano, it would have been necessary for her to go to the Conservatory of Paris to perfect her art. But she took two more years of harmony at the Conservatory of Dijon. Private lessons of general education were intensified, but too late, alas, to bear their fruits. We do not know their frequency, but music continued to take most of her time. At eighteen Elizabeth also studied English, and at this time she found a real enjoyment in sewing lessons as she loved beautiful clothes.

As a daughter of an officer and wife of one, used to moving, Mme. Catez loved to travel. From the age of eight at least, Elizabeth, with her mother and sister, took long trips during the summer vacations. They often went South, where Mme. Catez had spent her youth; there were prolonged sojourns in Saint Hilaire, where the Abbé Angles had been curate for some fifteen years, and at Carlipa, where the Rolland aunts lived. Four times at least the Catez spent their vacations in Lorraine, the Jura, and the Vosges.

In her letters (for example to Alice Chervau, Marie-Louise Maurel, and Françoise de Sourdon), Elizabeth spoke of her en-

thusiasm for the beauty of nature, the mountains and the sea;
she expressed her joy at seeing her friends, at playing tennis and
croquet, of joining in musical sessions. Everywhere she was loved.
A person who was with her only a few days summed up her
memories sixty years later: "Very lively, endowed with great
charm, she enthusiastically shared in the diversions of our age
. . . Elizabeth was too attractive for one to forget her."

But there were not only girl friends, there were also young
men. The *Souvenirs* is deliberately vague on this subject: ". . . her
charming appearance aroused many hopes around her. . . ."

"Without Making a Face"

Here we invite the reader to read in Volume III our introduction to the *Diary* which she wrote at the age of eighteen and
nineteen; it is, so to speak, part of this biographical sketch.

Let us simply recall that March 26, during the great mission
preached in Dijon, Mme. Catez finally consented to her daughter's entrance into Carmel—but not for two years. Five days
later, "full of excitement," Mme. Catez came to speak to her of
a "superb match," even though that day was Good Friday. Sabeth reaffirmed her total adherence to Jesus (D 124 and P 69 on
the same day).

From her *Diary* we can infer that the young girl, without ever
having made a vow of obedience like her neighbors, the Carmelites, had many occasions to practice it. But soon Mme. Catez
lifted her former ban on speaking with the Sisters (the Externs
and the Prioress) of Carmel. Elizabeth asked for admission in
June 1899. Nevertheless, earlier, faced with her mother's opposition and, above all, the question of conscience that her mother's ill health raised, Elizabeth had completely agreed to fulfill
the concrete will of the Lord, even if it went contrary to her own
plans for the monastic life. In her hope she lived in total abandonment, throwing herself "without making a face" (the expression is her confessor's) into her situation as a young layperson in the world.

So she continued to travel and meet her friends in Dijon and
elsewhere. She dressed elegantly and her hairstyles were impec-

cable. She was noticed in the circle of military families and at the dances where one met many people; Mgr. Brunhes, future Bishop of Montpellier, boasted of having danced with her in his youth. And the more perceptive men said to themselves: "She is not for us; look at her expression."

Sabeth radiated his Love. During a dancing party one evening, a lady suddenly said to her: "Elizabeth, you see God." Her whole being was orientated towards him. When Charles Hallo, Marie-Louise's brother, complimented her on her talents, she answered teasingly: "Charles, you annoy me!"

Her passion was Jesus, to "share" his joys and his griefs, to be near him and to give him absolutely everything. As she did not yet live in his presence in Carmel, she, like Catherine of Siena, interiorized her "cell":

> May my life be a continual prayer, a long act of *love. May nothing* distract me from You, neither noise nor diversions. O my Master, I would so love to live with You in silence. But what I love above all is to do Your will, and since You want me to still remain in the world, I submit with all my heart *for love of You*. I offer You the cell of my heart; may it be Your little Bethany. Come rest there; I love You so. . . . I would like to console You, and I offer myself to You as a victim, O my Master, for You, with You. (PN 5)

The word "victim" used here is owed to Thérèse of Lisieux. In 1899 one of the first conquests of *The Story of a Soul* was Elizabeth: Thérèse helped her to rid herself of all that still remained of Jansenism in her image of God. But above all, it was the mystical experience of divine love that often inundated her heart which was the best antidote for her fears. Already, before her entrance into Carmel, Elizabeth had given God this title which would remain very dear to her: the God "Who is All Love."

Elizabeth of the Trinity

In her heart the young girl dreamed of taking the name of *Elizabeth of Jesus* in Carmel. Not without sacrifice did she accept *Elizabeth of the Trinity* which the Prioress proposed to her in memory of a Carmelite of Beaune.

July 1, 1900, we find this name for the first time in Letter 28 which she addressed to another aspirant to Carmel, Marguerite Gollot. Shortly before, Elizabeth had met for the first time Père Vallée, Prior of the Dominicans of Dijon, a highly esteemed preacher in Carmel. The long conversation with this Father, whom she saw again several times before her entrance, intensely encouraged her to believe in the God "Who is all Love" who dwelt in her, a presence she had felt so strongly. The priest gave her wings to continue her rapid course. Not that he had revealed to her the reality of the indwelling of God in her soul for she was already living that. But she was surely enriched by what P. Vallée told her of the love that, not only Jesus, but God—Father, Word and Holy Spirit—bore for her. How she must have drunk in these words; she who had written two years before on the day of Pentecost, 1898, in speaking of the Holy Spirit whom she "invoked each day" and from whom she awaited the fulfillment of all her desires:

> Holy Spirit, Goodness, Supreme Beauty!
> O You Whom I adore, O You Whom I love!
> Consume with Your divine flames
> This body and this heart and this soul!
> This spouse of the Trinity
> Who desires only Your will! (P 54)

During the summer of 1900, this "spouse of the Trinity" said her last goodbye to the world in the course of a three-month trip. One last time the meetings and parties began again in Dijon, but also the apostolate to which she gave herself in the parishes of Saint-Michel and Saint-Pierre: the youth club for the children of the workers at the tobacco factory, catechism for the children who were preparing for their first communion, visits to their parents and to the sick, choir rehearsals.

Time passed quickly; her twenty-first birthday and her entrance into Carmel drew near. Elizabeth went through a period of aridity in her search for God. She suffered. And even more than that, she "suffered from making others suffer" (L 67): her mother and sister counted the days they had left with their Sabeth. "My poor darlings whom I am crucifying," she groaned (L 71). Later, Canon Angles would call to mind the "two loves" which, like a horizontal and vertical beam, formed a cross in Elizabeth's heart: "Love of God and love for her mother whom she cherished passionately." But the daughter of the officer did not retreat before the greatest sacrifices if it was to respond to the highest Love.

Marie of Jesus knew the value of her young postulant, and she decided to take her with her to the foundation of Paray-le-Monial. Elizabeth's trunks were already there when, at the last moment, they consented to leave her in the Carmel of Dijon out of consideration for Mme. Catez.

Those were heart-rending hours, that last evening, that last night together.

But August 2, 1901, also brought to Elizabeth the profound peace of at last being able to say yes to Jesus who wanted her in Carmel. That very morning she wrote again to Canon Angles: "We are going to receive communion at the eight o'clock Mass, and after that, when He is in my heart, mama will lead me to the enclosure door!"

When He is in my heart.... She ended, "I feel that I am wholly His, that I am keeping back nothing. I throw myself into His arms like a little child" (L 81).

Before leaving forever the house on Rue Prieur-de-la-Côte-d'Or, she knelt before the portrait of her father and asked him for a last blessing.

C.D.M.

NOTES

1. See Plan 5 in Volume III.
2. Cf. our introduction to the *Poems*, Volume III.
3. Cf. CE 16 in PAT.

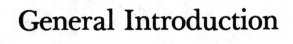

General Introduction

General Introduction

On the threshold of the twentieth century, Elizabeth of the Trinity's hidden life and her witness rooted in a divine world were a silent but real message which was welcomed by many spiritually-minded men and women. A daughter of her times, Elizabeth anticipated, without being aware of it, the spirituality of the Church under several aspects.

Prophet of God

Let us avoid two pitfalls when speaking of her contribution to Christian spirituality. First of all, it is not a question of attributing to Elizabeth of the Trinity exclusive rights in the renewal and deepening of spiritual life which she helped and continues to help effect. That would manifestly contradict the remarkable detachment she showed in giving little importance to the subjective resonances of the graces she received, but rather aligning herself with the great masters like Paul and John, John of the Cross, and Ruysbroeck. We must not isolate Elizabeth from the wider underlying currents (little known to her but well known to the Spirit), although, and wholly unaware of it, on certain points she was in advance of her times.

For example, how can we fail to compare her charismatic attraction for the New Testament with the biblical renewal that was slowly opening up, which Père Lagrange pioneered in the years 1890–1900: founding the Ecole Biblique of Jerusalem, the *Revue Biblique*, and the collection "Etudes Bibliques?"

On observing that Elizabeth, like John of the Cross, builds her spirituality on the objective foundation of Scripture and Faith, how can we fail to recognize this same movement in the authors of the nineteenth century such as Newman and Gay, and again, Faber and Lacordaire?

When we hear Elizabeth call herself "Praise of Glory," how
can we fail to think of the liturgical movement Dom Guéranger
and his monks of Solesmes endeavored for half a century to make
prevail over a too sentimental devotion, overly concerned with
states of soul?

When admiring her contemplative thirst for God, how can
we forget that whole mystical invasion at the end of the nineteenth century and the first decades of the twentieth, with re-
nowned representatives in Elizabeth's country such as Thérèse
of Lisieux and Charles de Foucauld?

Finally, if Elizabeth contributed, without realizing it, to a
spirituality of the laity, why separate this from the great evangelical awakening, that of the social movement in Western
Europe, which was supported by many of the laity long before
Leo XIII's encyclical, *Rerum Novarum*, in 1891?

Daniel-Rops understood this well: "Would not one of the most
surprising paradoxes of our national history be this: that France,
officially atheist, has been wholly penetrated with mysticism and
that an immense current of fervor is circulating underground
before surfacing through hundreds of springs?"[1]

The second pitfall to avoid would be to make Elizabeth a
prophet on *all* points of view!

We recognize in her a complete and traditional formation in
the customs, formulas, and conventions of the religious life at
the beginning of the twentieth century — exceptional only by the
quality of love that animated her. This religious life had been
well tested by the social pressure of the French state but had not
yet been confronted with modern challenges and new values
brought about by a better knowledge of man and the world, and
our technological era.

We also notice that Elizabeth's language, personal, simple
and affectionate, assumes in places a somewhat solemn style,
which does not at all correspond to her personality, although it
is filled with conviction, and, more than once, with a biblical
inspiration unsuspected at first sight. We have here a remnant
of the influence that Père Vallée's oratorical style exercised over
her for a short time, which the young religious had not yet completely assimilated. When we recall that her premature death at

the age of twenty-six did not allow her time to discover *fully* her personal style and vocabulary, we can only admire her manner of mystical expression and that "language which we wonder where she learned it," as the former rector of the University of Lyon, Pierre Dadolle, Bishop of Dijon, said in his foreword to the first edition of the *Souvenirs* (S IX).

We also see, against a background of Jansenism, from which Elizabeth was able to free herself magnificently—and to free others!—an appreciation of suffering, which, though inspired by quite positive views,[2] is "dated" in its expression. But can one ever speak well of this mystery?

Although traditional, several elements of her teaching, of which we will attempt to give an overall view in our work *Elizabeth or Love is There* (AL), are nevertheless very beautiful. Here all we will try to see is how this mystic enriched the spirituality of her time and still can enrich our own.

1. First of all, there is her *personal charism of sound interiority and attention to God*—a charism with many facets. Her lofty idea of God does not merely erect a hierarchy of values that culminates in God, the Prime Value, but it also impels her to leave everything, as far as that is possible, in order to devote herself (and with what ardor!) to a life of adoration freely given. The contemplative life, lived with intensity and faith, leads to the reality of God; the authenticity of Elizabeth's love reinforces the credibility of this statement.

Even in Carmel where the search for God (which is at the same time an ecclesial prayer) was so insistently recommended by Teresa of Avila, the quality of Elizabeth's constant recollection was impressive. Theoretically we might question what part is played here by a nature very gifted for contemplation and wonder, by a generosity which prefers God to the egotistic expressions of self, and again, by a supernatural charism destined for our enrichment: in reality all these composites are harmoniously united in this young woman. Elizabeth Catez by her fidelity to a charism displayed through all her gifts of heart and grace is a *prophet*. But she also became a *saint*, that is, faithful to the Gospel down to the very fibers of concrete existence, by the total exploitation of a gift that is placed in every human heart: love.

It seems to us that Elizabeth of the Trinity again presents a prophetic aspect by the gentleness and flexibility with which she lived this impressive recollection. There is nothing harsh, hard, or irritating about her—apart from a few short periods of transition, for she, too, must have had to struggle. In her silence there is a freedom which she had already acquired as a young lay person. Her neighbor does not feel rejected, but, on the contrary, drawn to her Mystery. We detect in her an exceptional combination of the mystical and the human, of attention to God and a deep sense of friendship; her relationship with her prioress, Germaine of Jesus, would be just one of the clearest examples of this. She learned that at the Master's school—first of all, perhaps, in his visits to Bethany which Elizabeth so loved to contemplate. She glimpsed it in God's heart: "Heaven is unity," she said a little before her death (S 254). If the witnesses repeat in chorus the epithet "recollected," they add others to it: simple, joyous, amiable, obliging. To understand thoroughly this prophet of the presence of God, we must never separate her *writings*, in which she inculcates the nearness of God, from her daily *life*. Writings, words, and actions are all one sheaf.

As a contemplative her role will not be to speak, to act, nor to appear abroad. Her task is "to remain at the Source": "There are two words which sum up for me all holiness, all apostolate: Union and Love" (L 191). Although Elizabeth experiences less of a need to reaffirm the apostolic usefulness of her life than her sister Thérèse of Lisieux does—a more lively disposition and more winning personality—she also knows she is "in the great body of the Church" (L 191). In making profession of the contemplative life, Elizabeth remains the same as the young girl who at the time of her *Diary* poured herself out for "souls" and prayed as fervently for the conversion of M. Chapuis as Thérèse did for Pranzini. Elizabeth carries in her heart the conviction that a daughter of Teresa of Avila "must be apostolic: all her prayers, all her sacrifices tend to this!" (L 136) When she prays in *O My God, Trinity Whom I Adore* (PN 15) to be more fully incorporated into the mystical Body of Christ, into his enlarged humanity, "that I may be another humanity for Him," she considers Christ coming into her not only as "Adorer" but also "as Restorer and as Savior" so that he can renew in her "His *whole* Mystery."

"The Glory of God" and "the Church" the dying nun will state these two ends of her life with the same ardor: "O Love!. . . Consume all my substance for your glory; let it distill drop by drop for your Church" (S 256–57).

2. Elizabeth also surpasses the current spirituality of her day by *her enthusiastic and loving approach to the Trinity*. She is overcome with wonder before God who, however exalted and immense he may be, is not alone in his majesty but is a Community of Love: Three in a union which surpasses all understanding—creating man and inviting him to live and act in him who is Love. For her the holiness of God radiates an infinite love! To draw near him is to be freed from the evil that is in us, to be enkindled with the fire of the Spirit.

It will not be her task to reflect theologically on the mystery of the intra-Trinitarian life. Rather her vocation will consist in thanksgiving for the love of the "Three," in wonderment of their beauty, and in the irrevocable gift of self to the least expression of their desire. What Elizabeth emphasizes before all is the mercy of the Trinity, its "philanthropia" as St. Paul says (Tt 3:4), "his love for men." Elizabeth loves so much to speak of God who is "all Love," continually bending over the work of his hands. He never leaves us; he dwells in us; he wants to be loved by us; he wants to give us life—forever; he wants to transform us into himself, to deify us. It is Heaven "that the Holy Spirit creates in you," she exclaims (L 239)!

With the eyes of her heart she follows the ascending and descending double movement of the dynamics of God's love for us. (This is to express figuratively what cannot be separated in God.) The Father sends his Son among us; Jesus perpetuates his human work, his love, and his presence in the Church, especially through the Eucharist. They send us the enabling Spirit so that the life of Jesus may manifest itself in our life and radiate through us to others. If they dwell in us, it is not just to make us happy by our faith in their love and nearness, but above all that, patiently and in free collaboration, our existence may be transfigured in-

to a life as "forgetful and freed of self" as Mary's was (LR 40) for
the good of others. Then the Spirit will sing ever more earnestly
in our hearts "the praise" of the God of Love (Ep 1:12).

In her Trinitarian approach, Elizabeth always remains Chris-
tocentric. Since her childhood she had been deeply touched by
the total gift of self that Jesus manifests on the Cross and in the
Eucharist. Her prayer as a Carmelite will be, above all, listening
to the "Master." And in the evening of her life, the mystic will
utter these moving words, pressing her profession crucifix to her
heart: "We have loved each other so much" (S 246). Her transformation in God will come about through conformity to the
Crucified and Risen One.

3. In her own way, Elizabeth was also a pioneer in the redis-
covery of *Scripture as the charter of Christian life.* Today it is
hard for us to understand how different the situation was at the
beginning of the twentieth century. At that time the Bible was
much less known and read by Catholics. During the preparation
of this edition, priests often told us: "What we received then in
our course on Holy Scripture was quite impoverished, Elizabeth
is the one who opened up St. Paul to me."

Obviously Paul was not unknown. But the Holy Spirit developed in the heart of this inadequately educated young woman a
special charism for understanding the inner meaning, for de-
lighting in and living the magnificent designs of divine love that
Paul and John unfolded before her wondering eyes. Without
having read exegetical works, rather poor and rare in her day,
she penetrated the texts by an inner intuition and translated
them into life. She based her contemplation and her doctrine on
the revealed word, made lifegiving by her contact with the Word
of God. This is what gives her writings vigor and wholeness, depth
and horizon. In all simplicity and clarity they are inscribed in
the fundamental perspectives of Christianity. If we had to describe her person and her mysticism in one word, we would say
right away that Elizabeth is thoroughly "Christian." She moves
"in the objectivity of the message and the universality of the
mystery of Christ," as Hans Ur von Balthasar says so well.[3]

This does not mean to say that she expatiates on all the aspects
of Christianity. That was not at all her intention. Her whole

work is a spontaneous outpouring occasioned by concrete circumstances; she lets her heart speak on what seems to her most beautiful in life: impassioned friendship for Christ, response to the love God manifests for us. She never had a synthesis in mind, although she had a profound intuition of the essential.

Thus, for example, she develops the practice of charity less than Thérèse of Lisieux does (who was favored by having written an autobiography, a kind of "book" which lent itself more easily to structuring) just as Thérèse speaks less explicitly of the presence of God. But what charity *in action* in Elizabeth's community relationships, or in her correspondence, so warm and attentive to the psychology of each one, with his joys, his vulnerable points, his sufferings, and his hidden thirst for God which she wanted to both quench and quicken! We repeat: the understanding of her message is inseparable from the knowledge of her life. Her writings, moreover, would never have had that force, that accent of authenticity, that resonance without the "lived" atmosphere from which they emanated. The supreme witness of Elizabeth of the Trinity is her way of living.

4. Elizabeth, a nun "to the hilt," to use Lacordaire's expression, which was quoted in her presence, paradoxically had her own word to say about the *spirituality of the laity*—a task that she should pursue more than ever in our day!

Elizabeth's contribution here is situated at the most fundamental level of lay spirituality. While affirming her happiness in her Carmelite vocation, the mystic goes beyond external forms to enlarge on the common riches of every Christian, whether in the monastery or in the midst of the world with its multiple activities: God's desire to give himself to us, our baptism, the Eucharist, our destiny beyond death, the universal presence of God, the reality of the "Three" in us, the joy of being a beloved child of the God of Love, a joy which impels us to give ourselves to others. In this way her message assumes a universal meaning.

Besides, we should not forget that many of her writings were destined for lay people. Among her fifty-nine correspondents there are six priests or seminarians, thirteen religious, but forty lay people (thirty-one in her letters from Carmel). She corresponds with a widow, mothers of families, a young man, her doctor, her friends. And all understood very well what Elizabeth wanted to tell them. The only boundaries separating them were the external ones.

Neither must we forget, in fact it is even important enough to emphasize it, that Elizabeth lived as a young lay person what she later extols as a Carmelite. Before her entrance into Carmel, this simple young girl, whether on trips, in a group, at home, or at the piano, already lived "within"; she felt drawn by the presence of God and she responded to it with an unlimited generosity. A considerable part of her writings date precisely from this period of her youth. This edition is privileged to publish them for the first time and to show us a young saint in the world attentive to others, who already lived her "passion for God" (L 136) in the "little cell" of her heart!

Like Thérèse of Lisieux, and partly under her influence, Elizabeth rejects a certain exotic conception of "holiness" and repeats that to live fully the Gospel, special conditions and extraordinary manifestations are not required. When she was asked on entering Carmel: "What is your ideal of holiness?", she answered, "To live by love." And "the quickest way to attain it?", "To become very little, to surrender oneself irrevocably" (PN 12). Five years later, when she composed her little treatise *Heaven in Faith* for her sister Guite, young mother of two children — she will have nine — she will say for "every soul": "Each incident, each event, each suffering as well as each joy is a sacrament which gives God to it" (HF 10).

A little later, a few weeks before she died, her mother was speaking to her of the possible departure of the community into exile and assured her that she would not let her sick daughter leave. Elizabeth of the Trinity, the contemplative who so loved the solitude of her Carmel, answered, "Yes, Mama, if it is God's will, I will go home with you to die. . . ."[4]

Elizabeth's Thought on Her Posthumous Mission

Eleven days before her death, Elizabeth wrote: "I think that in Heaven my mission will be to draw souls by helping them to go out of themselves in order to cling to God by a wholly simple and loving movement, and to keep them in this great silence within which will allow God to communicate Himself to them and to transform them into Himself" (L 335).

For a long time she had already been fulfilling a mission. Her "large heart overflowing with love" (L 295) predisposed her to share with others what seemed to her most dear and most important in this life. Her experience of God and the discovery of his word became an open inheritance.

Especially during her eight months in the infirmary, she felt as though impelled to express the essential, as though charged with speaking of the ultimate truth: "In the light of eternity God makes me understand many things, and I come to tell you as though it were coming from Him . . . " (L 324). The desire to communicate sometimes assumes a universal breadth: "Ah, I wish I could tell everyone what sources of strength, of peace and of happiness they would find if they would only consent to live in this intimacy" (L 302). "I wish I could make myself heard by everyone in order to tell them of the vanity, of the nothingness of what passes, unless it is done for God" (L 340).

Her message bears many names. It is a "program of life" (GV 9), an "ideal" (L 324), even her "recipe" (L 317). But also her "secret" and her "testament" (L 333), "my doctrine" (L 273) and even, indirectly, "my grace" (L 293). In her heart something is "happening similar to" Jesus' sentiments on the eve of his death (L 315) and, in the last weeks, Elizabeth says goodbye with a whole series of letter-testaments.

The idea of a spiritual motherhood after her death continues to develop, and promises to help those whom she loves multiply (L 324, 326, 330, 331, 333, 334, 335, 340, 341). "Call me," the dying nun says to her "little brother," Charles Hallo whom "she will love even more in Heaven!" "Yes, call your little sister. In this way you will increase her happiness in Heaven; she will be so glad to help you. . . ." (L 342) And to Doctor Barbier: "It is my turn now; I feel my mission beginning on your behalf" (L 340).

In her spiritual testament for Mother Germaine, Elizabeth feels commissioned by God to transmit a message and to exercise later a "priesthood" on earth. She calls herself God's messenger who reveals to Mother Germaine "what her God in the hours of profound recollection and of unifying contact, makes her understand". "If you knew," she wrote, "with what certitude I understand God's plan for your soul; it appears to me as in a great light, and I understand also that in Heaven I will fulfill in my turn a priesthood over your soul. It is Love who associates me with his work in you. . . ." (LL 1-3)

Sometimes her posthumous mission concerns a material or moral protection, but more often a deepening of life with God. We saw this in the solemn declaration of Letter 335, quoted at the beginning of this section. We notice it again, for example, in Letter 333 to Antoinette de Bobet: "I leave you my faith in the presence of God, of the God who is all Love dwelling in our souls. I confide to you: it is this intimacy with Him 'within' which has been the beautiful sun illuminating my life, making it already an anticipated Heaven; it is what sustains me today in my suffering."

A Visible Mediation

Did Elizabeth consider only a purely spiritual activity after her death without a visible mediation? It is hard to believe this. She must have forseen that the memory of her example and at least some of her writings and sayings would serve as a means for her mission.

To understand this, let us recall that, after the death of a Carmelite, it was customary to send an obituary circular to all the French Carmels and friends abroad. In it the sister's life was briefly related, while bringing out her gifts and virtues, and suggesting sometimes delicately her limitations. Each Carmelite knew this. Some were opposed to it and asked not to have a circular—out of humility, it was almost invariably explained. But most had no objection to it. For example, Thérèse of Lisieux said: "I really want a 'circular' because I have always thought that I must pay for the Office of the Dead that each Carmelite will say for me. I can't understand why some don't want a circular; it's so nice to get acquainted with each other and to know something about those with whom we will live eternally."[5]

Elizabeth was of this opinion. Mother Germaine relates: "Three weeks before her death when I was writing in her presence, she interrupted me to say with her usual smile and profound look: 'I'm happy to think that you will write my circular.' And since, surprised by such an unexpected reflection on her part, I objected that I wouldn't have much to say about a religious who had only lived in Carmel for five years, she told me: 'I will help you.' I answered: 'Very well. I will take you at your word. I am counting on you.' Then she said, 'We will do it together'" (PO 66).

This must not have been the first time that Elizabeth thought about her circular. In the first half of August 1906, when she had finished her spiritual treatise *Heaven in Faith*, the notebook intended for Guite remained in Mother Germaine's hands; Elizabeth certainly knew this. And when a little later, the Prioress asked her to compose a retreat for her this time, in which she could incorporate her personal ideas to a greater degree, Elizabeth must have easily guessed that the Prioress would use these writings for the circular, all the more so since Mother Germaine had been expecting the imminent death of her young Sister for at least three months. This clearly results from a letter of May 17, 1906, to Canon Angles (cf. note 1 of L 271) where Mother Germaine says in regard to the visit that day of Mme. Catez to her young daughter: "It is probably the last time that they will see each other on earth." When Elizabeth writes in a letter of July 16: "I think I will soon leave Carmel for Heaven," Mother Germaine adds: "I think so too" (L 297).

Convinced of Elizabeth's sanctity, which she does not fail to bring out in her circular, did Mother Germaine, great admirer of *The Story of a Soul* by Thérèse of Lisieux, already have the idea that one day she would likewise write Elizabeth's life? Did Elizabeth ever suspect it? This is only an hypothesis. But she certainly noticed the veneration which began to surround her during her illness.[6]

It is very probable that the use of the word "mission" in its posthumous perspective[7] owes its origin in Elizabeth to an explicit comparison with the posthumous "mission" of Thérèse of Lisieux.[8]

The *Souvenirs* of 1935 (pp. 234–235) adds a note from Mother Germaine (who died before the appearance of this edition): "When we asked her how she intended 'to spend her eternity,' and if, like the 'Little Thérèse,' she would 'come down' to earth for the good of souls, she replied: 'Oh! no, indeed, as soon as I reach the threshold of Paradise, I will rush like a little rocket into the bosom of 'my Three'; a Praise of Glory can have no other place for eternity and I will plunge ever deeper into it. . . .' Then, after a little pause, with her eyes closed and her hands joined, she added: 'However, if God grants my request, I think that in Heaven my mission will be to draw souls into *interior recollection*' . . . and she developed her idea in the words quoted in the above letter" (L 335).[9]

Marie of the Trinity, Sub-Prioress in Elizabeth's time, also affirms: "In regard to her heavenly mission, I heard the Servant of God state several times that her mission would not be the same as that of Sister Thérèse of the Child Jesus, but that she would be concealed, hidden, wholly interior" (PO 185).

After all it matters little to know whether the term "mission" and the effort to condense its content were set in motion by Thérèse's example. What is important is that this mission was prepared by and reflected in the life and witness of the Carmelite of Dijon.

Like two beacons which singularly illuminate this message, we find again in the last days, these counsels: "Let us live of love so that we may die of love and glorify the God Who is all Love" (L 335) and, "Let yourself be loved . . . ," that insistent invitation on the threshold of Heaven (LL).

The "Circular" and the "Souvenirs"

The Circular

A little after Elizabeth's death, November 9th, 1906, Mother Germaine began to write the obituary circular: "Fifteen days after her death," she stated, with "an extraordinary ease that led me to finish this work very rapidly" (PO 66). However, the circular will be signed only the 18th of December and sent around Christmas.[10] It contained fourteen pages in-quarto printed in small type.[11]

The Prioress consulted many sources in the course of this work:[12] "Thank you for your last letters," she wrote Guite, December 1, 1906. "I needed this whole dossier these days, but I am going to put it into the hands of my little copyist so that I can return it to you very soon, I hope." However, these letters were not used. The documents cited are the *Last Retreat, Heaven in Faith,* the *Diary,* some verses from the *Poems* of her youth, Letter 314 to her mother and Letter 323[a] to a friend. Guite's "dossier" was thus completed by other documents from Carmel, from the immediate family, and from some friends of Dijon, and in particular, by conversations with Mme. Catez who furnished details on Elizabeth's youth. When the Prioress sent the *Circular* to Guite, the 24th of December, she confessed: "It seems to me that I have said nothing in these twelve [in reality fourteen] pages, there was so much to be said; it is rather a sketch than a life of a soul, and I have already gone well beyond the usual limits of our circulars. But no one will complain of it, and for my part, I have found profound joys and true graces in the course of this little work done with my holy child."

Responses full of gratitude from the Carmels were expressed as early as December 28, 1906, and were often accompanied by a request for one or more extra copies. The first printing (of which we do not know the number) was not sufficient and on the 18th of January, Mother Germaine wrote to Marie Bouveret: "I'm not surprised at the effect of her Circular. It is the same in the Carmels from whom we receive daily the most consoling letters. . . . Today I can reserve a copy for you as I have been obliged to resort to a second printing. . . ."

Three months later, April 16, 1907, Sister Agnes wrote to the Carmel of Angers: "as for a Circular, alas, there are no more left, not even one! Even the Carmel of Saigon is asking for three! . . . But you will like the notice even more."

The Preparation of the "Souvenirs"

A "notice".... This is how Elizabeth's biography, later to be
called the *Souvenirs,** was designated at the beginning. Two
years later the Introduction will attribute the birth of this book
to the responses provoked by the reading of the *Circular,*[13] but
the project dated well in advance of its diffusion.

Mother Germaine sent a copy of the *Circular* to Mme. Catez
on December 24, 1906, and wrote, "If I have not spoken more of
her family, it was to conform to the customs of the Order, but
we can make up for this in a notice and I will whisper many
things to its author on this point."

Fifteen days later, a letter of January 7, 1907, to Guite shows
that Mother Germaine was already actively occupied with the
future biography: "Tell your dear Mama [that] she could do
me a great service in the preparation of the necessary materials
for the work I want to undertake for the honor of our little saint
by jotting down some notes from time to time (in order not to
tire herself), first of all about Elizabeth's maternal and paternal
family, and the place of origin on both sides. Then, as I believe I
have already asked you,[14] a few memories of her childhood,
trips, education, etc. I think it would be useful also to ask Abbé
Sellenet[15] to send us a brief account of his memories of this
soul...."

Mother Germaine must have continued her search for information, for in the Archives of the Dijon Carmel are preserved
several important documents which give some very early testimonies.[16] These are the precious substructures (nonedited) of
the *Souvenirs.* The Prioress also asked for (or received spontaneously) letters written by Elizabeth to different correspondents. On the 22nd of February she announced to Guite that she
"will set to work" on the 4th of March, after her annual retreat.
A letter of the 9th of March to Mme. Catez shows that the gath-
ering of materials which are called here "our documents" is
being actively pursued.[17]

---

*Published in English under the title *The Praise of Glory: Reminiscences of Sister Elizabeth
of the Trinity,* The Newman Press, Westminster, Maryland (1962). [translator's note]

But Mother Prioress had little time to do any serious writing! Sister Agnes wrote to Angers on the 16th of April: ". . . you will like the notice even more. Our good Mother is so busy that she has hardly any opportunity to work on it!" On October 23, 1907, Germaine completed her second term as prioress, and Sister Agnes could write to Angers that evening: "I hope this blessed notice will soon be published now that our good Mother will have more leisure to work on it."

And in fact the writing began. The following January 6th, Sister Agnes conveyed the good news: "This blessed notice! It is under way. Be patient. I asked Mother Germaine of Jesus what date I could promise it to you and she said to tell you that at Christmas she left Elizabeth at her first Communion, and since then she has been tranquilly making her thanksgiving, as the occupations of the good mother provisor [Germaine had become the bursar] do not permit her to work on it. She hopes to take it up again soon."

In the following months two letters reveal in what spirit the *Souvenirs* were written. First of all a concern for sobriety. On the 19th of January, 1908, Mother Germaine wrote to Abbé Jaillet: "The little work is begun: we are limiting ourselves to quite simply stating the facts so that the praise can emerge on its own without us trying to praise her ourselves." Then, a desire to be truthful, sometimes even to the point of scruple. This can be seen in an answer from the Carmel of Anderlecht[18] of June 7th, 1908: "I want to tell you my dear Mother, how very happy we all are to learn that we will soon receive the notice. . . . Our dear Mother was afraid that the suppression of the familiar *tu** could not be legitimately done; although the evidence of this little infraction of our customs is somewhat unfortunate, we must, before all, be scrupulously exact."

"Finally our 'Souvenirs' is finished!", Mother Germaine wrote to Mme. Catez October 15, 1908. "Blessed be God! The whole work needs to be minutely reread from beginning to end, which

---

*It was an old custom in Carmel to suppress the use of the familiar *tu* at the time of religious profession. It was for special reasons that they were maintained in Sister Elizabeth of the Trinity's correspondence. [Note from the French edition of the *Souvenirs*, p. 73, Tr.]

I hope to do after the retreat[19].... Our little saint is so alive and so beautiful in it! What a soul!" The introduction to the book bears the date of February 11, 1909. The manuscript then remained several weeks at the bishopric where Bishop Dadolle enthusiastically approved it.

Afterwards the manuscript was sent to the Jobard Printing Shop in Dijon. On the 10th of March 1909, Sister Agnes was able to tell Angers: "... the notice is now in the press [doubtless she meant to say the type was being set up]; but the Bishop wants to see the first proof again so he can write his letter of approbation. We are threatened with a new examination at the bishopric.... the Bishop read the manuscript and was extremely edified; he said that she is a saint and a soul of genius." On the 19th of March Mother Germaine announced to the Carmel of Anderlecht: "Her little notice will be published soon.... Yesterday, our Bishop sent word that he had read our manuscript several times. His Excellency 'canonizes' our dear little sister, ... [he] wants to return the manuscript personally...." The Carmel of Anderlecht answered on the 29th of March: "... we join with you in giving a little tug to the wings of the Bishop's angels."

But Bishop Dadolle's letter of approbation will not be signed until the 24th of September. The book came off the press at the very beginning of October 1909, for from the 6th the Carmels began to send thanks for the copy they received. Elizabeth had been dead nearly three years.

The Contribution of the "Souvenirs"

The paperback volume (of X + 368 pages, in the format 22 x 14.3 cm., and at the price of 3.50 F) bears as the complete title: *Soeur Elisabeth de la Trinité, religieuse Carmélite, 1880–1906. Souvenirs.* Following Bishop Dadolle's letter of approbation, Elizabeth's life is set forth in seventeen chapters. The appendix contains her *Last Retreat*, her prayer, *O My God, Trinity Whom I Adore*, 23 letters or fragments of letters, 17 poems,[20] and a letter from Abbé D[onin] to Mme. Catez. No trace remains of the original manuscript or its first outlines.

"I wrote this book on my knees," Mother Germaine said,[21] suggesting by that, not only her admiration before God's work in Elizabeth but primarily how much trouble the work had cost her.

In consulting the sources which she used, we could also say that it was written with much love and with ... "scissors"! The personal recollections of this major witness are enriched by those of Mme. Catez, the Sisters, friends, Canon Angles and Père Vallée, but above all by ample extracts from Elizabeth's *Diary*, and still more by extracts from her *Letters*.

Thus the biography became, as it were, an autobiography. Moreover, Mother Germaine had explained this in her introduction: "Faithful echo of her soul, her correspondence needed only to be arranged in the order of the facts to be related to let her most often describe herself" (S 5). And the first reader, Bishop Dadolle, said of these "epistolary conferences": "She pours out her soul with a delightful simplicity, freshness, and serenity. The thought is always substantial and exact; the lofty sentiment which wells up in it, giving it life and movement, continually clothes her expressions with a truly extraordinary strength or grace" (S IX–X).

Without being a masterpiece, the biography was successful enough. The fabric of events is harmoniously interwoven with the threads of a spiritual growth, although the outline of this evolution might be debatable. Even though the *Souvenirs* is written in the somewhat sentimental style of the period, the book leaves an overall impression of veracity.

We could have expected that from Mother Germaine. Our long contact with her correspondence and her history confirms the impression that her community and friends have kept of her: a noble and truthful person, respectful of others, somewhat timid and reserved, but with a very generous spirit of self-sacrifice. Concerned for monastic fervor and fidelity to the spirit of Carmel, she had sufficient discernment to grant a few minor exceptions at the necessary time, and enough talent to create in her community a family spirit characterized by joy and simplicity. Rather than an organizer or a born leader, she was a true Mother for her Sisters. It is hardly necessary to say that Mother Germaine effaces herself in the *Souvenirs* behind the memory of Elizabeth and her writings; it will be first of all Elizabeth's life and the texts themselves which will insure the success of this book. As for Elizabeth's confidences to her only Prioress and Mistress of Novices, quoted here at a distance of several months or years, we cannot expect a strict fidelity as if they had been recorded on tape, but they are presented to us in the best possible condition, given Mother Germaine's spirit of truthfulness and her respect, not to say veneration before God's work in Elizabeth.

What shall we say about the textual fidelity of the texts of Elizabeth quoted in the *Souvenirs?* It does not contradict what we have just observed: that the texts are not wholly authentic. Mother Germaine was not preparing a complete or critical edition, and the example of Mother Agnes revising the writings of Thérèse of Lisieux is there to remind us that at the beginning of the twentieth century there were less scruples on this plane than today.

Nevertheless, the modifications that Mother Germaine makes in Elizabeth's writings are much less numerous and less important than in Thérèse's case. She limited herself to unimportant omissions of passages, names, little expressions of affection or familiarity, and superfluous words. There are selections from the letters, small explanatory additions, some retouches of style, the replacement of certain words by synonyms to vary the writings. These interventions are a little more important in the poems in order to correct the rhythm in the more obvious cases.

In short, these small changes have no influence on the thought and are no obstacle, so to speak, to the understanding of Elizabeth. But strictly speaking, the texts cited in the *Souvenirs* are not quite authentic. The edition of 1927 informs us that "the texts cited have been minutely collated" (p. VI). But in those days they surely had another idea of minuteness than we have today, and the corrections are quite incomplete, especially in the *Poems.*

From the historical point of view it must be admitted that the *Souvenirs* is not exempt from errors, which proceed sometimes from the sources, sometimes from the lack of dates on most of Elizabeth's letters. Moreover, we have the impression that Mother Germaine, in all honesty, did not attach a primary importance to this aspect: she readily mixes documents of different periods; in like manner the spiritual perspectives overlap and the considerable period of Elizabeth's spiritual itinerary is blurred, whereas in this itinerary if a little of everything is everywhere, everything is not everywhere in the same way!

The fact that Mother Germaine had known Elizabeth in the monastery only as a young Carmelite, who was quite advanced in the ways of recollection and holiness, creates certain lacunae in the *Souvenirs*. Like the other panel of a diptych, we would have liked to see the mystical aspect completed by a more *human* approach to Elizabeth; there was so much tenderness in this young woman! The *Souvenirs* could have placed more emphasis on little characteristics of Elizabeth's charity, consideration, helpfulness, and joy both in her life as a layperson as well as in her community life. Other witnesses will tell us more about these, but the major witness, Mother Germaine, does not speak much about them except in general affirmations.

Besides, it was not in her nature to linger over concrete details of the past. In her correspondence after Elizabeth's death we look for them in vain. Thus a large number of incidents which portray life have disappeared. If Thérèse of Lisieux had lived with Elizabeth and would have spoken of her, she would surely have emphasized more her daily conduct in the little events of community life. But Mother Germaine had the great merit of recognizing, testing, and strengthening the gift of mystical life which the Lord granted to Elizabeth.

Being a very spiritual person, the Prioress strongly emphasized this aspect. For her Elizabeth is an angel who spent five and a half years in the Carmel of Dijon. Moreover, we must own that the adjective "angelical" is not missing from the *Souvenirs* (S 125, 222, 249, 255, 260, 262). The impression of a certain "angelization" is increased still more by the frequent use of the word "child"[22] — an expression obviously quite a la mode at that time in the mouths of Mother Superiors. It is true that Elizabeth possessed "the simplicity of a child" (S 256); or as Père Vallée said: "From childhood she possessed an instinctive artlessness and penetration. Wholly candid, frank and simple, she was completely absorbed in the things of God...." (S 81). But it should have been emphasized more fully that this was "a second childhood," as Paul Ricoeur said, a Johannine "rebirth" (Jn 3). It seems to us that Mother Germaine did not know how to bring out all the richness of her saint. But we thank her for the immense devotion that animated her work "on her knees". The *Souvenirs* remains an indispensable stage in the understanding of Elizabeth of the Trinity.

The Diffusion of the "Souvenirs"

The *Souvenirs* circulated rapidly. Less than five months after its publication Mother Germaine wrote to Anderlecht on February 10, 1910: "Its success surpasses our expectations, and the mission of *Laudem gloriae* ["Praise of Glory," the surname Elizabeth gave herself] is affirmed in a very comforting manner in all parts of the world. Faced with the dispersion of our 1,500 copies, we were a little hesitant on what course to take. But today we believe that we must actively busy ourselves with a second edition."

On the 22nd of June, Sister Agnes announced to the Carmel of Angers: "The second edition ran out quickly — and from everywhere such comforting news comes to us for the glory of God."

And around the 10th of August she noted in the Monastery's book of chronicles: "In less than a year three thousand copies have literally disappeared. Mother Germaine of Jesus is preparing a third edition."

On February 21, 1911, Mother Germaine wrote again to Anderlecht: "Our third edition of the "Souvenirs" appeared last December 20th;[23] it has vanished. 800 copies in two months. . . . "

On November 6th of the same year the Prioress informed Anderlecht: "Our fourth edition, published five weeks ago, went even more rapidly than the preceding ones; it is unbelievable."

The following year, 1912, it had reached the fifth edition. In his letter of approbation of October 15th, Monsignor Monestès, the new bishop of Dijon affirmed: "God has made the fervent Carmelite an apostle of a permanent Pentecost of the Holy Spirit in souls."

The printings increased and, despite the First World War, the new bishop, Monsignor Landrieux, could announce in 1919 that they had reached 25,000.

A year later it was at 33,000; in 1927, 65,000; in 1935, 80,000. The diffusion of the *Souvenirs* and its translations would have been much greater still if Père Philipon's work, of which we will speak, had not taken over from the *Souvenirs* since 1939. The sixteenth[24] edition (1956) of Mother Germaine's book, however, will exceed 100,000 copies.[25]

It is difficult to make a complete list of the translations of the *Souvenirs*, which appeared in at least ten languages: English, German, Dutch, Italian, Spanish, Portuguese, Ruthenian,

Czech, Japanese, and Polish. Elizabeth's Retreats were also translated into Arabic, Korean, Vietnamese, and partially into Russian.[26] We must include besides the translations of the texts of Elizabeth contained in P. Philipon's books.

The different editions of the *Souvenirs* did not vary greatly in their content: some letters of approbation were added, then, in 1915, parts of the spiritual treatise *Heaven in Faith*. There were a few retouches and the choice of the poems changed a little. However, the edition of 1927 underwent a more extensive revision.[27] Subsequently, the pages concerning Elizabeth's posthumous influence varied still more.

A "Doctrinal" and "Spiritual" Approach to the "Complete" Works

In the course of the years the renown of Elizabeth's holiness increased continually and spread throughout the world; the desire to see her canonized also increased. We do not intend to set forth here the history of her cause for canonization; we will limit ourselves to the history of her writings.

The Collection of the Writings in View of the Beatification

On May 23, 1931, Msgr. Petit de Julleville, Bishop of Dijon, announced the opening of the informative process for the beatification of Sister Elizabeth of the Trinity, and ordered that all the known writings of the Carmelite be submitted to the tribunal of process: ". . . that is, everything that she wrote with her own hand, that she dictated to others, or that had been written at her direction: whether it concerns printed works or manuscripts or simple opuscules, short writings, meditations, personal notes, intimate diaries, letters, notes to others, and the like; whether these writings refer to the period that preceded her entrance into Carmel or to that which followed this entrance."[28] The transcription of the documents thus collected was done at Carmel. In 1931 four Sisters set to work.

The difficult art of exact transcription was, in Elizabeth's case, made still more arduous by her nearly illegible hand over a long period, the feebleness of her handwriting during her illness, her bad punctuation, spelling errors, and irregularity in the use of capital letters. Also, her practice of continuing her letters by often filling up the margins of the preceding pages, or in writing crosswise over the horizontal lines, and, finally, often the inferior quality of the paper.

Then, there are the spontaneous reactions of the copyists, introducing a correction, supplying a word forgotten by Elizabeth, abbreviating what she wrote out, or vice-versa, omitting an underlining, beginning a new paragraph where Elizabeth did not, or vice-versa. There are also involuntary omissions: a word, an expression, a phrase, and sometimes a whole fragment.

As Elizabeth did not date many of her letters, a certain effort was made to indicate the estimated year in the margin, sometimes committing considerable errors in this: Letter 181 will even be postdated fifteen days after Elizabeth's death!

Thus, as the present edition shows, the inventory of the writings in such a case could not be complete.

All these defects, however, had only a relative importance in view of the end sought: to permit a judgement on the faith and virtues of the candidate for beatification. Canon Deberre, ecclesiastical notary, in collating (doubtless rapidly to judge by the rhythm of his approbations) the copies with the originals, sought only to detect forgotten words. Confronted with the same difficulties as the copyists, his work of investigation remains incomplete.[29]

Profiting by the presence of the documents in their monastery, the Carmelites transcribed many of the writings for their own archives. These are the manuscript "Notebooks,"[30] which we will refer to occasionally. They present the same defects but have often been improved over the years by, among others, Père Philipon.

Père Philipon's Book

The arrival in Dijon of P. Marie-Michel Philipon gave a new impetus to the study and diffusion of Elizabeth's message. Even if our knowledge has evolved since then, we cannot be too grateful to him for the work which he did at that time.

Père Philipon himself explained the origin of his famous book, *The Spiritual Doctrine of Sister Elizabeth of the Trinity*.[31] Having entered the Dominicans at the age of twenty-two, he soon read the *Souvenirs* which brought him "an immense light." For his doctoral thesis in theology he chose as his theme "The Indwelling of the Trinity in the Soul." When he became a young professor of philosophy at the Dominican College of Saint-Maximin he loved to treat of the mystery of the Trinity in his preaching. He reread the *Souvenirs* and decided to write on Elizabeth.

Desiring to gather more documentary evidence, he called on the Carmel of Dijon for the first time in August 1933. Mother Germaine received him somewhat reticently, but Father's earnestness succeeded in gaining the Prioress' complete confidence.

In July 1934 P. Philipon returned to Carmel. He related in 1937: "We compared all the writings with the autographs, except for a few rare letters which escaped us, but of which we were able to obtain a certified copy conforming to the original. . . . Pen in hand we questioned as many witnesses as possible."[32]

An attentive examination of this file on Elizabeth which he bequeathed to the Archives of the Carmel of Dijon after his death permits us to become acquainted with his method of work. As his fundamental text, P. Philipon utilized the Notebooks of Carmel. He compared them with the originals: there are corrections in his handwriting and often the mention "saw the original." We note that he realized immediately he could not and should not be disturbed by Elizabeth's poor punctuation, her irregular use of capital letters, and her spelling errors. He does not make any corrections in the Notebooks, but he emends them in his books. He pursues first of all forgotten words or phrases—without, however, finding all of them.

Three years after their transcription for the Process, many of the autographs were returned to their owners as had been provided for in Bishop Petit de Julleville's ordinance. But P. Philipon could easily recover at least those that were in Dijon.[33] He collated the texts of which he did not have the original with the copy from the Process: in the margins of the Notebooks of Carmel we can still see where he inserted references to the pages of the Process. For the *Last Retreat* and *Heaven in Faith* he used the texts already printed.

He then had a typewritten copy of the Notebooks of Carmel thus emended made for his personal use. He rearranged the texts in a better chronological order, although still quite inadequate and imprecise. Thus a considerable dossier was obtained.

The numerous texts that P. Philipon cites are not far from being authentic in these circumstances; however, small divergences even at the mere level of words are not absent. In the text alone of the *Last Retreat* published in *The Spiritual Doctrine*, there are at least some fifty of them.

Later P. Philipon will draw from his dossier a selection of texts, published under the title *Spiritual Writings*,[34] of which he said: "This work, published in 1948, cost me no effort. Without ever having reread my book on *The Spiritual Doctrine*, or having gone over the documents again, I recalled these texts, as present to my soul as if I had never left them."

Evaluation

It is certain that *The Spiritual Doctrine* by P. Philipon answered a need and an expectation at the time of its publication. The *Souvenirs* had penetrated into a number of libraries of priests, seminarians, convents, and lay people. The prayer, *O My God, Trinity Whom I Adore*, had covered the whole world.[35] The richness of Elizabeth the mystic was recognized.[36] However a doctrinal synthesis was lacking. *The Spiritual Doctrine* sought to fill this gap, and that is why this book received an enthusiastic welcome.

Marie-Michel Philipon, a young professor, recognized in Elizabeth an "essentially doctrinal spirituality." Subscribing to the assertion of Bishop Sagot du Vauroux that "what is most remarkable in the life of Sister Elizabeth of the Trinity is the exact conformity of her views, inclinations, interior life, and words, with the surest principles of mystical theology,"[37] he defined the meaning of his work as "a theologian's view of a soul and a doctrine" (p. 20). Or, as he said in another place: "On each point of doctrine to be analyzed it was possible to indicate with certitude and exactness to what principles of mystical theology the movements of this privileged soul were related, and what aspects of dogma had most profoundly nourished her interior life" (p. 23).

In fact, in *The Spiritual Doctrine* we meet a "related" Elizabeth—related to a spiritual and theological doctrine that the author progressively develops by brief explanations in the traditional theological vocabulary of his time. The clear divisions must have been appreciated, although in Elizabeth's case they are sometimes a little artificial, especially in the long chapter on the gifts of the Holy Spirit. The regular recourse to John of the Cross, Teresa of Avila, Thomas Aquinas and other saints—less regularly to the Bible and the history of the Church—certainly opened up horizons.

The backbone of the doctrine set forth—the Trinity, baptismal grace, divine indwelling, praise, conformity to Christ—gave a dogmatic foundation and unity to the texts chosen from Elizabeth. The book left an impression of solidity. There were also some innovations on the level of information. The few pages on her youth contributed several unknown facts, and in the remainder of the book there are little confidences from Mother Germaine and the other Sisters. Above all there were quite a few unedited texts, besides the numerous texts already familiar from the *Souvenirs*. In an appendix of nearly sixty pages, P. Philipon included the long letter of September 1906 to Françoise de Sourdon, *Heaven in Faith,* and the *Last Retreat,* which he had already abundantly cited in the course of the book. Inserted into a theological system, Elizabeth's texts certainly contributed much to the great success of P. Philipon's work.

Today we are in a position to perceive more easily the defects of this meritorious approach. While influenced by his readings of the *Souvenirs,* P. Philipon was equally influenced by his direct contacts with its author, Mother Germaine, the major witness, whose complete confidence he had gained and "to whom I owe the best of this book," as he wrote in the dedication of the copy he sent to the Carmel of Dijon. He explains this in the Introduction to *The Spiritual Doctrine*: "Nothing could have been more invaluable to us in the preparation of this work than the confidences and long hours of private conversation with Mother Germaine about one who was truly 'her child'; many times we had the inestimable consolation of receiving *full confirmation* from her on the conclusions that we drew from an

attentive analysis of the documents.[38] All the essential points of
this book were resolved in perfect agreement with her." (p. 21)

But we have spoken of the tendency to a certain "angelization"
which we noticed in Mother Germaine's biography of Elizabeth.
The Spiritual Doctrine continues to present us with the image of
an Elizabeth that is somewhat one-sidedly lofty and mystical.
The theological digressions on the Trinity and the work of the
Holy Spirit succeed in making her even more sublime. Elizabeth's
rich humanity remains in the background and her spiritual life
rests on too narrow a human foundation. Her community life in
Carmel (about which P. Philipon could still have gathered invaluable information from Mother Germaine) is, proportion-
ately, brought out very little. Finally, we are surprised that the
author profited so little from his inquiry of the witnesses whose
replies are preserved in his dossier in ACD. But perhaps the
explanation is to be found in the radical curtailing that the editor imposed on his first biographical chapter.[39] We notice in
particular large gaps in the study of Elizabeth as a lay person—
child or young girl—and yet, there would have been much to
"relate." The first nineteen years, three-fourths of her life, are
exhausted in a dozen pages. Now, in our opinion, Elizabeth's
Christian and mystical life must be taken seriously very early.

P. Philipon's doctrinal approach will obviously orientate his
choice of Elizabeth's texts. The same views also govern the selections and suppressions in the *Spiritual Writings*. In the two
books the young girl's *Diary* is scarcely mentioned;[40] the *Letters
of her Youth* are treated somewhat better. As for her *Poems*, of
which the *Spiritual Doctrine* cites only a few lines, P. Philipon
did not see that the key to their reading is that of spirituality,
which makes them a real "intimate journal" in which a whole
spiritual itinerary is revealed.[41]

As regards Elizabeth's humanity, the valuable insights of
Marie Dominique Poinsenet's book[42] make it, so to speak, the
complement of the *Spiritual Doctrine*. But it appeared thirty
years later, and the two books are characteristic of two different
eras and sensibilities.

On the *historical* level also P. Philipon's study presents some
lacunae: the dating of the letters, whose accuracy leaves much

to be desired, and the postponement of the beginning of Elizabeth's mystical life until the age of nineteen, as we have already said. Consequently, there is an overemphasis on the importance of her first meeting with P. Vallée, hence this absolute assertion: "From this day on everything was transformed and illuminated; she had found her way. Henceforth the Trinity will be her only life through everything. . . ." (pp. 38–39)

Another "thesis" that influences this approach is the erroneous date and meaning attributed to Elizabeth's discovery of her vocation as "Praise of Glory." Basing it on the sole witness of Sister Aimee of Jesus, thirty years after the facts, when the witness was almost eighty, P. Philipon situates the discovery "during the summer of 1905" (p. 54); "during the spring or summer of 1905," he said elsewhere (p. 128). Now Elizabeth already speaks of it in a letter of January 25, 1904.[43] The discrepancy of a year and a half out of the five years and some months she spent in Carmel is considerable.

Yet it is interesting to read a kind of retrospective self-criticism at a distance of thirty years, in which the author notes the fascination for the doctrinal aspect that he had formerly experienced: "A real reversal of perspectives took place in my thought. When, about thirty years ago, I began my research on Sister Elizabeth of the Trinity I was attracted especially by the simplicity and sublimity of her doctrine. My psychological inquiry of the witnesses of her life had aimed simply at assuring myself of the authenticity of her virtue so as to better understand the origins and meaning of her doctrine on the indwelling of the Trinity in the soul and on her supreme vocation as Praise of Glory. My dominant preoccupation remained the explanation of her doctrine. . . . After thirty-five years of experience with souls . . . what impresses me in Elizabeth of the Trinity, *even more than her doctrine, is the heroicity of her virtues.* I am convinced that from her earliest childhood she practiced the Christian virtues in an eminent, sometimes heroic, way."[44]

But at that point in the history of the study of Elizabeth, what reader would have then perceived signs indicated so obscurely? And the quality of P. Philipon's approach, which we have pointed out, assured that his work would be a great success. It underwent twelve editions in French and was translated into nine languages,[45] of which several were the object of various re-editions. In this way a number of Elizabeth's texts were widely diffused.

In the years 1960-1970, P. Philipon's work had less success, doubtless partly due to the "hagiographical strike" which was one of the characteristics of the spirituality of this period. In the following years, the witness of the saints stirred up a revival of interest, as the centenaries of Thérèse of Lisieux (1973) and Bernadette (1979) proved.

Towards the "Complete Works"

A "chance" visit to the Carmel of Dijon, November 6, 1977, gave us a renewed contact with Elizabeth of the Trinity, whose texts collected by P. Philipon we had read. Shortly afterwards, the idea of a complete edition of her writings imposed itself on us.

At that time we did not know what an unknown world was hidden behind this project; what joys, what encounters, and what work also. Since April 1978, our stays in Dijon became more frequent and prolonged. We discovered Elizabeth in a new and more complete light.

The first task, which we could never have brought to a successful conclusion without the untiring devotion of our Sisters of Dijon, was to define and explore what we have designated as ACD (Archives of the Carmel of Dijon). For a number of years the Carmelites, under the energetic impetus of Sister Marie of the Blessed Sacrament, have unceasingly and lovingly been compiling everything that pertains to their elder Sister from the beginning of the century.

In 1954 the Archives of Elizabeth were considerably enriched. In that year, Mme. Chevignard, Elizabeth's sister and an admirable Christian,[46] left, at the age of 42, a widow with nine children, died in Dijon. Her children then decided to bequeath to Carmel everything that was still a memento of Elizabeth: photos and pictures, objects and books that had belonged to her, the autographs of the writings that were in Guite's possession, copybooks, notebooks, and loose sheets on which she had copied prayers and texts before her entrance into Carmel, some music copybooks, and also nineteen school copybooks that not only give an idea of her educational formation and an overall view of the evolution of her writing as a child and as a young girl, but also contain fifty-four composition exercises, spaced over six years, some of which are very revealing of the psychology, activities, and milieu of the young girl.[47]

This donation to the Archives of Carmel also contained a series of letters from Mother Germaine to Guite and Mme. Catez, several of which date from Elizabeth's last illness and the first years after her death besides a long series of letters of condolence, or of testimony, addressed to the same at the time of Elizabeth's death or shortly after; and finally, a fragment of Mme. Catez's diary before her marriage, some letters written by her to her parents or to her husband which contain many details about Elizabeth as a small child, a series of letters which Canon Angles wrote her — always with some reference to Elizabeth — some letters from friends of Mme. Catez and Elizabeth and still other more official documents. In all of these[48] there can be found little nuggets of gold for Elizabeth's history.

But if we have spoken of the archives of Elizabeth of the Carmel of Dijon, let no one expect archives that are well localized, classified, and indexed. The lack of time in the life of a Carmelite dedicated to prayer, community life, daily work, and also the successive enrichment of the archives never permitted this systematic work of organization.

Thanks to the authorizations of the Carmelites and Monsignor Decourtray, Bishop of Dijon, it was possible for us to discover and explore one after the other: storerooms, cupboards, chests, boxes, packages, files, records, and envelopes — large and small. We gradually became familiar with the buildings where Elizabeth had lived; we saw the habits she wore, the objects and books she used, her photos, and the official books of the monastery (books of chronicles, accounts, elections, professions, and clothings). We examined many testimonies received with a view to writing the *Souvenirs* or to promoting the beatification of Elizabeth. Gradually a number of unknown writings found their way back to their owners. We had to study the history of Elizabeth and its context, her milieu, her city, her Carmel, her diocese, and her country at the beginning of the twentieth century. We often had to consult the Carmelites, especially Sister Elizabeth of Jesus, first niece of Elizabeth of the Trinity (of whom she often spoke in her correspondence of the last years), who later entered the Carmel of Dijon. We also had to visit and consult other archives, seek other information, interrogate witnesses of the witnesses.

But the principal work obviously concerned the numerous *writings* that Elizabeth of the Trinity left: her original writings as well as texts which she copied both as a lay person and as a Carmelite.

The Autographs and Their Origin

Inventory

Here is the list of writings, known to this day, which Elizabeth left us. We will exclude here the texts that she *copied* of which we will speak in PAT.

There are preserved:

—her *Diary*, written in three notebooks brought together into one tome

—4 SPIRITUAL TREATISES:

    I. *Heaven in Faith*, written in a notebook

    II. *The Greatness of our Vocation*, in the form of a letter

    III. *Last Retreat*, in a notebook

    IV. *Let Yourself Be Loved*, in the form of a letter

—17 PERSONAL NOTES on loose sheets, except for PN 13 and 14, written in her "personal notebook" and PN 7 and 12, of which the originals are lost

—124 POEMS (counting 1a), P 1a to 72 are written in two notebooks; the others are on loose sheets

—LISTS OF REFERENCES from the Bible or other authors, which are found in the appendix of our Volume II

—346 LETTERS (counting L 80a, 197a, 323a, and 328a rediscovered recently and also Spiritual Treatises II and IV, originally written in the form of a letter)

Besides these writings which are all published in these *Complete Works*, we must also mention:
— 54 COMPOSITION EXERCISES, written in school copybooks
— a notebook containing the account of her EXCURSIONS IN THE JURA IN 1895, which is also a composition exercise
— a notebook containing some SCHOOL EXERCISES IN POETRY

These writings, though often close to the reality which the young Elizabeth lived, also contain some elements of imagination proper to compositions, therefore we have not integrated them into the *Complete Works* but have assigned them to the documentary volume PAT. There one will also find the notes Elizabeth took of three retreats preached at Carmel: summaries and her *personal* choice of another's ideas.

We estimate that *nearly two-thirds* of Elizabeth's writings have never been published. We will speak of the autographs of the *Diary*, the *Spiritual Treatises*, the *Personal Notes*, and the *Poems* in their introductions and notes. Here we limit ourselves to the 346 *Letters*.

Letters Preserved and Letters Lost

By "letter" we mean every text in prose (except for the prayers), whatever its length, addressed to another person.

How is it that so many letters have been preserved of a young woman who died at the age of twenty-six?

Let us remark first of all that letters used to play a much more important role than they do now in our era of telephones and motorized transports. Also letters that had been received were kept much longer than in our age encumbered with papers! But the question remains.

Four complementary responses must be given: (1) Elizabeth had an overflowing, communicative, and very affectionate heart: "I have a grateful soul," she liked to say (Circ 14). So she easily took up her pen to tell of her affection and gratitude (which, in the infirmary, will lead her to write a number of short poems). (2) She was much loved by her correspondents, and her letters were for them the testimony of her friendship. (3) Her letters had such a content that they loved to reread them as messages born in the presence of God. (4) Elizabeth was considered very close to God, and soon as "a little saint"; her letters became "relics."

However, many letters were lost. Her best friend, Marie-Louise Hallo, who, during Elizabeth's lifetime, was absent from Dijon for three prolonged periods, confessed: "Unfortunately, I have very few of Elizabeth's letters. I infinitely regret having torn up some of them as they were too personal."[49] Likewise Mother Marie of Jesus, Prioress of Carmel at the time of Elizabeth's entrance, said, "A prolonged stay in the South [summer 1900] marked the year before her entrance; we exchanged some letters which I regret having burned." When she became Prioress of the new foundation of Paray-le-Monial, Elizabeth wrote her more than the two letters that have been preserved.[50] Sister Odile of Paray-le-Monial, whom Elizabeth had known, first as an extern Sister than as a non-choir Sister within the cloister in the Carmel of Dijon, affirmed, "I burned all her letters except for the last one."[51] And Anne-Marie d'Avout, a younger friend of Elizabeth said, "Unfortunately I burned all the documents or letters coming from Elizabeth."[52] Nevertheless, later one was discovered, as well as a letter to her mother, which allows us to suppose that Elizabeth wrote her occasionally from Carmel.

It is also certain that during her youth Elizabeth exchanged letters with very good friends such as Yvonne de Rostang, from Tarbes,[53] and Gabrielle Montpellier, from Limoux,[54] or with friends of her mother. Also the young Manitin Auburtin who met Elizabeth in September 1900 testified, "we wrote each other for awhile. . . . Elizabeth was too attractive a person to forget."[55] At the same time her sister, Elizabeth Auburtin (Mme. de Montleau) began to correspond with her namesake.[56]

It is equally certain there were letters to Mme. Massiet,[57] Mme. Angles,[58] Mme. de Maizieres[59] and Mme. de Vathaire[60] that have been lost, very probably also to Marie-Louise Maurel[61] and perhaps even to the Rolland aunts.[62]

Even in Carmel how many notes to her Prioress and her Sisters have disappeared! Little notes about work written during the times of silence or for a Sister who was not available at the time; a pledge of prayers, or a greeting on the occasion of a feast or anniversary. They could have taught us much about Elizabeth's loving and spiritual relationship with her Sisters of whom she said before her clothing, "I love them so!" (S 94) We can presume that several poems addressed to them have also disappeared.

In the month of December 1979 we had written here that it would be the least of our surprises if more letters were recovered. Two days later we received one addressed to Mme. Avout and another to her daughter Anne-Marie (L 197a and 328a), letters that were missing from all the inventories.

The Writing of Letters in Carmel

We will not linger over the origin of her letters from her childhood and adolescence. At first they accompanied her mother's letters (L 1-3); they were written on the occasion of a New Year (L 4-5); later they enthusiastically describe her trips; and in the last three years before her entrance into Carmel they were the expression of her friendly heart (twenty-four letters to Marie-Louise Maurel; ten to Françoise de Sourdon) or of her spiritual desires (five letters to Canon Angles; twenty-one to Marguerite Gollot). Elizabeth wrote them for the most part on her desk in her room (cf. CE 11).

In Carmel one did not write as often as one wished. Out of a spirit of solitude, correspondence was spaced, and out of a spirit of obedience, permission was always asked of the Prioress. According to the rules then in force, both incoming and outgoing correspondence was, in principle, read by the Prioress (except correspondence with ecclesiastical superiors and spiritual directors — but Elizabeth never had any in Carmel).

As for *frequency*, the Carmelite could write her parents, brothers and sisters each month, only every three months to other relatives and friends; and if one had a visit to the parlor, allowed at the same rhythm and conditions, this visit replaced a letter. So Elizabeth wrote her mother and sister — who faithfully took advantage of the parlor visits — chiefly during their absences, trips or vacations.

However, exceptions were always possible for an illness, a trial, a birth or a death. Mother Germaine also allowed Elizabeth to visit her lonely mother by letter, or to cheer up one of her many friends, or again to thank a donor for a gift received for the community. During the first months of her postulancy and during her last illness, obviously the exceptions will be more numerous.

In Lent and Advent all correspondence and all parlor visits were more strictly excluded. A serious reason was needed to break this silence. Exceptions will be very rare in Elizabeth's correspondence.[63]

During the week the Carmelite's day was well filled with community acts and work.[64] On Sundays and feast days the Blessed Sacrament was exposed in the Oratory until 5:00 P.M. Elizabeth loved to spend all her free time there. So she usually wrote her letters *during the free hour from 8:00 to 9:00 P.M.*[65] Seated on her little chair, she held her "desk" (L 88) on her knees, as she had no table.[66] This little wooden box contained an inkwell. At that hour she could seldom still profit from the natural light of evening that came through the small window overlooking the quadrangle. Ordinarily she had to use her kerosene lamp. She had to get used to it, and the new postulant confessed, "I don't know what I'm scribbling for I can hardly see with our little lamp" (L 90). But the advantage was that the ink could be dried in the small flame so as to turn the page more quickly, which was not without danger: "Please excuse this paper," Elizabeth wrote to Guite, "I put it closer to our lamp so that it would dry more quickly and I burned the bottom of the page" (L 117).

In winter the small cell had no heat of any kind. The cold did not help either the beauty of the writing or the rhythm. Elizabeth's skin was very sensitive and she easily developed chilblains on her face and hands. In a photograph taken in January 1903, she can be seen with some of her fingers wrapped in bandages, which made it all the more difficult to hold a pen! But the generous Carmelite remedies it with humor: "As for the cold, I would not know it was winter if I did not see the beautiful curtains God has hung at our little window. If you could see how lovely our cloister is with its frosted panes!" (L 109) Or again there is the moving explanation of Letter 156, love of the Crucified One makes us forget "sacrifices like this," and then in a very understanding tone, ". . . I am no more generous than you are, only you are ill, whereas I am in good health." Only once, during the last winter of her life, a little before her health gave way definitively, do we hear her excuse herself, "Please excuse this writing [poorly formed], but we have no heat, and I cannot hold my pen" (L 263).

The Poverty of the Paper

Let us say a word about the paper on which the autographs were written which shows us a way poverty was formerly lived in Carmel.

Most of the time Elizabeth used "white" ruled paper, the different qualities of which, according to our tastes, range from poor to very poor. They are sheets of 26.8 × 21.6 cm. or a few millimeters less; the lines, often somewhat oblique, lead us to think that the Carmelites received this paper as a gift.

Elizabeth seldom used the whole sheet in this large size; however, the "dear little aunts" of Carlipa, one of whom was somewhat deaf, the other somewhat blind, were given more consideration. Out of the twelve letters addressed to them from Carmel, eight were large sheets. But the most "spoiled" in this matter was Mme. Angles who was always ill.

Most of the time Elizabeth tore this large sheet in two, folded it once again and thus obtained four pages of around 13.4 x 10.8 cm. which she almost always filled up completely. It is true she left a space between each line, but on the other hand she often continued along the margins of the first page and sometimes even to the fourth! Still other times the large sheets were torn into irregular fragments, sometimes three-quarters of a sheet. The strip of paper which was left served to complete a new letter.

Beginning with the autumn of 1905, Elizabeth often used a whiter paper, of better quality, ruled in small rectangles, of which some sheets still bore the name of the donor: the notary Madon of Dijon.[67]

At other times it was old stationery,[68] pieces of paper in different sizes,[69] where one can see the irregular edges cut with scissors.[70] Sometimes it was paper that was almost as thick as cardboard (L 244). Messages could also be found on the back of a picture, on a calling card with the name scratched out (L 245, 251) or not scratched out if it was used for communication within the Carmel (L 100, 328), a wedding invitation (L 260) or a death notice;[71] the two sheets are glued together if the name of the deceased is still there (L 243).

Like the paper of the prayer *O My God, Trinity Whom I Adore* (PN 15), which was torn out of a notebook, some letters are written on a sheet taken from an old notebook[72] or account book.[73] Elizabeth wrote before her entrance and for her personal use: Personal Note 2 on the back of a letter that she had received, Personal Note 4 on the back of an invitation to a choir recital and Personal Note 5 on the back of a bill for coal. Likewise from Carmel, she will write parts of her letters on the back of an advertisement for paper (end of L 236), or for fire and life insurance (end of L 280). The little note, Letter 282, cut in the form of a trapezoid, is written on the back of a chocolate wrapper, "Milka Suchard."

For several letters or notes she even employed old wrapping paper that had already been used as the numerous folds prove.[74] These marks of poverty appear not only in her letters to her Carmelite sisters but also to her mother and to Guite, and are more and more frequent during her final illness (beginning with L 266). The letters to Guite will break all records with earthen-colored wrapping paper for Letter 292 and 298 — the so deeply moving Letter 298.

If before her entrance Elizabeth often used green, blue-grey or even violet writing paper, in Carmel there will be all the nuances of grey, yellowish, and white tints, without ever attaining a true white. Her *Poems from Carmel*, on the other hand, were often written on the back of small green leaflets which the Abbé Sauvé, director of the Major Seminary of Dijon, used to publicize his various "Dogmatic Elevations" and which he "bequeathed" regularly to Carmel. Something to encourage writers!

des Saints. St Paul dans ses magnifiques
épîtres ne prêche pas autre chose que
ce Mystère de la charité du Christ
aussi est-ce à lui que j'emprunte la
parole pour vous adresser mes vœux
"Que le Père de N. S. Jésus Christ vous
accorde selon les richesses de sa gloire que
vous soyez fortifié dans l'homme intérieur
par son Esprit. que J. C. habite dans
votre cœur par la foi. que vous soyez
enraciné et fondé en la charité en sorte
que vous puissiez comprendre avec tous les
saints quelle est la largeur, la longueur
la hauteur et la profondeur, et connaître

1. Letter 191, January 25, 1904.
   Below is a part of Letter 192, January 27, 1904.
   (Length of the first line of the original is 121 mm.)

2. Composition
   Exercise 13,
   May 21, 1894.

3. Diary 18,
   March 4,
   1899.

4. Diary 137,
   January 23,
   1900.

5. Letter 89,
   August 30,
   1901.

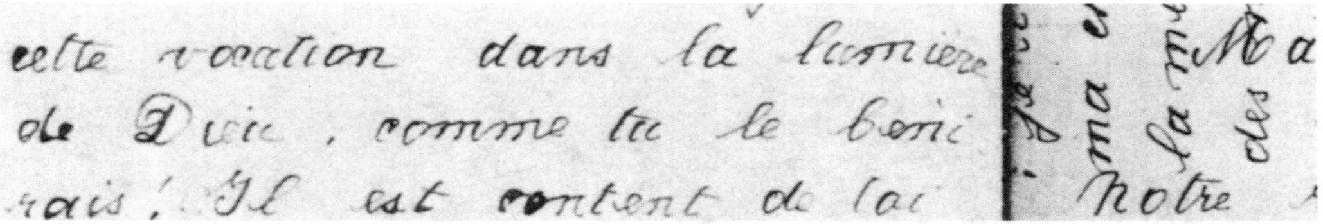

[Handwritten sample 6]

cette réaction dans la lumière
de Dieu, comme tu le béni-
rais. Il est content de toi

6. Letter 159,
March,
1903.

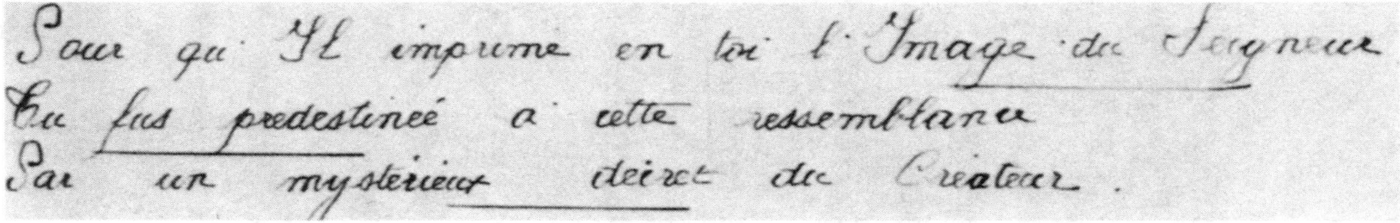

[Handwritten sample 7]

Sais que Il imprima en toi l'Image du Seigneur
Il fut prédestiné à cette ressemblance
Sais un mystérieux décret du Créateur.

7. Poem 93,
July 25,
1905.

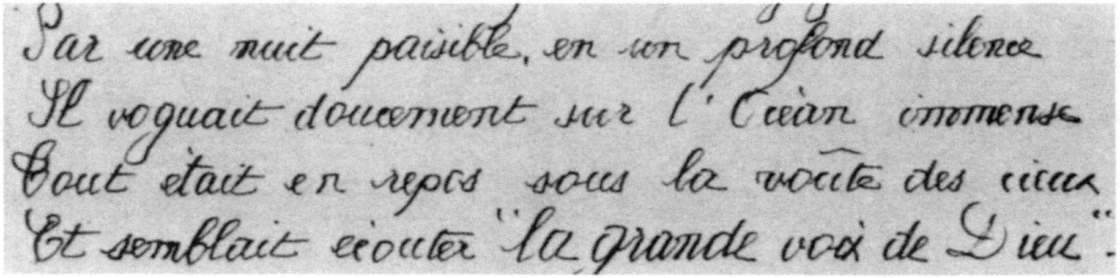

[Handwritten sample 8]

Par une nuit paisible, en un profond silence
Il voguait doucement sur l'Océan immense
Tout était en repos sous la voûte des cieux
Et semblait écouter "La grande voix de Dieu".

8. Poem 115 for
September 24,
1906.

J. M + J. T.

O mon Dieu Trinité que j'adore
aidez moi à m'oublier entièrement
pour m'établir en Vous immobile
et paisible comme si déjà mon
âme était dans l'éternité; que
rien ne puisse troubler ma paix ni
me faire sortir de vous ô mon Immua-
ble, mais que chaque minute m'em-
porte plus loin dans la profondeur
de votre Mystère. Pacifiez mon âme
faites en votre ciel, votre demeure aimée
et le lieu de votre repos; que je
ne vous y laisse jamais seul. mais que
je sois là toute entière, toute éveillée
en ma foi. tout adorante. toute
livrée à votre Action créatrice.
O mon Christ aimé. crucifié par
amour. je voudrais être une épouse
pour votre cœur. je voudrais vous cou-

9. Personal Note 15, November 21, 1904.

The Dating of the Letters

The *Diary, Spiritual Treatises,* most of the *Poems,* and the *Personal Notes*[75] offer no difficulty on the chronological level because Elizabeth dated them, or else the date is easily found. The dating of the *Letters,* on the other hand, proved very complex from the beginning.

To establish Elizabeth of the Trinity's spiritual itinerary precisely, especially in her brief and intense life as a Carmelite, it was necessary to resolve this chronological problem with maximum care; to amass or mix up the documents could only lead to inexact conclusions.

The reader will become aware of the problem on examining the very poor chronological indications that Elizabeth furnishes at the head of her letters. (These are not to be confused with the most accurate dates possible that we ourselves have added, in brackets, at the head of the letter. In most instances we have justified this more complete dating in the first notes, in which we have omitted other unnecessary proofs.)

Here is a table of chronological indications that Elizabeth left us for her letters:

—complete date: fourteen times
—mention of the *day of the week* + the *day of the month* + the *month,* without the year (for ex. "Wednesday, November 19"): twenty-five times
—mention of the *day of the month* + the *month,* without the year (for ex. "August 4"): seventy-one times
—mention of the *month* + the *year* (for ex. "January 1901"): three times
—mention of the *day of the week* + the *month* (for ex. "Friday, June"): once
—mention of the *day of the week* + the *day of the month,* without the month or year (for ex. "Saturday 30"): twice
—mention of the *month* alone (for ex. "August"): four times
—mention of the *day of the week* alone (for ex. "Thursday"): sixty-one times
—nothing at all: 165 times

Let us point out that other hands, most often the recipients themselves, have completed or added the date on the autographs *later*, in part or completely.

Apart from Mme. de Sourdon and Abbé Chevignard who seem to be the most precise, there are a number of inaccuracies in the others. It is the same with the chronological references that the numerous witnesses give; we must use them with pru- dence. One knows the limits of perception, of memory, of recall of facts — sometimes after long years. The incomplete notations and subjective interpretations, omissions, involuntary misrepre- sentations, personal sentiment, all this hardly permits a history of absolute exactness. The past cannot be entirely recovered, even when it is a matter of determining a fact as precise and ob- jective as a date. Many times, even in our own work, we have recalled the wise precautions of René Laurentin in his research on Lourdes — [76] the object of an even more complex historical study.

Our first task was to collect all the autographs still accessible. This was indispensable not only in order to establish the authen- tic text of this edition, but also in order to fix their dates, as we shall see.

Besides the autographs of the *Diary*, the *Spiritual Treatises*, the *Personal Notes*,[77] and the *Poems*,[78] we were able to collect and study 293 autographs, sixteen photocopies,[79] thirty manu- script copies,[80] and seven printed copies[81] of the *Letters*.

Reference Points

Our research was based on an ensemble of reference points, some of which could be used for almost every letter.

1. It is easy to see if the letter dates before or after her *entrance into Carmel* by the use of her religious name in the signature; this is an indication which, however, does not always afford an absolute certainty.[82]

2. In Carmel, the initials r.c.i. (unworthy Carmelite religious) after the signature, show that Elizabeth had already made her profession, the 11th of January, 1903. Its absence does not nec- essarily prove that the letter was written *before* her profession, for it is not uncommon that the professed omit it.

3. The indication of the *day of the week* + *the day of the month* (for ex. "Sunday, May 19" in L 55) permits us to determine easily the year, for this juncture would occur only every six years.

4. The *contents* of the letter often furnish indications for its period or its precise date of origin. In a series of letters to the same correspondent there is sometimes a logical connection: thanking for something asked for in a previous letter, the realization of a promise made earlier. Another source can inform us concerning the time of a trip, a meeting, a retreat, or conference, or vacations spent at a certain place which the letter speaks of. Or else there is an allusion to a particular year that is beginning, a liturgical or historical event, a feast day, an event in the family, the circle of friends, or the monastery. We completed the chronological precisions of ACD with information drawn from city halls, various archives, or families of the correspondents.[83]

5. A dozen times the *postmark* on the envelope preserved reveals the day on which the letter was sent. Sometimes an envelope Elizabeth had received was turned inside out in order to use it a second time. Even if her letter to her family or friends in Dijon was not sent by mail but delivered, for example by one of the Extern Sisters, the postmark on the inside indicates that Elizabeth's letter is posterior to this date.

6. Even the writing paper has a story to tell! We have said that Elizabeth often tore one of the large ruled sheets in two before writing her letter on it. If we compare some of the autographs, we can see that we have two halves of the same sheet: the torn edges fit together perfectly and the lines (often oblique) of the ruled paper match! (See the first photo in this volume with note 1 of L 191.) As the Carmelites, in their concern for poverty, kept only a little paper at a time, there is every chance that the two letters date from the same period, perhaps the same day.

7. The *ink* also reveals the period of the letter. Here we have a little secret of convents at the beginning of this century: in those days ink was not bought ready-made. It was the Sister Provisor who "made" the community ink by pouring water into a bottle

on the ink powder that had been purchased; and the Sisters went regularly to fill their little inkwell at the common bottle. The powder could vary in color (or else two different kinds of ink could be mixed), and thus the autographs are of various tints: pale copper, black, dark copper, "pure copper," blue-grey, black again (some years after Elizabeth's death purple will triumph). If at first sight all this seems to depend on the special-ized services of the police, when one has frequented Elizabeth's autographs for a long time, one can regroup them according to different periods solely on the basis of the ink used.[84] With a margin of prudence, however, for Elizabeth did not always write in her cell—she could also have drawn from the inkwell at the "turn"[85] where she spent several hours a day after her pro-fession. We have examples of two different kinds of ink for the same day or the same autograph.[86]

8. Let us not lay emphasis on the finer *pen* Elizabeth used beginning with Letter 258. But it is important to point out that all the letters during her eight months in the infirmary will be written in *pencil*, excepting those addressed to the Prioress —which were in ink—a custom of respect from which Elizabeth did not want to excuse herself.

9. We would surely have found priceless chronological ref-erences and information in the *letters from correspondents* who answered Elizabeth or whom she answered. But in a spirit of detachment, it was the custom in the Carmel of Dijon not to keep them. Only a few, by chance, escaped destruction.[87]

10. And there is a tenth witness, so eloquent for one who has studied Elizabeth's autographs for a long time: her very *hand-writing*. An extraordinary evolution in her handwriting permits us, with just a single glance, to determine within a year—more or less—the period of an autograph, especially after Elizabeth's fifteenth year.[88]

Her Writing

The numerous autographs that flowed from her pen during her short life constitute a marvelous display of the evolution of her handwriting, marked by two rather spectacular interventions.

The artist's fingers that, at the piano, rendered Elizabeth's emotions with such finesse also revealed her inmost feelings when she wrote. We have only to compare quickly examples 2, 3, 1, and 9 of the specimens of her writing reproduced in this volume to get a clear idea of the development of her writing, in which several stages can be distinguished.

1. The first is that in which the child learns penmanship. In her school copy-books she imitates reproduced models.[89] Despite the method, the search for a personal handwriting wins out.[90] Elizabeth never achieves a completely regular handwriting, but at fifteen and sixteen her writing has become round and legible, rather classic. The ink sketch of Composition Exercise 38 shows, however, that it is the fruit of application.

2. At seventeen, her handwriting evolves towards what could be called "an artist's handwriting"—large, pointed, and hooked. Did her mother urge her in this direction?[91] The evolution is slow but it is completed in the second half of 1898; it attains its maximum of illegibility and intricacy in the first half of 1899 when Elizabeth completes her nineteenth year. Example 3 (inset) shows us a specimen from her *Diary*. It is very hard to distinguish an *a* from an *o*, a *v* from an *n*, an *m* from *vi*; we must read the context. And what intricacy for the capital letters *I* and *J* (see the word *Jésus* in example 3)! The capitals are preceded by an "eye," a completely superfluous little circle;[92] after this little circle the pen descends, rises, descends and rises again to descend definitively and complete the capital. What gymnastics! But later, in August[93] this "eye," which for six years had preceded the capitals *I* and *J*, disappears forever (see the word "janvier" in example 4).

The second part of the *Diary*, written in January 1900 (see example 4) shows, moreover, that the "artist's writing" has become simplified throughout and has gained in legibility. The capitals *M* and *N* surmounted by a loop (see "Mardi" in example 4) lose it towards the middle of 1900. Her whole handwriting continues to become simpler (compare with example 5).

However, Elizabeth will have difficulty ridding herself of this pointed writing; and she retains a little complex about it! In the seven months that preceded her entrance into Carmel, a year and a half after the maximum illegibility of her "artist's writing," she excuses herself no less than ten times:[94] "You will need much time to decipher this letter with my horrible hand-writing," she wrote to Canon Angles (L 38); she speaks again of a "horrible scrawl" (L 45), of an "awful letter" (L 69), of an "epistle (which) I am ashamed to send you" (L 55).

In Carmel she is still "scribbling" (L 90). Towards the middle of 1902 her writing, which has become more disjointed, seems to reflect the difficulties through which she was passing. The Sisters became aware of her writing problems; and Marie of the Trinity, her former Sub-Prioress, relates how it was remedied: "On entering Carmel, the dear postulant had a handwriting which was very fashionable at that time for artists but not very religious. So her Prioress wanted her to change it. A Sister [doubt-less Sister Agnes], who has a rather classic handwriting, round and regular, gave her some lessons...."[95]

3. According to the autographs this little course took place after her profession, during Lent of 1903. Sister Elizabeth ap-plied herself to it with an ardor that only the saints know how to put into the smallest things — here, doubtless, somewhat humil-iating. The result is already visible in example 6, the first auto-graph that announces the new writing. The transformation is soon accomplished; and the penmanship, beautiful, round and regular, attains its apogee in the second half of 1903. Example 1, Letter 191 of January 25, 1904, although probably written with "cold hands" on this winter evening, is a good example of it.[96]

4. Nevertheless, this handwriting will also, slowly and un-consciously, undergo a profound modification especially in the sense of a simplification — in particular, a restriction of flour-ishes in the capital letters! Three factors play a role here: (a) physical fatigue — already from the summer of 1904 the hand has become less steady; the nearer Elizabeth approaches the autumn of 1906 when she will die, the more shaky and weak her hand becomes; at the end it will be sheer will power that drags it over the paper; (b) a natural diminution of application which becomes a secondary concern; (c) a simplification of soul which goes more and more to the essential and is reflected in the sim-

plification of this writing which had never been Elizabeth's "natural" expression. The autograph of *O My God, Trinity Whom I Adore* of November 1904 (see example 9) already reflects this whole process.

These evolutions are never completely abrupt; there are steps forward and backward, but over a space of time the change is obvious.

Two examples. The capital *P* (which often appears in the name of St. Paul) is, at the beginning of the new penmanship, rich in loops[97] (see two specimens in example 1); towards the end of 1904 it becomes simplified most often as a printed *P* (see the word "Pacifiez" in example 9); but from the middle of 1905 it is almost converted into a capital *S* (see examples 7 and 8)— and that with great consistency.[98]

Another example. In the new handwriting the *a, o, g* and *q,* have in general, many loops tightly closed at the top; also the lower loop of the *g, j* and *y*. The nearer Elizabeth approaches death the more the majority of these letters will be open, as can be seen quite well from example 8. Doubtless it is a consequence of her weakness but also the symbol of her desire to no longer be attached to earth—to let go—and to open towards Heaven.

After a long contact with Elizabeth of the Trinity's autographs it is impossible to confuse the documents of 1902 with those of 1904 or 1906.

Our Options for Establishing the Text

Once the texts are deciphered and the letters dated, other difficulties arise in giving a correct edition, which are due to Elizabeth's defective literary education.

Because of her studies at the Conservatory, begun at the age of eight, [99] there was not much time for the teaching she received at home. The little Elizabeth spent long hours at the piano each day. Her mother wished above all to assure her daughters a career as a music teacher. To judge from her school copybooks, it was only after having obtained her first prize at the piano at the age of thirteen that Elizabeth began a more intensive course of study. But it was then too late to remedy completely the handicaps due to this late education. Moreover, her instructor, Mlle. Forey, does not seem to have been one of the more demanding teachers. As a result of this, all her life Elizabeth will make many mistakes in spelling[100] and in grammar; and her punctuation will be rather capricious.

This posed a problem for the establishment of the text of the *Complete Works*. Should we push the demands of literary criticism to the point of scrupulously reproducing all these encumbering mistakes while considerably weighing down the critical apparatus? Should we retain the poor punctuation and thus make the reading difficult? Would the advantages be in proportion to the effort required of the reader?

We did not think so. Elizabeth's writings did not have the stormy history of those of Thérèse of Lisieux, to which Mother Agnes had added a number of corrections and personal modifications, and which, obviously, necessitated an edition as faithful as possible. Besides, we cannot say that Elizabeth was a master writer whose original punctuation would have revealed certain secrets of style.

As she did not intend these spelling errors nor this punctuation, to reproduce them would present no interest, except anecdotal for the reader, so we decided to correct the spelling and to modify slightly the punctuation, of which we will give here at least an idea.

Spelling Errors

First of all we must not consider as errors in spelling Elizabeth's peculiarities in her handwriting. Her accents and the dots over the i's generally fly high and wide, and just as she often turns her commas to the right rather than to the left, so her grave accents often slant to the left: for example we often read instead of "chère mère": "cheré meré"!

In general, it was rather by hearing than by seeing that the words were impressed on the young musician's memory, who as a young child had never really learned the instinctive reaction of good spelling. We also have the impression that, from the intensity of her emotion and her contact with others, her attention was fixed much more on whom or about whom she was writing than on the visual image of her writing. Likewise she seems to be entirely *in* what she is reading, scarcely paying any attention to the printed image of the words under her eyes. How else can we explain the remarkable consistency with which she wrote, hundreds of times, this word "Maître" which she so loved, without the circumflex accent?[101] Even "Jésus" must often do without the acute accent![102]

If anyone wants to undertake a thesis on "the saints and their mistakes in spelling," we can offer him the following remarks concerning Elizabeth Catez, the pianist who let herself be guided by sound:

— Frequent confusion between the infinitive (oublier), the imperative plural (oubliez) and the past participle (oubliée).

— Confusion between words of the same pronunciation: "ou" and "où"; "quelle" and "qu'elle"; "avait" and "avais"; "m'est" and "met"; "voir" and "voire"; "ai" and "aie"; "peux" and "peut"; "l'a" and "la," etc.

— Errors concerning nasal sounds: "enmène" (often); "cepandant"; "fonds" for "fond"; confusion between "quand," "quant" and "qu'en";

— Errors in the use of apostrophes and hyphens: "n'est-ce-pas" (often) "ta maladie ne t-a-t-elle pas";

— A number of mistakes in the accents: "penetrée," "ici-bàs" (often), "cloitre," "abime," "apparaitre," "fraiche," "cloture," "prophête," "repeter," "predestination," "reflêter," "celeste";

— Omission of a letter in certain words with double consonants: "embarassée," "inénarable," "consomer," "solenels," "enseveli-sez," "affectionée," "incessament";

— But on the other hand, redoubling a single consonant: "datte" (for date), "sottisses," "dissonnances," and, with an admirable consistency, redoubling the s (doubtless because of a slightly more stressed pronunciation) in "anniverssaire" and "inssondable"; we also find "indispenssable" and "occassion".

Along this line, Elizabeth stumbles again over difficult words like "Ressurection" (L 162) or "assenscions" (LR 44). But when she speaks of the mystère insaisissable de la mort" in Letter 238

she trips so thoroughly that she commits four mistakes in just
one word: "inssaissisabbe" later adding the syllable "sa" at first
omitted!

"Psalmodie" was another very difficult word. Already in 1898
she had written "psaumodie" (P 53) after having corrected a little earlier the word "plalmodies" (P 49); in a notebook of copied
texts we find "pslamadies." The one who writes psalms is sometimes called "the plasmiste" (L 242); some weeks later she corrects it to "pslalmiste" (L 263).

Other difficult words: "hazard" (L 335), "phisyques" (L 249),
"genoux" (L 60), "extention" (LR 8), "symphatie" (D 88, L 305),
and "antiphatie" (D 88 and 97). But we can see that sometimes
she corrects herself; too great a zeal makes her then change
"langage" to "language" (L 238).

We pass over in silence her mistakes in Latin when Elizabeth
begins to decline words in this language. Doubtless she would
answer us, "Je m'imamigine" (L 298) that it doesn't matter! In
any case it is not serious, for "a Carmelite supposes a being completely divinized"![103]

The Punctuation

Here also we must not confuse poor punctuation with peculiarities in her handwriting. When the period intended to dot an i
flies too far and stops over the final period of the sentence, it
produces a false colon. And if an accent overhangs the final
period, we obtain a false exclamation point! Moreover, the poor
quality of the paper can suggest periods and commas when in
reality it is only small spots on the paper.

Apart from that, the punctuation is quite defective, and the
sentences are sometimes interminable. Besides, the commas are
often so small that it is difficult to distinguish them from the
period, and we often have to guess. Again, if only Elizabeth
would have always written a capital in starting a new sentence,
but in her youth she often begins with a small letter! Later, it
will sometimes be difficult to distinguish the capital letters from
the small letters for *A* and *O*.

Towards the end of her life, especially when she wrote in pencil, the signs of punctuation are lighter still; and physical weakness leads her to neglect them more and more. Then we must try to enter into her thought and complete the punctuation as needed. We have done this with extreme respect for the verity of her thought and have, by preference, left her sentences in all their length.

The Capital Letters

Our third option was to conform the use of capitals. It is very difficult to say what is the secret that governs the presence or absence of the capital for appositions to Christ when Elizabeth writes in her *Diary* "Amour" fourteen times and "amour" nine times; or "vie" ten times and "Vie" six times: sometimes the two words appear next to each other, one with a capital and one with a small letter. Why is Jesus in turn the bien-aimé, the Bien-aimé, the bien-Aimé and the Bien-Aimé? And are we to attach an importance to the use of capital or small letters when she speaks to Germaine de Gemeaux of "Love, this Infinite love" and when she counsels her: "Let us wake in Love, all day let us surrender ourselves to Love, . . . and again let us sleep in Love" (L 172), only to reveal several days later to Canon Angles that her happiness is "to wake in love, to move in love, to sleep in love" (L 177)?

So throughout we have unified the most dominant tendencies in Elizabeth: capitals for the appositions of God and Christ; capitals for the qualities that define the being of God;[104] capitals for the synonyms of Heaven.[105]

In the personal pronouns that represent God there is again great confusion: Elizabeth very often writes He and Him but you and thee, when speaking of God. We have retained what is truly characteristic of her: He, The One, and Him: and in the plural, Them and Those. Canon Angles will testify: "She always called Christ—with a heavenly accent—*Him*!"[106] For her it was a word full of resonances and light, a word that shines!* And she almost always writes it with a capital letter.[107]

As for Elizabeth's circle of acquaintances, there is also great confusion;[108] we have chosen to consistently employ small letters.

---

* "shines": "Him" in French is *Lui*; the verb "to shine" is *luire*. [Translator's note]

Other Conventions

To facilitate the reading, we have printed out the abbreviations that Elizabeth often used, especially at the end of her life (pr, vs, ns, M. and Me, qqs., tante F., M.L.), as well as the numbers, leaving only abbreviations of the signature which might have significance.

The words which she underlines twice are printed in SMALL CAPITALS, and the words underlined three times in LARGE CAPITALS.[109]

Even though Elizabeth underlines only part of the words (see example 7),[110] we print them entirely in *italics*, as well as the words that she enlarged, giving them in this way a special emphasis (see "la grande voix de Dieu" in example 8).

We have completed the *inverted commas* when they were omitted at the beginning or end of a quotation, and we have respected Elizabeth's paragraphs, which are sometimes difficult to discern when the preceding paragraph ends exactly at the end of a line. Sometimes Elizabeth suggests a new paragraph by leaving a large space between two sentences, or by putting a very obvious horizontal dash.

Elizabeth and the Influences to Which She Was Exposed

We do not intend to make a thorough study here of the influences to which Elizabeth of the Trinity was exposed; they appear in our notes of her writings and an idea of them can be formed from the indices that are at the end of Volume II.

We would like simply to point out that she read the great authors in editions different from the ones we use today. That was the way God "passed by." In referring to the editions of today, we run the risk of projecting onto Elizabeth influences that she did not know and of not seeing those whose traces she bore.

For example, when Elizabeth discovered *The Story of a Soul* of Thérèse of Lisieux in 1899, it was the second edition[111] which had been thoroughly revised by Mother Agnes and is somewhat removed from the authentic edition of the manuscripts we possess today. The famous "chapter XI" incorporated the end of the present Ms. C and a great part of Ms. B. It was a magnificent ending which deeply affected the soul of the young Elizabeth. When we read "Thérèse," we must often understand: "Thérèse + (some) Agnes."

It is the same for St. Paul; Elizabeth read him especially in the translation by Canon Gaume,[112] which was augmented by numerous apologetic notes destined to make our "dear heretics" realize how wrong they were. Thus "Paul" is "Paul + Vulgate + Gaume." (Our biblical references will always follow the Vulgate numbering because of this.)

St. John of the Cross, whose *Spiritual Canticle* and *Living Flame*[113] she so savored, were known to her in the well-written but rather free translation of the Carmelites of Paris. For St. Teresa of Avila, she used (most of the time) the translation of Bouix.[114]

The case is somewhat more complicated for the anthology of Ruysbroeck,[115] which so delighted Elizabeth in the months of June-September 1906 during her final illness. Ernest Hello had translated into *French* the *Latin* translation Surius made from the *Old Dutch* of Ruysbroeck. But Surius did not always base himself on the authentic texts of Ruysbroeck, and consequently Elizabeth will quote passages attributed to the Flemish mystic which in reality are from one of his disciples, Godfried van Wevel.[116] Thus Ruysbroeck in Elizabeth is "Ruysbroeck, or sometimes Godfried van Wevel + Surius + Hello." Likewise Angela di Foligno[117] = "Angela di Foligno (her secretary, Brother Arnaud) + Hello."

Père Vallée

We must make special mention of the Dominican Father, Irénée Vallée whom Elizabeth met several times. The first was fourteen months before her entrance. Also, she had read some of his sermons before as well as after she entered.[118] She saw him again several times in Carmel and made a retreat under him in 1902.

The real influence of Père Vallée, which, in our opinion, was not as great as that of Paul, John of the Cross, or the two Tere-

sas, has nothing in common with the myth which would like to
make Elizabeth the mouthpiece of the Dominican preacher. We
will examine the question more thoroughly in AL; we limit
ourselves here to the following remarks.

"Père Vallée" is already a rather complex concept. Far less an
original thinker than an eloquent preacher, he is himself a cru-
cible in which numerous influences have mingled, and he continued to enrich himself by his readings and his contacts. For it
to be really complete, someday a little study should be made on
the influence of Elizabeth of the Trinity (especially after her
death) on the thought of Père Vallée, who was so legitimately
proud of her whom he readily called his "daughter".

Elizabeth was not the only one to appreciate the Father Prior
of the Dominicans of Dijon. He was very highly regarded and
likewise listened to in the Carmel. Several Sisters had him as
their spiritual director. He frequently preached there on great
feasts and was asked to give the community retreats of 1897,
1900, and 1902; Elizabeth read the texts of the first two retreats
that she had not attended. He also willingly gave the texts (often
printed) of his sermons given elsewhere. Thus P. Vallée communicated to the Carmel of Dijon, in a theological vocabulary
full of a personal oratorical style, a spiritual and dogmatic richness. There already existed a whole "Valléen background" in
the Carmel of Dijon before Elizabeth entered. So she drew from
this "background". Sister Marie of the Trinity and Sister Agnes
of Jesus and Mary, both directed by P. Vallée, contributed to
introducing her to it. Mother Germaine, Prioress and Mistress
of Novices, greatly esteemed the Father and doubtless encouraged the reading of his sermons; but her own personal spirituality and vocabulary were more purely "teresian" — and we must
understand by this word also Thérèse of Lisieux whom Mother
Germaine particularly loved. What, at first sight, can seem a
"Valléen" influence is often only secondary in Elizabeth. It was
strongest in 1901-02.

Later, other influences will prevail although Elizabeth still
quotes P. Vallée in her letters to Abbé Chevignard, a Dominican tertiary.

Elizabeth's Originality

Elizabeth had a very good auditory memory. From her child-hood she had spent hours at her piano each day, listening to the sounds with a refined ear and assimilating the rhythm of the pieces that she played. Thus this memory was capable of very faithfully rendering the sermons of the Mission of 1899 (see her *Diary*), and the accents, and turns of phrases of P. Vallée.

But in the end, this receptivity is not so much a question of "memory." It is her heart inflamed by love of God and all that concerns God that makes her "listen" — the word she so loved — as an ardent contemplative: first to P. Vallée, then to Mother Germaine, and later to the greatest masters of the spiritual life. But above all, she listened to her "Master" par excellence, Jesus, who sends his Spirit into this young heart that is so penetrable and avid for Life. "O Word eternal, Word of my God, I want to spend my life in listening to You. . . ." (PN 15)

"May our life flow into His. . . . There let us become silent that we may listen to Him who has so much to tell us . . . that we may hear everything that is being sung in His soul." (L 164)

The level of expression, the level of thought existed in Eliza-beth as they do in all of us who are enriched by our contacts, our reading, and our teachers. Dead at twenty-six, Elizabeth did not have the time, despite the richness of her heart, to attain a wholly personal style nor, despite her intelligence, a wholly origi-nal expression of her mystical life. But if we search not for the form in the man but the *man* in his form, we see that Elizabeth of the Trinity is situated at another level: that of holiness, of the experience of life in God — a lived experience. She is not a pro-fessor of theology, not even of mysticial theology; she is a witness of grace in action!

Elizabeth Catez read relatively little. But she contemplated at length the pages of the incarnation of Christ, his death, his life-giving Eucharist, the infinite Charity that educates us to a life in God, with God, for God — and for others. She particularly de-lighted in walking in the garden of the New Testament; above all in St. Paul and St. John, fascinated by the wide horizons that these two guides opened up before her wondering eyes. This gives to her writings a very broad and "Christian" base and makes them "relevant" for every believer who seeks a close relationship with God in the depths of his heart, and finds it again at the surface of each day.

Testimony

Elizabeth's writings belong first of all to the order of witnessing, to be understood in the context of her unwritten acts and words. A witness does not want to prove but to share. Either you are touched by it or you reject it. Or you begin to question.

This does not exclude that there is to be found in the writings of this young mystic, not a ready-made "doctrine" but an underlying doctrinal foundation. "The structure of her spiritual universe, the content and the style of her theological thought," wrote Hans Urs von Balthasar, "are of an intensity and a flawless consistency."[119]

We would like to end this general introduction with the lines that this theologian sent us after receiving Volume III of the *Complete Works,* and which express our own expectation: "This profusion of new texts will help to awaken a general interest in Elizabeth. The Christian people knows well what it owes its Saints!"

Conrad De Meester

NOTES

1. *Mystiques de France. Textes choisis et commentés,* Ed. Corrêa, 14e éd., pp. 283-284.

2. Cf. Our introduction to the first section of the *Letters from Carmel.*

3. *Elisabeth de la Trinité et sa mission spirituelle,* Seuil, 1960, p. 79.

4. Cf. RB 1 in PAT.

5. *Derniers Entretiens* DDB-Cerf, 1971, p. 214 (27.5.1). Cf. *Thérèse of Lisieux St., Her Last Conversations,* trans, by John Clark, O.C.D., ICS Publications, p. 102.

6. Cf. AL. An impressive verification: almost all the numerous letters of condolence that the family received on the occasion of Elizabeth's death used the word "Saint" (cf. PAT). Cf. also S 261: "As soon as the news of her death spread through the town, people crowded to Carmel, eager to contemplate her whom all called *the little saint. . . .*"

7. To be sure she had already used the word in an earthly perspective: the mission of the Carmelite (P 86, L 250, 256) or of a priest (L 250) or of a mother (L 186).

8. Cf. HA, p. 235. We cite the second edition of *Histoire d'une Ame* (HA).

9. Mother Germaine places the conversation "at the time when this letter was written" (*Souvenirs*, ed. 1935, p. 234).

10. The first responses of the Carmels, preserved in ACD, are dated from the 28th of December.

11. It is almost impossible to find; we will republish it in PAT.

12. It is possible to reconstitute satisfactorily the genesis of the *Circular* and the *Souvenirs* thanks to the letters of Mother Germaine to Mme. Catez and to Guite (ACD) and to the Carmel of Anderlecht (Archives of the Carmel of Clamart), to the letters of Sisters Agnes of Jesus and Mary of the Carmel of Dijon to the Carmel of Angers (Archives of the Carmel of Angers) and to the answers from the Carmel of Anderlecht (ACD).

13. Responses provoked in a way by the *Circular* itself: "But we must restrict ourselves and keep these confidences for the day when God will be pleased to extend the influence of His 'Praise of Glory'" (Circ. 3).

14. From a letter of the same day to Mme. Catez it seems that this request was very probably made during a conversaton in the parlor around the 1st of January.

15. Her confessor at the parish church of Saint-Michel, from the age of eleven to seventeen. Elizabeth loved "his firm and severe direction," as she called it in her *Diary* (D 5). Abbè Sellenet's answer to Mother Germaine's request is found in PAT.

16. For example, from Marie-Louise Hallo, Germaine Gemeaux, Louise Demoulin. They are found in PAT.

17. Mother Germaine writes: "I am returning to you, very dear Madame, the letters entrusted to us and which, after copying, we are sending back to you complete and intact, I believe." [It probably concerns Elizabeth's letters to her mother.] "I am also returning your letters that were addressed to you [letters of condolence and testimony after Elizabeth's death] keeping only four that could complete 'our documents' for the notice. One from the good Canon [Angles], one from the Curé of Saulieu [Abbè Sellenet], one from Abbé Chaboisseau [the priest who baptised Elizabeth at the military camp of Avor, in Farges-en-Septaine] and the fourth from Mme. de Bobet. I am keeping them very carefully with the one of yesterday (P. Vallée, very beautiful) and the religious Weekly [with the funeral oration for M. Catez, which will be cited in S 9]." For all these documents which were returned to the Archives of the Dijon Carmel in 1954 (cf. *infra*, pp. 48-49), see PAT.

18. This was the first Carmel founded in France in 1604, at Paris, Rue d'Enfer (successively Rue Denfert and Rue Henri-Barbusse). In 1901 they had to take refuge in Anderlecht (Belgium). In 1920 they returned to France and established themselves at Clamart near Paris. Since they were the first foundation in France and had an illustrious history, many Carmels naturally consulted them on the subject of Carmelite customs.

19. Preached by P. Vallée, from the evening of the 16th to the morning of the 25th of October 1908.

20. These are: Poems 83, 86, 96, 88, 91, 89, 80, 94, 95, 100, 104, 109, 120, 115, 118, 106, 122. The (selections from) the letters in the appendix were addressed to Françoise de Sourdon, Canon Angles, Mme. Angles, Germaine de Gemeaux, Mme. Farrat and Mme. de Sourdon.

21. Mother Marie of St. John, who became prioress after Mother Germaine's death, testified: "Mother Germaine had a difficult time writing it. She told me 'I wrote the *Souvenirs* on my knees weeping'" (PO 464). The same Prioress had explained this already in the obituary circular (p. 7) of Mother Germaine (completed June 16, 1935), when speaking of the *Souvenirs* ". . . the works of God are brought to birth in suffering and humiliation; the more fruitful they are to be, the more the Lord demands a persevering and confident effort in the beginnings. Also, our dear Mother needed a special grace to complete the work undertaken, for there was no lack of difficulties and trials. She was no longer Prioress as the new elections had just placed back at the head of the community the revered Mother Marie of the Heart of Jesus. Since she had not known Elizabeth of the Trinity intimately and her views were not quite the same as those of our dear Mother, she did not at first understand the designs of the Lord. Without letting herself be upset, and remaining humble and perfectly obedient, but with the assurance that God was asking it of her, our Mother set to work. She wrote this work of devotion and tears 'on her knees,' continually praying to obtain light from the Holy Spirit. No one will know what anguish and affliction it cost her maternal heart. Bishop Dadolle, our Superior, supported her with his fatherly encouragement and helped her with his wise advice." According to the recollections of the Carmelites of Dijon, the difficulty mentioned was occasioned especially by the fact that Mother Germaine, who had become bursar of the Monastery, was very busy (we heard this, moreover, in the preceding pages), and her Prioress thought that the work of the *Souvenirs* demanded too much time. There is also Mother Marie of St. John's explanation: "of a practical nature, she [Mother Marie of the Heart of Jesus, whose brother, Bishop Herzog, would later become the first postulator of Elizabeth's Cause. . . .] felt that it was a waste of time" (PO 464). In the same place Mother Marie of St. John affirms again: "[Mother Germaine] had each chapter sent to the bishopric and the Bishop supported her." But this detail, a late recollection of 1948, cannot be confirmed as Mother Marie of St. John did not enter Carmel until 1915.

22. Elizabeth is called the "poor child" (S 251), "the happy child" (S 96, 178, 277), "the beloved child" (S 247), "the generous child" (S 172, 213), the "holy child" (S 182, 248, 260) and most often, "the dear child" (S 139, 177, 188, 206, 213, 217, 228, 249, 253, 255, 258).

23. But the cover of this "Third edition" bears 1911 as the date.

24. We have found sixteen editions: twelve in the *large* format, (22 x 14.3 cm.) and four in the *small* format (16.8 x 11 cm. — without the Letters and Poems; the last edition in the small format, of 1956, is complete and measures 18 x 11.3 cm.). We give between parentheses the printing they reached when this is indicated on the cover. (It is not certain, however, that the printings in the *small* format were included in this number, for Bishop Landrieux remarks in his approbation for the *ninth* edition that it is "the seventh which reached 25,000": thus he did not take into consideration the two editions in the *small*

format.) Here then is the order: (1) 1909; (2) 1910; (3) 1911; (4) also 1911; (5) 1912; (6) 1915; (7) 1917; (small format); the year is suggested by the announcement in a small *Extrait des Souvenirs*, which we will speak of later, of this "popular edition"; the price given is 2.25 F; in reality it will be 3.25 F (unless it concerns another printing, all trace of which has been lost); (8) 1918 (small format, the year is indicated in pencil on the copy preserved in ACD); (9) 1919 (25,000); (10) 1920 (33,000; it is to be noted that this same number also figures on other copies that bear the year 1921 on the cover: it is then the same printing, but with two different covers); (11)? (40,000); (12) 1927 (65,000); (13) 1930 (small format); (14) 1935 (80,000); (15) 1946 (95,000); (16) 1956 (small format). Let us also mention that the cover indicates as editor the Carmel of Dijon, but for the last two editions, les Editions de Saint-Paul, Paris. The Carmel of Dijon edited in 1917 (imprimatur) a small *Extrait des Souvenirs: Soeur Elisabeth de la Trinité*, 15 x 10 cm., 38 pp., re-edited in 1925. Then, in 1938 (imprimatur): *Une Louange de gloire. Soeur Elisabeth de la Trinité*, 15.1 x 9.7 cm., 38 pp. These two brochures had a large circulation but there are no figures for them. It is not possible to speak here of the numerous pamphlets and pictures diffused since Elizabeth's death.

25. Although the cover bears the number 96,000 (which is unlikely since in 1946 it had already reached 95,000) the text indicates (p. 231) that the *Souvenirs* "exceeded 100,000 for France alone" (that is, for the edition in the French language).

26. We took these facts concerning the translations from P. Simeone Tomás-Fernandez, *Bibliografia della Serva di Dio Elisabetta della Trinità*, Roma, Postulazione generale OCD, 1974.

27. What is most striking is the introduction of a new chapter, the XVIIIth, on Elizabeth's posthumous influence. But the "Foreword" for this new edition mentions still other modifications: "We have profited by this new edition to collate minutely the texts cited. Some fragments of the letters had been transposed to facilitate the connection of facts referring to the same subject. We believed it our duty to replace them in their chronological order. Some reminiscences of friends of our venerated Sister, new selections from her *Diary*, several unedited letters, and a supplementary chapter containing letters of appreciation concerning the spirituality and life of Sister Elizabeth of the Trinity, testimonies of veneration, and, finally, some accounts of facts which came to our knowledge after 1909 are the modifications of the new edition of the *Souvenirs.*"

28. *La Vie Diocésaine. Revue de l'activité catholique dans le diocèse de Dijon*, no. 79, May 23, 1931, p. 244.

29. Let us mention that the dossier of the writings reassembled in view of the beatification, in better order, was translated into Italian by Giovanni Dante under the title *Scritti* (Roma, Postulazione generale dei carmelitani scalzi, 1967). The Spanish edition of Fr. Alfonso Aparicio, *Obras Completas* (Burgos, El Monte Carmelo, 1969; new edition 1979) already shows a considerable progress due to the fact that the translator worked for several weeks on the autographs themselves at the Carmel of Dijon. In our edition which concerns the French originals, we will abstain from all criticism, textual or otherwise, concerning their translations.

30. The Notebooks are arbitrarily numbered. Notebook 6, which contains the letters to Mme. Catez, Guite, Abbé Chevignard, and the letter to Abbé Jaillet (to which were later added some other letters or fragments addressed to the same), seems to be quite old: it was written by Sister Agnes (who, in any case, left the Carmel of Dijon in 1920 for the Carmel of Toulouse) in the ink characteristic of the first year after Elizabeth's death. There is also a letter that Bishop Dadolle addressed to Mme. Catez November 18, 1906. Could it be the transcription that the "little copyist" (very probably the young Sister Agnes, considering her numerous transactions in the preceding years) made of "this whole dossier" entrusted to them by Guite, and of which Mother Germaine's letter of December 1, 1906, that we have already cited, speaks? Notebook 7 contains the *Diary*, probably in the hand of Sister Marie of the Immaculate Conception, in the same copper-colored ink as the preceding notebook. This copy is also probably quite old. There also exists a very early copy of the letters to Mme. Farrat made by Mme. Catez; on the other hand, it was only around 1967 that Sister Marie of the Blessed Sacrament, the Prioress, had the letters to Canon Angles typed.

31. With a preface by R. P. Garrigou-Lagrange, Desclée De Brouwer, s.d. (published in 1939, according to "the preface for the 2nd edition"), 354 pp. We will cite from the 9th edition (1947). Père Philipon relates the origin of his book in a typewritten note which is found in his dossier in ACD; he published these pages, slightly revised, in *En présence de Dieu. Elisabeth de la Trinité* ("Présence du Carmel," 7), DDB 1966, pp. 185-187, 208-211. But the Introduction to *The Spiritual Doctrine* also gives some information on the origin of this book.

32. *Spiritual Doctrine*, p. 21. The result of his inquiry will be found in PAT.

33. A letter of December 30, 1935, from Marguerite Gollot to P. Philipon, who met him August 13, 1935, and a letter from Mme. Farrat of February 18, 1936, prove that the author was continuing his inquiry. The two letters speak of pictures or letters of Elizabeth that were to be sent to him. According to the Farrat family, the autographs of Elizabeth's letters to Mme. Farrat must have been lost after P. Philipon received them.

34. *Ecrits spirituels d' Elisabeth de la Trinité* ("La Vigne du Carmel"), Seuil 1949, 255 pp., translated into Italian, English, and Swedish.

35. Let us mention a commentary that was several times re-edited and translated into several languages: Dom Eugène Vandeur, OSB, *O mon Dieu, Trinité que j'adore. Prière de Soeur Elisabeth de la Trinité, carmélite, commentée. Elévations* (Louvain, Abbeye de Mont-César), 1923. A more modest commentary appeard in 1942, also re-edited several times and translated: Maurice De Meulemeester, C.SS.R., *O mon Dieu, Trinité que j'adore. Commentaire ascétique de la prière de Soeur Elisabeth de la Trinité, du Carmel de Dijon*, Louvain, Imprimerie Saint-Alphonse.

36. On this subject one can consult the edition of the *Souvenirs* of 1935, in particular, chapter 18.

37. Letter of December 24, 1909, published for the first time in the third edition of the *Souvenirs* in 1911. The phrase quoted is on p. XIII.

38. Let us remark, however, that Mother Germaine died November 30, 1934. The introduction to the book was signed March 7, 1937.

39. He says in a typewritten note mentioned in note 31: "On reading this first

chapter, the literary censor of the house Desclée De Brouwer, M. Stanislas Fumet, made this criticism: 'Too long for a doctrinal study; too short for a biography.' In a few minutes I cut out seventeen pages from the typewritten text and thus lightened returned it to him."

40. Some sixty lines in the *Spiritual Writings,* and some one hundred in *The Spiritual Doctrine.*

41. Cf. our introduction to the *Poems.*

42. *Cette présence de Dieu en toi... Elizabeth Catez. Soeur Elisabeth de la Trinité o.c.d.,* Editions Saint-Paul, Paris-Fribourg, 1969, 240 pp.

43. See note 1 of L 191. P. Philipon was so convinced of his thesis "Praise of Glory = spring or summer of 1905" that he even changed the (exact) date on the autograph of this letter, affixed by Abbé Chevignard, by putting *December* 25 (still insufficient, it is true, to illustrate his thesis). He also changed the date on the copy in Notebook 7 of ACD in the same sense. He attributes to this so-called discovery of 1905 an excessive importance: "For a long time she was caught up in herself and was unable to free herself. God will deliver her through a personal intervention...." (p. 127) "Laudem Gloriae marks another stage incomparably superior: the sole concern for His glory." (p. 129)

44. *En présence de Dieu,* op. cit., p. 208.

45. According to the *Bibliografia*: Italian, Portuguese, Dutch, English, German, Japanese, Spanish, Croatian, and Polish.

46. It is fitting to evoke here for a moment the memory of this woman of great faith who died May 7, 1954. We will do it by quoting from an extract of a letter to her daughter Chantal, a Dominican religious nurse of the poor, written February 20, 1946 on the occasion of her sixty-third birthday: "In looking back over these sixty-three years, I see many sufferings but above all, many graces and much love on God's part, and my heart overflows with gratitude. I do not find the time long when I am alone: I always have "Janua Coeli" ["Gate of Heaven": the little statue of the Blessed Virgin which Elizabeth had with her in the last phase of her illness]. The Lord has taken his share of my children [a priest, four consecrated to the Lord, three married, and a child who died at ten], and I value this choice. It is my comfort, when I see that I am not performing any useful apostolate, to rely on that of my children and their activity. Tuesday is for you; while you work I sit in my armchair and pray for you. Janua Coeli is near me, and I speak to her of you. I offer my fatigue so that you may have the strength to climb those flights of stairs."

47. These copybooks were found in the attic. We are publishing the composition exercises in PAT.

48. One will find in PAT everything that would be useful for knowing the character and history of Elizabeth.

49. RB 7 in PAT. L 87 speaks of a letter (lost).

50. Letter to Mother Germaine; cf. PAT.

51. EP in PAT.

52. PA 644.

53. Elizabeth speaks of Yvonne in L 10-11 of 1896. And in 1898: "... my dear Yvonne whom I so love" (L 16). "If only you knew what a lovely girl she is —and with such marvelous personality...." (L 14) She will address several letters to "Yvonne" as "composition exercises": CE 22, 39, 51.

54. Cf. L 11 of 1896: "I have found my dear friend Gabrielle Montpellier; she is twenty-one and a charming girl." And P 17: "Gabby, my dear friend, I think of you constantly." PN 2 is written on the back of a letter from Gabrielle (same writing as in the letter of condolence in which she signs her married name).

55. She became Mme. Sirlonge; she wrote this testimony February 9, 1958; cf. PAT.

56. Cf. L 89; the letter received is preserved.

57. Cf. L 95.

58. Cf. L 131.

59. Cf. L 257.

60. Cf. L 287.

61. September 17, 1901, Elizabeth prepared "a whole packet of mail for Labastide" where Marie-Louise will be married on the 30th.

62. Cf. L 154, with note 5.

63. L 99, 109, 159, 186, 196, 197, 214, 215, 226, 265.

64. Cf. the Horarium at the end of Volume II.

65. Many letters testify to this.

66. There was a "board" attached to the wall (cf. L 168, n.7); but as can be seen from L 88, Elizabeth wrote on the portable "desk."

67. L 305, 309, 314.

68. For ex. L 99, 133, 135, 139, 189, 205.

69. L 118-120, 127, 134, a fragment of 178, 281, 319, 321.

70. L 213, 233, 234, 273...

71. Parts of L 302, 308, 314.

72. L 113 and a fragment of L 123.

73. L 285, 287, first half of 288.

74. L 253, 283, 327, end of 300, of 302, and of 309. There is still preserved in ACD an envelope containing similar papers that Elizabeth kept in reserve.

75. For the *Poems* and the *Personal Notes* we have added an asterisk after the date when it was given by Elizabeth herself.

76. Cf. *Lourdes, Histoire authentique des apparitions*, tome I, Lethielleux 1961, pp. 21-38.

77. Except PN 7 (manuscript copy), and PN 12 (printed copy).

78. Except P 88 (photocopy).

79. L 11, 13, 94, 96, 106, 112, 155, 160, 165, 169, 174, 241, 256, 261, 274, 307.

80. L 6, 7, 8, 9, 14, 15, 46, 78, 80, 83, 104, 147, 158, 163, 195, 218, 228, 250, 259, 276, 277, 286, 289, 293, 326, 331, 332, 336, 341, 342. Strictly speaking, we could add to this L 266, and 340 (counted among the "autographs") which are letters dictated by Elizabeth and written by Mother Germaine. L 341 and 342 were also dictated to Mother Germaine, but the originals have disappeared.

81. L 114, 152, 255, 279, 299, 323a, 339.

82. Before her entrance into Carmel she already signed almost all her letters to Marguerite Gollot, an aspirant to Carmel, with her future religious name. But after that she sometimes signs only her baptismal name.

83. It is a pleasant duty to thank all those who furnished us with information for this edition: MM. Pierre Gras (Municipal Library of Dijon); Bernard Savouret (Municipal Archives of Dijon); General Porret (Historical Service of the Army); PP. André Duval (Archives O.P.); Hughes Beylard (Archives S.J.); Gilbert Humbert (Archives C.SS.R.); Joseph Baudry and Louis Marie du Christ (Archives O.C.D.); Jean Marilier (Archives Bishopric of Dijon); the Chevignard family, and in particular M. Bernard Chevignard; the Carmels of Paray-le-Monial, Clamart, Angers, Lisieux, Amiens, Saint-Sever, Mons, Kain, Avranches, Rheims; the Visitation of Dijon and of Orthez; my brother Carmelites, Pancrace Martens, Gaston de Kerpel, Emmanuel Renault, Guy Gaucher, Jean Lammens, Jesus Castellano, Valentino Macca, Simeon Tomás-Fernandez, Benoît Langlois; MM. and PP. Albert Patfoort, O.P., P. Thomas Camelot, O.P., Maurice Buil, René Lefebvre, André and Maurice Philbée, Jean Sender, Jacques Nourissat, Emile Sellenet, Bernard Card, Chan. Bruneau, Pierre de Gonneville, M. Huftier, André Darbon, O.P., Michel Florent, O.P., Paul Marsil, P.Bl., Emile De Roover, O.Praem., Michel Farin, S.J., René Bonhoure, Otto Steiner, Pierre Descouvemont, Michel Veys, Gilbert Larsonneur, M.S.Th., Philippe Ledoux, O.S.B., André Vidal; Srs. Cécile, O.C.D., Geneviève, O.P., Andrée Mullot, Marie-Cécile (Ste Famille, Pezens), Marie-Roger (Providence de Portieux), Simone Tournier (N.D. du Bon-Secours de Troyes), Gabrielle (Gardes-malades de Beaune); Mme. Rocher; Mme. Elisabeth de Jacquelot; MM. P. de Saint-Péreuze, P. de La Robertie, le Marquis de Saint-Seine, Patrick Jouffroy; Mlles. Marie Dussap, Elisabeth d'Arbaumont, Marie-Thérèse Van Oosterhout; the photographers Thérèse Laureyns and A. Fasquel; all those who enriched the archives of Elizabeth; and, last but not least, les Editions du Cerf and l'Imprimerie Saint-Paul de Bar-le-Duc.

84. Here is the history of her ink in Carmel. Let us point out that the same tints could give colors that differ slightly according to the capacity of absorption, more or less great, of the paper used. (1) *Pale copper color*: L 84-110, with the exception of L 99 in black ink, perhaps written in the "novitiate" (cf. Plan 1, no. 19, in Volume II) where there was also an inkwell. (2) *Black* ink: L 111-148. (3) *Deep copper color*: L 149-180 (4) *Pure copper color*: L 181-192. (5) *Pure copper color but a little darker* (less visible than in 3):L 193-203. (6) *Blue-grey color:* L 204-247. (7) *Black with a base of copper*: L 248-265. Later, in the infirmary, the letters, with the exception of those to Mother Germaine, are in pencil. There is only one autograph preserved in *purple* ink: L 284. And another in *red* ink: P 121.

85. Cf. Plan 1, no. 21, in Volume II.

86. Using a finer pen and the pure copper-colored ink (color 4), Elizabeth wrote L 200, probably in the "turn" a little after L 199 of the same day. She began L 167 with the same pen and ink and continued it in her "cell" before "Matins" with the usual pen and ink (color 3!) of this period, beginning with "C'est dommage . . .". The first words of L 221 ("Que Jésus nous . . .") are also from the same pen and ink; the rest is with her customary heavier pen and with ink color 6. L 246 is also written with two different kinds of ink. L 251 was written elsewhere than in her cell.

87. A letter from Elizabeth de Montléau of August 1901; a letter from

Canon Angles of July 22, 1903, and one of May 19, 1906. Elizabeth must have passed them on to her mother. They are found in PAT. There is also a short letter from Sister Louise de Gonzague, Carmelite of Dijon, a telegram of December 8, 1901, from Abbé Chaboisseau, and a few pictures received. One letter and a dozen messages from different friends written *before* her entrance have been preserved.

88. It is a little more difficult to judge concerning the autographs written in *pencil* (a number of texts copied), sometimes in rough draft.

89. For example, in a copybook of November 1893. In October 1895 (at age fifteen) she fills up a fourth, and in October 1895, a fifth "writing copybook" of the Godchaux Method: "Ruled Writing Copybooks With Printed and Graduated Models." (This method is contained in twelve copybooks.) Elizabeth probably used others besides these two.

90. Let us take an example. In the school copybook of June 1892–January 1893, the bar of the letter d is always straight. In the copybook of November 6, 1893–May 9, 1894, the bar remains straight (type 1), but in February 1894, it slants to the left (type 2); before long it often ends in a loop as it crosses the vertical bar (type 3), only to eliminate this loop a little later, keeping only the vertical bar and a stroke to the right (type 4). It is this type 4 (which can be seen in example 2 of the reproductions of her handwriting in the inset) which becomes general in the month of May 1894. But after the vacations, Elizabeth has completely reverted to the d of type 1. From May 1895, however, the d of type 4 gains the ascendancy, dominates again during her vacations, to disappear at the end of October (very probably under the influence of the writing exercises—see preceding note), where she reverts again to type 1. Type 4 will not appear again, but a year later type 2 (slanted to the left) is then the most frequent. If we now examine the autograph of PN 2 ("Timetable of the Passion," cf. Volume III), we see that the nineteen d minuscules all belong to type 4. At the same time, the thirteen t's belong to type 1 (see example 2, inset): the horizontal bar intersects the vertical bar. This PN 2, not dated, can only belong to the first period of the d of type 4 (May–October 1894) where we also encounter our t! (In the second period of the d of type 4, the t is generally different, *no longer intersecting* the vertical bar, but simply starting from it towards the right.) The overall image of the writings of these two periods is, moreover, different. The date "1887–1890" which appears in the *Souvenirs* beginning in 1927 (p. 12) is surely in error, unless it concerns another "timetable."

91. This is what tradition affirms. All her life Guite will retain this artist's handwriting, but it is much more legible. We find it often in this period.

92. It appears from the second half of 1893.

93. We can see clearly the new Capital *J* in L 24 to Marie-Louise Maurel, of August 12, 1899, and also in the autograph of P 69 and 70 which were composed earlier; but the overall image of the writings of these poems is already so different from P 68 that we can only deduce from it that Elizabeth copied P 69–70 in her Poetry Notebook later.

94. Cf. L 38, 41, 45, 50,53,54,55,65,69,70. And even earlier in L 12 and 13; but in this period, 1896–97, her writing was much more legible.

95. Letter to Père Beaubis, June 6, 1953. In it Marie of the Trinity deplores that the lessons caused Elizabeth's handwriting to lose "all personal character." Let us note, however, that this handwriting recaptures in great part that of the end of 1895 while perfecting it. In this very handwriting, many personal traits will manifest themselves, as we shall explain.

96. Note that from the first half of 1903 the *f* has lost forever its lower loop (see examples 7 to 9). Before April 1903, there was always a loop. By this fact alone, this letter *f* is a priceless chronological reference.

97. Most of the time, three loops: one in completing the vertical bar (which begins from the top) and two in beginning and completing the crown of the *P*. For another example of flourishes compare the word "Père" in example 1.

98. Other capital letters are also greatly simplified, like the *D* (compare examples 6, 8, and 9; the upper loop disappears), the *R*, and the *M*.

99. Cf. the Biographical sketch, p.11.

100. But we also find it in the letters of her contemporaries.

101. For this word she usually ingnores the circumflex accent, except in L 278. Also it might be a correction by someone else, for the letters to Germaine Gemeaux have been arranged several times in pencil by someone else's hand (cf. note 110). In any case in the same letter the word recurs twice more without the circumflex accent.

102. Towards the end of her life, Elizabeth will purposely abbreviate "J. Christ."

103. Cf. L 178. It is very probably an unknown hand that corrected it later.

104. For example, "God is Love," but also his Mystery, his Heart, his Cross. Note that the adjective is often capitalized; as in "Infinite Love."

105. For example, Father's House, Heavenly City, Fatherland, Divine Dwelling.

106. RB 5 in PAT.

107. On the other hand we always found "the good God" with a small *g*.

108. Nevertheless a "general" rule can be discerned (although Elizabeth is often unfaithful to it), which is doubtless the fruit of a spontaneous interior movement: she frequently writes with a capital what concerns the person whom she is addressing, and with a small letter, what concerns a third person. A fictitious example: She could write Marguerite Gollot: "Dear Friend, I saw your Sister who met my mother. Greetings to your Mother." But to Guite she could write: "My little Sister, I saw your friend and her sister. Their mother is well. They send greetings to our Mother."

109. Sometimes she puts a second or third line, not *under* the word but *above* it, thus framing it as it were.

110. Elizabeth's habit of underlining only partially enables us to recognize that the numerous underlinings in the letters to Mme. de Bobet are not hers. Mme. de Bobet underlined very distinctly, word by word, the sentences of Elizabeth which had particularly touched her. Likewise in what concerns the parentheses in the autographs of the letters to Germaine de Gemeaux, which probably indicate some passages to be omitted when read in public. Elizabeth very rarely used parentheses.

111. Soeur Thérèse de l'Enfant-Jésus et de la sainte Face. *Histoire d'une*

Ame, écrite par elle-même. Lettres-Poésies, Paris-Bar-le-Duc-Fribourg. Librairies de l'Oeuvre de Saint-Paul, 1899, XL + 488 pp. It is the second edition which remains at the head of the series until 1907, thus during all of Elizabeth's life.

112. *Manuel du Chrétien. Nouveau Testament, Psaumes, Imitation*, éd. du chanoine Gaume, Paris, Gaume et Cie, 1896, LXXVI + 1041 + 214 + 214 pp.

113. *Vie et Oeuvres de . . . Saint Jean de la Croix*. Trad. nouvelle . . . par le soins des Carmélites de Paris. Tome IV, *Le Cantique spirituel* et *La vive Flamme d'amour*, Paris, H. Oudin, 1892, 3e ed., 674 pp.

114. *Oeuvres de Sainte Thérèse, traduites, d'après les manuscrits originaux* par le P. Marcel Bouix, s.j., Paris, Julien, Lanier et Cie, 3 tomes, 1852-56. It is not certain that Elizabeth read the three volumes.

115. *Rusbrock l' admirable. Oeuvres choisies*. Traduit par Ernest Hello, Paris, Perrin et Cie, 1902, nlle ed., LXIV 253 pp.

116. In *D. Joannis Rusbrochii . . . opera omnia* (Cologne, 1552), Surius (+ 1578) had attributed to Ruysbroeck (+ 1381) the book *Van den XII dogheden* (On the twelve virtues) composed by a disciple and confrere of Ruysbroeck, Godfried van Wevel (+ 1396), who was often inspired by his master. On this question cf. S. Axters, *Geschiedenis van de vroomheid in de Nederlanden*, tome II, De Sikkel, Anvers, 1953, pp. 329-39. In Hello's anthology the following pages (quoted by Elizabeth!) are from Godfried van Wevel: 97-103 (Humility), 112-22 (On interior detachment), except for a passage from pp. 119-21, not quoted by Elizabeth, 169-70. This having been said, our abbreviations *Ru* will refer simply to the anthology of Hello, the one in which Elizabeth read him.

117. *Le Livre des visions et instructions de la bienheureuse Angèle de Foligno*. Traduit par Ernest Hello, DDB et Cie, 1895, 3e ed., 286 pp.

118. Cf. L 54 (note 2), 133 (note 4), 145 (note 2).

119. *Elisabeth de la Trinité et sa mission spirituelle*, Paris, Seuil, 1960, p. 24. This French translation, reviewed by the author, contains certain nuances in regard to the original, *Elizabeth von Dijon, und ihre geistliche Sendung*, Jakob Hegner, Köln-Olten, 1952. (Reprinted in *Schwestern im Geist. Therese von Lisieux und Elisabeth von Dijon*, Johannes Verlag, Einsiedeln, 1970.) This rich study could only be based at that time on the *Souvenirs* and the texts edited by P. Philipon, the limits of which we have already described.

Major Spiritual Writings

I

HEAVEN IN FAITH

Introduction

Elizabeth of the Trinity has still three months to live when, in the first half of August 1906, she writes the first of her four spiritual treatises. The disease ruthlessly pursues its course; Elizabeth knows that death is now inevitable and imminent. She has an intense desire to see God and a faith that seems unshakable. Her mother related that, during their first meeting after the serious crisis at the end of March and the beginning of April, "Elizabeth did not hide her regret at not having gone to Heaven! . . . Never did she give me one word of hope of a cure; she felt that the Master was calling her."[1] But her heart overflowed with tenderness for her own, and it is of this tenderness that *Heaven in Faith* will be born.

These pages were conceived as a "surprise" for Guite, their recipient, who will know of this initiative only two months after her sister's death, as we shall see. Could Elizabeth have done better than to leave to Guite, for whom she "felt the heart of a little mother" (L 204), a lasting written souvenir which contains a solid and wholly spiritual nourishment? The *Letters from Carmel* reveal the level the friendship and exchanges between the two sisters had already attained.

A Musical Unity

Elizabeth will organize her souvenir as a "retreat" of *ten* days, like the Carmelites make each year. Each day will have its two "prayers."

The retreat has a *precise end*, the only one that Elizabeth still

pursues: "During this retreat . . . the object of which is to make
us more like our adored Master, and more than that, to become
so one with Him that we can say: I live no longer I but He lives in
me. . . ." (HF 28) The *way to be followed* is specified: union
with God (in Christ) by a return to the center of our soul where,
since our baptism, the Trinity opens a dwelling for us; this implies a prayerful and assiduous searching, full of loving attention to the hidden God who is the great Present One, and requires the total gift of love that dies to all egoism. This whole
search for God is animated by the awareness that he loves us and
visits us through his Eucharist, his word, the secret touches of
his grace, and his concrete desires for us scattered throughout
our life; Christ is in all this; he is the way which leads us and the
image which draws us; living thus, we will become, like Mary, a
true "praise of glory" of God.

The unity of this treatise is less methodical and structural
than psychological and musical. The great leitmotif of union
with God, always differently orchestrated, runs through this
whole symphony. The unity of these pages is that of the life
which has inspired them: having reached the spiritual summits,
Elizabeth of the Trinity, the saint and mystic, is translating the
great theme of these pages by a radical and persevering gift to
the hidden God who she knows is present, who is her consuming
Fire, transforming her being into him, and who will soon unveil
his Face forever.

To be able to appreciate the true value of this retreat, we
must hear within us the echo that each word, each quotation,
touched by faith, awoke in Elizabeth. But all these resonances,
all these dreams, all these decisions here expressed are summed
up in the first and last lines of this treatise: the overture and
finale of the symphony. Everything is developed, beginning
with the solemn intonation, full of evangelical tones: " 'Father, I
will that where I am they also whom You have given Me may be
with Me. . . .' He wills that where He is we should be also, not
only for eternity, but already in time. . . ." (HF) Everything will
be concentrated in the final chords: "In the Heaven of Glory the
Blessed have no rest day or night saying: Holy, holy, holy. . . . In
the heaven of her soul, the praise of glory has already begun her

work of eternity." (HF 44) It is a profoundly Christian and contemplative hymn that we listen to here.

For *"Every Soul"* (HF 10)

Contemplative does not necessarily mean cloistered. The nun Elizabeth is aware throughout these pages that she is addressing a young mother with two children, married to a banker. She considers that neither the home nor encounters[2] with others should prevent Guite from being united with God who is present everywhere. Have we not all "received . . . the spirit of adoption as children in which we cry out: Abba, Father" (HF 31)? "The Trinity, this is our home. . . . " (HF 2)

By little touches, the Carmelite extends her aspirations for union with God to every Christian. When she speaks of the inner freedom required to "live in close union with God" and teaches that a soul must be "stripped and withdrawn from all things," she adds in parenthesis and underlines *"(in spirit)"* (HF 11). Descent into the depths "is not an external separation from external things but a solitude of spirit" (HF 7). Elizabeth explains that the "Remain in Me" that Jesus addresses to all is an "order" and a "wish" valid "for you with everyone and everything" (HF 3). When we choose love that is forgetful of self, we "find everywhere the secret of growing in love even in our relations . . . with the world (and) in the midst of the cares of life" (HF 16). If one goes to "everything with the same attitude of soul that our holy Master would have" (HF 27), then everything becomes "a sacrament which gives God to it" (HF 10). And Elizabeth recalls to the young mother Mary's example in awaiting her Child: "In what peace, in what recollection Mary lent herself to everything she did! How even the most trivial things were divinized by her!" (HF 40)

The only explicit allusion to the religious life found here serves again to make it relative and to emphasize the fundamental and common Christian value which is love.[3] It is in the plural that Elizabeth writes to her married sister: " . . . to correspond to our vocation and to become perfect *Praises of Glory* of the Most Holy Trinity."[4] Whether in the cloister or in the world, Elizabeth recognizes only one Christian way, that of love in everything, and of attention to God present and prevenient.

A Mosaic in an Apse

Elizabeth never said to herself: "I am going to write a 'spiritual treatise.'" Her original idea was simply to give pleasure to Guite by leaving her a souvenir written in her hand and, at the same time, to do her some good. She is not concerned either with being original or quoting her sources; the references to authors[5] are freely made at will. In this perspective who will prevent her from strewing these pages with beautiful texts borrowed from others if they have already expressed very well what she wants to say? For her to use Scripture and the mystics with whom she felt in unison is not an indication of a lack of inventiveness but a richness of listening, a desire to be objective; we will return to this point in the introduction to the *Last Retreat*.

Among biblical authors St. Paul—the "great St. Paul" (L 304), "St. Paul, my dear saint" (L 306), she writes in the letters of these days—obviously occupies the first place. Then comes St. John.

The first non-biblical author that she quotes is St. John of the Cross: "This beautiful book gives joy to my soul, which finds in it a wholly substantial nourishment," she had written again two weeks before (L 299). But to choose texts of John of the Cross is for Elizabeth one more way of giving pleasure to her sister whom she had initiated with success into the reading of the mystical doctor by giving her her own book: "I am very pleased that you love St. John of the Cross; I was sure you would for I know *my child*" (L 239).

But the author who appears most often in this retreat is Ruysbroeck. For five or six weeks Elizabeth had been plunging enthusiastically into the reading of this great Flemish mystic. It is a "wonderful" book (L 288), "magnificent" (L 300), it contains "magnificent things" (L 292). Elizabeth wants to share with her sister certain pages, certain horizons, discovered in the book that their mother had given her.

In this retreat we also find quotations or reminsicences of other authors: Lacordaire, Bossuet, a text attributed to Albert the Great, Teresa of Avila, a letter recently received from P. Vallée, a note from Canon Gaume found in her *Manual for Christians*. . . .

If in this way Elizabeth assembles as it were a mosaic of beautiful texts, the apse which is to contain them is indeed her own! For, and we must emphasize it, these are but selections: between the first and tenth "day," where much is in her own vein, along with the remarkable description of the "praise of glory" (HF 43–44), we will find personal passages that are very revealing. The borrowed passages themselves sometimes reveal very original adaptations. And, finally, there is a choice and a structuring of texts which serve as a vehicle for the convictions and desires that dwell in the depths of her being. Their inspiration is hers. We sense that Elizabeth had first savored and prayed these texts for a long time in true *lectio divina*. Where there is often not originality of thought, there is an originality of heart and of contemplative gaze.

Description and History

Elizabeth wrote her retreat in a notebook, 18.3 × 10.7 cm., with ruled paper and a hardback cover bound in black oilcloth. The notebook contains 114 pages.[6] Elizabeth began on page two leaving the first page blank; she filled the notebook up to page 70, leaving the following 44 pages blank.

Although it cannot be proven with certitude, the analogy with the *Last Retreat* makes it probable that the invalid had proportioned her efforts and in fact spread out the writing over "ten days." She wrote with her cherished books by her side: the long extracts prove it for her excellent memory would not have sufficed of itself to remember them. The texts chosen reflect her recent reading, perhaps of the same day. Elizabeth could have taken a few notes in advance, but nothing indicates that she made a rough copy.

Heaven in Faith was written in *the first half of August 1906*. It precedes the *Last Retreat* begun on the 16th. In HF 20 the "sixth day" Elizabeth quotes a passage from P. Vallée's letter written from Belgium the 5th of August; she surely had not received it before August 7; besides she could have quoted it several days later. The Marian tenor of the "tenth day" is perhaps inspired by the feast of the Assumption, although this cannot be affirmed.[7]

Elizabeth certainly asked permission from her Prioress to write this retreat and use this notebook. Thus Mother Germaine knew of it and will temporarily keep the notebook when Elizabeth gives it to her. So Elizabeth did not have the opportunity to explain to her sister the "literary genre" of her text or to tell her that she had largely drawn from Ruysbroeck and John of the Cross. In fact Guite will not learn of the existence of this "surprise" until the month of January 1907. On January 7th, Mother Germaine wrote her: "Did I tell you the other day about the little retreat notebook that Elizabeth prepared for you as a final souvenir last summer? Your dear Mother will tell you about it. You must be so busy these days...." The same day she wrote to Mme. Catez "... I am going to send you a little retreat notebook that she prepared during the last days of her exile for her dear Marguerite. She asked me to send it to her as a last souvenir. She had in mind her sister's soul and that of her nieces but she thought that the soul of her beloved mother would also joyfully find in it this wholly profound movement of faith and love.... I kept this treasure so long because I needed it for my little work...."[8]

Guite's ignorance concerning the existence of this notebook warns us therefore to interpret in a very broad sense Mother Germaine's remark that Elizabeth wrote this retreat "to answer the desire of a soul very dear to her who had begged her to initiate her into the secret of the interior life, to help her *find heaven on earth.*"[9]

This is the title Mother Germaine will give the little spiritual treatise which Elizabeth left without a title: "How to Find Heaven on Earth." Considering the title too long, P. Philipon dropped the first three words in his books and entitled the retreat "Heaven on Earth." But that is an overemphasis of the thought of an Elizabeth ravaged by disease and physical suffering.

If it is best to abbreviate the title given by Mother Germaine, still we would like to keep the idea of "how we can find ..."; the answer is, faith (cf. HF 19-20). If Elizabeth sometimes affirms she has found her "Heaven on earth" (L 122; cf. L 133) because we carry this Heaven within our soul (*ibid* and HF 32, 44), this Heaven is under the "veil of faith which covers it" (HF 19). Elizabeth then states more precisely, in speaking of "Heaven in faith" (L 143, 165, 169, 274): "How good faith is; it is Heaven in darkness" (L 162). She had understood that well when she made her profession in pure faith after hours of confusion "overwhelmed with anguish" (L 152). "During the night that preceded the great day [of her profession], while I was in choir waiting for the Bridegroom, I realized that my Heaven had begun on earth; Heaven in faith, with suffering and immolation for Him whom I love!" (L 169)

The treatise, in partial form, revised and stripped especially of the quotations from Ruysbroeck, appeared in the *Souvenirs* beginning with the edition of 1915. It will remain in this version (even after being collated with the original text in 1927) in all editions of the *Souvenirs* and P. Philipon's books, and also in the second edition (partial one of 1911[10]) of the short work *Reflections and Thoughts in the Form of Retreats*,[11] which underwent at least seven editions. That of 1942 gives the integral text for the first time. In the text we are going to read we, of course, are the ones who introduced the page numbering.[12]

NOTES

1. RB 2 in PAT. Cf. also L 266.
2. Guite relates: "Last winter [1905-1906] I had to go to a party, and I told her that the prospect of it was not very pleasant. She answered, 'As for me, I am very glad that you are going to this party for at least there will be one there who will love God and keep Him company. So you must look very beautiful!'" (RB 3 in PAT).
3. Cf. the passage of Ruysbroeck on the "way of life or the clothing" in HF 24.
4. HF 41; also in the plural in HF 44.
5. Here is a list of *explicit references* to her sources (we omit the references to the word of the "Master" and also vague references to Scripture suggested by the quotation marks that Elizabeth inserts herself); *St. Paul*, 19 times (HF 2, 4, 11, 13, 14, 19, 20, 23, 26, 27 [3x], 28 [2x], 31, 35, 41, 42 [2x]); *St. John*, 5

times (HF 2, 14, 22, 31, 38); *St. John of the Cross*, 4 times (HF 5, 6, 19, 42); *Isaiah*, twice (HF 1, 34); *David*, twice (HF 16, 23); *"the prophet"* twice (it is Hosea in HF 3 and Ezechiel in HF 26); *St. Peter*, once (HF 27); *St. John Baptist*, once (HF 38); *Bossuet*, once (HF 22); *Lacordaire*, once (HF 6); a *pious author* twice (it is pseudo-Albert the Great in HF 25 and Ruysbroeck in HF 40). The expression "pious author" was current in the Carmel of Dijon at that time. Note also that Elizabeth never writes the name of Ruysbroeck (or "Rusbrock" as Ernest Hello wrote): perhaps this foreign name intimidated her pen.

6. Without counting the two sheets glued against the flyleaf at the front and back of the notebook. Elizabeth tore out a sheet (which would have been pp. 3-4) after the words "l'Essence divine invisibile": from HF 1. Did she make an error? The bottom half will be used to write P 108. Notice also that the black ink with a copper base gives way after the words "Celui qui arrive" from HF 17, to a pale copper-colored ink. This treatise is entirely written in ink.

7. Note that between L 304 and L 305, there are exactly *ten days* of silence in her correspondence.

8. Notably the *Circular*. Thirty years later Guite will recall that "after Elizabeth's death" Mother Germaine gave her the notebook and said, "She prepared it as a last remembrance" (cf. PS in PAT).

9. In the Foreword (p. 3) of the opuscule cited *infra*, note 10. Also in the *Souvenirs* of 1915, p. 305.

10. In a letter of May 20, 1911, the Carmel of Zarauz (exiled from Bordeaux) expressed its desire to see "the last retreat printed separately: . . . such a sublime commentary on certain passages of Holy Scripture." Mother Germaine noted down concerning this letter (which supposes that this partially printed edition was still unknown), "One complimentary copy, Retreat, 1st ed." She sent it in fact for the Carmel of Zarauz acknowledges receipt of the "printed matter" on June 7th: ". . . what a nice surprise." A letter of July 8, 1911, from the Carmel of Westburn indicates the same suggestion and the same pleasure, "What a nice surprise! How grateful we are to you for having acceded to our humble but ardent desires concerning this marvellous retreat. . . . We never tire of reading and rereading these remarkable pages from the pen of one who is practically a child. . . ." September 14, the Carmel of Turin will order "three copies of the last *Retraite* of Laudem gloriae" (which cost 0.40 F). It was a small book of 34 pages called *Dernière retraite de Laudem gloriae*. But as in the *Souvenirs* of 1909 and 1910, the "fifteenth day" is missing (cf. *infra*, p. 145, n.13).

11. The present state of our research assures us that there were at least seven editions: (1) 1911 (with only LR; cf. preceding note). (2) Between October 6, 1911 and March 31, 1915, since this edition bears the imprimatur of Jacques-Ludovicus [Monestès], Bishop of Dijon during this period (Carmel of Dijon, 17 x 11.3 cm., s.d., 64 p.). (3) Between February 2, 1916 and November 11, 1926 (s.d., 64 p.) for it bears the imprimatur of Maurice [Landrieux], then Bishop of Dijon. (4) Between these same dates for it has the same imprimatur. Only a *photo* of Elizabeth has replaced the *picture* reproduced in the preceding edition. It was on a copy that Mother Germaine listed the corrections (which would

appear in the *Souvenirs* from 1927 on); (5) 1930, 64 p. (imprimatur of E. Marigny, vicar-general); (6) 1942, 76 p. (s.d., but the imprimatur of October 11, 1942, of G. Jacquin, vicar-general); (7) 1968, 84 p. (imprimatur of May 15, 1968, of R. Lefebvre, vicar-general).

12. We therefore began a fresh paragraph before the numbers 2, 4, 6, 8, 10, 12, 14, 16, 25, 27, 29, 30, 32, 33, 34, 42, and 44.

HEAVEN IN FAITH

Text

First Day

First Prayer

1. "Father, I will that where I am they also whom You have given Me may be with Me, in order that they may behold My glory which You have given Me, because You have loved Me before the creation of the world."[1] Such is Christ's last wish, His supreme prayer before returning to His Father. He wills that where He is we should be also, not only for eternity, but already in time, which is eternity begun and still in progress. It is important then to know where we must live with Him in order to realize His divine dream. "The place where the Son of God is hidden is the bosom of the Father, or the divine Essence, invisible to every mortal eye, unattainable by every human intellect,"[2] as Isaiah said: "Truly You are a hidden God."[3] And yet His will is that we should be established in Him, that we should live where He lives, in the unity of love; that we should be, so to speak, His own shadow.[4]

2. By baptism, says St. Paul, we have been united to Jesus Christ.[5] And again: "God seated us together in Heaven in Christ Jesus, that He might show in the ages to come the riches of His grace."[6] And further on: "You are no longer guests or strangers, but you belong to the City of saints and the House of God."[7] The Trinity—this is our dwelling, our "home," the Father's house that we must never leave. The Master said one day: "The slave does not remain with the household forever, but the son[8] remains there forever" (St. John).[9]

Second prayer

3. "Remain in Me."[10] It is the Word of God who gives this order, expresses this wish. Remain in Me, not for a few moments,

a few hours which must pass away, but *"remain . . . "* per-
manently, habitually, Remain in Me, pray in Me, adore in Me,
love in Me, suffer in Me, work and act in Me. Remain in Me so
that you may be able to encounter anyone or anything; penetrate
further still into these depths. This is truly the "solitude into
which God wants to allure the soul that He may speak to it," as
the prophet sang.[11]

4. In order to understand this very mysterious saying, we must
not, so to speak, stop at the surface, but enter ever deeper into
the divine Being through recollection. "I pursue my course,"[12]
exclaimed St. Paul; so must we descend daily this pathway of
the Abyss[13] which is God; let us slide down this slope[14] in wholly
loving confidence. "Abyss calls to abyss."[15] It is there in the very
depths that the divine impact[16] takes place, where the abyss of
our nothingness encounters the Abyss of mercy,[17] the immensity
of the all[18] of God. There we will find the strength to die to ourselves and, losing all vestige of self, we will be changed into
love. . . . "Blessed are those who die in the Lord"![19]

Second Day

First prayer
5. "The kingdom of God is within you."[1] Awhile ago God in-
vited us to "remain in Him," to live spiritually in His glorious
heritage,[2] and now He reveals to us that we do not have to go out
of ourselves to find Him: "The kingdom of God is within"! . . .
St. John of the Cross says that "it is in the substance of the soul
where neither the devil nor the world can reach"[3] that God gives
Himself to it; then "all its movements are divine, and although
they are from God they also belong to the soul, because God
works them in it and with it."[4]

6. The same saint also says that "God is the center of the soul.
So when the soul with all" its "strength will know God perfectly,
love and enjoy Him fully, then it will have reached the deepest
center that can be attained in Him." Before attaining this, the
soul is already "in God who is its center," "but it is not yet in its
deepest center, for it can still go further. Since love is what unites

us to God, the more intense this love is, the more deeply the soul enters into God and the more it is centered in Him. When it "possesses even one degree of love it is already in its center"; but when this love has attained its perfection, the soul will have penetrated into its *deepest* center. There it will be transformed to the point of becoming very like God."[5] To this soul living within can be addressed the words of Père Lacordaire to St. Mary Magdalene: "No longer ask for the Master among those on earth or in Heaven, for He is your soul and your soul is He."[6]

Second prayer

7. "Hurry and come down, for I must stay in your house today."[7] The Master unceasingly repeats this word to our soul which He once addressed to Zacchaeus. "Hurry and come down." But what is this descent that He demands of us except an entering more deeply into our interior abyss?[8] This act is not "an external separation from external things," but a "solitude of spirit,"[9] a detachment from all that is not God.

8. "As long as our will has fancies that are foreign to divine union, whims that are now yes, now no, we are like children; we do not advance with giant steps in love for fire has not yet burnt up all the alloy; the gold is not pure; we are still seeking ourselves; God has not consumed" all our hostility to Him. But when the boiling cauldron has consumed "every imperfect love, every imperfect sorrow, every imperfect fear," "then love is perfect and the golden ring of our alliance is larger than Heaven and earth. This is the secret cellar in which love places his elect," this "love leads us by ways and paths known to him alone; and he leads us with no turning back, for we will not retrace our steps."[10]

Third Day

First prayer

9. "If anyone loves Me, he will keep My word and My Father will love him, and We will come to him and make our home *in him*."[1]

The Master once more expresses His desire to dwell in us. "If anyone loves Me"! It is love that attracts, that draws God to His creatures: not a sensible love but that love "strong as death that deep waters cannot quench."[2]

10. "Because I love My Father, I do always the things that are pleasing to Him."[3] Thus spoke our holy Master, and every soul who wants to live close to Him must also live this maxim. The divine good pleasure[4] must be its food,[5] its daily bread; it must let itself be immolated by all the Father's wishes in the likeness of His adored Christ. Each incident, each event, each suffering, as well as each joy, is a sacrament which gives God to it; so it no longer makes a distinction between these things; it surmounts them, goes beyond them to rest in its Master, above all things. It "exalts" Him high on the "mountain of its heart," yes, "higher than His gifts, His consolation, higher than the sweetness that descends from Him."[6] "The property of love is never to seek self, to keep back nothing, but to give everything to the one it loves."[7] "Blessed the soul that loves" in truth; "the Lord has become its captive through love"![8]

Second prayer

11. "You have died and your life is hidden with Christ in God."[9] St. Paul comes to bring us a light to guide us on the pathway of the abyss. "You have died"! What does that mean but that the soul that aspires to live close to God "in the invincible fortress of holy recollection"[10] must be "set apart, stripped, and withdrawn from all things"[11] (*in spirit*). This soul "finds within itself a simple ascending movement of love to God, whatever creatures may do; it is invincible to things which" pass away, "for it transcends them, seeking God alone."[12]

12. "Quotidie morior."[13] "I die daily." I decrease,[14] I renounce self more each day so that Christ may increase in me and be exalted; I "remain" very little "in the depths of my poverty." I see "my nothingness, my misery, my weakness; I perceive that I am incapable of progress, of perseverance; I see the multitude of my shortcomings, my defects; I appear in my indigence." "I fall down in my misery, confessing my distress, and I display it before the mercy"[15] of my Master. "Quotidie morior." I place the joy of

my soul (as to the will, not sensible feelings) in everything that can immolate, destroy, or humble me, for I want to make room for my Master. I live no longer I, but He lives in me:[16] I no longer want "to live my own life, but to be transformed in Jesus Christ so that my life may be more divine than human,"[17] so that the Father in bending attentively over me can recognize the image[18] of His beloved Son in whom He has placed all His delight.[19]

Fourth Day

First prayer

13. "Deus ignis consumens."[1] Our God, wrote St. Paul, is a consuming Fire, that is "a fire of love" which destroys, which "transforms into itself everything that it touches."[2] "The delights of the divine enkindling[3] are renewed in our depths by an unremitting activity: the enkindling of love in a mutual and eternal satisfaction. It is a renewal that takes place at every moment in the bond of love."[4] Certain souls "have chosen this refuge to rest there eternally, and this is the silence in which, somehow, they have lost themselves." "Freed from their prison, they sail on the Ocean of Divinity without any creature being an obstacle or hindrance to them."[5]

14. For these souls, the mystical death of which St. Paul spoke yesterday becomes so simple and sweet! They think much less of the work of destruction and detachment that remains for them to do than of plunging into the Furnace of love burning within them which is none other than the Holy Spirit, the same Love which in the Trinity is the bond between the Father and His Word. They "enter into Him by living faith, and there, in simplicity and peace" they are "carried away by Him" beyond all things, beyond sensible pleasures, "into the sacred darkness" and are "transformed into the divine image."[6] They live, in St. John's expression, in "communion"[7] with the Three adorable Persons, "sharing" their life, and this is "the contemplative life"; this contemplation "leads to possession."[8] "Now this simple possession is eternal life savored in the unfathomable abode. It is there, beyond reason, that the profound tranquillity of the divine immutability awaits us."[9]

Second prayer

15. "I have come to cast fire upon the earth and how I long to see it burn."[10] It is the Master Himself who expresses His desire to see the fire of love enkindled. In fact, "all our works and all our labors are nothing in His sight. We can neither give Him anything nor satisfy His only desire, which is to exalt the dignity of our soul." Nothing pleases Him so much as to see it "grow." "Now nothing can exalt it so much as to become in some way the equal of God; that is why He demands from the soul the tribute of its love, as the property of love is to make the lover equal to the beloved as much as possible. The soul in possession of this love" "appears on an equal footing with Christ because their mutual affection renders everything common to both."[11] "I have called you My friends because all things that I have heard from My Father I have made known to you."[12]

16. But to attain to this love the soul must first be "entirely surrendered,"[13] its "will must be calmly lost in God's will"[14] so that its "inclinations," "its faculties" "move only in this love and for the sake of this love. I do everything with love, I suffer everything with love: this is what David meant when he sang, 'I will keep all my strength for You.'"[15] Then "love fills it so completely, absorbs it and protects it" so well "that everywhere it finds the secret of growing in love," "even in its relations with the world";[16] "in the midst of life's cares it can rightly say: 'My only occupation is loving'!..."[17]

Fifth Day

First prayer

17. "Behold, I stand at the door and knock. If any man listens to My voice and opens the door to Me, I will come in to him and sup with him, and he with Me."[1] Blessed the ears of the soul alert enough, recollected enough to hear this voice of the Word of God; blessed also the eyes[2] of this soul which in the light of a deep and living faith can witness the "coming" of the Master into His intimate sanctuary. But what then is this coming? "It is an unceasing generation, an enduring hymn of praise." Christ

"comes with His treasures, but such is the mystery of the divine swiftness that He is continually coming, always for the first time as if He had never come; for His coming, independent of time, consists in an eternal *"now,"*[3] and an eternal desire eternally renews the joys of the coming. The delights that He brings are infinite, since they are Himself." "The capacity of the soul, enlarged by the coming of the Master, seems to go out of itself in order to pass through the walls into the immensity of Him who comes; and a phenomenon occurs: God, who is in our depths, receives God coming to us, and God contemplates God! God in whom beatitude consists."[4]

Second prayer
18. "He who eats My flesh and drinks My blood, remains in Me and I in him."[5] "The first sign of love is this: that Jesus has given us His flesh to eat and His blood to drink." "The property of love is to be always giving and always receiving. Now the love" of Christ[6] is "generous. All that He has, all that He is, He gives; all that we have, all that we are, He takes away. He asks for more than we of ourselves are capable of giving. He has an immense hunger which wants to devour us absolutely. He enters even into the marrow of our bones, and the more lovingly we allow Him to do so, the more fully we savor Him." "He knows that we are poor, but He pays no heed to it and does not spare us. He Himself becomes in us His own bread, first burning up, in His love, all our vices, faults, and sins. Then when He sees that we are pure, He comes like a gaping vulture that is going to devour everything. He wants to consume our life in order to change it into His own; ours, full of vices, His, full of grace and glory and all prepared for us, if only we will renounce ourselves. Even if our eyes were good enough to see this avid appetite of Christ who hungers for our salvation, all our efforts would not prevent us from disappearing into His open mouth." Now "this sounds absurd, but those who love will understand!" When we receive Christ "with interior devotion, His blood, full of warmth and glory, flows into our veins and a fire is enkindled in our depths." "We receive the likeness of His virtues, and He lives in us and we in Him. He gives us His soul with the fullness of grace, by which

the soul perseveres in love and praise of the Father"! "Love draws its object into itself; we draw Jesus into ourselves; Jesus draws us into Himself. Then carried above ourselves into love's interior," seeking God, "we go to meet Him, to meet His Spirit, which is His love, and this love burns us, consumes us, and draws us into unity where beatitude awaits us." "Jesus meant this when He said:[7] 'With great desire have I desired to eat this pasch with you.' "[8]

Sixth Day

First prayer

19. "To approach God we must believe."[1] Thus speaks St. Paul. He also says, "Faith is the substance of things to be hoped for, the evidence of things not seen."[2] That is "faith makes so present and so certain future goods, that by it, they take on existence in our soul and subsist there before we have fruition of them."[3] St. John of the Cross says that it serves as "feet" to go "to God,"[4] and that it is "possession in an obscure manner."[5] "It alone can give us true light" concerning Him whom we love, and our soul must "choose it as the means to reach blessed union."[6] "It pours out in torrents in the depths of our being all spiritual goods. Christ, speaking to the Samaritan woman, indicated faith when He promised to all those who would believe in Him that He would give them 'a fountain of water springing up unto life everlasting.' "[7] "Thus even in this life faith gives us God, covered, it is true, with a veil but nonetheless God Himself."[8] "When that which is perfect comes," that is, clear vision, then "that which is imperfect," in other words, knowledge given through faith, "will receive all its perfection."[9]

20. "We have come to know and to believe in the love God has for us."[10] That is our great act of faith, the way to repay our God love for love; it is "the mystery hidden"[11] in the Father's heart, of which St. Paul speaks, which, at last, we penetrate and our whole soul thrills!"[11a] When it can believe in this "exceeding love"[12] which envelops it, we may say of it as was said of Moses, "He was unshakable in faith as if he had seen the Invisible."[13] It

no longer rests in inclinations or feelings; it matters little to the
soul whether it feels God or not, whether He sends it joy or suffering: it believes in His love. The more it is tried, the more its
faith increases because it passes over all obstacles, as it were, to
go rest in the heart of infinite Love who can perform only works
of love. So also to this soul wholly awakened in its faith[14] the
Master's voice can say in intimate secrecy the words He once addressed to Mary Magdalene: "Go in peace, your faith has saved
you."[15]

Second prayer
  21. "If your eye is single, your whole body will be full of
light."[16] What is this single eye of which the Master speaks but
this "simplicity of intention" which "gathers into unity all the
scattered forces of the soul and unites the spirit itself to God. It
is simplicity which gives God honor and praise; it is simplicity
which presents and offers the virtues to Him. Then, penetrating
and permeating itself, permeating and penetrating all creatures,
it finds God in its depths. It is the principle and end of virtues,
their splendor and their glory. I call simplicity of intention that
which seeks only God and refers all things to Him." "This is
what places man in the presence of God; it is simplicity that gives
him light and courage; it is simplicity that empties and frees the
soul from all fear today and on the day of judgement." "It is the
interior slope" and "the fountain of the whole spiritual life." "It
crushes evil nature under foot, it gives peace, it imposes silence
on the useless noises within us." It is simplicity that "hourly increases our divine likeness. And then, without the aid of inter-
mediaries, it is simplicity again that will transport us into the
depths where God dwells and will give us the repose of the abyss.
The inheritance which eternity has prepared for us will be given
us by simplicity. All the life of the spirits, all their virtue, consists— with the divine likeness—in simplicity, and their final rest
is spent on the heights in simplicity also." "And according to the
measure of its love, each spirit possesses a more or less profound
search for God in its own depths."[17] The simple soul, "rising by
virtue of its interior gaze, enters into itself and contemplates in
its own abyss the sanctuary where it is touched"[18] by the touch of

the Holy Trinity. Thus it has penetrated into its depths "to the very foundation which is the gate of life eternal."[19]

Seventh Day

First prayer

22. "God chose us in Him before creation, that we should be holy and immaculate in His presence, in love."[1]

"The Holy Trinity created us in its image, according to the eternal design that it possessed in its bosom before the world was created,"[2] in this "beginning without beginning" of which Bossuet speaks[3] following St. John: "In principio erat Verbum."[4] In the beginning was the Word; and we could add: in the beginning was nothing, for God in His eternal solitude already carried us in His thought.[5] "The Father contemplates Himself" "in the abyss of His fecundity, and by the very act of comprehending Himself He engendered another person, the Son, His eternal Word. The archetype of all creatures who had not yet issued out of the void eternally dwelt in Him, and God saw them and contemplated them in their type in Himself. This eternal life which our archetypes possessed without us in God, is the cause of our creation."

23. "Our created essence asks to be rejoined with its principle."[6] The Word, "the Splendor of the Father, is the eternal archetype after which creatures are designed on the day of their creation." This is "why God wills that, freed from ourselves, we should stretch out our arms towards our exemplar and possess it," "rising" above all things "towards our model." "This contemplation opens" the soul "to unexpected horizons." "In a certain manner it possesses the crown towards which it aspires."[7] "The immense riches that God possesses by nature, we may possess by virtue of love, by His dwelling in us and by our dwelling in Him."[8] "It is by virtue of this immense love"[9] that we are drawn into the depths of the "intimate sanctuary" where God "imprints on us a true image of His majesty."[10] Thus it is, thanks to love and through love, as the Apostle says, that we can be holy and immaculate in God's presence,[11] and can sing with David:

"I will be unblemished and I will guard myself from the depths of sinfulness within me."[12]

Second prayer

24. "Be holy for I am holy."[13] It is the Lord who speaks. "Whatever may be our way of life or the clothing we wear, each of us must be the holy one of God."[14] Who then is "the most holy"? "The one who is most loving, who gazes longest on God and who most fully satisfies the desires of His gaze."[15] How do we satisfy the desires of God's gaze but by remaining "simply and lovingly"[16] turned towards Him so that He may reflect His own image as the sun is reflected through a pure crystal.[17] "Let us make man in our own image and likeness":[18] such was the great desire in the Heart of our God. "Without the likeness which comes from grace, eternal damnation awaits us. When God sees that we are prepared to receive His grace, His generous goodness is ready to give us the gift that will give us His likeness. Our aptitude for receiving His grace depends on the inner integrity with which we move towards Him." And then God, "bringing us His gifts," can "give Himself, imprint on us His likeness, forgive and free us."[19]

25. "The highest perfection in this life," says a pious author,[20] "consists in remaining so closely united to God that the soul with all its faculties and its powers is recollected in God," "that its affections united in the joy of love find rest only in possession of the Creator. The image of God imprinted in the soul is formed by reason, memory, and will. As long as these faculties do not bear the perfect image of God, they do not resemble Him as on the day of creation. The form of the soul is God who must imprint Himself there like the seal on wax, like the stamp on its object. Now this is not fully realized unless the intellect is completely enlightened by knowledge of God, the will captivated by love of the supreme good, and the memory fully absorbed in contemplation and enjoyment of eternal happiness." "And as the glory of the blessed is nothing else than the perfect possession of this state, it is obvious that the initial possession of these blessings constitutes perfection in this life."[21] To "realize this ideal"[22] we must "keep recollected within ourselves," "remain silently in God's presence," "while the soul immerses itself, expands,

becomes enkindled and melts in Him, with an unlimited fullness."

Eighth Day

[*First prayer*]

26. "Those whom God has foreknown, He has also predestined to become conformed to the image of His divine Son. . . . And those whom He has predestined, He has also called; and those whom He has called He has also justified; and those whom He has justified He has also glorified. What then shall we say after that? If God is for us, who can be against us? . . . Who will separate me from the love of Christ?"[1] This is how the mystery of predestination, the mystery of divine election appeared to the enlightened gaze of the Apostle. "Those whom He has foreknown." Are not we of that number? Cannot God say to our soul what He once said through the voice of His prophet: "I passed by you and saw you. I saw that the time had come for you to be loved. I spread my garment over you. I swore to you to protect you, and I made a covenant with you, and you became mine."[2]

27. Yes, we have become His through baptism, that is what Paul means by these words: "He called them"; yes, called to receive the seal of the Holy Trinity; at the same time we have been made, in the words of St. Peter, "sharers in the divine nature,"[3] we have received "a beginning of His existence"[4]. . . . Then, He has justified us by His sacraments, by His direct "touches" in our contemplation "in the depths" of our soul;[5] justified us also by faith[6] and according to the measure of our faith in the redemption that Jesus Christ has acquired for us. And finally, He wants to glorify us, and for that reason, says St. Paul, He "has made us worthy to share in the inheritance of the saints in light,"[7] but we will be glorified in the measure in which we will have been conformed to the image of His divine Son.[8] So let us contemplate this adored Image, let us remain unceasingly under its radiance so that it may imprint itself on us; let us go to everyting with the same attitude of soul that our holy Master would have. Then we

will realize the great plan by which God has "resolved in Himself to restore all things in Christ."[9]

Second prayer

28. "It seems to me that all is loss since I have known the excelling knowledge of my Lord Jesus Christ. For love of Him I have forfeited everything. I have accounted all else rubbish that I may gain Christ. What I want is to know Him, to share in His sufferings, to become like Him in His death. I pursue my course striving to attain what He has destined me for by taking hold of me. My whole concern is to forget what is behind and to strain forward constantly to what is ahead. I run straight to the goal, to the vocation to which God has called me in Christ Jesus."[10] That is: I want only to be identified with Him: "Mihi vivere Christus est," "Christ is my life!"[11]

All the intensity of St. Paul's soul is poured out in these lines. The object of this retreat[12] is to make us more like our adored Master, and even more, to become so one with Him that we may say: "I live no longer I, but He lives in me. And the life that I now live in this body of death, I live in the faith of the Son of God, who loved me and gave Himself up for me."[13] Oh! Let us study this divine Model: His knowledge, the Apostle tells us, is so "excelling."[14]

29. And when He first came into the world what did He say? "You no longer delight in holocausts; so I have assumed a body and I come, O God, to do Your will."[15] During the thirty-three years of His life this will became so completely His daily bread, that at the moment of handing over His soul into His Father's hands, He could say to Him: "All is accomplished,"[16] yes, all Your desires, *all* have been realized, that is why "I have glorified You on earth."[17] When Jesus Christ spoke to His apostles of this food which they did not know, He explained to them "that it was to do the will of Him who sent Me."[18] Also He could say: "I am never alone. He who sent Me is always with Me because I do always the things that are pleasing to Him."[19]

30. Let us lovingly eat this bread of the will of God. If sometimes His will is more crucifying, we can doubtless say with our adored Master: "Father, if it is possible, let this cup pass me by,"

but we will add immediately: "Yet not as I will, but as You will";[20] and in strength and serenity, with the divine Crucified, we will also climb our calvary singing in the depths of our hearts and raising a hymn of thanksgiving to the Father. For those who march on this way of sorrows are those "whom He foreknew and predestined to be conformed to the image of His divine Son,"[21] the One crucified by love!

Ninth Day

[First prayer]

31. "God has predestined us to the adoption of children through Jesus Christ, in union with Him, according to the decree of His will, to make the glory of His grace blaze forth, by which He has justified us in His beloved Son. In whose blood we have redemption, the remission of our sins, according to the riches of His grace, which has abounded beyond measure in us in all wisdom and prudence...."[1] "The soul now a true daughter of God is, in the words of the Apostle, moved by the Holy Spirit Himself: 'All who are led by the Spirit of God are children of God.' "[2] And again: "We have not received a spirit of slavery to be still led by fear, but the spirit of adoption as children in which we cry out: Abba, Father! The Spirit Himself gives witness with our spirit that we are children of God. But if we are children, we are heirs as well; I mean heirs of God and co-heirs with Jesus Christ if only we suffer with Him so as to be glorified with Him."[3] "It is to bring us to this abyss of glory[4] that God has created us in His image and likeness."[5]

"See," says St. John, "what manner of love the Father has bestowed on us, that we should be called children of God; and such we are.... Now we are the children of God, and we have not yet seen what we shall be. We know that when He appears, we shall be like Him, for we shall see Him just as He is. And everyone who has this hope in Him makes himself holy, just as He Himself is holy."[6]

32. This is the measure of the holiness of the children of God: "to be holy as God, to be holy with the holiness of God";[7] and we

do this by living close to Him in the depths of the bottomless abyss[8] "within." "Then the soul seems in some way to resemble God Who, even though He delights in all things, yet does not delight in them as much as He does in Himself, for He possesses within Himself a supereminent good before which all others disappear. Thus all the joys which the soul receives are so many reminders inviting her to enjoy by preference the good she already possesses and to which nothing else can compare."[9] "Our Father Who art in Heaven...."[10] It is in "this little heaven"[11] that He has made in the center of our soul that we must seek Him and above all where we must remain.[12]

33. Christ said one day to the Samaritan woman that "the Father seeks true adorers in spirit and truth."[13] To give joy to His Heart, let us be these true adorers. Let us adore Him in "spirit," that is, with our hearts and our thoughts fixed on Him, and our mind filled with His knowledge imparted by the light of faith. Let us adore Him in "truth," that is, by our works for it is above all by our actions that we show we are true:[14] this is to do always what is pleasing to the Father[15] whose children we are. And finally, let us "adore in spirit and in truth," that is, *through* Jesus Christ and with Jesus Christ, for He alone is the true Adorer in spirit and truth.

34. Then we will be daughters[16] of God; we will "know with an experiential knowledge the truth of these words of Isaiah: 'You will be carried at the breast and He will caress you on His knees.'" In fact "God seems to be wholly occupied with overwhelming the soul with caresses and marks of affection like a mother who brings up her child and feeds it with her own milk."[17] Oh! Let us be attentive to the mysterious voice of our Father! "My daughter," He says, "give Me your heart."[18]

Second prayer

35. "God who is rich in mercy, impelled by His exceeding love, even when we were dead because of our sins, has brought us back to life in Christ Jesus...."[19] "Because all have sinned and have need of the glory of God, they are justified freely by His grace, through the redemption which is in Christ, whom God has set forth as a propitiation for sins, showing both that He

is just and that He makes just him who has *faith* in Him"[20] (St. Paul).

"Sin is such a terrifying evil that in order to seek any good whatsoever, or to avoid any evil whatsoever, no sin should be committed." "Now we have committed very many." How can we keep from "fainting in adoration when we plunge into the abyss of mercy and the eyes of our soul are fixed upon this fact: God has taken away our sins."[21] He said so Himself: "I will blot out all their iniquities and I will no longer remember their sins."[22]

"The Lord, in His mercy, willed to turn our sins against themselves to our advantage; He found a way to make them useful for us, to convert them in our hands into a means of salvation. But do not let this diminish in any way our horror of sinning, nor our sorrow for having sinned. But our sins" "have become a source of humility for us."[23]

36. When the soul "considers deep within itself, its eyes burning with love, the immensity of God, His fidelity, the proofs of His love, His favors which can add nothing to His happiness; then, looking at itself it sees its crimes against this immense Lord, it turns to its own center with such self-contempt that it does not know how it can endure its horror."[24] "The best thing for it to do is to complain to God, its Friend, of the strength of its self-love which betrays it by not letting it place itself as low as it would wish. It resigns itself to the will of God, and in self-abnegation, finds true, invincible, and perfect peace, which nothing can disturb. For it has plunged into such a deep abyss that no one will seek it there."[25]

37. "If anyone should affirm to me that to find the bottom of the abyss is to be immersed in humility, I would not contradict him. However, it seems to me that to be plunged into humility is to be plunged into God, for God is the bottom of the abyss. That is why humility, like charity, is always capable of increasing."[26] "Since a humble heart is the vessel needed, the vessel capable of containing the grace God wants to pour into it," let us be "humble."[27] "The humble can never rank God high enough nor themselves low enough. But here is the wonder: their weakness turns into wisdom, and the imperfection of their acts, always insufficient in their eyes, will be the greatest delight of their life.

Whoever possesses humility has no need of many words to be instructed; God tells him more things than he can learn; such was the case with the Lord's disciples."²⁸

Tenth Day

[*First prayer*]

38. "Si scires donum Dei. . . ."¹ "If you knew the gift of God," Christ said one evening to the Samaritan woman. But what is this gift of God if not Himself? And, the beloved disciple tells us: "He came to His own and His own did not accept Him."² St. John the Baptist could still say to many souls these words of reproach: "There is one in the midst of you, '*in you*,' whom you do not know."³

39. "If you knew the gift of God. . . ." There is one who knew this gift of God, one who did not lose one particle of it, one who was so pure, so luminous that she seemed to be the Light itself: "Speculum justitiae."⁴ One whose life was so simple, so lost in God that there is hardly anything we can say about it.

"Virgo fidelis":⁵ that is, Faithful Virgin, "who kept all these things in her heart."⁶ She remained so little, so recollected in God's presence, in the seclusion of the temple, that she drew down upon herself the delight of the Holy Trinity: "Because He has looked upon the lowliness of His servant, henceforth all generations shall call me blessed!"⁷ The Father bending down to this beautiful creature, who was so unaware of her own beauty, willed that she be the Mother in time of Him whose Father He is in eternity. Then the Spirit of love who presides over all of God's works came upon her; the Virgin said her *fiat*: "Behold the servant of the Lord, be it done to me according to Your word,"⁸ and the greatest of mysteries was accomplished. By the descent of the Word in her, Mary became forever God's prey.

40. It seems to me that the attitude of the Virgin during the months that elapsed between the Annunciation and the Nativity is the model for interior souls, those whom God has chosen to live within, in the depths of the bottomless abyss. In what peace, in what recollection Mary lent herself to everything she did! How

even the most trivial things were divinized by her! For through it
all the Virgin remained the adorer of the gift of God![9] This did
not prevent her from spending herself outwardly when it was a
matter of charity; the Gospel tells us that Mary went in haste to
the mountains of Judea to visit her cousin Elizabeth.[10] Never did
the ineffable vision that she contemplated within herself in any
way diminish her outward charity. For, a pious author says, if
contemplation "continues towards praise and towards the eternity of its Lord, it possesses unity and will not lose it. If an order
from Heaven arrives, contemplation turns towards men, sympa-
thizes with their needs, is inclined towards all their miseries; it
must cry and be fruitful. It illuminates like fire, and like it, it
burns, absorbs and devours, lifting up to Heaven what it has de-
voured. And when it has finished its work here below, it rises,
burning with its fire, and takes up again the road on high."[11]

Second prayer.
41. "We have been predestined by the decree of Him who
works all things according to the counsel of His will, so that we
may be *the praise of His glory.*"[12]
It is St. Paul who tells us this, St. Paul who was instructed by
God Himself. How do we realize this great dream of the Heart of
our God, this immutable will for our souls? In a word, how do
we correspond to our vocation and become perfect *Praises of
Glory* of the Most Holy Trinity?
42. "In Heaven" each soul is a praise of glory of the Father, the
Word, and the Holy Spirit, for each soul is established in pure
love and "lives no longer its own life, but the life of God."[13] Then
it knows Him, St. Paul says, as it is known by Him.[14] In other
words "its intellect is the intellect of God, its will the will of God,
its love the very love of God. In reality it is the Spirit of love and
of strength who transforms the soul, for to Him it has been given
to supply what is lacking to the soul," as St. Paul says again.[15]
"He works in it this glorious transformation." St. John of the
Cross affirms that "the soul surrendered to love, through the
strength of the Holy Spirit, is not far from being raised to the
degree of which we have just spoken,"[16] even here below! This is
what I call a perfect praise of glory!

43. A praise of glory is a soul that lives in God, that loves Him with a pure and disinterested love, without seeking itself in the sweetness of this love; that loves Him beyond all His gifts and even though it would not have received anything from Him, it desires the good of the Object thus loved. Now how do we *effectively* desire and will good to God if not in accomplishing His will since this will orders everything for His greater glory? Thus the soul must surrender itself to this will completely, passionately, so as to will nothing else but what God wills.

A praise of glory is a soul of silence that remains like a lyre under the mysterious touch of the Holy Spirit so that He may draw from it divine harmonies; it knows that suffering is a string that produces still more beautiful sounds; so it loves to see this string on its instrument that it may more delightfully move the Heart of its God.

A praise of glory is a soul that gazes on God in faith and simplicity; it is a reflector of all that He is; it is like a bottomless abyss into which He can flow and expand; it is also like a crystal through which He can radiate and contemplate all His perfections and His own splendor.[17] A soul which thus permits the divine Being to satisfy in itself His need to communicate "all that He is and all that He has,"[18] is in reality the praise of glory of all His gifts.

Finally, a praise of glory is one who is always giving thanks. Each of her acts, her movements, her thoughts, her aspirations, at the same time that they are rooting her more deeply in love, are like an echo of the eternal Sanctus.

44. In the Heaven of glory the blessed have no rest "day or night, saying: Holy, holy, holy is the Lord God Almighty .... They fall down and worship Him who lives forever and ever...."[19]

In the heaven of her soul, the praise of glory has already begun her work of eternity. Her song is uninterrupted, for she is under the action of the Holy Spirit who effects everything in her;[20] and although she is not always aware of it, for the weakness of nature does not allow her to be established in God without distractions, she always sings, she always adores, for she has, so to speak, wholly passed into praise and love in her passion for the glory of her God. In the heaven of our soul let us be praises of glory of the Holy Trinity, praises of love of our Immaculate Mother. One day the veil will fall, we will be introduced into the eternal courts, and there we will sing in the bosom of infinite Love. And God will give us "the new name promised to the Victor."[21] What will it be?

LAUDEM GLORIAE[22]

NOTES

First Day

1. Jn 17:24.
2. SC 22 Cf. *Complete Works of St. John of the Cross*, trans. Kieran Kavanaugh, O.C.D. and Otilio Rodriguez, O.C.D. (Washington: ICS Publications, 1973) St. 1:3, p. 417.
3. Is 45:15, cited in SC 22.
4. "His own shadow": the image is inspired by Ru 81: "Our shadow accompanies us everywhere. . . . That is the way love follows God. . . ."
5. "By baptism" "united": cf. Rm 6:4-5.
6. Ep 2:6-7.
7. Ep 2:19.
8. Elizabeth wrote "Son" with a capital letter. But since her intention was universal, we corrected it to a small letter.
9. Jn 8:35.
10. Jn 15:4.
11. Cf. Hs 2:14. This verse (very well-known) is also found in SC 376-377 and LF 566. Cf. *Collected Works*, SC, St 35:1, p. 543, LF, St 3:34, p. 623.
12. Cf. Ph 3:12.
13. At this period the image of the abyss in Elizabeth comes especially from Ruysbroeck (here Ru 52-53). Cf. L 292, n.2.
14. The "slope of love": Ru 52. The "slope of humility": Ru 101.
15. Ps 41:8. Cited in Ru 53.
16. Cf. Ru 40: "The impact takes place in the depths. . . ."
17. This image combines Ang 234 (". . . the double abyss, where the divine Immensity encounters the nothingness of man," also cited in GV 5) and (less pronounced) Ru 2, cited in L 298.
18. Cf. the "todo" of God in John of the Cross face to face with the "nada" (our nothingness) of man.
19. Ap 14:13.

Second Day

1. Lk 17:21.
2. Cf. Ep 1:18.
3. LF 462. Cf. *Collected Works*, St. 1:9, p. 582.
4. LF 463. Cf. *Collected Works*, St. 1:9, p. 582.
5. LF 465-466. Cf. *Collected Works*, St. 1:13, p. 583.
6. Ru 9.
7. Lk 19:5.
8. Although the expression "interior abyss" (which we find again in L 292) is in Ru 158, Elizabeth is clearly echoing Ru 3-5 where there is a commentary on Zacchaeus and in which "*this* rapid *descent* which God *demands* is simply an immersion in the *abyss* of the Divinity." (We have italicized the words which she repeats.)
9. Ru 118.
10. This whole passage is taken from Ru 157-159, with some omissions.

Third Day

1. Jn 14:23.
2. Ct 8:6-7.
3. Jn 14:31 and 8:29.
4. The expression, quite well-known, is found for example in SC 114, 228, 309, 310.
5. The reference to the example of Jesus in the following lines proves that Elizabeth is thinking of Jn 4:32.
6. Ru 9.
7. SC 351 (cf. *Collected Works*, St 32:2, p. 535). Elizabeth says "Seek self" instead of "Being occupied with self, of wanting nothing for self" of John of the Cross.
8. SC 350. Cf. *Collected Works*, St 32:1, p. 534.
9. Col 3:3.
10. SC 439 (cf. *Collected Works*, St 40:3. p. 564). Literally: "the fortress, the invincible citadel of interior recollection." Cf. L 284, n.6.
11. SC 439. Literally: "set apart, stripped, alone, withdrawn from all creatures." Cf. *Collected Works*, St 40:2, p. 563.
12. Ru 117.
13. "I die daily": 1 Co 15:31.
14. A reminiscence of Jn 3:30 (which she cites in LR 39): "He must increase and I must decrease" (trans. from her *Manual*).
15. Cf. Ru 1-2. Ruysbroeck speaks of the just man. Elizabeth changes "he" and "his" to "I" and "my".
16. Cf. Ga 2:20, cited in Sc 127 (cf. following note).
17. Cf. SC 127 (cf.*Collected Works*, St 12:8, pp. 455-456). John of the Cross speaks of St. Paul, but Elizabeth changes "his" to "my".
18. Cf. Rm 8:29: "the image of His Son," often quoted by her.
19. Cf. Mt 17:5. Cf. PN 15, with n. 31.

Fourth Day

1. "God is a consuming fire": Heb 12:29, citing Dt 4:24, quoted in LF 490 (cf. following note).

2. LF 490. Cf. *Collected Works*, St 2:2, p. 596.

3. Ruysbroeck wrote: "embrassement" (embrace), but Elizabeth twice changes it to "embrasement" (enkindling) thus prolonging the image of fire which she had just used. An unknown hand has added a second s.

4. Ru 72.

5. Cf. Ru 72-73. Elizabeth omits the word "dark" after "silence". In the second part she changes "we" to "they".

6. Cf. Ru 144-145. Quoting freely, Elizabeth changes, above all, "we" to "they".

7. Cf. 1 Jn 1:3.

8. Cf. Ru 145.

9. Ru 147.

10. Lk 12:49.

11. Sc 307-308. Cf. *Collected Works*, St 28:1, p. 520.

12. Jn 15:15, cited in SC 308 (cf. preceding note).

13. SC 308. Cf. *Collected Works*, St 28:2, pp. 520.

14. Cf SC 314. Cf. *Collected Works*, St 28:10, pp. 522-523.

15. Ps 58:10, cited (without "all") in SC 313. Everything between quotation marks starting with "inclinations" is taken from SC 313.

16. SC 306, with some grammatical adaptations. Cf. *Collected Works*, St 27:8, pp. 519-520.

17. SC 313.

Fifth Day

1. Ap 3:20.

2. Cf. Mt 13:16.

3. Elizabeth enlarges (as in the typography of Ru 64) the word *now* and sets it off with quotation marks.

4. This whole passage on "the coming" of the Master is taken from Ru 64-65 (with some insignificant omissions). She replaces the expression "Spouse" of Ruysbroeck by her own cherished name "Master" (twice) and "Christ" (once). In HF 18 she will change it once to "He". Did she do this because of Guite who is married (to a human "spouse")?

5. Jn 6:56.

6. The text of Ruysbroeck which we have already been reading since "The first sign . . ." reads here: "Now the love of Jesus is avid and generous." Elizabeth omits the expression "avid" (which nevertheless she will copy further on). She also changes the name of "Jesus" to "Christ".

7. This whole number HF 18, from "The first sign . . ." is taken from Ru 151-154, with some omissions.

8. Lk 22:15, this text is also part of the citation of Ru 154.

Sixth Day

1. Heb 11:6.
2. Heb 11:1.
3. Note to Heb 11:1 of Canon Gaume in Elizabeth's Manual, p. 838.
4. SC 31. Cf. *Collected Works*, St 1:11, p. 420.
5. SC 122. Literally: "The possession of truth in an obscure manner." Cf. *Collected Works*, St 12:3, p. 454.
6. SC 121. Cf. *Collected Works*, St 12:2, pp. 453–454.
7. SC 122, containing Jn 4:14.
8. SC 124. Cf. *Collected Works*, St 12:4, p. 454.
9. SC 126, containing 1 Co 13:10. Cf. *Collected Works*, St 12:6, p. 455.
10. 1 Jn 4:16.
11. 'The mystery hidden': Col 1:26.
11a. Elizabeth quotes here from memory the letter recently received from P. Vallée (cf. L 304, n. 10); here is the original passage: "We have known the love God has for us, *and we have believed in it.* . . . To believe that we are loved like that is our great act of faith; it is the way to repay our crucified God love for love; it is the 'mystery hidden' in God's heart for all ages and finally penetrated, and our whole heart thrills under the life which overflows into it—and for which it was made."
12. Ep 2:4.
13. Heb 11:27.
14. Cf. PN 15.
15. Lk 7:50.
16. Mt 6:22.
17. Almost this whole number 21 from "simplicity of intention," is taken from Ru 33–35, with some omissions, among others, the more difficult words "transcendence" and "essence."
18. Ru 36. Ru 35-6 speaks of "the touch" of Christ; Elizabeth adds her personal note: "touch of the Holy Trinity. . . ."
19. Ru 37.

Seventh Day

1. Ep 1:4.
2. Ru 68.
3. *Elévations à Dieu sur tous les mystères de la religion chrétienne*, Besançon-Lille-Paris, 1845, p. 250: "*in the beginning*, without beginning, before all beginning, beyond all beginning. . . ."
4. Jn 1:1.
5. Doubtless Elizabeth means to say that in one sense there had not been a beginning since from all eternity God was already thinking of us.
6. From "The Father contemplates. . . ." is taken from Ru 67.
7. Ru 67-69 (*passim*), with certain grammatical adaptations.
8. Ru 66.

9. Ru 66.
10. Ru 70. Literally: "imprints on the ravished soul," etc.
11. Cf. Ep 1:4.
12. Ps 17:24 (v. 26 in the *Manual* which gives this translation).
13. 1 P 1:16, citing Lv 11:44–45.
14. Ru 157.
15. Ru 113.
16. LF 564. Cf. *Collected Works*, St 3:33, p. 622.
17. Cf. L 269, n.11.
18. Gn 1:26.
19. Ru 48, with some grammatical adaptations at the end.
20. This "pious author" is first of all St. Albert the Great, *De l'Union avec Dieu*, Fribourg, Saint-Paul, 1895, 136 pp. But Martin Grabmann (cf. *Benediktinische Monastschrift*, 2, 1920, pp. 201ff) has shown that this treatise is in reality by a Benedictine monk Jean de Castel. See art. *Johannes von Kastl*, in *Lexikon für Theologie und Kirche*, V. col. 1049. Note that in this whole number 25, Elizabeth is merely copying her "retreat devotion" of 1904 (explanation, cf. PN 16, n. 1).
21. *Op. cit.*, pp. 10–13. Elizabeth says "perfect image" instead of "perfect imprint" of the text.
22. *Op. cit.*, p. 4, with some grammatical adaptations.

Eighth Day

1. Rm 8:29–31, 35. Elizabeth writes "me" instead of "us," a moving personal accent in the midst of the great sufferings she had already experienced.
2. Ez 16:8. Elizabeth follows the translation of SC 252, in the feminine ("soul").
3. 2 P 1:4.
4. Heb 3:14.
5. Elizabeth refers to SC 211–212. Cf. *Collected Works*, ST 19:4–5, p. 489.
6. Cf. Rm 5:1.
7. Col 1:12.
8. Cf. Rm 8:29.
9. Cf. Ep 1:9–10.
10. Ph 3:8, 10–14.
11. Ph 1:21.
12. Elizabeth explains here the center and end of this retreat which she will give Guite: union with God through union and conformity to Christ.
13. Ga 2:20.
14. Cf. Ph 3:8.
15. Heb 10:5–7 (paraphrase).
16. Jn 19:30.
17. Jn 17:4.
18. Jn 4:34.

19. Jn 8:29.
20. Mt 26:39.
21. Rm 8:29.

Ninth Day

1. Ep 1:5-8.
2. LF 523, containing Rm 8:14. Cf. *Collected Works*, St II:34, p. 608.
3. Rm 8:15-17.
4. This whole phrase with the biblical allusion is from SC 423. (cf. *Collected Works*, St, 39:4, p. 558).
5. Cf. Gn 1:26.
6. 1 Jn 3:1a, 2-3.
7. Echo of 1 Jn 3:3, which she has just quoted.
8. "Bottomless Abyss": Elizabeth's formula which she will repeat in HF 43 and LR 1.
9. SC 229-230. (Cf. *Collected Works*, St 21:12, p. 493. Elizabeth omits "substantial and permanent goods" after the word "possesses".
10. Mt 6:9.
11. Cf. Teresa of Avila, *The Way of Perfection*, chap 28 (29 in Bouix trans. vol. III, p. 202 which we cite here): "Those who can thus enclose themselves in this little heaven of their soul where He dwells. . . ." Teresa is commenting on the Our Father (which Elizabeth has just quoted); she also had a great love for the Samaritan woman, and put the emphasis on "works" and "acts" (cf. notes 13 and 14). Elizabeth enters here more explicitly into St. Teresa's thought.
12. Reminiscence of SC, St 1: it is "in the inmost depths of the soul" that we must "seek" God (SC 26) and "remain" (SC 29) with Him. Cf. *Collected Works*, St 1:3, p. 417; St 1:9, p. 419.
13. Cf. Jn 4:23.
14. Teresa of Avila insisted on this, and it was well known in Carmel. For ex. *Interior Castle*, III, 1 (trans. Bouix, t. III. pp. 377-378 and *ibid* VII, 4 (pp. 611-613).
15. Cf. Jn 8:29.
16. "Daughters," in the feminine. Elizabeth always thinks of Guite. In the citation of SC which follows, child is also in the feminine ("la") as seen below in Pr 23:26.
17. SC 299, with grammatical adaptations, containing Is 66:12. Cf. *Collected Works*, St 27:1. p. 517.
18. Pr 23:26.
19. Cf. Ep 2:4-5.
20. Rm 3:23-26.
21. Ru 169. Elizabeth omits "neither mortal nor venial" after the word "committed".
22. Is 43:25.
23. Ru 169-170.
24. Ru 97. Elizabeth changes "man" of Ruysbroeck (and the grammatical

structure in the masculine) to "soul." Slight omissions: among others, the word "essence" (of God).

25. Ru 98. Same change to the feminine as in the preceding note.

26. Ru 99. With a slight omission. Elizabeth adds the "me" in "affirm to me".

27. Ru 100, with slight omissions.

28. Ru 102. With omissions.

Tenth Day

1. Jn 4:10.

2. Jn 1:11.

3. Jn 1:26. Elizabeth adds and underlines, putting it between quotation marks '*in you*'. This is a reminiscence of Lk 17:21 (which she quotes several times and which she loved so much): "The kingdom of God is within you." This is how her *Manual* translated it according to the exegesis of the time. The "within" had a strong resonance for Elizabeth.

4. "Mirror of justice," from the Litany of Loretto.

5. "Faithful Virgin," from the Litany of Loretto.

6. Cf. Lk 2:19 and 51.

7. Lk 1:48.

8. Lk 1:38.

9. Cf. "The Virgin remains the wholly adoring one of the gift of God": a text that she had written on a little piece of embroidery work made by her during her illness. Cf. L 286, n.4.

10. Cf. Lk 1:39-40.

11. Ru 224. Elizabeth calls here "contemplation" what Ruysbroeck calls "freedom": free will under the gift of fortitude.

12. Ep 1:11-12. Elizabeth enlarges the words (here in italics) "the praise of His glory" as in the following paragraph and at the end (cf. n.22).

13. Cf. SC 127. Cf. *Collected Works*, St 12:8, pp. 455-456.

14. Cf. 1 Co 13:12, cited in SC 408 (cf. n.16).

15. In this long quotation from SC (cf. following note), Elizabeth adds this allusion to Rm 8:26 of her dear St. Paul.

16. Cf. SC 408-409, from "her intellect . . ." *Collected Works*, St 38:3. p. 554. It will be noted that Elizabeth, in gleaning these texts, omits the expression "in the spiritual marriage". Is it because Guite is married or because of personal discretion?

17. Cf. LF 615: (Cf. *Collected Works*, St 3:77, p. 640) "we could call it a crystal which, penetrated by the rays of the sun, reflects back its own splendors." For the image of the crystal see also L 269, n.11.

18. LF 529 (Cf. *Collected Works*, St 3:1, p. 610). Cf. also Ru 68, where the Father gives His Son "all that He has and all that He is" ("except the personal relation of the Father").

19. Ap 4:8, 10.

20. Probable reminiscence of 1 Co 12:11: "It is one and the same Spirit who effects all these things...."

21. Cf. Ap 2:17.

22. Elizabeth enlarges the name she gives herself *Laudem gloriae* (here in italics) and writes it in the middle of the line. On this name, cf. L 250, n. 16 and 17.

II

THE GREATNESS
OF OUR VOCATION

Introduction

Although the *Last Retreat* was written a few days earlier than the pages we are going to read, we have put it in third place, for it combines the more mystical tone of *Heaven in Faith* and the more ascetical tone of *The Greatness of Our Vocation*.

This "spiritual treatise" of September, 1906, is written to a young girl of Dijon; Françoise de Sourdon, age nineteen. The bonds of a long friendship already united her to Elizabeth, as the twenty-six letters that Elizabeth addressed to her witness, and which cover a period of more than eight years.[1]

Elizabeth sees a little of herself in the young Françoise: "You have a temperament like mine, so I know what you can do" (L 98). But Françoise does not know how to direct her vitality as well as Elizabeth does, who often has to call her to order in a friendly way.

A difference of seven years in age gives Elizabeth's friendship a certain maternal aspect and, once a Carmelite, she will spontaneously call herself Françoise's "little mother" (for example L 98, 128). We recognize this note of tenderness in the pages which follow, her very last letter, with the play on her name "Framboise" [Raspberry] and the use of the familiar "tu." If witnesses describe for us a somewhat capricious child who clung to her before her entrance, Elizabeth had, nonetheless, a keen sympathy for the young girl of whom she said: "What a character!" (L 178)

Here as in *Heaven in Faith*, the suffering Carmelite does not
lose sight of her correspondent, which gives to these pages two
particular characteristics adapted to Françoise's personality.

First of all, a tone of *magnanimity*, and Elizabeth feels that
the best of Françoise is capable of attaining it. Four years before
she had already written her: "I understand that you need an
ideal, something that will draw you out of yourself and raise you
to greater heights. But, you see, there is only One; it is *He*, the
Only Truth! Ah, if you only knew Him a little as your Sabeth
does! He *fascinates*, He sweeps you away; under His gaze the
horizon becomes so beautiful, so vast, so luminous. . . . My dear
one, do you want to turn with me towards this sublime Ideal? It
is no fiction but a reality." (L 128)

And finally, an *ascetic* note, for Françoise does not possess
Guite's maturity and inner richness. She must still conquer herself. So Elizabeth cannot tell her as much about her desires for
mystical union. In fact, the "questions" (GV 2) Françoise asked
have somewhat oriented the response. If the explanation is more
ascetical, and thus is a good complement to *Heaven in Faith*,
the end proposed remains just as lofty.

The letter to Françoise becomes a long meditation, a little
treatise:[2] "Let's *treat* humility first of all . . ." begins Elizabeth
on a serious note (GV 2).

These pages turn around the axis of humility-magnanimity.
Humility leads us to the forgetfulness of ourselves, to the death
of the old man, in order to make us free, happy, and Christlike.
Conscious of our "greatness" (GV 4), we will follow Christ, our
image and model. Associated in his Passion, for the Church, we
can draw near "our eternal predestination" (GV 9).

We have entitled these pages *The Greatness of Our Vocation*,
because of the horizons they open up. A year earlier, Elizabeth
had already written: "Oh, Framboise, how God has enriched us
with His gifts; He has predestined us to divine adoption and
thus to be heirs of His heritage of glory!" (L 238) A few days before, moreover, she was again speaking of "the greatness" of
"this vocation" (LR 36).

Around the 9th of September, 1906,[3] Elizabeth completed in
pencil the three ruled sheets folded in two;[4] it had taken her

"many days." The writing betrays her physical exhaustion, especially at the end. She is already "extremely weak; I feel as if I were going to faint at any moment." But we notice the touch of humor when she describes her long letter as a "journal."[5] She feels her young life is being harvested—she herself uses the image of the "sickle," but her faith tells her that it is "love" that is consuming her (GV 7). Two months before her death, she writes from the infirmary: "I feel already as if I were almost in heaven in my little cell, alone with Him alone, bearing my cross with my Master" (GV 13).

NOTES

1. The first one is letter 16 of August 9, 1898 (Vol III).

2. Just as Ms B of Thérèse of Lisieux was originally a letter to her sister Marie. The *Souvenirs*, from the first edition, gives a special place to "this beautiful letter" and quotes it integrally (pp. 222-228). P. Philipon also makes it a separate little chapter in his book.

3. Cf. L 310, n.1. Note the great resemblance between the first seven lines of GV 7 and L 309, also written around the 9th of September.

4. Two sheets, 26.8 x 21.5 cm. and a fragment of 26.8 x 14.6 cm. By folding them in two Elizabeth obtained twelve pages. In numbering the paragraphs, we began fresh paragraphs with numbers 2, 3, 5, 6, 7, 8, 10, 11, and 12.

5. Same title for her long and very beautiful letter to Guite, L 298 of July 16, 1906.

THE GREATNESS
OF OUR VOCATION
Text

J.M. + J.T.

1. Here comes Sabeth at last to sit down by her dearest Framboise and visit—with her *pencil*! I say pencil for the heart-to-heart communion was established long ago, and we are now as one. How I love our evening rendez-vous;[1] it is like the prelude of that communion from Heaven to earth that will be established between our souls. It seems to me that I am like a mother bending attentively over her favorite child: I raise my eyes and look at God, and then I lower them on you, exposing you to the rays of His Love. Framboise, I do not use words when I speak to Him of you but He understands me even better for He prefers my silence. My dearest child, I wish I were a saint so that I could help you here below while waiting to do it from Heaven. What I would not endure in order to obtain for you the graces of strength that you need.

2. I want to answer your questions. Let's treat humility first; I have read some splendid pages on it in the book I spoke to you about.[2] The pious author says that nothing can "disturb" the humble. He possesses "invincible peace for he has plunged into such an abyss that no one would go that far to look for him."[3] He also says that the humble person finds his greatest pleasure in life in feeling his own "weakness" "before God."[4] Little Framboise, pride is not something that is destroyed with one good blow of the sword! Doubtless, certain heroic acts of humility, such as we read of in the lives of the saints, give it, if not a mortal blow, at least one that considerably weakens it; but without that grace we must put it to death each day! "Quotidie morior," exclaimed St. Paul, "I die daily!"[5]

3. Framboise, this doctrine of dying to self is the law for every Christian, for Christ said: "If anyone wants to follow Me, let him take up his cross and deny himself."[6] But this doctrine which seems so austere, takes on a delightful sweetness when we consider the outcome of this death—life in God in place of our life of sin and misery. That is what St. Paul meant when he wrote: "Strip off the old man and clothe yourselves anew in the image of Him who created you."[7] This image is God Himself. Do you recall His wish which He so clearly expressed on the day of creation: "Let us make man in our image and likeness"?[8] Oh! you see, if we would think more about the origin of our soul, things here below would seem so childish[9] that we would have only contempt for them. St. Peter writes in one of his epistles that "we have been made sharers in His divine nature."[10] And St. Paul recommends that we "hold firm to the end this beginning of His existence which He has given us."[11]

4. It seems to me the soul that is aware of its greatness enters into that "holy freedom of the children of God" of which the Apostle speaks,[12] that is, it transcends all things, including self. The freest soul, I think, is the one most forgetful of self. If anyone were to ask me the secret of happiness, I would say it is to no longer think of self, to deny oneself always. That is a good way to kill pride: let it starve to death! You see, pride is love of ourselves; well, love of God must be so strong that it extinguishes all our self-love. St. Augustine says we have two cities within us, the city of God and the city of SELF.[13] To the extent that the first increases, the second will be destroyed. A soul that lives by faith in God's presence, that has this "single eye" that Christ speaks of in the Gospel,[14] that is, a purity of "intention" that seeks only God;[15] this soul, it seems to me, would also live in humility: it would recognize His gifts to it—for "humility is truth"[16]—but it would attribute nothing to itself, referring all to God as the Blessed Virgin did.

5. Framboise, all the movements of pride that you feel within yourself, only become faults when the will takes part in them! Without that, although you may suffer much, you are not offending God. Doubtless self-love is at the bottom[16a] of those faults which, as you say, you commit without thinking, but that,

my poor darling, is, in a way, part of us. . . . What God asks of
you is never to entertain deliberately any thought of pride, and
never to act on the inspiration of pride, for this is wrong. And
yet, if you find yourself doing either of these, you must not become discouraged, for again, it is pride which is irritated.[17] You
must "display your misery"[18] like Magdalene at the Master's feet,
and ask Him to set you free. He so loves to see a soul recognize its
weakness. Then, as a great saint said, "The abyss of God's immensity encounters the abyss of the creature's nothingness,"[19]
and God embraces this nothingness.

6. My dearest child, it is not pride to think that you do not
want to live an easy life; I truly believe that God wants your life
to be spent in a realm where the air breathed is divine. Oh! You
see, I have a profound compassion for souls that live only for this
world and its trivialities; I consider them as slaves, and I wish I
could tell them: Shake off the yoke that weighs you down; what
are you doing[20] with these bonds that chain you to yourself and
to things less than yourself? It seems to me that the happy ones
of this world are those who have enough contempt and forgetfulness of self to choose the Cross as their lot! What delightful
peace we experience when we place our joy in suffering!

7. "In my own flesh I fill up what is lacking in the passion of
Christ for the sake of His body, which is the Church."[21] The
apostle finds his happiness in this! The thought pursues me and
I confess that I experience a profound inner joy in thinking that
God has chosen to associate me in the passion of His Christ. This
way of Calvary I climb each day seems to me more like the path
of Beatitude! Have you ever seen those pictures depicting death
reaping with his sickle? Well, that is my condition; I seem to feel
myself being destroyed like that. Sometimes it is painful for
nature and I can assure you that if I were to remain at that level,
I would feel only my cowardice in the face of suffering. But that
is looking at things from the human point of view! Very quickly
"I open the eye of my soul in the light of faith."[21 a] And this faith
tells me that it is love who is destroying me, who is slowly consuming me; then I feel a tremendous joy, and I surrender myself
to Him as His prey.[22]

8. Framboise, to attain the ideal life of the soul, I believe we must live on the supernatural level, that is, we must never act "naturally." We must become aware that God dwells within us and do everything with Him, then we are never commonplace, even when performing the most ordinary tasks, for we do not live in these things, we go beyond them! A supernatural soul never deals with secondary causes but with God alone. Oh! How its life is simplified, how it resembles the life of the blessed, how it is freed from self and from all things! Everything for it is reduced to unity, to that "one thing necessary,"[23] of which the Master spoke to Magdalene. Then the soul is truly great, truly free, for it has *"enclosed its will in God's."*[24]

9. My Framboise, when we contemplate our eternal predestination, visible things seem so worthless. Listen to St. Paul: "Those whom God has foreknown, He has also predestined to be conformed to the image of His Son."[25] (That is not all, my little one, you are going to see that you are one of the number of the "known"!) "And those He has known He has called": it is baptism which has made you a child of adoption,[26] which has stamped you with the seal of the Holy Trinity! "And those whom He has called, He has also justified": how often you have been justified by the sacrament of penance and by all those touches of God in your soul, without you even being aware of it!

"And those whom He justified, He has also glorified." That is what awaits you in eternity! But remember that our degree of glory will depend on the degree of grace in which God finds us at the moment of death; allow Him to complete His work of predestination in you. To do this listen to St. Paul again who will give you a program of life.

10. "Walk in Jesus Christ, rooted in Him, built up on Him, strengthened in faith and growing in Him in thanksgiving."[27] Yes, little child of my heart and soul, walk in Jesus Christ: you need this broad road, for you were not made for the narrow paths of here below! Be *rooted* in Him. This implies being uprooted from self, or doing everything as if you were, by denying self each time you meet it. *Be built* up on Him, high above everything that is passing, there where everything is pure, everything is luminous.

11. Be *strengthened in faith*, that is, never act except in the great light of God, never according to impressions or your imagination. Believe that He loves you, that He wants to help you in the struggles you have to undergo. Believe in His love, His *exceeding* love,[28] as St. Paul says. Nourish your soul on the great thoughts of faith which will reveal to you all its richness and the end for which God has created you! If you live like this, your piety will never be a nervous exaltation as you fear but will be *true*. Truth is so beautiful, the truth of love. "He loved me and gave Himself up for me."[29] That, my little child, is what it means to be true!

12. And, finally, *grow in thanksgiving*.[30] That is the last word of the program and is but the consequence of it. If you walk rooted in Christ, strengthened in your faith, you will live in thanksgiving: the love of the sons of God! I wonder how a soul that has sounded the depths of love the Heart of God has *"for it"* could be anything but joyful in every suffering and sorrow. Remember that "He has chosen you in Him before the creation of the world to be immaculate and pure in His presence in love";[31] again it is St. Paul who says this. So do not fear struggles or temptations: "When I am weak," exclaimed the Apostle, "it is then I am strong, for the strength of Jesus Christ dwells in me."[32]

13. I wonder what our Reverend Mother is going to think when she sees this journal. She does not let me write any more for I am extremely weak, and I feel as if I would faint at any moment. This will probably be the last[33] letter from your Sabeth; it has taken her many days to write, and that explains its incoherence. And yet this evening I cannot bring myself to leave you. I am in solitude; it is seven-thirty, and the community is at recreation. As for me, I feel already as if I were almost in heaven here in my little cell, alone with Him alone, bearing my cross with my Master. Framboise, my happiness increases along with my suffering! If you only knew how delicious the dregs are at the bottom of the chalice prepared by my Heavenly Father!

A Dieu, beloved Framboise; I cannot go on. And in the silence of our rendez-vous you will guess, you will understand, what I do not tell you. I send you a kiss. I love you as a mother loves her little child. A Dieu my little one. "In the shadow of His wings may He guard you from all evil."³⁴

> S.M. Eliz. of the Trinity
> Laudem Gloriae
> (This will be my new name in Heaven.)

A very respectful and loving remembrance to your dear mama and regards to dear Marie-Louise.

NOTES

1. Cf. L 310, n.2.
2. The anthology of Ruysbroeck (cf. L 288, n.7). "Spoke": during a visit in the infirmary parlor a little before the 2nd of August (cf. L 302).
3. Ru 98.
4. Ru 99.
5. 1 Co 15:31.
6. Mt 16:24.
7. Cf. Col 3:9-10.
8. Gn 1:26.
9. Perhaps this word came to her mind because she is writing to Françoise whose caprices she sometimes had to criticize (cf. L 98, 123, 128, 167).
10. Cf. 2 P 1:4.
11. Cf. Heb 3:14.
12. Cf. Rm 8:21.
13. *De Civitate Dei, passim.* Whereas Augustine speaks of the city of God and the earthly city, Elizabeth applies it to the "self" (which she underlines above and below) probably referring to what P. Fages said (after praising this book) in the 9th conference of his Retreat for the Community in 1904: "St. Augustine does not hesitate to say that we have within us two cities which are: divine love and self-love." *De Civitate* 14:28 indicates them only as *cause*.
14. Mt 6:22, cited in Ru 34 (cf. the following note).
15. Ru 34.
16. Cf. Teresa of Avila, *The Interior Castle*, VI, 10 (trans. Bouix, III, p. 566) "Humility is nothing else than walking in the truth".
16a. Elizabeth wrote *"fonds"* (instead of "fond") but it is probably a mistake in spelling, as in HF 32 in speaking of "l'abîme sans fonds"; she corrects it herself in HF 36.
17. The manuscript is mutilated here but the words can easily be restored

"s'irrite," "Madeleine," "qu'il," "reconnaitre." And on the back, in number 7:
"Dieu" (the word is almost entirely effaced but is attested by the first copies),
"passion."

18. The proximity of the quotation from Angela di Foligno (cf. the following note) shows that it is probably a reminiscence of Ang 115 (where the expression is repeated twice) rather than of Ru 2, a text, moreover, already cited
in HF 12 (cf. *ibid.*, n.15).

19. Cf. Ang 234: "... the double abyss, where the divine Immensity encounters the nothingness of man." Elizabeth seems to be quoting from
memory.

20. While expressing a very personal conviction, Elizabeth is probably re-
calling the exclamation of St. John of the Cross in SC 425-426 (cf. *Collected
Works*, St. 39:7, p. 559), where he speaks of the "glorious destinies" of man:
"O souls created for these wonders and called to realize them in yourselves,
what are you doing? In what miserable nothings are you wasting your time?
Your ambitions are but baseness...."

21. Col 1:24.

21a. "To open the eye of the understanding (the soul) in the light of faith":
formula of Catherine of Siena. Cf. L 199, n.9.

22. Cf. PN 15. On the origin of the use of "prey" in Thérèse of Lisieux, cf. L
125, n.3.

23. Cf. Lk 10:42.

24. Cf. Ru 157.

25. Rm 8:29. Then she also develops verse 30.

26. Cf. Rm 8:15. On this role of baptism, cf. Rm 6:3-4.

27. Col 2:6-7, a citation that she gradually develops.

28. Cf. Ep 2:4.

29. Ga 2:20.

30. Elizabeth writes: "croisse." She underlines *rooted* and *built up*. So, logically, we did the same for *strengthened in faith* and *grow in thanksgiving*, the
words taken from St. Paul.

31. Cf. Ep 1:4. Notice that Elizabeth puts the words of St. Paul in the feminine singular to adapt them to her correspondent.

32. Cf. 2 Co 12:10, 9.

33. It is in fact her last letter to Françoise. The writing reveals Elizabeth's
physical exhaustion.

34. Cf. Ps 90:4, 10, 11.

III

LAST RETREAT
Introduction

From her cell in the infirmary, the 14th of August, 1906, Elizabeth of the Trinity announces to Mother Marie of Jesus (Prioress of the Carmel of Paray-le-Monial, and her former Prioress at the time of her entrance in Carmel, who had just recently come to Dijon) that tomorrow evening she will begin her annual retreat. She knows all too well it is the last one. "I am delighted to meet you on my great journey. I leave with the Blessed Virgin on the eve of her Assumption to prepare myself for eternal life. Our Mother [Mother Germaine] did me so much good by telling me that this retreat would be my novitiate for Heaven, and that on the 8th of December [fifth anniversary of her clothing], if the Blessed Virgin sees that I am ready, she will clothe me in her mantle of glory. Beatitude attracts me more and more; between my Master and me that is all we talk about, and His whole work is to prepare me for eternal life" (L 306). The same idea recurs in Letter 307 the next day.

Elizabeth had "asked for the grace of a retreat" until the "31st of August."[1] The Prioress, who has had in her hand for just a few days the notebook of *Heaven in Faith*, and who for some time now has been thinking of the obituary circular that she must soon write on the young dying nun,[2] in her turn makes an apparently innocent request, "that she simply note down any spiritual insights[3] that she received." Elizabeth "understood and smilingly agreed."[4]

Description and Dating

A little notebook,[5] written in ink, entrusts to us the account of her spiritual insights.

It was not until the 24th of September[6] that Elizabeth gave up

131

her notes to her Prioress, wrapped in very poor brown paper (preserved) which contains this inscription: "The last retreat of Laudem Gloriae."[7] Is it a "title" (one which, in fact, is fitting) as Mother Germaine suggests?[8] Or is it not rather a simple *chronological indication*, as we are inclined to think: "this retreat has been my last, soon I will be no more"?[9]

On opening the notebook we read at the top of the first page before the text begins: "Thursday, August 16. First day," and nothing else; Elizabeth gives no title. As in *Heaven in Faith*, this absence indicates at least a great lack of pretension.

The "16th day" brings us logically to the 31st of August for the conclusion of the retreat; the text seems in fact to be quite in keeping with the liturgy of that day, the Dedication of the Churches of Carmel.[10] However, Elizabeth does not give up her notebook until the 24th of September and this "sixteenth day" also reflects, as it were, Poem 115, prepared for this same date.[11]

So we could ask ourselves if the writing really was completed on the 31st of August or if it were continued afterwards. Or again, if the notebook is a second redaction from a first copy which Elizabeth perhaps destroyed. It is impossible to solve these questions, but it seems very probable that the writing actually coincided with the sixteen days of the retreat and was written directly in the notebook.[12]

The *handwriting*, painstaking and laborious, witnesses to Elizabeth's physical exhaustion.

Somewhat revised, the text was published in the first edition of the *Souvenirs* in 1909.[13]

A Retreat of an Invalid

Because of Elizabeth's illness, her retreat does not proceed as in other years. On the one hand she no longer goes with the community to the Divine Office and meals; on the other hand the solitude and silence during the day cannot be as absolute. There are visits from the infirmarians who bring the little nourishment that she can still take, make the bed for the exhausted invalid, clean the room, and take care of her. And there are also the physician's visits. One other Sister at least (very old, who will die

five days after Elizabeth) is also living in the infirmary. Elizabeth
has seen her mother again in the infirmary parlor during these
days (cf. L 308, n.3): she did not want to tell her family about
her retreat[14] in order not to deprive them of the consolation of
one more visit before her approaching death. During this period
she does not always stay in her cell but takes advantage of the
"good weather" to "go out on the terrace."[15]

Elizabeth spends her days in prayer, reading, silence, and
rest. It is in the evening, when there is less likelihood of being
interrupted by the visits of the infirmarians, that she writes her
retreat notes.[16] Mother Germaine says that these pages were
"written during the course of painfully sleepless nights, and in
the grip of such violent pains that the poor child felt as if she
would faint" (S 215). The little lamp by whose light she writes
down her thoughts[17] is like a symbol of her desire to offer herself
to "the consuming fire" of God (LR 19), enlightened only by
"the beautiful light of faith . . . which alone should light my way
as I go to meet the Bridegroom" (LR 10).

The retreat notes do not necessarily indicate her prayer of
that day, nor the quoted texts, her daily reading. Elizabeth's
prayer is made up much less of ideas than of a loving, persevering, believing attention to a Presence who dwells in her
and a Love which claims her. It is the *totality* of thoughts expressed in the *Last Retreat* which illustrates her interior life at
this time.

Keys to Reading

Without claiming to exhaust the wealth of these very dense pages,
we will content ourselves with indicating some indispensable
keys to reading for a good understanding.

1. *An autobiographical background.* If the "days" and
"prayers" of *Heaven in Faith*, written *in the form* of a retreat,
wish simply to offer material for reflection close to the reality
Elizabeth was living, the *Last Retreat*, on the other hand, has a
real autobiographical richness and a chronological significance.
It translates the dominant spiritual realities of these sixteen days
of retreat, just as Mother Germaine had desired.

"Sister Elizabeth told her Mother Prioress one day that she had tried to explain in this little collection of notes how she understood her work of praise of glory."[18] Moreover, that is what she herself wrote during this retreat: "to learn" this work (LR 1), "to conform my life . . . that I may fulfill my work of "Laudem Gloriae" (LR 9; cf 20). "Laudem Gloriae" repeated in the *Last Retreat* 25 and 42, really is the personal name that she chose for herself; it is not the "soul" in general, but Elizabeth Catez, Elizabeth of the Trinity. Each time that we see here the personal pronouns "I," "me," or the possessives "my," "mine," we must give them their full personal weight. And when we meet the expression "soul" we must understand once more "I," "Elizabeth."

Basing herself on the conversations which she had with Elizabeth during or after her retreat, Mother Germaine, in an excellent position to verify the agreement between what was written and what was lived, assures us: "During these blessed days . . . her beloved Master spoke to her . . . not in words,[19] but by opening up new horizons. . . . It would have been difficult for her to put down in writing what she received from God in the simple yet profound manner of which we have spoken. Nevertheless, it seems in looking over these pages written by this predestined soul, we could entitle them 'Personal Souvenirs'" (S212-15).

Elizabeth does not speak as a theoretician (whether of theology or mysticism, it does not matter); she gives a testimony. Even more than her *Poems*, the *Last Retreat* belongs to the genre of diary.

2. This autobiographical background better explains, for three reasons, *the presence of suffering* in the *Last Retreat*.

The recurrence of increased physical suffering[20] necessitates an unceasingly reaffirmed and deepened identification with the Crucified One. For she suffers cruelly. Recently she confessed to Mother Marie of Jesus: "When I lie down on my little bed, I think that I am going up to my altar and I tell Him, 'My God, feel free to do what ever You want!' Sometimes anguish overcomes me but then I gently calm myself and say to Him, 'My God, that does not count.'"[21] When she tries to eat a little more than usual, the consequences are very painful: "That upset my stomach, increased my vomitings and so forth" (L 305). "I am attentive to my stomach and, for love of God, I do what I can to not let it die of hunger" (L 309), she wrote a few days after her retreat. "I am extremely weak; I feel as if I would faint at any moment" (L 310). Never did they give her either sedatives or morphine. So it is hardly a hyperbole when she writes in her retreat: "He has substituted me for Himself on the cross" (LR 41). But it is moving to rediscover in the bride climbing to Calvary with her crucified King (LR 13) the young girl of seventeen and eighteen who confessed she was "proud and happy to climb Calvary,"[22] eager to "share" the crosses of the Beloved.[23] The desire to accept suffering is sustained by an attitude of faith (LR 10, 34), even in the face of "abandonment, helplessness, and anguish" (LR 39), and by "a wholly confident faith" in the reiterated forgiveness of God (LR 31).

What is she to do with her suffering? During her prolonged retreat she seeks to live out the answer in an even better way, the answer she had clearly given a few hours before: "This is what I am going to be taught: conformity, identity with my adored Master, the One crucified by love. Then I can fulfill my work as praise of glory. . . ."[24] As Mother Germaine emphasizes, what her Master tells her during these days ("not in words") concerns "His Passion"; the new horizons which He opens up to her are "the love hidden in the Cross." He makes her "understand that her dreams of union will find their realization in suffering"; "more than ever ravished by love," Elizabeth submits with her whole heart (S 212–13). All this is vigorously reflected in her notes, and conformity to Christ crucified also encompasses the redemptive value of suffering for the Church.[25]

Finally, we might wonder if the desire not to increase the pain of her family led Elizabeth to limit herself in *Heaven in Faith*, destined for Guite, to some general considerations on suffering. But with Mother Germaine she has nothing to hide in this domain.

3. Suffering impels Elizabeth to *a pronounced Christocentrism*. Physical pain, joined to a voluntary search of the death of the old man (LR 24), is lucidly placed at the service of the ideal of conformity with "the One crucified by love" (LR 1). Before being "transformed from glory to glory in the image of the Divine Being," we must become "conformed to the image of the

Word Incarnate, the One crucified by love" (LR 12). No name
for God recurs as frequently as "Master," that is, Christ. The
center does not exclude the totality of her vision of God: Elizabeth of the Trinity knows that she is "the daughter of God, the
bride of Christ, temple of the Holy Spirit" (LR 25), but first of
all: bride! In the extension of her Christocentrism is Mary.
"This Mother of grace will form" Elizabeth's soul in the image of
"her first-born, the Son of the Eternal One" (LR 2). Mary, who
was beneath the cross of Jesus, is also close to the invalid: "to
teach me to suffer as He did" (LR 41).

4. In speaking of the *Last Retreat*, Mother Germaine called
Elizabeth the soul of one idea":[26] the central idea which she
untiringly repeats of *union with God on earth as in Heaven!*
Conformity to Christ takes place in faith, a total entry into his
concrete desires, even in crucifying circumstances, *and* loving
attention to his Presence in the very depths of Elizabeth's recollected heart. She wants "to walk without deviating from this
magnificent road of the presence of God" (LR 23); this requires
interior silence and forgetfulness of self. As in *Heaven in Faith*,
this union with God even in this life is expressly formulated in the
first and last "day": these are the piles that support the bridge. In
the middle of the *Last Retreat*, the seventh and eighth "day," a
new formulation of this union without prospect of end will be as
the third support of the bridge. Read with particular attention
the first ten lines of the *Last Retreat* 1, 17, 20, and 42.

As in *Heaven in Faith*, a profound musical unity[27] underlies
the *Last Retreat*. The union sought for is at the service of the song
of *praise*. The great perspectives of eternity, often opened up by
St. Paul, are enriched by those of St. John in the Apocalypse.[28]
This can be no surprise: Elizabeth is writing the last pages of the
book of her life, and she will soon pass from the earthly Jerusalem
to the heavenly Jerusalem. In this last phase of her life, there is
already a presence of Heaven, an abundant life of God. It will
be noted with what ease, in some way connatural, Elizabeth
moves in *Heaven in Faith* and the *Last Retreat* among the passages of St. John of the Cross who speaks of the high mystical
degrees of the spiritual betrothal and spiritual marriage. Her
most profound aspirations coincide with the Pauline vision of

conformity to Christ and the Johannine vision of praise and adoration, as it is expressed in the Apocalypse. Like John, Elizabeth has become a prophet of the divine. Soon she will hear the voice of the Bridegroom say "Come!" Like the singer John, the musician Elizabeth intones a hymn that will never end: "Since my soul is a heaven where I live while awaiting the heavenly Jerusalem, this heaven also must sing the glory of the Eternal, *nothing* but the glory of the Eternal" (LR 17).

5. Now we can better understand the meaning of the *biblical citations*. When Mother Germaine, who already possessed the notebook of *Heaven in Faith*, asked Elizabeth to write her reflections of these days of solitude, she doubtless suggested to her not to take such long extracts from Ruysbroeck or others but to speak from the depths of her own heart. This Elizabeth will do, but not without frequent recourse to Scripture.[29]

Elizabeth is dazzled by the magnificent divine reality that is expressed there. To open Scripture is to plunge into the truth; it is to have recourse to the objectivity of faith which must govern our whole spiritual journey. There we find God's "plan" for us (LR 32 and 6), His "mystery" (LR 2) and His "secret" (LR 6 and 2), the "dream" (LR 8) and "desire" of the Creator (LR 23). There we find the "explanations" (LR 6) of His "counsel" (LR 32 and 23), and "will" (LR 22), of "the work" of Christ (LR 31) and of our "vocation" (LR 36). Scripture shows us "the way" (LR 24) and a "rule of life" (LR 32), it "teaches" us (LR 37), "instructs" us (LR 29 and 32), and in it we can "study this divine Model" (LR 37). Scripture is the "word". . . sharper than any two-edged sword" (LR 27). There is something "strong and magnificent" to be found there, she had said not long before (L 305).

This adherence to Scripture enables Elizabeth to establish herself in faith, beyond "feelings, memories, impressions, etc., —the *self*, in a word!" (LR 26) It gives a note of virility that well suits this officer's daughter, the spiritual daughter of Teresa of Avila and John of the Cross. Mother Germaine still recalls these days of retreat. "Never did we discover her being turned in on self" (Circ 9).

Like Mary (Elizabeth repeats it twice, LR 2 and 40), she keeps in her heart and ponders what she hears and reads in Scripture.

She nourishes herself on the Word of God and the prophets which are given for our teaching; she assimilates it in her own flesh. When she brings forth the Word again, it has become her own, soaked in her heart, sometimes in the blood of her suffering. To quote Scripture, especially in a retreat, is for Elizabeth to repeat to herself her Master's "call" (LR 26), to listen to Him again like Mary Magdalene seated at His feet. Had she not promised in her prayer *O My God, Trinity Whom I Adore*: "O Word eternal, Word of my God, I want to spend my life listening to You, I want to become wholly teachable so that I may learn all from You" (PN 15)? The Word was stored in the *depths* of her heart, and it is from there that it resounds; history, so to speak, is transcended. "'Be perfect as your heavenly Father is perfect.' When my Master makes me understand these words in the depths of my soul, it seems to me that He is asking me to live like the Father 'in an eternal present'" (LR 25). Here, to quote Scripture is to marvel, to beat in unison, to say yes and commit oneself, to disappear in the Beloved. Here, to quote Scripture is, in the last analysis, to pray.

Is the *Last Retreat* a "masterpiece"? We do not like that word in this context. It makes us think too much of something that one *does*. The *Last Retreat* is *born* of a thirst for total truth in God, of a donation down to the most intimate fibers of the heart to the "One crucified by love." It is not a "beautiful" spiritual treatise that we are going to read. It is a cry of love before the "exceeding love" of God (LR 34), a cry issuing from the "depths of the bottomless abyss" (LR 1). The Breath of God passes from the heart to the pen.

NOTES

1. S 212–13. The indication "three weeks" of Circ 9 is thus too generous for these sixteen days.

2. Cf. *supra*, p. 31.

3. S 214. "At our request, she jotted down the lights from her retreat," says Circ 10.

4. "I have this detail from Mother Germaine herself," notes P. Philipon in *The Spiritual Doctrine* . . . , *op. cit.*, p. 132.

5. 12.8 x 8.5 cm. containing 58 ruled sheets, that is, 116 pages. Elizabeth writes only three lines on p. 115 and leaves p. 116 blank (as well as p. 45).

Whereas at the beginning she writes only on every other line of the ruled paper, beginning with LR 39 ("which we draw . . .") and up to and including LR 41, she compresses her handwriting and writes on each line for fear that the notebook will not suffice. She resumes her normal writing for the sixteenth day. The hardback cover is bound in black oilcloth. In numbering the paragraphs we began new paragraphs with nos. 4, 8, 10, 16, 23, 28, 33, 34, 43 and 44.

6. She gives up this notebook "prepared with all the loving attentions of a daughter's heart, on the occasion of an anniversary" (S 214-15). This was the twelfth anniversary of Mother Germaine's profession; the tradition of the Carmel of Dijon confirms this. The "loving attentions" are P 115 and 116, and L 316.

7. This is also probably what Elizabeth said in giving up her notebook (S 214).

8. "Title given by our dear Sister" she wrote in the foreword of the second edition of the opuscule LR (cf. *supra*, p. 92, n. 11).

9. If Elizabeth had envisaged it as a title, would she not have spontaneously written "last retreat" instead of "*The* last retreat" (moreover, Mother Germaine herself omits *The*—a revealing omission)?

10. Cf. LR 42, n. 3.

11. In comparing LR 44 and P 115, we find in both texts the quotation "Immensus Pater, etc., " "a spacious place," the idea of the descent, the "repose" in the "Trinity" eternally. But there are also differences, and the expression "a spacious place" already appeared in LR 16 and 27.

12. The punctuation, full of errors, and some thirty corrections, erasures, additions, almost always insignificant, simple expressions of her fatigue (see however an important correction, LR 31, n. 14), argue for a single and immediate redaction. The small additions of words show that Elizabeth reread her texts. As for the synchronization of the "days" of the notebook and the actual days of the retreat, we can exclude the possibility that a hypothetical (and improbable) redaction after the 31st of August, might have been made later than September 14th. Otherwise Elizabeth would surely have quoted Angela di Foligno's thought on the suffering Christ which so impressed her at this time: "Where does He dwell but in suffering?" (cf. L 311, n. 3) The texts of the *Souvenirs* which we will read later also argue in the same sense, although the *Souvenirs* does not respect historical facts which overlap each other more than once. Mother Germaine's veracity is quite apart from her sense of historiography.

13. The "fifteenth day" is missing in the editions of 1909 and 1910 (and in the first edition of the opuscule mentioned in n. 8). In the Souvenirs of 1911, p. 299, Mother Germaine explains why: she had already "given in several places extracts" from this fifteenth day.

14. She does not tell her mother either before (L 305), nor during (L 308). She did not speak of it to Guite as in preceding years (cf. L 211 and 245): Mother Germaine's letter to Mme. Catez on August 29, shows that Guite would like to come the 31st. Mother Germaine, who does not breathe a word about the retreat, asks only that she come the 1st of September.

15. Cf. Mother Germaine's letter of August 29th, in PAT. For "the terrace" and "the infirmary" see in Volume II, Plan 2, nos. 3 to 11.

16. One recalls the account of Thérèse of Lisieux during her illness (but not in retreat it is true), relating good-humoredly how her Sisters, whom she did not want to learn about the nature of her work, came constantly to interrupt her in the writing of her autobiography (MS C, 17 r°/v°). It is understandable that Elizabeth would want to keep her work secret, except from her Prioress who came to give her her blessing around 10:30 P.M., as she did to the other Sisters also according to the usual custom.

17. Cf. Mother Germaine's testimony (PO 86).

18. Mother Germaine in the Foreword cited in n. 8.

19. Cf. what Elizabeth wrote in LR 25: "When my Master makes me understand these words in the depths of my soul...."

20. Cf. our introduction to the fourth section of *Letters from Carmel*, in Volume II.

21. Cf. L 306, n. 1.

22. For ex. in the *Poems of her Youth*, P 39, with n. 5 (Volume III).

23. Cf. in her *Diary*, D 7, with n. 13 (Volume III).

24. L 307. Cf. L 306 of the evening before: "I so want the Father to be able to recognize in me the image of the One crucified by love...."

25. She wants to be "one of the redeemed who in its turn must redeem other souls" (LR 13). She knows she is associated in Christ's "work of redemption" (LR 13 and 41). She repeats Col. 1:24; that she "suffers in her body what is lacking in the passion of Christ, for the sake of His body, which is the Church" (LR 13 and 41, as well as in the letters of this period).

26. In a note of LR, p. 7 of the opuscule indicated in n. 8.

27. Cf. *supra*, p.86.

28. In particular the fourth, fifth, sixth and eighth "days". Cf. S 211: "At this time the most beautiful passages of the Apocalypse captivated Sister Elizabeth...."

29. Here is the list of *explicit* citations, more numerous than in HF (while omitting references to the words of the "Master" and also vague allusions to Scripture suggested by Elizabeth's quotation marks): *St. Paul* 40 times (LR 2, 3, 5, 6 [2x], 7 [2x], 8, 9, 11, 13 [2x], 16, 20, 21, 22 [2x], 23 [2x], 24, 25, 26, 27, 28 [2x], 29 [2x], 30 [2x], 32 [2x], 33 [2x], 34 [2x], 36, 37, 38, 40, 43); *St. John* 4 times (LR 2, 9, 15, 22); *St. Peter* twice (LR 22, 29); *John the Baptist* once (LR 39); *Isaiah* once (LR 8); *Song of Songs* once (LR 1); *Prophet Hosea* once (LR 27); *Psalms* 18 times (under different names: David, psalmist, prophet, royal-prophet, a psalm; cf. LR 34, n. 12; strictly speaking she is mistaken only once in LR 12): LR 10, 12, 16, 17 [2x], 18, 20, 21 [2x], 25 [2x], 27, 33, 34, 38, 39, 43, 44; *St. Dionysius* (the pseudo-Aeropagite) once (LR 26); the *Rule of Carmel* once (LR 3); *John of the Cross* 4 times (LR 19, 21, 28, 43); *P. Lacordaire* once (LR 21); *Ruysbroeck* 4 times (under the expressions "pious author" in LR 7, "great mystic" in LR 11, "a mystic" in LR 21, "pious writer" in LR 28).

LAST RETREAT
Text

First Day

Thursday August 16

1. "Nescivi."[1] "I no longer knew anything." This is what the "bride of the Canticles" sings after having been brought into the "inner cellar."[2] It seems to me that this must also be the refrain of a praise of glory on this first day of retreat in which the Master makes her penetrate the depths of the bottomless abyss so that He may teach her to fulfill the work which will be hers for eternity and which she must already perform in time, which is eternity begun and still in progress.[3] "Nescivi"! I no longer know anything, I do not want to know anything except "to know *Him*, to share in His sufferings, to become like Him in His death."[4] "Those whom God has foreknown He has also predestined to become conformed to the image of His divine Son,"[5] the One crucified by love. When I am wholly identified with this divine Exemplar,[6] when I have wholly passed into Him and He into me, then I will fulfill my eternal vocation: the one for which God has "chosen me in Him"[7] "in principio," the one I will continue "in aeternum" when, immersed in the bosom of my Trinity, I will be the unceasing praise of His glory, Laudem gloriae ejus.[8]

2. "No one has seen the Father," St John tells us, "except the Son and those to whom the Son chooses to reveal Him."[9] It seems to me that we can also say, "No one has penetrated the depths of the mystery of Christ except the Blessed Virgin." John and Mary Magdalene penetrated deeply this mystery; St. Paul often speaks of "the understanding of it which was given to him";[10] and yet, how all the saints remain in the shadows when we look at the Blessed Virgin's light!

This is the unspeakable "secret" that she kept in mind and pondered in her heart"[11] which no tongue can tell or pen describe! This Mother of grace[12] will form my soul so that her little child will be a living,[13] "striking" image of her first-born,[14] the Son of the Eternal, He who was the perfect praise of His Father's glory.

Second Day

3. "My soul is always in my hands."[1] My Master sang this in His soul, and that is why in the midst of all His anguish He always remained the calm and strong One. My soul is always in my hands! What does that mean but this complete self-possession in the presence of the peaceful One? There is another of Christ's songs that I would like to repeat unceasingly: "I shall keep my strength for you."[2] My Rule tells me: "In silence will your strength be."[3] It seems to me, therefore, that to keep one's strength for the Lord is to unify one's whole being by means of interior silence, to collect all one's powers in order to "employ" them in "the one work of love,"[4] to have this "single eye" which allows the light of God to enlighten us.[5] A soul that debates with its self, that is taken up with its feelings, and pursues useless thoughts[6] and desires, scatters its forces,[6a] for it is not wholly directed toward God. Its lyre does not vibrate in unison and when the Master plays it, He cannot draw from it divine harmonies, for it is still too human and discordant. The soul that still keeps something for self in its "inner kingdom,"[7] whose powers are not "enclosed"[8] in God, cannot be a perfect praise of glory; it is not fit to sing uninterruptedly this "canticum magnum" of which St. Paul speaks[9] since unity does not reign in it. Instead of persevering in praise through everything in simplicity, it must continually adjust the strings of its instrument which are all a little out of tune.

4. How indispensable this beautiful inner unity is for the soul that wants to live here below the life of the blessed, that is, of simple beings, of spirits. It seems to me the Master had that in mind when He spoke to Mary Magdalene of the "Unum necessarium."[10] How well that great saint understood this! "The eye of her soul enlightened by faith"[10a] recognized her God beneath the veil of His humanity; and in silence, in the unity of her powers, "She listened to what He told her."[11] She could sing, "My soul is always in my hands," and also this little word: "Nescivi"! Yes, she knew nothing but *Him*! There could be noise and excitement around her: "Nescivi"! They could accuse her: "Nescivi"! Neither empty self-esteem nor exterior things could draw her out of her "sacred silence."[12]

5. It is the same for the soul that has entered into the "fortress of holy recollection":[13] the eye of its soul, opened in the light of faith, discovers its God present, living within it; in turn it remains so present to Him, in beautiful simplicity,[14] that He guards it with a jealous care. Then disturbances from without and tempests from within may arise; its self-esteem may be wounded: "Nescivi"! God may hide Himself, withdraw His sensible grace: "Nescivi." Or, as St. Paul writes: "For love of Him I have forfeited everything."[15] Then the Master is free, free to flow into the soul, to give Himself "according to His measure."[16] And the soul thus simplified, unified, becomes the throne of the Unchanging One, since "unity is the throne of the Holy Trinity."[17]

Third Day

6. "We have been predestined by the decree of Him who works all things according to the counsel of His will, so that we may be the praise of His glory."[1] It is St. Paul who announces to us this divine election, St. Paul who penetrated so deeply the "mystery hidden from eternity in the heart of God."[2] Then he gives us light on this vocation to which we are called. "God," he says, "chose us *in Him* before creation that we might be holy and immaculate in His presence, in love."[3] If I compare these two explanations[4] of the divine and eternal unchanging plan, I conclude from them that in order to fulfil worthily my work of Laudem Gloriae, I must remain "in the presence of God" through everything; and that is not all: the Apostle tells us "in charitate," that is, in God, "Deus Charitas est . . .";[5] and it is contact with the divine Being that will make me "holy and immaculate" in His eyes. . . .

7. I relate all this to the beautiful virtue of simplicity of which a pious author wrote: "It gives the soul the repose of the abyss,"[6] that is, rest in God, the unfathomable Abyss, prelude and echo of the eternal sabbath[7] of which St. Paul spoke when he said, "We then who have believed shall enter into this rest."[8]

The glorified have this repose of the abyss because they contemplate God in the simplicity of His essence. "They know Him," says St. Paul again, "as they are known by Him,"[9] that is, by intuitive vision, a simple gaze; and that is why, the great saint continues, "they are transformed from brightness to brightness into His very Image by the power of His Spirit";[10] then they are an unceasing praise of glory of the divine Being who contemplates in them His own splendor.[11]

8. It seems to me that it would give immense joy to the Heart of God if we would perfect in the heaven of our soul this occupation of the blessed and cling to Him by this simple contemplation which resembles that of man in the state of innocence before original sin when God created him "in His image and likeness."[12] Such was the Creator's dream: to be able to contemplate Himself in His creature and see reflected there all His perfections, all His beauty as through a pure and flawless crystal.[13] Is not that a kind of extension of His own glory?

The soul, by the simplicity of the gaze which it fixes on its divine object, finds itself set apart[14] from all that surrounds it, set apart also and above all from itself. Then it is resplendent with this "knowledge of the glory of God,"[15] of which the Apostle speaks, because it permits the divine Being to be reflected in it, "and all His attributes are communicated to it."[16] Truly this soul is the praise of glory of all His gifts; through everything, even the most commonplace acts, it sings the canticum magnum, the canticum novum...,[17] and this canticle thrills God to His very depths.

"Your light," we can say with Isaiah, "shall rise up in darkness, and your darkness shall be as the noonday. The Lord will give you rest continually, and will fill your soul with His brightness; He will strengthen your bones, and you shall be like a watered garden, and like a fountain of water whose waters shall not fail.... I will lift you above the high places of the earth...."[18]

Fourth Day

9. Yesterday St. Paul lifted the veil a little and allowed me to gaze on "the inheritance of the saints in light,"[1] that I might see what their occupation is and try, as far as possible, to conform my life to theirs so as to carry out my work of "Laudem Gloriae."

Today it is St. John, the disciple whom Jesus loved,[2] who partially opens "the eternal gates"[3] for me, that I may rest my soul in "the heavenly Jerusalem, sweet vision of peace!"[4] First of all he tells me there are no lights in the city "for the glory of God has illuminated it, and its lamp is the Lamb"....[5]

If I want my interior city[6] to have some similarity and likeness to that "of the King of eternal ages"[7] and to receive this great illumination from God, I must extinguish every other light and, as in the holy city, the Lamb must be "its only light."

10. Here faith, the beautiful light of faith appears. It alone should light my way as I go to meet the Bridegroom. The psalmist sings that He "hides Himself in darkness,"[8] then in another place he seems to contradict himself by saying that "light surrounds Him like a cloak."[9] What stands out for me in this apparent contradiction is that I must immerse myself in "the sacred darkness"[10] by putting all my powers in darkness and emptiness; then I will meet my Master, and "the light that surrounds Him like a cloak" will envelop me also, for He wants His bride to be luminous with His light, His light *alone, "which is the glory of God."*

It was said of Moses that he was "unshakable in his faith, as if he had seen the Invisible."[11] It seems to me that this should be the attitude of a praise of glory who wishes to continue her hymn of thanksgiving through everything: "unshakable in her faith, as if she had seen the Invisible"; unshakable in her faith in His "exceeding love."[12] "We have known the love of God for us, and we have believed in it."[13]

11. "Faith", St. Paul says, "is the substance of things to be hoped for, the evidence of things not seen."[14]

What does it matter to the soul that is absorbed in recollection of the light which these words create in it, whether it feels or does not feel, whether it is in darkness or light, whether it enjoys or does not enjoy. It feels a kind of embarrassment in making any distinction between these things; and when it still feels affected by them, it holds itself in deep contempt for its lack of love and quickly looks to its Master that He might set it free. In the expression of a great mystic it "exalts" Him "on the highest summit of the mountain of its heart, above the sweetness and consolations that descend from Him for it has resolved to go beyond everything to be united with Him whom it loves."[15] It seems to me that to this soul, unshakable in its faith in the God of Love, may be addressed these words of the Prince of Apostles, "Because you believe you will be filled with an unshakable and glorified joy."[16]

Fifth Day

12. "I saw a great multitude which no man could number. . . . These are they who have come out of the great tribulation and have washed their robes and made them white in the Blood of the Lamb. Therefore they are before the throne of God, and serve Him day and night in His temple, and He who sits upon the throne will dwell with them. They shall neither hunger nor thirst anymore, neither shall the sun strike them nor any heat. For the Lamb will be their shepherd, and He will lead them to the fountains of the waters of life, and God will wipe away every tear from their eyes. . . ."[1]

All these elect who have palms in their hands,[2] and who are wholly bathed in the great light[3] of God, have had first to pass through the "great tribulation," to know this sorrow "immense as the sea,"[4] of which the psalmist sang. Before contemplating "with uncovered face the glory of the Lord,"[5] they have shared in the annihilation of His Christ; before being "transformed from brightness to brightness in the image of the divine Being,"[6] they have been conformed to the image of the Word Incarnate, the One crucified by love.

13. The soul that wants to serve God day and night in His temple—I mean this inner sanctuary of which St. Paul speaks when he says, "The temple of God is holy and you are that temple,"[7] this soul must be resolved to share *fully* in its Master's passion. It is one of the redeemed who in its turn must redeem other souls, and for that reason it will sing on its lyre: "I glory in the Cross of Jesus Christ."[8] "With Christ I am nailed to the Cross. . . ."[8a] And again, "I suffer in my body what is lacking in the passion of Christ for the sake of His body, which is the Church."[9]

"The queen stood at your right hand":[10] such is the attitude of this soul; she walks the way of Calvary at the right of her crucified, annihilated, humiliated King, yet always so strong, so calm, so full of majesty as He goes to His passion "to make the glory of His grace blaze forth" according to that so strong expression of St. Paul.[11] He wants to associate His Bride in His work of redemption and this sorrowful way which she follows seems like the path of Beatitude to her, not only because it leads there but also because her holy Master makes her realize that she must go beyond the bitterness in suffering to find in it, as He did, her rest.

14. Then she can serve God *"day and night in His temple"*! Neither trials from without nor from within can make her leave the holy fortress in which the Master has enclosed her. She no longer feels *"hunger or thirst,"* for in spite of her consuming desire for Beatitude, she is satisfied by this food which was her Master's: "the will of the Father."[12] *"She no longer feels the heat of the sun,"* that is, she no longer suffers from suffering. Then the Lamb can *"lead her to the fountain of life,"* where He wills, as He wills, for she does not look at the paths on which she is walking; she simply gazes at the Shepherd who is leading her.[13] God bends lovingly over this soul, His adopted daughter, who is so conformed to the image of His Son, the "firstborn among all creatures,"[14] and recognizes her as one of those whom He has "predestined, called, justified."[15] And His fatherly heart thrills as He thinks of consumating His work,[16] that is, of "glorifying"[17] her by bringing her into His kingdom,[18] there to sing for ages unending "the praise of His glory."[19]

Sixth Day

15. "And I saw, and behold, the Lamb was standing upon Mount Sion, and with Him a hundred and forty-four thousand having His name and the name of His Father written on their foreheads. And I heard a voice like a voice of many waters, and like a voice of loud thunder; and the voice that I heard was as of several harpers playing on their harps. And they were singing as

it were a new song before the throne; and no one could learn the song except those hundred and forty-four thousand, for they were virgins. These follow the Lamb wherever He goes. . . . "[1]

There are some who even here below belong to this "generation pure as the light";[2] they already bear on their foreheads the name of the Lamb and of His Father. *"The name of the Lamb"*:[3] by their resemblance and conformity with Him whom St. John calls "the Faithful and True"[4] and whom he shows us "clothed in a robe stained with blood";[5] these also are the faithful and true, and their robe is stained with the blood of their constant sacrifice. *"The name of His Father"*: because He radiates in them the beauty of His perfections. All His divine attributes are reflected in these souls, and they are like so many strings which vibrate and sing *"the new song."* They *"also follow the Lamb whereever He goes,"* not only on the highways that are broad and easy to travel but down the thorny paths, along the brambly ways. That is why these souls are *virgins*, that is, free, set apart, stripped;[6] free from all save their love,[7] set apart from everything, especially themselves, stripped of all things both in the supernatural order as well as in the natural order.

16. What a going out from self that implies! What a death! Let us say with St. Paul, "Quotidie morior."[8] The great saint wrote to the Colossians, "You have died and your life is hidden with Christ in God."[9]

That is the condition: we must be dead! Without that we may be hidden in God at certain moments; but we do not LIVE habitually in this divine Being because all our emotions, self-seekings and the rest, come to draw us out of Him.

The soul that gazes steadfastly on its Master with this "single eye which fills the whole body with light"[10] is kept "from the depths of iniquity within it" of which the prophet complains.[11] The Lord has brought it into "this spacious place"[12] which is nothing else than Himself; there everything is pure, everything is holy!

O blessed death in God! O sweet and gentle loss of self in the beloved Being which permits the creature to cry out: "I live, no longer I, but Christ lives in me. And the life that I now live in this body of death, I live in the faith of the Son of God, who loved me and gave Himself up for me."[13]

Seventh Day

17. "Coeli enarrant gloriam Dei."[1] This is what the heavens are telling: the glory of God.

Since my soul is a heaven in which I live while awaiting the "heavenly Jerusalem,"[2] this heaven too must sing the glory of the Eternal, *nothing* but the glory of the Eternal.

"Day to day passes on this message."[3] All God's lights, all His communications to my soul are this "day which passes on to day the message of His glory." "The command of the Lord is clear," sings the psalmist, "enlightening the eye. . . ."[4] Consequently, my fidelity in corresponding with each of His decrees, with each of His interior commands, makes me live in His light; it too is a "message which passes on His glory." But this is the sweet wonder: "Yahweh, he who looks at you is radiant!",[5] the prophet exclaims. The soul that by the depth of its interior gaze contemplates its God through everything in that simplicity which sets it apart from all else is a *"radiant"* soul: it is "a day that passes on to day the message of His glory".

18. "Night to night announces it."[6] How very consoling that is! My weaknesses, my dislikes, my mediocrity, my faults themselves tell the glory of the Eternal! My sufferings of soul or body also tell the glory of my Master! David sang: "How shall I make a return to the Lord for all the good He has done for me?" This: "I will take up the cup of salvation."[7] If I take up this cup crimsoned with the Blood of my Master and, in wholly joyous thanksgiving, I mingle my blood with that of the holy Victim, it is in some way made infinite and can give magnificent praise to the Father. Then my suffering is "a message which passes on the glory" of the Eternal.

19. "There (in the soul that tells His glory) He has pitched a tent for the Sun."[8] The sun is the Word, the "Bridegroom." If He finds my soul empty of all that is not contained in these two words—His love, His glory, then He chooses it to be "His bridal chamber"; He "rushes" in "like a giant racing triumphantly on his course" and I cannot "escape His heat."[9] He is this "consuming fire"[10] which will effect the blessed transformation of which St. John of the Cross speaks when he says: "Each seems to be the other and the two are but one":[11] a "praise of glory"[12] of the Father!

Eighth Day

20. "And they do not rest day and night, saying, Holy holy, holy is the Lord God Almighty, who was, and who is, and who will be for ages unending.... And they fall down and worship Him and they cast down their crowns before the throne, saying, Worthy are you, O Lord, to receive glory and honor and power...."[1]

How can I imitate in the heaven of my soul this unceasing occupation of the blessed in the Heaven of glory? How can I sustain this uninterrupted praise and adoration? St. Paul gives me light on this when he writes to his followers his wish that "the Father would strengthen them inwardly with power through His Spirit so that Christ would dwell through faith in their hearts, and so that they would be rooted and grounded in love."[2] To be rooted and grounded in love: such, it seems to me, is the condition for worthily fulfilling its work as praise of glory. The soul that penetrates and dwells in these "depths of God" of which the royal prophets sings,[3] and thus does everything "in Him, with Him, by Him and for Him" with that limpid gaze which gives it a certain resemblance to the simple Being, this soul, by each of its movements, it aspirations, as well as by each of its acts, however ordinary they may be, "is rooted" more deeply in Him whom it loves. Everything within it pays homage to the thrice-holy God: it is so to speak a perpetual Sanctus, an unceasing praise of glory!

21. "They fall down and adore, they cast down their crowns ...." First of all the soul should "fall down," should plunge into the abyss of its nothingness, sinking so deeply into it that in the beautiful expression of a mystic, it finds "true, unchanging, and perfect peace which no one can disturb, for it has plunged so low that no one will look for it there."[4]

Then it can "adore." Adoration, ah! That is a word from Heaven! It seems to me it can be defined as the ecstasy of love. It is love overcome by the beauty, the strength, the immense grandeur of the Object loved, and it "falls down in a kind of faint"[5] in an utterly profound silence, that silence of which David spoke when he exclaimed: "Silence is Your praise!"[6] Yes, this is the most beautiful praise since it is sung eternally in the bosom of the tranquil Trinity; and it is also the "last effort of the soul that overflows and can say no more ..." (Lacordaire).[7]

"Adore the Lord, for He is holy,"[8] the Psalmist says. And again: "They will adore Him always because of Himself."[9] The soul that is absorbed in recollection of these thoughts, that penetrates them with "this mind of God"[10] of which St. Paul speaks, lives in an anticipated Heaven, beyond all that passes, beyond the clouds, beyond itself! It knows that He whom it adores possesses in Himself all happiness and all glory and, "casting its crown" before Him as the blessed do, it despises self, loses sight of self, and finds its beatitude in that of the adored Being, in the midst of every suffering and sorrow. For it has left self, it has "*passed*"[11] into Another. It seems to me that in this attitude of adoration the soul "resembles those wells" of which St. John of the Cross speaks,[12] which receive "the waters that flow down from Lebanon," and we can say on seeing it: "The impetus of the river delights the City of God."[13]

Ninth Day

22. "Be holy for I am holy."[1] Who then is this who can give such a command? ... He Himself has revealed His name, the name proper to Him, which He alone can bear: "I am Who Am,"[2] He said to Moses, the only living One, the principle of all the other beings. "In Him," the Apostle says, "we live and move and have our being."[3] "Be holy for I am holy"! It seems to me that this is the very same wish expressed on the day of creation when God said: "Let us make man in Our image and likeness."[4] It is always the desire of the Creator to identify and to associate His creature with Himself! St. Peter says "that we have been made sharers in the divine nature";[5] St. Paul recommends that we hold on to "this beginning of His existence"[6] which He has given us; and the disciple of love tells us: "Now we are the children of God, and we have not yet seen what we shall be. We know that when He appears, we shall be like Him, for we shall see Him just as He is. And everyone who has this hope in Him makes himself holy, *just as He Himself is holy.*"[7] To be holy as God is holy, such is, it seems, the measure of the children of His love! Did not the Master say: "Be perfect as your heavenly Father is perfect"?[8]

23. Speaking to Abraham God said: "Walk in My presence and be perfect."[8a] This then is the way to achieve this perfection that our Heavenly Father asks of us! St. Paul, after having immersed himself in the divine counsels,[9] revealed exactly this to us when he wrote "God has chosen us in Him before the creation of the world, that we might be holy and immaculate *in His presence* in love."[9a] It is also by the light of this same saint that I will be enlightened so that I might walk without deviating from this magnificent road of the presence of God on which the soul journeys "alone with the Alone,"[10] led by the "strength of His right arm,"[11] "under the protection of His wings, without fearing the terror of the night nor the arrow that flies by day, nor the evil that stalks in darkness, nor the attacks of the noonday devil...."[12]

24. "Strip off the old man in whom you lived your former life," he tells me, "and put on the new man, who has been created according to God in justice and holiness."[13] This is the way set forth; we have only to strip off self to follow it as God wills! To strip off self, to die to self, to lose sight of self. It seems to me the Master meant this when He said: "If anyone wants to follow Me, let him take up his cross and deny himself."[14] "If you live according to the flesh," the Apostle also says, "you will die, but if you put to death in the spirit the works of the flesh, you will live."[15] This is the death that God asks for and of which it is said: "Death has been swallowed up in victory."[16] "O death," says the Lord, "I will be your death";[17] that is: O soul, my adopted daughter, look at Me and you will forget yourself; flow entirely into My Being, come die in Me that I may live in you!

Tenth Day

25. "Be perfect as your heavenly Father is perfect."[1] When my Master makes me understand these words in the depths of my soul, it seems to me that He is asking me to live like the Father "in an eternal present," "with no before, no after," but wholly in the unity of my being in this "eternal now."[2] What is this present? This is what David tells me: "They will adore Him always because of Himself."[3]

This is the eternal present in which Laudem Gloriae must be established. But for her to be truly in this attitude of adoration, so that she can sing, "I will awake the dawn,"[4] she must also be able to say with St. Paul, "For love of Him I have forfeited everything";[5] that is: because of Him, that I may adore Him always, I am "alone, set apart, stripped" of all things, both with regard to the natural as well as the supernatural gifts of God. For a soul that is not thus "destroyed and freed"[6] from self will of necessity be trivial and natural at certain moments, and that is not worthy of a daughter of God, a spouse of Christ, a temple of the Holy Spirit. To guard against this natural life the soul must be wholly vigilant in her faith[7] with her gaze turned towards the Master. Then she "can walk," as the royal prophet sings, "in the integrity of her heart within her house."[8] Then she "will adore her God always because of Himself" and will live, like Him, in that eternal present where He lives. . . .

26. "Be perfect as your heavenly Father is perfect." "God," says St. Dionysius, "is the great solitary."[9] My Master asks me to imitate this perfection, to pay Him homage by being a great solitary. The divine Being lives in an eternal, immense solitude. He never leaves it, though concerning Himself with the needs of His creatures, for He never leaves Himself; and this solitude is nothing else than His divinity.

So that nothing may draw me out of this beautiful silence within, I must always maintain the same dispositions, the same solitude, the same withdrawal, the same stripping of self! If my desires, my fears, my joys or my sorrows, if all the movements proceeding from these "four passions"[10] are not perfectly directed to God, I will not be solitary: there will be noise within me. There must be peace, "sleep of the powers,"[11] the unity of being. "Listen, my daughter, lend your ear, forget your people and your father's house, and the King will become enamoured of your beauty."[12]

It seems to me that this call is an invitation to silence: listen . . . lend your ear. . . . But to listen we must forget "our father's house," that is, everything that pertains to the natural life, this life to which the Apostle refers when he says: "If you live according to the flesh, you will die."[13] To forget "your people" is more difficult, I think, for this people is everything which is, so to speak, part of us: our feelings, our memories, our impressions, etc., the *self*, in a word! We must forget it, abandon it, and when the soul has made this break, when it is free from all that, the King is enamoured of its beauty. For beauty is unity, at least it is the unity of God!

Eleventh Day (continued)[1]

27. "The Lord brought me into a spacious place, because He was gracious toward me...."[2] The Creator, seeing the beautiful silence which reigns in His creature, and gazing on her wholly recollected in her interior solitude, is enamoured of her beauty and leads her into this immense, infinite solitude, into this "spacious place" sung of by the prophet, which is nothing else but Himself: "I will enter into the depths of the power of God."[3] Speaking through his prophet, the Lord said: "I will lead her into solitude and speak to her heart."[4] The soul has entered into this vast solitude in which God will make Himself heard! "His word," St. Paul says, "is living and active, and more penetrating than a two-edged sword: extending even to the division of soul and spirit, even of joints and marrow."[5] It is His word then that will directly achieve the work of stripping in the soul; for it has this particular characteristic, that it effects and creates what it intends,[6] provided however that the soul consents to let this be done.

28. But it is not enough just to listen to this word, we must keep it![7] And it is in keeping it that the soul will be "sanctified in the truth," and that is the desire of the Master: "Sanctify them in the truth, your word is truth."[8] To the one who keeps His word has He not made this promise: "My Father will love him and we will come to him and make our home *in him*"?[9] It is the whole Trinity who dwells in the soul that loves them in truth, that is, by keeping their word! And when this soul has realized its riches, all the natural or supernatural joys that can come to it from creatures or from God Himself are only an invitation to re-enter into itself in order to enjoy the substantial Good that it possesses, which is nothing else than God Himself. And thus it has, St. John of the Cross says, a certain resemblance to the divine Being.[10]

"Be perfect as your heavenly Father is perfect." St. Paul tells me "that He works all things according to the counsel of His will,"[11] and my Master asks me also to pay Him homage in this regard: "to do all things according to the counsel of His will." Never to let myself be ruled by impressions, by the first impulses of nature, but to let the will gain self-mastery.... And for this will to be free, it must be, in the expression of a pious writer, "enclosed in God's will."[12] Then I will be "moved by His Spirit,"[13] as St. Paul says. I will do only what is divine, only what is eternal, and, like my Unchanging One, I will live even here below in an eternal present.

Twelfth Day

29. "Verbum caro factum est et habitavit in nobis."[1] God has said: "Be holy, for I am holy."[1a] But He remained hidden in His inaccessible [light[2]] and the creature needed to have Him descend to it, to live its life, so that following in His footsteps,[3] it can thus ascend to Him and become holy with His holiness. "I sanctify myself for them that they also may be sanctified in the truth."[4] Here I am in the presence "of a mystery hidden from ages and generations," the "mystery which is Christ": "your hope of glory," says St. Paul! And he adds that "the understanding of this mystery" was given to him.[6] So it is from the great Apostle that I am going to learn how I may possess this knowledge which, in his expression, "surpasses all other knowledge: the knowledge of the love of Christ Jesus."[7]

30. First of all he tells me that He is "my peace,"[8] that it is "through Him that I have access to the Father,"[9] for it has pleased this "Father of lights"[10] that "in Him all fullness should dwell, and that through Him He should reconcile to Himself all things, whether on the earth or in the heavens, making peace through the Blood of His Cross...."[11] "You have received of His fullness," the Apostle continues, "you were buried with Him in Baptism, and in Him you rose again through faith in the working of God.... He brought you to life along with Him, forgiving you all your sins, cancelling the decree of condemnation which weighed on you: He abolished it by nailing it to the Cross. Despoiling Princi-

palities and Powers, He victoriously led them away as captives, triumphing over them in Himself . . . ,"[12] "to present you holy, pure, and without reproach before Him. . . ."[13]

31. This is Christ's work in every soul of good[14] will and it is the work that His immense love, His *"exceeding love,"*[15] is eager to do in me. He wants to be my peace so that nothing can distract me or draw me out of "the invincible fortress of holy recollection."[16] It is there that He will give me "access to the Father" and will keep me as still and as peaceful in His presence as if my soul were already in eternity.[17] It is by the Blood of His Cross that He will make peace in my little heaven, so that it may truly be the repose of the Three. He will fill me with Himself; He will bury me with Him; He will make me live again with Him, by His life: "Mihi vivere Christus est"![18] And if I fall at every moment,[19] in a wholly confident faith I will be helped up by Him. I know that He will forgive me, that He will cancel out everything with a jealous care, and even more, He will "despoil" me, He will "free"[20] me from all my miseries, from everything that is an obstacle to the divine action. "He will lead away all my powers,"[21] making them His captives, triumphing over them in Himself. Then I will have wholly passed into Him and can say: "I no longer live. My Master lives in me"![22] And I will be *"holy, pure, without reproach"* in the Father's eyes.

Thirteenth Day

32. "Instaurare omnia in Christo."[1] Again it is St. Paul who instructs me, St. Paul who has just immersed himself in the great counsel of God[2] and who tells me "that He has resolved in Himself to restore all things in Christ."

So that I may personally realize this divine plan, it is again St. Paul who comes to my aid and who will himself draw up a rule of life for me. "Walk in Jesus Christ," he tells me, "be rooted in Him, built up in Him, strengthened in faith, growing more and more in Him through thanksgiving."[3]

33. *To walk in Jesus Christ* seems to me to mean to leave self, lose sight of self, give up self, in order to enter more deeply into

Him with every passing moment,[4] so deeply that one is *rooted* there; and to every event, to every circumstance we can fling this beautiful challenge: "Who will separate me from the love of Jesus Christ?"[5] When the soul is established in Him at such depths that its *roots* are also deeply thrust in, then the divine sap streams into it[6] and all this imperfect, commonplace, natural life is destroyed. Then, in the language of the Apostle, "that which is mortal is swallowed up by life."[7] The soul thus "stripped" of self and "clothed"[8] in Jesus Christ has nothing more to fear from exterior encounters or from interior difficulties, for these things, far from being an obstacle, serve only "to root it more deeply in the love"[9] of its Master. Through everything, despite everything, the soul can "adore Him always because of Himself."[10] For it is free, rid of self and everything else; it can sing with the psalmist: "Though an army encamp against me, I will not fear; though war be waged upon me I will trust in spite of everything; for Yahweh will hide me in the secrecy of His tent"[11] and this tent is nothing else but Himself. I think that is what St. Paul means when he says: "be rooted in Jesus Christ."

34. And now what does it mean *to be built up in Him?* The prophet[12] also sings "He has set me high upon a rock, now my head is held high above my enemies who surround me";[13] I think that this can well be taken as a figure of the soul "built up in Jesus Christ." He is that rock on which it is set high above self, the senses and nature, above consolations or sorrows, above all that is not *Him* alone. And there in complete self-control, it overcomes self, it goes beyond self and all else as well.

Next St. Paul advises me to *be strengthened in faith*: in that faith which never lets the soul doze but keeps it wholly vigilant beneath its Master's gaze, wholly absorbed in recollection of His creating word,[14] in that faith "in His exceeding love,"[15] which permits God, St. Paul tells me, to fill the soul "*with His fullness.*"[16]

35. Finally, he wants me "to grow in Jesus Christ through *thanksgiving*": for everything should end in this! "Father, I thank You!"[17] My Master sang this in His soul and He wants to hear the echo of it in mine! But I think that the "new song"[18] which will most charm and captivate my God is that of a soul stripped and freed from self, one in whom He can reflect all that He is, and

do all that He wills. This soul remains under His touch like a lyre, and all His gifts to it are like so many strings which vibrate to sing, day and night, the praise of His glory!

Fourteenth Day

36. "It seems to me that all is loss since I have known the excelling knowledge of my Lord, Jesus Christ. For love of Him I have forfeited everything; I have accounted all else rubbish that I may gain Christ, so as to be found in Him, not with my own justice but with the justice that comes from God through faith. What I want is to know Him, to share in His sufferings, to become like Him in His death. I pursue my course, striving to attain to what Christ has destined me for by taking hold of me; my whole concern is to forget what is behind and to strain forward constantly to what is ahead; I run straight to the goal . . ., to the prize of the heavenly vocation to which God has called me in Christ Jesus."[1] The Apostle has often revealed the greatness of this vocation: "God," he says, "has chosen us in Him before the creation of the world that we might be holy and immaculate in His presence in love. . . . We have been predestined by the decree of Him who works all things according to the counsel of His will, so that we may be the praise of His glory."[2]

37. But how do we respond to the dignity of this vocation? This is the secret: "Mihi vivere Christus est!. . . Vivo enim, jam non ego, vivit vero in me Christus. . . ."[3] We must be transformed into Jesus Christ; again it is St. Paul who teaches me this: "Those whom God has foreknown, He has predestined to be conformed to the image of His Son."[4]

It is important then that I study this divine Model so as to identify myself so closely with Him that I may unceasingly reveal Him to the eyes of the Father. First of all, what did He say when He came into the world? "Here I am, O God, I come to do your will."[5] I think that this prayer should be like the bride's heartbeat:[6] "Here *we* are, O Father, we come to do your will!"

38. The Master was truth itself in this first oblation! His life was as it were but the consequence of it! "My food," He liked to

say, "is to do the will of Him who sent Me."[7] It should also be that of the bride, and at the same time the sword that immolates her.... "If it is possible, let this cup pass me by, yet not as I will but as You will."[8] And then she will joyfully go in peace to every sacrifice with her Master, rejoicing to *"have been known"* by the Father since He crucifies her with His Son. "Your decrees are my inheritance forever; they are the joy of my heart":[9] my Master sang this in His soul, and it should echo resoundingly in that of the bride! It is by her constant fidelity to these *"decrees,"* whether exterior or interior, that she will "bear witness to the truth"[10] and will be able to say "He who sent me has not left me alone. He is always with me because I do always the things that are pleasing to Him."[11] And by never leaving Him, by remaining in closest contact with Him, she will radiate "this secret power"[12] which saves and delivers souls. Stripped and set free of self and all else, she can follow the Master to the mountain[13] to pray there with Him in her soul, "a prayer of God."[14] Then, still through the divine Adorer, He who is the great praise of glory to the Father, she will "ceaselessly offer a sacrifice of praise, that is, the fruit of lips praising His name"[15] (St. Paul). And, as the psalmist sings, she will praise Him "in the expansion of His power, and for the immensity of His grandeur."[16]

39. Then, when her hour of humiliation, of annihilation comes, she will recall this little phrase, "Jesus autem tacebat";[17] and she will be silent, "keeping all her strength for the Lord";[18] this strength which "we draw from silence."[19] And when the hour of abandonment, of desertion, and of anguish comes, the hour that drew from Christ this loud cry, "Why have You abandoned Me?"[20], she will recall this prayer: "that they may have in themselves the fulness of My joy";[21] and drinking to the dregs "the cup prepared by the Father,"[22] she will find a divine sweetness in its bitterness. Finally, after having said so often "I am thirsty,"[23] thirsty to possess You in glory, she will sing: "Everything is consumated; into Your hands I commend my spirit."[24] And the Father will come for her to "bring her into His inheritance,"[25] where in "the light she will see light."[26]

"Know that the Lord has marvellously glorified His Holy One," David sang.[27] Yes, the Holy One of God will have been glorified

in this soul, for He will have destroyed everything there to "clothe
it with Himself,"²⁸ and it will have lived in reality the words of
the Precursor: "He must increase and I must decrease."²⁹

Fifteenth Day

40. After Jesus Christ, doubtless at the distance that there is
between the Infinite and the finite, there is one who was also the
great praise of glory of the Holy Trinity. She responded fully to
the divine election of which the Apostle speaks: she was always
*"pure, immaculate, and without reproach"*¹ in the eyes of the
thrice-holy God. Her soul is so simple. Its movements are so profound that they cannot be detected. She seems to reproduce on
earth the life which is that of the divine Being, the simple Being.
And she is so transparent, so luminous that one would mistake
her for the light, yet she is but the "mirror" of the Sun of Justice:
"Speculum justitiae"!²
"The Virgin kept all these things in her heart":³ her whole
history can be summed up in these few words! It was within her
heart that she lived, and at such a depth that no human eye can
follow her. When I read in the Gospel "that Mary went in haste
to the hill country of Judea"⁴ to perform her loving service for
her cousin Elizabeth, I imagine her passing by so beautiful, so
calm and so majestic, so absorbed in recollection of the Word of
God within her. Like Him, her prayer was always this: *"Ecce,
here I am!"* Who? "The servant of the Lord,"⁵ the lowliest of His
creatures: she, His Mother! Her humility was so real for she was
always forgetful, unaware, freed from self. And she could sing:
"The Almighty has done great things for me, henceforth all
peoples will call me blessed."⁶
41. This Queen of virgins is also Queen of martyrs; but again
it was *in her heart* that the *sword pierced,*⁷ for with her everything took place within!... Oh! How beautiful she is to contemplate during her long martyrdom, so serene, enveloped in a
kind of majesty that radiates both strength and gentleness....
She learned from the Word Himself how those must suffer whom
the Father has chosen as victims, those whom He has decided to

associate with Himself in the great work of redemption, those whom He "has foreknown and predestined to be conformed to His Christ,"[8] crucified by love.

She is there at the foot of the Cross, *standing*, full of strength and courage, and here my Master says to me: "Ecce Mater tua."[9] He gives her to me for my Mother. . . . And now that He has returned to the Father and has substituted me for Himself on the Cross so that "I may suffer in my body what is lacking in His passion for the sake of His body, which is the Church,"[10] the Blessed Virgin is again there to teach me to suffer as He did, to tell me, to make me hear those last songs of His soul which no one else but she, His Mother, could overhear.

When I shall have said my "consummatum est,"[11] it is again she, "Janua coeli,"[12] who will lead me into the heavenly courts, whispering to me these mysterious words: "*Laetatus sum in his quae dicta sunt mihi, in domun Domini ibimus!*"[13]

Sixteenth Day

42. "As the thirsty doe longs for the springs of fresh water, so my soul longs for You, O God! My soul thirsts for the living God! When will I appear before His face? . . ."[1]

And yet, as "the sparrow has found a home," and "the turtle-dove a nest in which she may lay her young,"[2] so Laudem Gloriae has found while waiting to be brought to the holy Jerusalem, "beata pacis visio"[3] — her retreat, her beatitude, her anticipated Heaven in which she begins her life of eternity. "In God my soul is silent; my deliverance comes from Him. Yes, He is the rock in which I find salvation, my stronghold, I shall not be disturbed!"[4]

This is the mystery my lyre sings of today! My Master has said to me as to Zacchaeus: "Hurry and come down, for I must stay in your house today. . . ."[5] Hurry and come down, but where? Into the innermost depths of my being: after having forsaken self, withdrawn from self, been stripped of self, in a word, *without self*.

43. "I must stay in your house!" It is my Master who expresses this desire! My master who wants to dwell in me with the Father and His Spirit of love, so that, in the words of the beloved disciple,

I may have "communion"[6] with Them. "You are no longer guests or strangers, but you already belong to the House of God,"[7] says St. Paul. This is how I understand "belong to the House of God": it is in living in the bosom of the tranquil Trinity, in my interior abyss, in this "invincible fortress of holy recollection"[8] of which St. John of the Cross speaks!

David sang: "My soul falls down in a faint for the courts of the Lord."[9] I think that this should be the attitude of every soul that enters into its interior courts to contemplate its God and to come into closest contact with Him: it "falls down in a faint" in a divine swoon before this all-powerful Love, this infinite Majesty who dwells within it! It is not life that abandons the soul, but rather the soul that scorns this natural life and withdraws from it. . . . For it feels that this life is not worthy of His rich essence[10] so it dies and flows into its God.

44. Oh! How beautiful is this creature thus stripped, freed from self! It can "use the ascensions in its heart so that it may pass from this valley of tears" (that is, from all that is less than God) "to the place which is its goal,"[11] this "Spacious place,"[12] of which the psalmist sings, which is, it seems to me, the unfathomable Trinity "Immensus Pater, immensus Filius, immensus Spiritus sanctus!"[13] It ascends, it rises above the senses, above nature; it transcends itself; it goes beyond every joy and every pain and passes through the clouds, not stopping until it has penetrated *"into the interior"*[14] of Him whom it loves and who Himself will give it "the repose of the abyss".[15] And all that without leaving the holy fortress! The Master had said to it: "Hurry and *come down*. . . ."[16] It is also without leaving it that the soul will live, like the immutable Trinity, in an *eternal present*,[17] "adoring Him always because of Himself,"[18] and becoming by an always more simple, more unitive gaze, "the splendor of His glory,"[19] that is, the unceasing praise of glory of His adorable perfections.

NOTES

First Day

  1. Ct 6:11, cited (also in Latin) in SC 291 (cf. the following note).
  2. Cf. SC 291 and 292. (Cf. *Collected Works*, St 26:14, p. 514).
  3. Elizabeth loves this definition of time which she had already given in HF 1. Is it her own inspiration?

4. Cf. Ph 3:10.

5. Rm 8:29.

6. This term probably stems from her recent reading in Ruysbroeck, for ex. in Ru 44, 45, 46, 68. There, however, it concerns the exemplar of our spirit in God; here Elizabeth applies it to Christ of whom Paul has just said that He is our "image."

7. Cf. Ep 1:4. The "in principio" ("in the beginning") is inspired by this election "before the creation of the world" (in the same verse Ep 1:4), willed "for eternity."

8. Ep 1:12. On this name which Elizabeth gives herself, cf. L 250, n.16, and 17.

9. Quoting from memory, Elizabeth combines Jn 6:46 (or a reminiscence of Jn 1:18 or 1 Jn 4:12) and Mt 11:27 (whose beginning verse is very close to that of Jn).

10. Cf. Ep 3:3-4.

11. Cf. Lk 2:19.

12. From the Litany of Loretto. The Virgin venerated in the Carmel of Dijon (cf. Plan 1, no 8) was "Our Lady of Grace".

13. Elizabeth is probably thinking of SC 126 (cf. *Collected Works*, St 12:6, p. 455) in which John of the Cross describes how perfect love can "reproduce" "the features of the Beloved in such a vivid and intimate way", "such a striking resemblance", "a ravishing picture". She will quote this page in LR 19 (cf. *ibid.*, n.11).

14. Cf. Lk 2:7.

Second Day

1. Ps 118:109.

2. Ps 58:10, taken from SC 313 (Cf. *Collected Works*, St 28:8, p. 522). (Cf. HF 16, n. 15, and 16).

3. *Rule of Carmel*, partially citing Is 30:15, which Elizabeth abridges still more.

4. Cf. SC 313.

5. "The single eye" of Mt 6:22, found in the description of Ru 34 on "singleness of intention". Cf. HF 21, with n. 17.

6. A reminiscence of the doctrine on detachment set forth in SC 312 (Elizabeth has just referred to the following page 313, cf. n. 4) in which John of the Cross speaks of *"useless* things, of *taking up ones thoughts"* (the words that recur in Elizabeth are in italics) of "useless pastimes", and of a "host of other such useless things". Cf. *Collected Works*, St 28:7. p. 522.

6a. Cf. Ru 33: "Singleness of intention gathers together into unity of spirit the scattered forces of the soul. . . . "

7. LF 626 "the inner kingdom of the soul". Cf. *Collected Works*, St 4:5, p. 644.

8. Ru 157. Cf. GV 8.

9. "Great canticle". But St. Paul does not use this expression.

10. "The one thing necessary": cf. Lk 10:42.

10a. Catherine of Siena. Cf. L 199, n. 9.

11. Cf. Lk 10:39.

12. Ru 29.

13. Cf. SC 439. Literally: "the fortress, the unassailable citadel of interior recollection" (Cf. *Collected Works*, St 40:3, p. 64.) Cf. L 284, n.6.

14. Elizabeth, who has just sung in LR 3-4 of "beautiful inner unity," here calls it "beautiful simplicity," recalling pp. 33-37 of Ru which she had recently quoted at length in HF 21. She considers them so to speak as synonyms when writing: "the soul thus simplified, unified" or "an always more simple, more unitive gaze" (cf. *infra* 44).

15. Cf. Ph 3:8.

16. Expression of Catherine of Siena (Elizabeth heard it from P. Vallée (cf. L 291, n. 3); the Lord told her, "Your measure will be my measure." The thought was revived by P. Vallée's recent letter to Elizabeth (cf. L 304, n. 10) in which he wrote, "(Christ) is finally free to give Himself in His measure, to fill her with His grace...." Cf. also Ru 178: "He possesses God without measure and is possessed by Him."

17. Ru 178. Elizabeth adds "Holy." But whereas Ruysbroeck speaks of unity in God, Elizabeth changes the perspective by speaking of the unity of the perfect soul.

Third Day

1. Ep 1:11-12.

2. Cf. Ep 3:9.

3. Ep 1:4.

4. That is: the predestination to be praises of glory, and, also, to be that in the presence and love of God.

5. "God is Love": 1 Jn 4:16.

6. Cf. Ru 35: "(Simplicity of intention) will give us the repose of the abyss."

7. Cf. He 4:9 where the word "sabbath" appears in the trans. of the *Manual*. In a note Canon Gaume explains: "*Rest* means the true sabbath of God which we will celebrate eternally, the perfect rest after the labors of this life..." (p. 812). This is probably the origin of the expression "eternal sabbath" in Elizabeth as she is approaching her death.

8. Heb 4:3.

9. Cf. 1 Co 13:12.

10. Cf. 2 Co 3:18.

11. Cf. this same elaboration in HF 43 (on "praise of glory") with note 17. Canon Gaume notes in the margin of the verse cited: "This refers to Him who is the glory and splendor of the Father; like living mirrors we receive in ourselves and reflect the divine Image... (p. 622).

12. Gn. 1:26.

13. The crystal: cf. L269, n.11. Given the citation of note 16, Elizabeth is thinking here especially of LF 615.

14. "Set apart": on the echo of John of the Cross, cf. L 220, n. 4.

15. 2 Co 4:6.

16. Cf. LF 615 (cf. *Collected Works*, St 3:77. p. 640).

17. "The great canticle": cf. *supra*, LR 3, n. 9. "The new canticle": cf. Ap 14:3.

18. Is 58:10-11, 14, taken from SC 384-385. Cf. *Collected Works*, St 36:2, p. 546.

Fourth Day

1. Col 1:12.

2. Cf. Jn 13:23.

3. Ps 23:7 and 9.

4. Cf. hymn *Caelestis urbs Jerusalem* from Vespers of the Common of the Dedication of a Church.

5. Ap 21:23. The same verse (and not v.11, since it speaks of the *only* light) is repeated further on.

6. Elizabeth interiorizes "the holy city, the new Jerusalem" (Ap 21:2) in the "heaven of the soul," as she will do *infra*, 17. (To be compared with "the city of the soul" in SC 206 [cf. *Collected Works*, St 18:7, p. 484]).

7. 1 Tm 1:17. Elizabeth writes "immortels" (unless this was added by an unknown hand). We correct it after St. Paul, as S 272 of 1909 had already done.

8. Cf. Ps 17:12 (v. 13 in her *Manual*).

9. Ps 103:2.

10. Ru 73 and 145.

11. Cf. Heb 11:27.

12. Cf. Ep 2:4.

13. 1 Jn 4:16.

14. Heb 11:1.

15. This phrase is taken from Ru 9-10. The expression "exalts": Ru 9.

16. 1 P 1:8. Elizabeth really writes "(joie) glorifiée," as in the text of Peter and that of her *Manual*.

Fifth Day

1. Ap 7:9, 14-17. The text is repeated in the course of the following lines.

2. Cf. Ap 7:9.

3. "Great light": Is 9:2. Lesson from Christmas Matins. But the expression appears here in the context of the light of God of the apocalyptic city (cf. *supra*, 9).

4. It is the prophet Jeremiah and not the "psalmist": Lm 2:13. Lesson from Matins of Good Friday.

5. 2 Co 3:18.

6. Cf. 2 Co 3:18.

7. 1 Co 3:17.

8. Cf. Ga 6:14.

8a. Ga. 2:19. "Clouée" in the feminine, it is the redeemed and redeeming soul; it is also Elizabeth suffering on "the altar of her bed." Cf. her testimony to Marie of Jesus some weeks before, in L 306, n.1; and soon to her Mother in L 309.

9. Cf. Col 1:24.

10. Ps 44:11.

11. Ep 1:6.

12. Cf. Jn 4:32-34.

13. Cf. Ps 22:3-4.

14. Although the expression that Elizabeth places in quotation marks comes directly from Col 1:15, the Carmelite is surely thinking at the same time of Rm 8:29 (which she loved so) " . . . conformed to the image of His Son, so that He might be the first-born among many brothers." The word "conformed" of Elizabeth and her following citation prove it.

15. Cf. Rm 8:30.

16. Cf. Jn 17:4.

17. Jn 17:4.

18. Cf. Col 1:13; " . . . brought into the kingdom of His Beloved Son."

19. Ep 1:12.

Sixth Day

1. Ap 14:1-4, with some omissions in v. 3-4.

2. Sg 4:1. These words appear in the first antiphon of Matins of the Common of Virgins.

3. Further on Elizabeth underlines and puts between quotation marks: "*The name of His Father.*" For parallelism and the sake of clarity we do the same here.

4. Ap 19:11.

5. Ap 19:13.

6. The language here (as well as the distinction of the two orders) is inspired by John of the Cross. " . . . set apart, stripped . . ."; SC 439 (Cf. *Collected Works*, St 40:2, pp. 563-564). (Cf. also L 220, n.4).

7. "Free from all save their (or his) love": words attributed by Elizabeth to Mgr. Gay in L 199.

8. "I die daily": 1 Co 15:31.

9. Col 3:3.

10. Cf. Mt 6:22.

11. Cf. Ps 17:24.

12. Ps 17:20 (22 in the translation of her *Manual*).

13. Ga 2:20.

Seventh Day

1. "The heavens are telling the glory of God"; Ps 18:1. For this psalm Elizabeth will follow the trans. of Eyragues.

2. Heb 12:22.
3. Ps 18:3 (v. 2 in her *Manual*).
4. Ps 18:9.
5. Ps 33:6 (trans. Eyragues).
6. Ps 18:3 (v. 2 in her *Manual*).
7. Ps 115:3-4 (trans. from her *Manual*).
8. Ps 18:5.
9. The words between quotation marks are also taken from Ps 18:5-6 in Eyragues' translation. Note however that John of the Cross also explains (without referring to this psalm): "like the Bridegroom comes forth from His bridal chamber" (LF 635). (Cf. *Collected Works*, St 4:13, p. 648). It is there that Elizabeth could have read Ps 44:10, "The queen stood at your right hand . . ." in this translation which she cited two days previously, cf. *supra*, 13.
10. Cf. Heb 12:29, repeating Dt 4:24. John of the Cross cites it in SC 434 when speaking of the "transformation". Cf. *Collected Works*, St 39:14, p. 562.
11. SC 126. Cf. *Collected Works*, St 12:7, p. 455.
12. Ep 1:12.

Eighth Day

1. Ap 4:8, 10-11, with slight adaptations. The text will be repeated further on.
2. Cf. Ep 3:16-17.
3. The expression "depths of God" (which "the Spirit penetrates") is found in 1 Co 2:10, but the fact that Elizabeth attributes it to the "royal prophet" seems to reveal the presence of John of the Cross. In SC 391 (st. 36), he speaks of "the depth" (or the "depths" of God), which the soul (as in Elizabeth, and not "the Spirit," who *alone* can penetrate these depths in 1 Co 2:10-11) wishes "to penetrate and he reinforces his explanation by a phrase from the "Royal Prophet"; then he recommends — by referring to Ep 3:17, the text which Elizabeth just cited — "to be rooted in love" (SC 394). Cf. *Collected Works*, St 36: 13, p. 549.
4. Ru 98, with slight grammatical adaptations. But Elizabeth replaces the word "invincible" of Ruysbroeck with a term dear to her: "unchanging."
5. "To fall down in a faint": Ru 191, 231. The word "faint" recurs often in Ruysbroeck, for ex. Ru 99, 100, 178. (She had already copied the "to faint" of Ru 169 in HF 35). But we find "to fall down in a faint" in SC 109 (cf. *Collected Works*, St 11:4, p. 449), which even cites Ps 83:3 in this translation (different from the *Manual* or Eyragues), and again in LF 551 (cf. *Collected Works*, St 3:20, p. 618). The expression is also found in Ang 147, but Elizabeth has not yet really "discovered" this book at this time.)
6. Ps 65:1 (trans. Eyragues).
7. *Sainte Marie-Madeleine, op. cit.*, p. 83. Literally: ". . . her silence, which is an act of faith and humility is also the last effort of a soul that overflows and can say no more."
8. Ps 98:9.

9. Ps 71:15.

10. Cf. Rm 11:34 and 1 Co 2:16. Her *Manual* translates: "the mind of the Lord."

11. Elizabeth's quotation marks and underlining: does she mean to make an allusion? She had already used this expression in PN 13 of 1902, and quite recently, "wholly passed into" in HF 44, repeated in LR 31. She certainly could have heard it from P. Fages who said in his retreat of 1904, speaking of the gift of the Incarnation (first conference) "... I am immersed in the counsels of God. [And Elizabeth copied this thought in her personal notes of this retreat: cf. PAT.] Is that not enough to make you live in ecstasy, out of self, wholly passed into, wholly lost in the thought of God?"

12. LF 536. Cf. *Collected Works*, St 3:7, p. 613.

13. Ps 45:5, in the translation of LF 536.

Ninth Day

1. 1 P 1:16, citing Lv 11:44, 45.

2. Ex 3:14.

3. Ac 17:28.

4. Gn 1:26.

5. 2 P 1:4.

6. Heb 3:14.

7. 1 Jn 3:2–3.

8. Mt 5:48.

8a. Gn 17:1. This text was on the wall of the little staircase (cf. Plan 1, between no. 16 and 17).

9. Ep 1:11 speaks of the "counsel" in which St. Paul "immerses himself" as Elizabeth says. The same phrase is copied from P. Fages, cf. *supra*, 21, n.11. Coincidence or influence?

9a. Ep 1:4.

10. Teresa of Avila: cf. L 109, n.5.

11. Lk 1:51.

12. Cf. Ps 90:4–6. Elizabeth writes, as in her *Manual*, "demon *du* midi."

13. "He," that is, St. Paul: Ep 4:22, 24. Taken in this translation and form from LF 521–522. Cf. *Collected Works*, St 2:33. p. 607.

14. Cf. Mt 16:24.

15. Rm 8:13. Translation from LF 521. Cf. *Collected Works*, St 2:33, p. 607.

16. 1 Co 15:54; also from LF 524. Cf. *Collected Works*, St 2:34, p. 609.

17. Ho 13:14. With "the Lord says" at the end, just as in LF 524 (cf. *Collected Works*, St 2:34, p. 609). Probably Elizabeth had read and meditated this day on LF 520–527.

Tenth Day

1. Mt 5:48.

2. Ru 67: "God contemplates Himself in a simple gaze, with no before or after, in an eternal now."

3. Ps 71:15, repeated further on.

4. Cf. Ps 56:9 (trans. of Eyragues).

5. Cf. Ph 3:8.

6. Placed in quotation marks by Elizabeth, this formula is probably not a borrowing, but summarizes what she has just said, following John of the Cross: "... My soul is set apart, stripped, alone, withdrawn from all creatures, spiritual and material"... (SC 439) *Collected Works*, St 40:2, pp. 563-564.

7. Cf. PN 15.

8. Ps 100:3 in the trans. of the *Manual* which has "purity" instead of "integrity."

9. In the library of her Carmel there were the *Oeuvres de Denys l'Aréopagite*, translated by J. Dulac, Paris, Martin-Beaupré, 1865, 672 pp., as well as the little treatise *Théologie mystique* of Dionysius the Aréopagite (in the trans. of 1845 by Mgr Darboy) cited in L Chardon, *La Croix de Jésus*, t. II, Lethielleux, 1895, pp. 425-437. We did not find the citation there. Elizabeth is only summarizing the idea of the transcendence of God which is so strongly emphasized by Dionysius. She had surely heard of it. Apart from this allusion there is nothing to prove that she read anything by the Areopagite.

10. SC 441 (cf. *Collected Works*, St 40:4, p. 564). John of the Cross often speaks of these "four passions: joy, hope, sorrow, and fear" (SC 218), (cf. *Collected Works*, St 20:4, p. 489) for ex. again in SC 223-230 (cf. *Collected Works*, St 20: 9-13, pp. 491-493), SC 296-297 (cf. *Collected Works*, St 26:18, p. 516), 310 (cf. *Collected Works*, St 28:4, p. 521).

11. The expression "sleep of the powers" is in Teresa of Avila, *Life*, ch. 16 (trad. Bouix, tome I, 1857, p. 191). It is the third degree of prayer. However, it may be that Elizabeth is thinking rather of St 26 of the *Spiritual Canticle* on the inebriation of love after having drunk in the "inner cellar of the Beloved": "the three powers of the soul are inebriated together on their Beloved" (SC 287), (cf. *Collected Works*, St 26:8, p. 513). This is the strophe of the "Nescivi," the word with which this *Last Retreat* begins.

12. Cf. Ps 44:12-13.

13. Rm 8:13.

Eleventh Day

1. Elizabeth herself indicates: "(continued)."

2. Ps 17:20 (v. 22 in her *Manual*).

3. Ps 70:16.

4. Ho 2:14.

5. Heb 4:12.

6. Possibly Elizabeth is recalling here the doctrine of Teresa of Avila on "interior locutions" (*Interior Castle*, VI, 3) or that of John of the Cross on "substantial words" (*Ascent of Mount Carmel*, II, ch 31). Nothing proves that she read these pages, but this doctrine was quite familiar in Carmel.

7. Cf. Jn 14:23. Also perhaps Ja 1:22-23.

8. Jn 17:17.

9. Jn 14:23.

10. Cf. especially SC, strophe 39: "like God" (SC 422), (cf. *Collected Works*, St 39:4, p. 558), "truly gods, like God" (SC 425), (cf. *Collected Works*, St 39:6, p. 559). Also strophe 36: "more and more like the Beloved" (SC 387), (cf. *Collected Works*, St 36:4, p. 547) and strophe 12: "a striking resemblance" (SC 126), (cf. *Collected Works*, St 12:6, p. 455).

11. Ep 1:11.

12. Ru 157. Cf GV 8.

13. Rm 8:14.

Twelfth Day

1. "The Word was made flesh and dwelt among us": Jn 1:14.

1a. 1 P 1:16, citing Lv 11:44, 45.

2. "Inaccessible Light": cf. 1 Tm 6:16.

3. Cf. 1 P 2:21: ". . . Christ . . . left you an example that you might follow in His footsteps."

4. Jn 17:19.

5. Cf. Col 1:26–27.

6. Ep 3:4.

7. Cf. Ep 3:19.

8. Ep 2:14.

9. Ep 2:18.

10. Ja 1:17.

11. Col 1:19–20.

12. Col 2:10, 12–15, with some small omissions.

13. Col 1:22, repeated a little further on.

14. A first version follows here: "will, and that is what He wants to do in me, to be my peace so that nothing [here again a first version: "may stop me"] may draw me out of the bosom of the Father, so that I may remain there as still and as peaceful as if my soul were already in eternity." In these last words we recognize PN 15 ("O My God, Trinity Whom I Adore"). Did Elizabeth find that union with God expressed in this way resembled too greatly that of Christ "in the bosom of His Father"? Afterwards she glued a half-sheet over this first version and wrote a second definitive text. She made this correction *immediately*: the proof of it is that after the last word of the first version "eternity," the line remains blank. After the part that is pasted over her writing continues as usual.

15. Ep 2:4.

16. John of the Cross. Cf. L 284, n.6.

17. Cf. PN 15.

18. "For me to live is Christ": Ph 1:21.

19. Cf. *To Live by Love* by Thérèse of Lisieux, a poem that Elizabeth loved: "But if I fall at every passing hour: / helping me up . . . You [Jesus] will give me Your grace. . . ." Cf. L 214, n.9, as well as *infra*, 33, n.4.

20. In this context the word reveals an allusion to Rm 7:24: "Unhappy man that I am! Who will free me from this body of death?" Below, 35 and 44, Eliza-

beth repeats her biblical binomial "despoiling," "freed." "Despoiling" comes from Col 2:15

21. Taken from Col 2:15, cited *supra*, 30. Note that Elizabeth intends the word "powers" in a psychological sense: the powers of the soul.

22. Cf. Ga 2:20.

Thirteenth Day

1. "restores all things in Christ": Ep 1:10. She immediately cites it in French, Ep 1:9-10.

2. Cf. Ep 1:11 (see already *supra*, 23, n.9).

3. Col 2:6-7. Elizabeth applies this text to herself in the feminine; she will comment on it gradually. As she herself underlined the first three elements, we logically underline "to be strengthened in faith" and "thanksgiving."

4. "At each passing moment": a probable echo of Thérèse of Lisieux, cf. L 214, no.9.

5. Rm 8:35. Elizabeth writes "me" instead of "us."

6. Perhaps in the background there is the image of the vine and its branches, and the command of the Lord "Remain in me" ("established in Him" Elizabeth says). Cf. Jn 15:4-5.

7. 2Co 5:4.

8. We also find these words in 2Co 5:4, but she vitalizes them by and in the much richer context of Col 3:9-10: "Strip off the old man . . . and clothe yourselves in the new . . . in the image of Him who created you," and of Ga 3:27 (as well as Rm 13:14): "clothed in Jesus Christ."

9. A reminiscence this time of Ep 3:17: "rooted and grounded in love."

10. Ps 71:15.

11. Ps 26:3, 5 (trans. Eyragues).

12. Several times Elizabeth gives to the "psalmist" the name of "prophet". It will be noticed that, in the literature of that period, David is often called the king of the prophets.

13. Ps 26:5-6 (trans. Eyragues).

14. "Creating Word": expression that Elizabeth heard at Carmel, notably from P. Vallée, for ex., in his Discourse for the feast of St. John of the Cross, November 24, 1901, and twice in the fourth evening conference of the Retreat of 1902. The expression obviously refers to Gn 1.

15. Ep 2:4.

16. Ep 3:19.

17. Jn 11:41.

18. Ap 14:3.

Fourteenth Day

1. Ph 3:8-10, 12-14. Perhaps she copied here her "retreat devotion" of 1905 (PN 16). Adaptation of verse 10.

2. Ep 1:4, 11-12.

3. "Christ is my life! I live, no longer I, but Christ lives in me": a combination of Ph 1:21 and Ga 2:20.

4. Rm 8:29.

5. Heb 10:9, citing Ps 39:10-11.

6. First version crossed out: "the breathing."

7. Jn 4:34.

8. Mt 26:39.

9. Ps 118:111.

10. Cf. Jn 18:37.

11. Jn 8:29. Elizabeth writes: "seule," in the feminine.

12. Cf. Lk 6:19.

13. This refers to Lk 6:12, as the following note proves.

14. Lk 6:12: "He spent the night there in a prayer of God" (trans. of the *Manual*). Canon Gaume notes: "Literal translation; we could find no other way to express the force of the text" (p. 205).

15. Heb 13:15.

16. Ps 150:1-2 (trans. Eyragues).

17. "But Jesus was silent": Mt 26:63.

18. Cf. Ps 58:10 in translation of SC 313, cf. *Collected Works,* St 28:8, p. 522.

19. Cf. Is 30:15, cited in the *Rule of Carmel.*

20. Mt 27:46.

21. Jn 17:13.

22. Cf. Jn 18:11.

23. Jn 19:30.

24. Lk 23:46.

25. Cf. Col 1:12-13.

26. Cf. Ps 35:10.

27. Ps 4:4.

28. Cf. Ga 3:27. Cf. also *supra,* 33, n.8.

29. Jn 3:30.

Fifteenth Day

1. Col 1:22.

2. "Mirror of Justice": from the Litany of Loretto.

3. Lk 2:19 and 51.

4. Lk 1:39.

5. Lk 1:38.

6. Lk 1:49, 48.

7. Cf. Lk 2:35.

8. Cf. Rm 8:29.

9. "Behold your mother": Jn 19:27.

10. Col 1:24.

11. "It is finished": Jn 19:30.

12. "Gate of Heaven": from the Litany of Loretto. This is the name that Elizabeth often gives the Blessed Virgin during the last months of her life (cf. S 204).

13. The handwriting is enlarged. "I rejoiced when they said to me: Let us go up to the house of the Lord": Ps 121:1 (we give the trans. of the *Manual*). Three times a day the Sisters recited this psalm as they entered Choir.

Sixteenth Day

1. Ps 41:1-2 (trans. Eyragues). Elizabeth adds the adjective "thirsty."
2. Ps 83:3.
3. "Blessed vision of peace": from the hymn *Coelestis urbs Jerusalem*: Vespers of the Common of the Dedication of a Church. Notice that having begun her *Last Retreat* on the sixteenth of August, the "sixteenth day" is the thirty-first, on which the Dedication of the Churches of Carmel was celebrated. The biblical texts cited in notes 2, 3, 5, 9, and 11 belong to the liturgy of this day.
4. Ps 61:2-3 (trans. Eyragues).
5. Lk 19:5.
6. 1 Jn 1:3.
7. Ep 2:19.
8. Cf. SC 439 (cf. *Collected Works*, St 40:3, p. 564). Cf. L 284, n.6.
9. Ps 83:3. But "falls down in a faint" is the translation she had read in SC 109 (cf. *supra*, 21, n.5).
10. That is, the divine life which is already given us and which awaits its full revelation. It is as much the doctrine of John and Paul as of John of the Cross which seems to be in the background here (in particular the death of love in LF 478-480) cf. *Collected Works*, St 1:30-31. pp. 593-594.
11. Cf. Ps 83:6 (according to her *Manual*) but Elizabeth herself seems to translate "ascensiones" (Latin) by ascensions (her Manual says "roads," Eyragues says "paths"). She does not go up, like the psalmist, to the earthly Jerusalem, but towards the heavenly city: hence her idea of "ascension"!
12. Ps 17:20.
13. "Immense Father, Immense Son, Immense Spirit": from the Athanasian *Creed* which was recited at Prime on the feast of the Trinity and often on Sundays.
14. Her underlining. She means: *into* the "house" of God, "into the bosom" of the Trinity, where she will enter by the act of "dying and flowing into her God," as she has just explained in 43, *supra*.
15. Ru 35.
16. In her explanation Elizabeth places the emphasis on "come down," that is "without leaving the holy fortress," but by entering further into her "interior abyss" (*supra*, 43). That is why for a good understanding of the text we have underlined the words *come down*. She "ascends" and "descends" at the same time: in both cases the movement is vertical.
17. Cf. the "eternal now" of Ru 64 and 67 already cited in HF 17.
18. Cf. Ps 71:15.
19. Heb 1:3. There it refers to Christ. In Heaven Elizabeth will be completely united to Him.

IV

LET YOURSELF BE LOVED
Introduction

L *et Yourself Be Loved* is a very rich text, but one that does
not easily yield up its "secrets," the word which Elizabeth
wrote on the little envelope[1] containing these deeply personal
lines[2] written during the last days of October 1906.[3] Before this
document was found in 1934 on the dead Prioress' table,[4] how
many times had she not examined its promise! It was in her
worn-out *Grace* Book[5] that we discovered the note (containing
the words of the Lord addressed to Bl. Angela di Foligno) that
accompanied and completed the message.[6]

We must read these pages in a triple light. In our General Introduction,[7] we have already placed in its *prophetic context* this
text written at the time when the testament letters were multi-
plying. Elizabeth's posthumous mission: to help others to live
"in communion with Love" (LL 4 and 6), takes on here an accent, more clearly formulated than ever, of abandoment and of
faithful return made to a wholly prevenient Love. We also note
Elizabeth's complete silence about her suffering, so completely
has it disappeared behind the message that Elizabeth wants to
communicate and the deep gratitude that she feels for the Prioress
who has been for her God's instrument.

We must also place these pages in the context of an *almost
sacramental spirituality* which developed greatly during her last
illness.[8] In the task of the Prioress, Elizabeth sees a *mediation*
like "another Christ." She is the "priest" who received the religious vows of the "victim" handing over her whole life to God;
again, it is the Prioress who helped her to offer her sufferings
and her approaching death (in conformity with the One

I Have Found God

crucified by love, and for the Church). After the apostolate that Mother Germaine exercised in Elizabeth's regard as her Mistress of Novices (the sharing of the bread of the Word is another aspect of her quasi-sacerdotal action) Elizabeth now assures her: "In my turn I am going to fulfill a priesthood over your soul. It is Love who associates me with His work in you, this time I will be your little Mother" (LL 3-4).

And finally, we must see them in a *deeply and nobly human context* for we sense behind these lines the loving concern that the Prioress carries in her heart. Desirous of leading her community to a high ideal, it is not without apprehension that she bears the burden of her responsibility. She, the timid and reserved one, must have felt in her heart, perhaps with anguish,[9] the request that the Lord addressed to the first Pastor of the Church: "Simon, son of John, do you love Me more than these?" (Jn 21:15). Elizabeth will reverse the perspective: "Let yourself be loved more than these"; an emphasis repeated six times, which justifies the title we have given these pages.

Germaine greatly loved the person and spirituality of Thérèse of Lisieux of whom, as mistress of novices, she had often spoken to Elizabeth. The disciple takes up the teaching of the mistress: the Thérèsian tone is manifest in this "vocation" of opening to prevenient and condescending Love.

Her very spiritual vision does not prevent Elizabeth from humanly feeling very close to her of whom she said she could not tell her "all she had been for her" (cf. LL 1). She had been the Prioress' first postulant, first novice, first professed,[10] and now the first one to die. When we see in how many ways these two women were close to each other, we can better surmise how much this closeness between them was founded in God. Elizabeth's message, human and mystical, has all the intensity of a last "A Dieu" — as she loved to write — which will be but the beginning of a new "intimacy" (LL 4), lived in God, present on earth as in heaven.

We must not see simply a *teaching* of Elizabeth in this predication of a divine and merciful love, but the expression of an attitude that had long been hers, although she often had to live it in faith: as a young lay woman she complained to Mother Marie of Jesus "of not doing anything (during prayer), so enraptured was she by Him who did everything."[11] "I have only to love Him, to let myself be loved," she wrote in 1903 (L 177). And during her illness in 1906: "There is a phrase from St. Paul that is like a summary of my life, and which could be written on every one of its moments: *Proper nimiam charitatem*. Yes, all these floods of graces are because He has loved me exceedingly" (L 280). This wholly confident *"Let Yourself Be Loved"* is like the pause in a long symphony of love, the first note of the eternal Sanctus.

Should we not also read these pages as an invitation to live "in communion with Love, believing in Love" (LL 4)?

NOTES

1. The little envelope, 11.1 x 7.2 cm., bears on the front the words: "Secrets for our Reverend Mother," and on the back a seal of red wax, a solemn symbol!

2. Two sheets of ruled paper, 26.9 x 10.4 cm. Folded in two they thus presented eight small pages which were folded again to fit in the envelope. The letter is written in ink. There was also a note of which we will speak in note 6. Since we numbered the pages, we began new paragraphs before numbers 3, 4, 5, and 6.

3. This is the date that Mother Germaine wrote on it. According to her Obituary Circular (pp. 6-7), Elizabeth had asked her Prioress "for some paper to write on" (and thus for the permission) before writing this last sign of her gratitude. Mother Germaine read these pages (as foreseen in LL 1) only after Elizabeth's death. According to an oral tradition of the Carmel of Dijon, she sometimes spoke of this letter but never allowed it to be read.

4. Cf. Mother Germaine's Obituary Circular, p. 7.

5. *The Blessing for Meals with Thanksgiving and other Prayers for the Use of Carmelite Religious.* Oudin, Poitiers, 1863, 217 pp. + 45 manuscript pages. Prioress eight times, Mother Germaine made much use of this book.

6. A little note, 10.4 x 6.5 cm., written on both sides in ink. Elizabeth first lightly ruled the paper with pencil and then framed the text in ink. The convergence of several elements makes us conclude that this little note belonged to LL: a) it is cut with scissors so as to fit in the little envelope; b) it is in the same writing and the same ink; c) the feebleness of the handwriting suggests a late period; d) the citations from Bl. Angela di Foligno also suggest the last days; e) the citations tie in very well with the theme of LL (cf. "loved by Him to this extent, in this way, loved by an unchanging and creative love. . .," LL 5); f) the "I" of Jesus implies also the "I" of Elizabeth present in Germaine, another theme of LL; both will be "in the depths of her soul" (LL 4 and 7);

g)the privileged place of the note in Mother Germaine's Grace Book; h) the absence of any other plausible explanation.

7. Cf. *supra*, pp. 28-30.

8. Cf. our work *Elisabeth ou l'Amour est là*.

9. Mother Germaine's Obituary Circular says, in connection with LL: "In fact, it seems that our venerated Sister Elizabeth of the Trinity had received an intimate revelation (enlightened by God) on the state of suffering that her beloved Mother was experiencing, the Lord having permitted this richly endowed soul to feel in her depths only poverty, humility and fear" (p. 7).

10. As a young professed, she remained three more years in the novitiate.

11. Cf. our introduction to the *Diary*, Volume III.

LET YOURSELF BE LOVED
Text

J.M. + J.T.

1. My Cherished Mother, my Holy Priest,[1] when you read these lines, your little Praise of Glory will no longer be singing on earth, but will be living in Love's immense furnace;[2] so you can believe her and listen to her as "the voice" of God. Cherished Mother, I would have liked to tell you all that you have been for me, but the hour is so serious, so solemn . . . and I don't want to delay over telling you things that I think lose something when trying to express them in words. What your child is coming to do is to reveal to you what she feels, or, to be more exact; what her God, in the hours of profound recollection, of unifying contact, makes her understand.

2. *"You are uncommonly loved,"*[3] loved by that love of preference that the Master had here below for some and which brought them so far. He does not say to you as to Peter: "Do you love Me more than these?"[4] Mother, listen to what He tells you: *"Let*[5] yourself be loved more than these! That is, without fearing that any obstacle will be a hindrance to it, for I am free to pour out My love on whom I wish! '*Let* yourself be loved more than these' is your vocation.[6] It is in being faithful to it that you will make Me happy for you will magnify the power of My love. This love can rebuild what you have destroyed. *Let* yourself be loved more than these."

3. Dearly loved Mother, if you knew with what assurance I understand God's plan for your soul; it appears to me as in an immense light, and I understand also that in Heaven I will fulfill in my turn a priesthood over your soul. It is Love who associates me with His work in you: Oh, Mother, how great and adorable it is on God's part! And how simple it is for you, and that is exactly what makes it so luminous! Mother, *let* yourself be loved more than the others; that explains everything and prevents the soul from being surprised. . . .

179

4. If you will allow her, your little host[7] will spend her Heaven in the depths[8] of your soul: she will keep you in communion[9] with Love, believing in Love; it will be the sign of her dwelling in you. Oh, in what intimacy we are going to live. Cherished Mother, let your life also be spent in the Heavens where I will sing in your name the eternal Sanctus:[10] I will do nothing before the throne of God without you; you know well that I bear your imprint and that something of yourself appeared with your child before the Face of God. I also ask you not to do anything without me; you have granted me this. I will come to live in you. This time I will be your little Mother. I will instruct you,[11] so that my vision will benefit you, that you may participate in it, and that you too, may live the life of the blessed!

5. Revered Mother, Mother consecrated for me from eternity,[12] as I leave, I bequeath to you this vocation which was mine in the heart of the Church Militant and which from now on I will unceasingly fulfill in the Church Triumphant: "*The Praise of Glory of the Holy Trinity.*"[13] Mother, "*let* yourself be loved more than these": it is in that way that your Master wills for you to be a praise of glory! He rejoices to build up[14] in you by His love and for His glory, and it is He alone who wants to work[15] in you, even though you will have done nothing to attract this grace except that which a creature can do: works of sin and misery . . . He loves you like that. He loves you "more than these." He will do everything in you. He will go to the end: for when a soul is loved by Him to this extent, in this way, loved by an unchanging and creative love, a free love which transforms as it pleases Him, oh, how far this soul will go!

6. Mother, the fidelity that the Master asks of you is to remain in communion with Love, flow into, be rooted[16] in this Love who wants to mark your soul with the seal of His power and His grandeur. You will never be commonplace if you are vigilant in love! But in the hours when you feel only oppression and lassitude, you will please Him even more if you faithfully *believe* that He is still working, that He is loving you just the same, and *even more*: because His love is *free* and that is how He wants to be *magnified* in you; and you will *let* yourself be loved "*more than these.*" That, I believe, is what this means. . . . Live in the

depths of your soul![17] My Master makes me understand very clearly that He wants to create marvellous things there: you are called to render homage to the simplicity[18] of the Divine Being and to magnify the power of His Love. Believe His "voice" and read these lines as if coming from Him.

[*Elizabeth now illustrates her convictions with a long quotation from Blessed Angela di Foligno. All these words are addressed by Jesus or the Holy Spirit to Blessed Angela.*[19]]

7. Oh! I love you, I love you more than anyone else in this valley! [of Spoleto].... It is "I"[20] who come, and I bring you unknown joy.... I will enter into the depths of your being.

O my spouse! I have rested and reposed in you; now possess[21] yourself and repose in Me!...

Love Me! All your life will please Me, provided that you love Me!... I will do great things in you; I will be made known in you, glorified, and praised in you!...

NOTES

1. On this appelation "priest," cf. L 320, n.3.
2. For "Love's furnace" and the background of Thérèse of Lisieux: cf. L 190, n.3.
3. Elizabeth enlarges these words that we put in italics. This expression comes perhaps from P. Vallée. In the Retreat that he preached for the community in 1902, we find the formula: "so uncommonly rich in love" (second morning conference), and "there is in God an uncommon tenderness" (fourth morning conference). Could he have used the expression again in the two sermons that he preached in Carmel's chapel on the 13th and 14th of October 1906, and in the conversation that he had then with Elizabeth? On the 10th of January, 1907, P. Vallée wrote to Mme. Catez that Elizabeth's last weeks were "so uncommonly, so divinely beautiful."
4. Jn 21:15.
5. Elizabeth emphasizes the word "let" three times in a row by enlarging it a little; the fourth time (at the end of 3) she even writes it with a capital after a *comma*. We put the word then, in *italics*, including the fifth and sixth time it occurs. Until the end of this paragraph 2 it is the Lord who is speaking ("Me," and "My").
6. Perhaps a reminiscence of the "vocation" of love according to Thérèse of Lisieux (HA p. 208)? Cf. *Story of a Soul*, p. 194. Cf. L 250, n.17.

7. "Host" that the Prioress-priest offered to God when she received her vows in 1903, and will offer in a few days when Elizabeth gives up her life: cf. L 320, n.3. [The French word *hostie* means both *victim* as well as *host*. Elizabeth intends both meanings here.Tr.]

8. Elizabeth will be there in Jesus in the sense of his promise to Angela di Foligno (Ang 59) which Elizabeth will quote *infra*, 7.

9. "Communion": a frequent allusion to 1 Jn 1:3 as in LL 6.

10. "Eternal Sanctus": cf. L 250, n.18.

11. As Mother Germaine, Elizabeth's mistress of novices and Prioress, had instructed her . . . "This time," it will be she who instructs her.

12. "From eternity": the background of the divine "election" "before creation" (Ep 1:4), the divine "predestination" "according to the counsel of his will" (Ep 1:11).

13. Cf. Ep 1:12. Elizabeth enlarges her writing. Here in italics.

14. Cf. Col 2:7.

15. Biblical expression taken from Ep 1:11 (cf. L 224), as in LL 6.

16. Cf. Ep 3:17.

17. Elizabeth will also be "in the depths of your soul" (cf. LL 4), with the Master.

18. "Simplicity" was a characteristic of Mother Germaine.

19. Cf. Ang 59-61. In the French the participles remain in the masculine: it is *Jesus* who is speaking. Elsewhere (cf. for ex. LR), Elizabeth uses the feminine when she applies these words to herself.

20. The word is in italics in Ang 59. Elizabeth enlarges it and puts it in quotation marks.

21. Ang 59 says here: "pose" (rest). Elizabeth writes "possède" (possess). We retain her nuance. Could it be an error in transcription as Mother Germaine supposed when later she wrote over it "pose"?

O MY GOD, TRINITY WHOM I ADORE[1]

November 21, 1904[2]

J.M. + J.T.

O my God, Trinity[3] whom I adore, help me to forget[4] myself entirely that I may be established in You as still[5] and as peaceful as if my soul were already in eternity. May nothing trouble my peace or make me leave You, O my Unchanging[6] One, but may each minute[7] carry me further into the depths of Your Mystery. Give peace to my soul;[8] make it Your heaven,[9] Your beloved dwelling[10] and Your resting place.[11] May I never leave You there alone but be wholly present, my faith wholly vigilant,[12] wholly adoring,[13] and wholly surrendered to Your creative Action.[14]

O my beloved Christ, crucified by love, I wish to be a bride[15] for Your Heart; I wish to cover You with glory;[15a] I wish to love You . . . even unto death![16] But I feel my weakness, and I ask[17] You to "clothe me with Yourself,"[18] to identify my soul with all the movements of Your Soul, to overwhelm me, to possess me,[18a] to substitute Yourself for me that my life may be but a radiance of Your Life. Come into me as Adorer, as Restorer, as Savior. O Eternal Word, Word of my God,[19] I want to spend my life in listening[19a] to You, to become wholly teachable[20] that I may learn all from You. Then, through all nights, all voids, all helplessness,[21] I want to gaze[22] on You always and remain in Your great light. O my beloved Star,[23] so fascinate me[24] that I may not withdraw from Your radiance.

O consuming Fire,[25] Spirit of Love, "come upon me,"[26] and create in my soul a kind of incarnation[27] of the Word: that I may be another humanity[28] for Him in which He can renew His whole Mystery. And You, O Father, bend lovingly over Your poor little[29] creature; "cover her with Your shadow,"[30] seeing in her only the "Beloved in whom You are well pleased."[31]

183

O my[32] Three, my All, my Beatitude, infinite Solitude,[33] Immensity in which I lose[34] myself, I surrender myself to You as Your prey.[35] Bury Yourself in me that I may bury[36] myself in You until I depart to contemplate in Your light the abyss of Your greatness.[37]

November 21, 1904

Annotations

1. This prayer is written in ink on a very thin sheet of paper, lightly ruled, 14.1 x 9.3 cm. The sheet has been detached from Elizabeth's "personal notebook" (cf. PN 13, n.1); the facing page is still there; the torn edges fit together and the two sheets show the same brown stains caused by a dried flower that Elizabeth kept in this place. Between the first two sheets a similar little flower is still to be found with the same stains. The autograph, dated but without a title, has nineteen lines of text on the front page (besides J.M. + J.T. at the top) and thirty-four lines on the back (not counting the date). From the very beginning of this sheet, Elizabeth had compressed her handwriting by writing two lines for every line of paper; thus she was aware that otherwise her prayer would have gone beyond the limits of the sheet. This also proves that she tore out the sheet *before* writing on it since the notebook still contains seven blank pages. Doubtless she detached the sheet in order to carry this prayer around in a book (for ex. her *Manual* or the *Spiritual Canticle* by St. John of the Cross) so that she could read it again more easily. The page is not folded. Did she make a rough copy? At first sight the compressed writing on the front would suggest that she had a clear idea of what was to follow; nevertheless several autographs of the letters show the same compactness on the back page, even from the first line (for ex. L 238, 241). It would seem more likely that there was no rough copy and that the prayer sprang from the fullness of her heart. The handwriting is peaceful and even; there is only one correction (cf. n.36). The edition of 1911 of the *Souvenirs* mentions for the first time, in a note, that "this prayer of Elizabeth of the Trinity was found without a title in her notes"

(p. 305). It already appeared in the first edition of 1909 (pp. 299-300), but the Obituary Circular dated December 18, 1906, did not yet mention it. In the annotation of this very rich prayer, our intention is only to explain the provenance, or preparation in her writings, of certain formulas and images.

2. Feast of Mary's Presentation in the Temple. On that day, after Mass, the Carmelites renewed their religious vows in the oratory. Elizabeth wrote her prayer in the course of the day or during the hour of great silence; there was no work on that day. It is very important to note that on that same morning the retreat preached by P. Fages, a Dominican, ended. Begun the evening of November 12th, it lasted for eight full days. The complete text is kept in ACD. In PAT one will find Elizabeth's personal notes with the corresponding passages, as well as the general scheme of the retreat. It was centered on "the Mystery of the Incarnation" or, as the preacher indicated, on "that beautiful, lovable figure, adorable above all, who is called Our Lord Jesus Christ" (p. 9). In our opinion, this retreat was more on the level of the audience than that of P. Vallée in 1902.

3. This prayer of Elizabeth, however personal it may be in its conception, is not without relation to two other prayers that she loved. First of all Thérèse of Lisieux's *Act of Oblation* which Elizabeth, with her good memory, must have known practically by heart. It begins with the same words: "O my God, (blessed Trinity)," and reveals a fundamental affinity of structure (cf. AL). Then, the prayer of St. Catherine of Siena, *O eternal Trinity* (*Dialogue*, chap 167, trans. Cartier, Paris, 1855, p. 224) which Elizabeth had copied (cf. L 115) and which she kept in her books. The conclusion of PN 15 alludes to the prayer of Catherine again (cf. n.37).

4. Elizabeth wrote: "oubliez."

5. "Still" (immobile): this word does not describe a physical attitude, much less a psychic inertia. It sums up, it seems, *an ideal* and *an attitude* of inner peace described in the *Spiritual Canticle* and the *Living Flame* of John of the Cross, a book "so desired" and so "precious" (L 106), which is the whole nourishment of my soul" (L 241). The word "still" reflects first of all *the ideal* of the transformation in God, of the spiritual marriage described in

SC, St 20-21, and 40. "The Son of God," the mystical Doctor explains (SC 217 ff), "established [this is the expression Elizabeth uses here but it was also dear to P. Vallée] the bride in perfect possession [cf. in Elizabeth the idea of the soul already in eternity] of peace" [Elizabeth wishes to be "peaceful"]. He then reviews all the spiritual faculties and the appetites with their passions showing how God "quiets" (SC 218) the restlessness and irritability that used to afflict it" (SC 219), "the fatigue and anguish occasioned by inordinate affections and activities," in short "their inordinate movements" (SC 234). It is to these "movements" (a word repeated six times in these pages 218-234) and it is in this sense that the ideal of Elizabeth is opposed when she wants to become "still" without inordinate movements: "May nothing trouble my peace," she says immediately after in her Prayer. It is not excluded that, by nature impulsive and choleric (cf. D 1 and 34; PN 12), she had remembered well what John of the Cross said about "anger" in particular: "An impulsive movement that troubles peace" (SC 234). Nevertheless, she is echoing here more probably Thérèse of Lisieux's "profession note" which she had copied before her entrance: "Let none of the things of earth trouble my peace" (HA p. 129). The word "still" also evokes and sums up for Elizabeth an *attitude* of spirit, notably the contemplative attitude of peaceful silence and loving attention during the graces of infused prayer which John of the Cross abundantly describes in LF III, 557-605. "Its attitude is to remain, so to speak, passive, without making any *movement* [italics ours], without applying itself to anything else than this loving, simple attention, fixed on its object alone, somewhat like one who opens his eyes to gaze lovingly. God then wants to commune with the soul by a simple and loving knowledge; the soul also, must receive it simply and lovingly . . . in complete detachment from all things, in absolute rest, in perfect calm, *like God Himself*" (LF 564-565; cf. in Elizabeth the idea of the soul already in eternity).

One must not be like children who "fidget with their feet" says John of the Cross (and Elizabeth will refer to this example in L 231) or like "a painting which might happen to move while the artist is painting it" (LF 604). Still: without "making me leave you," Elizabeth prays again. This is what she heard from P. Fages and noted down two days before: "The soul cannot leave Christ . . . ." (cf. PAT)

6. "Unchanging," a word with a Valléen background, but it must be interpreted in Elizabeth's sense: "He who always remains while all passes and all changes around us!" (L 107) "Unchanging Beauty" (L 121 and 212; P 84 and 85), "Unchanging Love" (L 210).

7. Cf. P 90 of the preceding month: "So that infinite Love / At each passing moment / May carry it [the soul] away and consume it in Him." Also the previous evening P. Fages said of the Blessed Virgin that, "at each moment she increased, she accumulated grace . . . ."

8. "Give peace" at a truly profound level, as the context demands. Perhaps a reminiscence of what Elizabeth had read in St 24 (p. 265) of the *Spiritual Canticle*, or the double repetition of the "dwelling at peace" in the poem the *Ascent of Mount Carmel* (St 1 and 2)? Cf. L 165: "Let us make for Him in our soul a dwelling wholly at peace."

9. The idea of "the heaven of the soul" abounds in her *Letters from Carmel* from the beginning. Notice in particular L 210 of August 21, 1904, in which is found the formula "the heaven of our soul." A few days earlier Elizabeth had noted down these words spoken by P. Fages: "the faculties of the soul must be as calm and peaceful as . . . a tranquil lake in which the whole sky is reflected." Notice in this phrase the word "peaceful" which she had already used in this prayer.

10. Cf. L 165, cited n.8. Nine days before she had written: "We will ask Him . . . to establish His dwelling in our souls" (L 213). Perhaps also a reminiscence of Jn 15.4: "*Dwell* in me, and *I in you*."

11. Allusion to Bethany (Lk 10). Cf. PN 5 and L 145, in which "Bethany" and "rest" are associated.

12. L 150 speaks of "wholly vigilant"; L 165 of "wholly vigilant in faith." The image is also, in part, indebted to P. Vallée, who spoke of the "wholly vigilant" soul (Retreat of 1900, second Conference) or "very vigilant in faith" (Retreat of 1902, second Conference in the evening) or "completely vigilant" (*ibid.*, fourth Conference in the morning).

13. "Adoring": we often find the expression in her previous writings (L 150, 204; P88). And "wholly adoring" in L 131, 135, 158, 185; P. 86, 90.

14. P. Fages often spoke in his retreat of "the action" and the "creation" of the Holy Spirit. But Elizabeth most probably learned this expression "creative action" from P. Vallée, who used it in his "Homily for the Veiling of Marie of the Trinity," in his Retreat of 1900 (twice) and in his Retreat of 1902 (four times).

15. Cf. PN 13.

15a. "to cover with glory": a probable reminiscence of Heb 2:7 and 9, where the "humiliated Christ (cf. "crucified" in Elizabeth's prayer) is then "crowned with glory," an expression in its turn taken from Ps 8:6. (She had also read in SC 113 the expression "clothe with glory" and in SC 153-154 "to fill with glory".) It was in January of this year that she formulated her desire to be a "praise of glory" of the Lord (L 191).

16. Note the fusion of two representatives of this total gift, Teresa of Avila and Thérèse of Lisieux, in L 169 (n.4) where Elizabeth writes "I wish to love you so . . . even unto death."

Her *Poems*, both those she wrote as a young girl as well as those she wrote as a Carmelite, often express this desire of loving unreservedly.

17. In her *Act of Oblation*, filled with the same desire of total love, Thérèse of Lisieux had used the same words: "But I feel my weakness, and I ask You . . ." (HA p. 249). We find the same manifestation of weakness and the same appeal to the substituting holiness of God, formulated in Thérèse's terms, in PN 4, 5, and L 149, 184, and 212.

18. Cf. Ga 3:27 ("to be clothed with Jesus Christ"). In her *Act of Oblation*, Thérèse of Lisieux had asked God "to be Yourself my holiness," but she also wanted to "be clothed with Your own Justice" (HA pp. 249-251).

18a. The two words "overwhelm" and "possess" (associated in the second morning Conference of the Retreat of 1902 of P. Vallée) are already found together in Elizabeth's writings: cf. L 185 and 192. As for the formula "identify my soul with all the movements of Your soul," it was already presented in full in L 156 and 175, and in part in L 121, 133, 138, and P 85. Cf. also the desire to be "transformed" in God, in L 164, 179 and 185.

19. We found in Elizabeth's Breviary a picture of Thérèse of Lisieux at the harp (Celine's design in 1901). All around it, in the hand of Sister Genevieve of Dijon, we read the second stanza — very Trinitarian — of *To Live by Love* (HA p. 330) which includes the expression "Word of my God". The invocation "Eternal Word" is obviously well known; let us note however that Elizabeth had copied it (cf. PAT) from Thérèse (*Only Jesus*): "My Only Love, Jesus, Word Eternal" (HA p. 362).

19a. At the top of her personal notes of P. Fages's retreat, Elizabeth had written this phrase that we do not find in the preacher's text: "I want to spend my life gazing on my living God" (cf. PAT). Was this her retreat resolution? Cf. also L 149: "A whole life to be spent in silence and adoration, a heart-to-heart with the Spouse!" and P 88 of Christmas 1903: "May I spend my life, O Word, in listening to you...."

20. "Teachable": an expression that P. Vallée used once in his Retreat of 1897, three times in that of 1900, and twice in that of 1902. In translating "Docibiles Dei," he makes reference to the Vulgate: Jn 6:45.

21. We recognize in "nights," "voids," "helplessness," accents of John of the Cross, but also (following him) of Thérèse of Lisieux in her description of the "poor little bird" who, "helpless" and in the "night" looks in the direction of the hidden sun (HA pp. 212-214; Ms B 4v°-5r°); cf. the following notes.

22. Cf. L 190, n.3. Thérèse says: "*I want* to remain there, *gazing* until death on my Divine Sun . . . the *Star* of Love." The sentence is preceded by the affirmation: "I dare to *gaze* on the Divine Sun of Love." She reaffirms: "As long as You [my Beloved *Star*] wish, I will remain with my eyes fixed on You: I want to be *fascinated* [Thérèse is the one who underlines] by Your divine gaze; I want to become the *prey* of Your Love" (HA pp. 212-214). We have italicized the words that recur in Elizabeth's Prayer. At the beginning of the year, Elizabeth had already written: ". . . if my gaze remains always fixed on Him, my luminous Star, oh, then all else disappears . . ." (L 190).

23. Cf. preceding note.

24. Cf. n.22.

25. Heb 12:29, citing Dt 4:24.

26. The quotaton marks indicate a borrowing. It concerns Lk 1:35: "The Holy Spirit will come upon you" (trans. in her *Manual*). Elizabeth was very fond of this passage. It is the central theme of P 79, and she had evoked it a month before in P 90. Notice however that the retreat which had just ended strongly emphasized the awareness of the work of the Spirit in souls. P. Fages had recalled the scene of the Annunciation ("the magnificent scene," p. 157) no less than *ten* times, in a rather elaborated manner. Three days before, in the eleventh Conference on "the operations of grace," he had concluded: "If you are awaiting the movement of life, formulate your request: 'Spirit of God, come upon me as you came upon the chaos of the world, as you came upon the Virgin Mary to create in her Our Lord.' Do you want the Word to live in you; do you want the Incarnation to bear its fruit in you? There is only one way. The Holy Spirit caused the Son of God to be conceived and grow in the womb of the Virgin. Well, it is He again who will cause Him to live and grow in you" (pp. 160-161). We will return to this in greater detail in AL.

27. Cf. the preceding note. In her Christmas poems, Elizabeth loved to evoke "the new incarnation" in us: P 75, 86, and soon P 91. Cf. also L 187: ". . . a birth no longer in the crib, but in my soul, in our souls. . . ."

28. The expression, which could have reached Elizabeth by various ways, is found in Mgr. Charles Gay, *De la Vie et des vertus chrétiennes considérées dans l'état religieux* (vol. I Poitiers-Paris, Oudin, 1874, p. 103): "You are another humanity for Jesus Christ. . . ." The text is applied directly to religious, but earlier he had already designated every Christian "a secondary humanity that Jesus deigns to join to His own" (p. 42).

29. The conjunction "poor little" is typical of Thérèse of Lisieux. Elizabeth uses it for the first time in her *Letters from Carmel* in L 190 (in which we note the Thérèsian passage of the gaze always fixed on the Star). This passage, already studied in notes 21 and 22, speaks of the "poor little bird" and, in a larger context, we find: "poor creature" (HA p. 202), "helpless and imperfect creature" (HA p. 209), "the littlest of creatures" (HA pp. 209-210), "weak creature" (HA p. 213). . . .

30. The context (see following note) reveals that Elizabeth is referring to the "overshadowing" of Mt 17:5 (scene of the Transfiguration of Jesus) rather than to Lk 1:35 (the Annunciation). In both cases the *Manual* translates it "to cover with his shadow."

31. Cf. Mt 17:5 where the *disciples* on Mount Tabor are "overshadowed with a cloud." Elizabeth must be thinking less explicitly of the scene of the baptism of Jesus in Mt 3:17: the presence of "the overshadowing" and the word "*all*" (my delight) are missing from it.

32. In her preceding letters and poems she often spoke of *these* or *the* "Three." Here we find "my" Three. Circ 4 affirms: ". . . 'her Three' was her expression."

33. "Solitude" in the sense of the transcendance of the Immanent: the Letters sing of the intimacy that He establishes with us. Note the juxtaposition of "Beatitude" and "Solitude." From the door of her cell, three meters away, Elizabeth could read the motto of Saint Bruno written on the wall: *O beata solitudo, O sola beatitudo!*

34. On the Thérèsian accent of "lose," cf. L 110, n.3. "The Immensity": "An immensity of love that inundates us on all sides", she wrote seven months before (cf. L 199 and n.13); and three months before: "It is like an abyss of love in which I lose myself" (L 208 and n.4).

35. Cf. n.22. Also L 125, n.3 and L 41, n.7.

36. A term equivalent to "hidden"; allusion to Col 3:3 (cf. L 158 n.5. Elizabeth first wrote: "Bury me . . ." then corrected it to "Bury Yourself in me." She wrote: "ensevelisez-vous."

37. Taken from the Prayer of St. Catherine of Siena (cf. n.2): ". . . because I have seen in Your light the abyss of Your greatness . . ." (the version copied by Elizabeth, cf. L 115).

OTHER BOOKS ABOUT
ELIZABETH OF THE TRINITY
FROM ICS PUBLICATIONS

Complete Works of Elizabeth of the Trinity, volume 2:
Letters from Carmel (1901–1906)

Translated by Anne Englund Nash

Paperback   394 pages   photos
ISBN: 978-1-939272-20-1

Light-Love-Life: Elizabeth of the Trinity

Conrad De Meester, O.C.D.,
translated by Aletheia Kane, O.C.D.,
edited by John Sullivan, O.C.D.

Oversize paperback   144 pages   photos
ISBN: 978-0-935216-07-3

He Is My Heaven: The Life of Elizabeth of the Trinity

Jennifer Moorcroft

Paperback   208 pages   photos
ISBN: 978-0-935216-25-7

For more information and to purchase these and other books,
visit our website at:
www.icspublications.org

About Us

ICS Publications, based in Washington, D.C., is the publishing house of the Institute of Carmelite Studies (ICS) and a ministry of the Discalced Carmelite Friars of the Washington Province (U.S.A.). The Institute of Carmelite Studies promotes research and publication in the field of Carmelite spirituality, especially about Carmelite saints and related topics. Its members are friars of the Washington Province.

Discalced Carmelites are a worldwide Roman Catholic religious order comprised of friars, nuns, and laity—men and women who are heirs to the teaching and way of life of Teresa of Avila and John of the Cross, dedicated to contemplation and to ministry in the church and the world.

Information about their way of life is available through local diocesan vocation offices, or from the Discalced Carmelite Friars vocation directors at the following addresses:

Washington Province:
1525 Carmel Road, Hubertus, WI 53033

California-Arizona Province:
P.O. Box 3420, San Jose, CA 95156

Oklahoma Province:
5151 Marylake Drive, Little Rock, AR 72206

Visit our websites at:

www.icspublications.org and *http://ocdfriarsvocation.org*

CITIES OF THE BIBLICAL WORLD

MEGIDD(

Graham I. Davies

Lecturer in Divinity
University of Cambridge

L

LUTTERWORTH PRESS
CAMBRIDGE

WILLIAM B. EERDMANS PUBLISHING COMPANY
GRAND RAPIDS, MICHIGAN

CITIES OF THE BIBLICAL WORLD

General Editor: Graham I. Davies,
Lecturer in Divinity, University of Cambridge

Other Titles:

Excavation in Palestine, Roger Moorey, Senior Assistant Keeper,
   Department of Antiquities, Ashmolean Museum, Oxford
Qumran, Philip R. Davies, Lecturer in Biblical Studies,
   University of Sheffield
Jericho, John R. Bartlett, Lecturer in Divinity and Fellow of
   Trinity College, Dublin
Ugarit (Ras Shamra), Adrian H. W. Curtis, Lecturer in Old
   Testament Studies, University of Manchester

British Library Cataloguing in Publication Data

Davies, G. I.
   Megiddo.
   1. Megiddo (Ancient city) 2. Israel—
   Antiquities 3. Excavations (Archaeology—
   Israel—Megiddo, Ancient city
   I. Title
   933   DS110.M4

   ISBN 0–7188–2586–1

First published in 1986 by
Lutterworth Press
7 All Saints' Passage
Cambridge CB2 3LS
Copyright © Graham I. Davies 1986

First American edition published 1986 through special arrangement with Lutterworth by Wm. B. Eerdmans
Publishing Co., 255 Jefferson S.E., Grand Rapids, MI 49503

ISBN 0–8028–0247–8

Photoset and printed in Great Britain by
Redwood Burn Limited, Trowbridge, Wiltshire

Contents

Preface   iv

Abbreviations and Notes to the Reader   vi

Chronological Table   viii

List of Illustrations   x

1. The Identification of Megiddo and its Geographical Setting   1

2. The Excavations at Tell el-Mutesellim (Megiddo)   12

3. The Earliest Settlements at Megiddo   25

4. Canaanite Megiddo   37

5. Israelite Megiddo   76

6. Megiddo under the Persians and Afterwards   107

Appendix: A Visit to the Site   113

Indexes   115

Preface

My interest in Megiddo could be said to have begun with some undergraduate essays which I wrote in 1969 under the guidance of Dame Kathleen Kenyon, when she was Principal of St Hugh's College, Oxford. It was a great privilege to be taught by her, and since then I have been fortunate in having my archaeological education extended through the help of a number of friends, especially David Ussishkin and Gabriel Barkay during the excavations at Lachish sponsored by Tel Aviv University. Nevertheless I remain essentially an observer of the archaeological scene and, while this book does contain one or two new suggestions, I have regarded it as my principal aim to draw together the conclusions already reached by others who are better qualified than I am to unravel the complicated history of this fascinating site. Of course the specialists do not always agree, and in a book of this size it is not possible to present every alternative theory to the reader in the detail which it deserves. Perhaps this small book, which is designed with non-specialists in mind, will also encourage a professional archaeologist to undertake the rewarding task of writing a comprehensive account of the site, which I suspect will occupy several large volumes. If so, I hope that my occasional references to the reports on the German excavations at the beginning of this century will serve as a reminder of their great interest and value.

In connection with the writing of this book I wish to express particular thanks to the following for their help: to Lutterworth Press, for their understanding, and patience with the consequent delay, when in the summer of 1982 I decided to change the subject of my contribution to the 'Cities of the Biblical World' series, and for their care and attention during the production of the book (here David Game deserves special mention); to the staff of the West Room of the University Library in Cambridge, for their cheerful assistance at all times; to the Managers of the Bethune-Baker and Hort Memorial Funds of Cambridge University, for grants which made it possible for me to consult the Megiddo archives in Chicago, and to Dr John Larsen, the Museum Archivist at the Oriental Institute, for his willing assistance with my enquiries; to Mr Robert Hamilton, formerly Director of Antiquities in Palestine, for sharing

iv

with me his recollections of the American excavations; to the Warden and Fellows of Merton College, Oxford, for electing me into a Visiting Research Fellowship for the Hilary Term, 1985, which enabled me to complete this book in the incomparable surroundings of that College; to Dr Roger Moorey of the Ashmolean Museum and Professor John Emerton of the University of Cambridge, for finding time to read the original manuscript and for many helpful suggestions; to Andrew Brown, whose skilful and intelligent draughtsmanship has produced such excellent drawings to accompany the text; and to Judith Hadley, for her meticulous checking of the proofs.

I am also grateful to Richard Cleave, of Pictorial Archive Inc., of Jerusalem, and Ted Todd, now in Rome, for permission to use photographs from their collections; to the British Academy for permission to reproduce figure 16 from Y. Yadin, *Hazor*, Schweich Lectures for 1971, figure 39; to the Deutscher Palästina-Verein and its President, Professor H. Donner, for permission to reproduce figures 9, 19 and 22 from the published reports on Schumacher's excavations; to A. and C. Black Ltd, for permission to cite a passage from *The Letters of Gertrude Bell*, originally published by Ernest Benn Limited in 1927; to Princeton University Press, for permission to quote extracts from *Ancient Near Eastern Texts Relating to the Old Testament*, ed. J. B. Pritchard, 3rd edition (1969); to the Ordnance Survey, for permission to base figure 12 on one of their maps; and to the Oriental Institute of the University of Chicago, for permission to reproduce numerous photographs and drawings from their publications, to cite extracts from the excavation diary of G. Loud, and to consult and make reference to other unpublished material in their archives.

Cambridge, February 1986   G.I. DAVIES

Abbreviations

AJSL	*American Journal of Semitic Languages and Literatures*, Chicago.
ANET	*Ancient Near Eastern Texts Relating to the Old Testament*, ed. J. B. Pritchard, 3rd. ed. (Princeton, 1969).
BA	*The Biblical Archaeologist*, Philadelphia.
BASOR	*Bulletin of the American Schools of Oriental Research*, Philadelphia.
IEJ	*Israel Exploration Journal*, Jerusalem.
OIP	*Oriental Institute Publications*, Chicago.
PEQ	*Palestine Exploration Quarterly*, London.
SAOC	*Studies in Ancient Oriental Civilisation*, Chicago.
ZDPV	*Zeitschrift der deutschen Palästina-Vereins*, Wiesbaden.

EB I etc. Early Bronze Age I etc. ⎫
MB I etc. Middle Bronze Age I etc. ⎬ (see Chronological Table)
LB I etc. Late Bronze Age I etc. ⎭

Notes to the Reader

1. The strata or archaeological layers referred to in this book are those defined by the American excavations (1925–39). The numbering begins with the top (i.e. latest) layer (I) and ends with the lowest (i.e. earliest) layer (XX). The symbol '−XX' refers to remains on and in the bedrock below the lowest complete layer. For fuller details (e.g. of dates) see the Chronological Table on p. viii–ix.

2. The suggestions for further reading at the end of each chapter are primarily

intended for students and others who need to consult the technical literature relating to the site. Those with a more general interest in archaeology could usefully consult:

Y. Aharoni, *The Land of the Bible*, 2nd ed. (Burns and Oates, London, 1979)

K. M. Kenyon, *Royal Cities of the Old Testament* (Barrie and Jenkins, London, 1971)

K. M. Kenyon, *Archaeology in the Holy Land*, 4th ed. (Ernest Benn, London, 1979)

Roger Moorey, *Excavation in Palestine* (Lutterworth Press, Cambridge, 1981)

Chronological Table

Archaeological Periods in Palestine	Megiddo Strata		Wider History
BC			BC
8500–4000 Neolithic			
	Stratum XX (early phase)		
4000–3100 Chalcolithic			
(3500–3100 Proto-urban)	Strata XX (later phase)–XIX		
3100–2700 Early Bronze Age I–II	Stratum XVIII		3200–2200 Egyptian Archaic Period and Old Kingdom
2700–2300 Early Bronze Age III	Strata XVII–XVI		
2300–2000 Early Bronze Age IV (or Middle Bronze I or Intermediate Early Bronze–Middle Bronze Period)	Strata XV–XIV		2200–2040 First Intermediate Period in Egypt
2000–1750 Middle Bronze Age I (or Middle Bronze IIA)	Stratum XIII		2040–1786 Egyptian Middle Kingdom
1750–1550 Middle Bronze Age II (or Middle Bronze IIB–C)	Strata XII–X		1786–1550 Second Intermediate Period in Egypt ('Hyksos')
	Stratum IX (AA)		
1550–1400 Late Bronze Age I		Strata IX–VIIB (BB)	1550–1070 Egyptian New Kingdom
			c. 1468 Invasion of Tuthmosis III
1400–1300 Late Bronze Age IIA	Stratum VIII (AA and DD)		
	Stratum VIIB (AA and DD)	Stratum VIIA (BB)	1364–1347 Reign of Amenophis IV/Akhenaten (Amarna period)
1300–1200 Late Bronze Age IIB	Stratum VIIA (AA and DD)		Arrival of Israelites and Philistines in Canaan

Archaeological Periods in Palestine	Megiddo Strata	Wider History
BC		BC
1200–900 Iron Age I (or 1200–1000)	Strata VIB–VIA	
	Stratum VB Stratum VA/IVB	1010–970 Reign of David 970–930 Reign of Solomon c.925 Invasion of Sheshonq I
900–600 Iron Age II	Stratum IVA Strata III–II	734–3 Invasions of Tiglath-Pileser III of Assyria Assyrian rule in Northern Palestine 640–609 Reign of Josiah
605–539 Babylonian Period 539–332 Persian Period 332–31 Hellenistic Period	Stratum I	332 Alexander the Great in Palestine
31–AD324 Roman Empire	New settlement at Lejjun (Caparcotnae/Legio/ Maximianopolis)	AD66–70 First Jewish Revolt AD132–5 Second Jewish Revolt

Note
The dates for the archaeological periods to the end of Iron Age II are round figures and necessarily approximate. The Megiddo strata are those defined by the American expedition (1925–39): as will be clear from the text of this book, they sometimes include finds of more than one period and the dates attributed to them here are only for general guidance. In some cases they reflect viewpoints adopted in this book with which some scholars would disagree. The dates in the third column are based (where there is disagreement) on the chronological systems referred to at the end of the appropriate chapters of this book.

List of Illustrations

Figure 1   Map of Palestine showing places referred to in the text (Andrew Brown)

Figure 2   Map of Megiddo and its surroundings (Andrew Brown)

Figure 3   Plan of American excavation areas (Andrew Brown; based on G. Loud, *Megiddo II*, figure 377, and P. L. O. Guy and R. M. Engberg, *Megiddo Tombs*, figure 2)

Figure 4   Drawings of (a) harpist and (b) horned animal incised on stones from the courtyard of the Chalcolithic shrine (Stratum XIX) (*Megiddo II*, plates 273.5 and 276.12)

Figure 5   The Early Bronze IV temples and the 'staircase-building' (3160) to the east (Andrew Brown; based on *Megiddo II*, figures 393–5)

Figure 6   Plan of a four-chambered shaft tomb (T.878) (Andrew Brown; based on *Megiddo Tombs*, figure 42)

Figure 7   Pottery from two shaft tombs (Andrew Brown; based on *Megiddo Tombs*, plates 20 and 22)

Figure 8   City wall and gate in Area AA (Stratum XIII), probably built *c*. 1850 BC (Andrew Brown; based on *Megiddo II*, figure 378)

Figure 9   Plan and section of 'Burial Chamber I' (G. Schumacher, *Tell el-Mutesellim I*, Tafel V)

Figure 10 The eastern quarter of Megiddo (Stratum X) towards the end of the Middle Bronze Age (Andrew Brown; based on *Megiddo II*, figure 400)

Figure 11 Bichrome pottery from Megiddo (*Megiddo II*, plate 53.1–2)

Figure 12 Map illustrating Tuthmosis III's battle at Megiddo (Andrew Brown; based on the Ordnance Survey 1:20 000 map of Palestine (1942), with permission)

Figure 13 Fortress and city gate of the fifteenth century BC (Stratum VIII) (Andrew Brown; based on *Megiddo II*, figure 382)

Figure 14 Plan of the two phases of Temple 2048 (Andrew Brown; based on *Megiddo II*, figures 401, 403 and 404)

Figure 15 Frieze of Philistine jug found in Stratum VIA (*Megiddo II*, plate 76)

Figure 16   Plan of the major structures in Strata VA/IVB and IVA (From Y. Yadin, *Hazor* (Schweich Lectures), figure 39)

Figure 17   Plan of Gate 2156 of the Solomonic period (*Megiddo II*, figure 105)

Figure 18   Fragment of a stele of Sheshonq I found at Megiddo (R. S. Lamon and G. M. Shipton, *Megiddo I*, figure 70)

Figure 19   Seals of (a) Shema and (b) Asaph (Andrew Brown; based on C. Watzinger, *Tell el-Mutesellim II*, figures 61 and 62)

Figure 20   Plan of Strata III and II. (Andrew Brown; based on *Megiddo I*, figures 71, 72, 89 and 95)

Figure 21   A selection of pottery from the Assyrian period (Andrew Brown; drawn from *Megiddo I*, plates 1.34, 2.58, 3.78, 9.7, 12, 23.15, 37.7)

Figure 22   Stamped brick fragment of the Sixth Legion found near the Roman theatre (Andrew Brown; based on *Tell el-Mutesellim I*, figure 261)

Plate 1   Tell el-Mutesellim from the south (R. L. W. Cleave: Pictorial Archive Inc., Jerusalem)

Plate 2   The plain of Esdraelon seen from the summit of Tell el-Mutesellim (G. I. Davies)

Plate 3   The Chalcolithic shrine seen from the north (G. I. Davies)

Plate 4   Round altar of Early Bronze Age II (G. I. Davies)

Plate 5   Copper 'ceremonial sword' of Stratum XVIII (*Megiddo II*, plate 283.1)

Plate 6   Temple 4040 of Early Bronze IV from the north-east (G. I. Davies)

Plate 7   Part of an inscribed statuette of the Egyptian official Thuthotep, found in the Late Bronze Age temple but to be dated c. 1900 BC (*Megiddo II*, plate 265)

Plate 8   Middle Bronze Age II bone inlays (*Megiddo II*, plate 193.9)

Plate 9   Gold and faience jewellery from tombs of the end of the Middle Bronze Age and the beginning of the Late Bronze Age (*Megiddo II*, plate 225.2, 3, 6 and 7)

Plate 10   Cultic objects from Temple 2048: (a) bronze figurine of deity overlaid with gold (b) clay liver model for divination (*Megiddo II*, plates 238.30 and 255.1)

Plate 11   Ivory casket from Stratum VIIA hoard (G. Loud, *Megiddo Ivories*, no. 1a)

Plate 12   Ivory board for the 'Game of 58 Holes', from Stratum VIIA hoard (*Megiddo Ivories*, no. 221)

Plate 13   Inscribed bronze statue base of Ramesses VI found buried in Stratum VIIB (*Megiddo II*, figure 374)

Plate 14 Bronze figurine of fighting god from the time of David (Stratum VB) (*Megiddo II*, plate 239.31)

Plate 15 'Manger' from the ninth-century 'stables' (E. P. Todd)

Plate 16 Section of the city wall of Stratum IV, showing 'offsets' and 'insets' (*Megiddo I*, figure 39)

Plate 17 Unit of the 'Northern Stables' of the ninth century (*Megiddo I*, figure 50)

Plate 18 The horizontal tunnel cut through the rock for the ninth-century water-system (G. I. Davies)

Plate 19 Cist grave of the Persian period with the covering slabs removed (*Megiddo I*, figure 107)

Plate 20 Tyrian silver didrachma, dated to the mid-fourth century BC (*Megiddo I*, figure 124.9)

Plate 21 Aerial view of the tell from the west: numbers refer to main features visible today – for key see *Appendix: A Visit to the Site* (R. L. W. Cleave: Pictorial Archive Inc., Jerusalem)

1

The Identification of Megiddo and its Geographical Setting

Tell el-Mutesellim ('the tell of the governor' in Arabic) is a large mound at the foot of the north-east flank of the Carmel ridge, about 40 km from the point where it juts out into the Mediterranean Sea. It lies on the south-west boundary of the great plain of Esdraelon (or Jezreel), which provides one of the very few easy cross-country routes from the coastal plain of Palestine to the Jordan valley, the sea of Galilee and the countries beyond. Just over a kilometre to the south there emerges into the plain the pass (Wadi Ara) which has been the most popular route across the neck of the Carmel ridge for travellers making these journeys and even, surprisingly at first glance, for many seeking to follow the coast road north. The shoreline around the tip of Carmel is so narrow, and the coast beyond it was once so marshy, that such travellers have at most periods of history chosen instead to cross by Wadi Ara to the plain of Jezreel and then make for Acco (Acre) by a more inland route.

Identification

This mound (plate 1), it is now known, contains the ruins of Megiddo, one of the great cities of ancient Palestine in the pre-Christian centuries. The modest settlements which are now to be found in this area make it difficult to imagine that there was once a line of great fortified cities along this edge of the plain, whose names are to be found in more than one Biblical passage, as well as in the literature of ancient Egypt, several of whose kings recorded in stone the names of the cities which they conquered in their invasions of their northern neighbour. The book of Joshua, for example, reports that

> In Issachar and Asher Manasseh had Beth-shean and its villages, and Ible-am and its villages, and the inhabitants of Dor and its villages, and the inhabitants of En-dor and its villages, and the inhabitants of Taanach and its villages, and the inhabitants of Megiddo and its villages. (17:11)

The identification of Tell el-Mutesellim as the site of Megiddo was not won without a struggle. For many centuries after it was abandoned *c.* 330 BC the

1

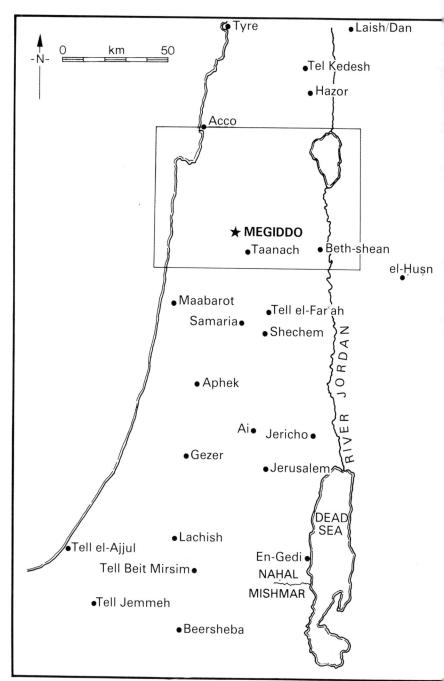

Figure 1 Map of Palestine showing places referred to in the text. (Andrew Brown)

Plate 1 Tell el-Mutesellim from the south (R. L. W. Cleave: Pictorial Archive Inc., Jerusalem)

location of Megiddo was forgotten. Jerome in the late fourth century AD had only a vague idea of where it was. The map of Marino Sanuto (fourteenth century) located it at Sububa, presumably the village known more recently as Ezbuba, 6 km south-east of the true site. This he may have deduced from the frequent connection in the Bible between Megiddo and Taanach, the name of Taanach being clearly preserved in the Arab village of Ti'inik 5 km south of Ezbuba. The first to come close to the true identification was Esthori Haparchi, a Jewish writer of the early fourteenth century. A native of France who subsequently studied in Spain, he emigrated to the Holy Land in 1313 and, after a brief stay in Jerusalem, settled at Beisan (Beth-shean) where he worked as a doctor. He was also, however, an enthusiastic and intelligent explorer and in 1322 he completed a book about the Holy Land called *Caphtor Wapherach*. In it there is the following brief reference to Megiddo: 'Let us return to Shunem: about two hours directly to the west of it is Megiddo, and it is (now) called Lejjun. One hour to the south of Megiddo is Taanach – its name has not changed.' (*Caphtor Wapherach* ed. Luncz, p. 293) Lejjun was an Arab village located a little over 1 km south of Tell el-Mutesellim (on its own origin and history see pp. 110–11). As far as we know, nobody had suggested this identification for Megiddo before, and unfortunately Haparchi does not give

3

his reasons for proposing it. It was subsequently forgotten and was put forward again as a new discovery over five hundred years later by Edward Robinson, the American biblical scholar and explorer, who visited the Holy Land in 1838 and 1852 and greatly advanced the science of biblical geography. (Robinson later discovered that his suggestion had been anticipated by Haparchi and also by two German writers who preceded him by only a few years.) On his first visit to Palestine he did not go to Lejjun, but it was pointed out to him as he crossed the plain some miles to the east. He recognised the Arabic name as a corruption of 'Legio', which had been the name of a well-known Roman city in this area, and he went on to give a series of reasons for locating Megiddo at the same spot, concluding: 'All these circumstances make out a strong case in favour of the identity of Legio and Megiddo; and leave in my own mind little doubt upon the point.' (*Biblical Researches*, 1st ed., vol. 3, p. 180.)

When he returned to Palestine in April 1852 Robinson actually visited not only Lejjun but Tell el-Mutesellim, and saw no reason to change his theory:

> The prospect from the Tell [i.e. Tell el-Mutesellim] is a noble one; embracing the whole of the glorious plain; than which there is not a richer upon earth.... A city situated either on the Tell or on the ridge behind it, would naturally give its name to the adjacent plain and waters; as we know was the case with Megiddo and Legio. The Tell would indeed present a splendid site for a city; *but there is no trace, of any kind to show that a city ever stood there*. Legio, as we shall see, was situated on a different spot (my italics). (*Biblical Researches*, 2nd ed., vol. 3, p. 117.)

It seems remarkable now that, after perceiving so clearly the strategic advantages of the tell's location, Robinson failed to identify it as the site of ancient Megiddo. We have to remember that he was quite unaware of the true nature of the tells whose existence he often reported in the course of his *Biblical Researches*. He had no idea that, as Flinders Petrie was to demonstrate so vividly in his excavations at Tell el-Hesi in 1890, each of these tells was a 'mound of many cities', built up over centuries by the superimposition of the ruins and debris of one period of occupation after another. Consequently he only identified the tells with ancient sites when he could discern ruins on them. At Tell el-Mutesellim there were no ruins – though Robinson may have missed some, because (as he tells us) the summit was 'now covered with a fine crop of wheat' – and so he concluded that it could not be an ancient site.

Before general agreement was reached on the precise location of Megiddo, Robinson's apparently successful detective-work was to find a very eminent and persistent critic in Claude Reignier Conder, the British army officer whose name (together with that of H. H. (later Lord) Kitchener) became most closely associated with the Palestine Exploration Fund's Survey of Western

Palestine. The latter bore fruit from 1881 onwards in the publication of the first really accurate map of Western Palestine and of three volumes of *Memoirs* describing the land and its antiquities. In the second volume of these *Memoirs* Conder vigorously rejected the identification of Megiddo with Lejjun, and proposed instead to locate Megiddo at Khirbet Mujedda', a large ruin on the western slopes of the Jordan valley, which he believed had accurately preserved the ancient name and which (according to him) enabled good sense to be made of the various biblical and other references to Megiddo. The pages of the *Quarterly Statement* of the Palestine Exploration Fund resounded with the salvoes of this controversy for a number of years and it was still sufficiently alive in 1892 for the young George Adam Smith to think it necessary to enter the lists against the eminent surveyor in a long footnote in *The Expositor*, the elements of which (in due course appropriately enlarged) were reproduced as an appendix to the chapter on Esdraelon in his famous *Historical Geography of the Holy Land*.

A location for Megiddo in the general vicinity of Lejjun is clearly indicated by the textual evidence, which has been augmented in modern times by discoveries of Egyptian and Canaanite texts. Several biblical passages mention Megiddo in connection with such places as Beth-shean, Taanach and Jezreel, all of which have been securely located by the preservation of the ancient name in an Arabic form (Joshua 17:11, Judges 1:27, 1 Kings 4:12, 2 Kings 9:27, 1 Chronicles 7:29): it follows from this that Megiddo must itself lie somewhere in north central Palestine. The possibilities are narrowed down by the fact that it is a place where Josiah could intercept Pharaoh Neco on his march north to Syria (2 Kings 23:29–30, 2 Chronicles 35:22), by its proximity to Taanach, which is evident both in the Bible (Judges 5:19) and in a Canaanite text of the fifteenth century BC (Taanach Letter 5), and by its choice as a refuge by Ahaziah of Judah as he fled from Jezreel before Jehu's attack from the east (2 Kings 9:27). That it was a little to the north of Taanach is proved by a statement in the annals of Tuthmosis III of Egypt, to the effect that the south wing of the Asiatic army defending Megiddo against him was at Taanach (*ANET*, p. 236). The same annals describe the details of the Pharaoh's approach to Megiddo in such a way as to leave no doubt that it was at or close to Lejjun. The precise identification with Tell el-Mutesellim follows from the archaeological evidence of the excavations, which has made it clear that it was here that a city of the Canaanite and Israelite periods was located, whereas at Lejjun only remains from the Roman period and later have been identified. We can therefore confidently say, despite the fact that the ancient name did not survive in this case and the absence to this day of any inscription from the site which mentions its name, that Tell el-Mutesellim is the site of ancient Megiddo.

5

Geographical Setting

The size of the mound was considerably underestimated by early visitors. The PEF Survey described it as 'a long flat-topped mound about 200 yards by 100 (or four acres)'. The true maximum dimensions of the summit, as given by Gottlieb Schumacher's topographical survey of 1903, are about 315 metres from east to west and 230 metres from north to south, and the surface area is upwards of twelve acres. The shape is somewhat irregular, like a pear, with

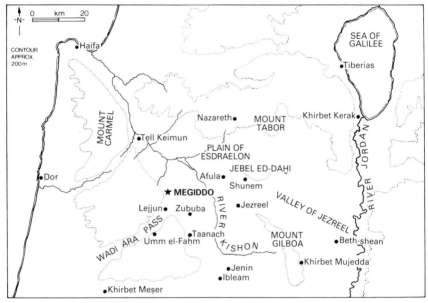

Figure 2 Map of Megiddo and its surroundings. (Andrew Brown)

the narrow end to the west. Before excavation began, the highest point of the mound, in the south-east corner, was about 175 metres above sea level, but in the north, where the main city gates proved to be, there was a hollow, whose lowest point was only about 155 metres above sea level. Below it, and providing a convenient access to the summit, was a flat terrace with some ancient remains, at an average of a little over 140 metres above sea level. Today a site museum and reception area for visitors is located there in buildings erected in the 1930s as the camp of the Chicago expedition.

The mound is situated near the northern end of a low ridge about 1.5 km long which is divided from the hills to the west by a shallow valley (called es-Suq el-Mindessi according to Schumacher's map) and bounded on the south by Wadi el-Lejjun. To the east the ground falls away to the Jezreel plain, which in this region lies about 120 metres above sea level. There is an abundant spring, Ain el-Kubbi, below the northern slopes of the terrace referred to above, but Schumacher commented on the swampy surroundings and the tendency of those who drank its water to contract fever, which deterred even the Bedouin from using it, and better water was to be found a little further away to the north-west at Ain er-Ruzz. Another spring used in antiquity was located in a cave on the south-west slopes of the mound proper.

Large cities (large whether by ancient standards or modern) do not grow up everywhere, but only where the surrounding territory is capable (or can be made capable) of supporting a large population and where particular factors, geographical or political, demand the presence of such centres. It is therefore possible to explain in large measure why cities developed at particular places at different epochs of history by making use of, on the one hand, scientific knowledge about the geology, geography and climate of an area and, on the other, historical information (both from texts and from archaeological excavations) about political conditions, wars, trade and so on. The nexus between settlement patterns and such factors also makes it possible to fill some of the many gaps in our historical evidence by inferring what must have been the case for city life to have been possible.

We have already noticed that Tell el-Mutesellim lies on the boundary of two geographical sub-regions of Palestine, the alluvial plain of Esdraelon (Jezreel) and the hills of the Carmel Ridge. The former (plate 2) is an almost triangular area which is bounded by the Carmel ridge on the south-west, the Nazareth hills on the north, and Mount Tabor, Jebel ed-Dahi ('Little Hermon' or the hill of Moreh) and Mount Gilboa on the east. It slopes very gently to the west (the drop is only about 25 metres in 25 km from south-east to north-west) and is drained by the various tributaries of the river Kishon (Nahr el-Muqatta'), into which a substantial quantity of water also runs off the surrounding hills. The river is one of the few perennial streams of Palestine, but it is no more than twenty feet across even at the point where it leaves Esdraelon near Tell el-Qassis. The problems of drainage caused by the flatness of the plain and its enclosed nature are accentuated in the eastern part by low ridges of basalt (marked today by the houses of the Israeli settlement of Hayogev) which cut into the plain from both sides north of Megiddo. The poor natural drainage used to make for difficult travel in winter and there are several reports from quite modern times of the problems faced by travellers, not to speak (for the present) of the embarrassment caused to Sisera's army according to the fifth

Plate 2   The plain of Esdraelon seen from the summit of Tell el-Mutesellim
(G. I. Davies)

chapter of the book of Judges. For example, the generally courageous travel-
ler Gertrude Bell wrote of a journey from Haifa to Jenin in February 1905:

> Moreover the road lay all across the Plain of Esdraelon (which is without doubt the
> widest plain in the world) and the mud was incredible. We waded sometimes for an
> hour at a time knee deep in clinging mud, the mules fell down, the donkeys almost
> disappeared ('By God!', said one of the muleteers, 'you could see nothing but his
> ears') and the horses grew wearier and wearier. (*Letters*, vol. 1, p. 176.)

This probably helps to account for the fact that in ancient times there were
very few settlements in the central part of the plain near the Kishon: the emptiness of the area between Megiddo, Afula, Jezreel and Jenin is particularly
striking. Coupled with the problem of drainage is the incidence of malaria,
which troubled the German excavators at Megiddo in 1903–5 and the Americans in the 1920s.

It would, however, be a mistake to exaggerate the consequences of these difficulties for the agricultural exploitation of the plain, and even for travel
within it, in ancient times. Genesis 49:15 speaks of the 'pleasantness' of the
land of Issachar, the tribal territory which most nearly corresponds to the
plain. The difficulties for travellers are largely seasonal, being severe only in
the winter months, and the basalt ridges north of Megiddo referred to earlier

provided an easier passage across the breadth of the plain which may well have been the regular road in that area in antiquity (rather than the present more easterly route to Afula). It could well be that in this as in other parts of the ancient world drainage schemes served to mitigate the consequences of the natural lie of the land. Certainly it is incorrect to suppose that the plain was uncultivable except in small areas until the 1920s, for the officers of the PEF Survey reported that in 1872 the great majority of the plain was under cultivation, the problem in recent times having been not the poor drainage but raiders and Bedouin encampments. Given the right political conditions it seems likely that large areas could have been under cultivation in antiquity. The absence of settlements is no objection, for cultivation could have been organised from the large cities on the edge of the plain, like Megiddo. One of the Amarna letters from Megiddo (see below, pp. 59–60) speaks of the ruler of Megiddo organising agricultural labourers even at Shunem, on the far side of the plain. Of the richness of the plain when it is cultivated there is no doubt, given the fertile alluvial soil and the ample rainfall. In the nineteenth century AD the main products were wheat, barley and millet, with a little sesame, castor-oil and cotton.

The hilly hinterland of Megiddo is of a different character north and south of Wadi Ara, because of the geology of the area. The hills to the south, known in modern times as the Sheikh Iskander hills or the Heights (Ramoth) of Manasseh, are of the same Cenomanian limestone as Mount Carmel itself and the bulk of the central hill country of Palestine. This is the type of stone preferred for building and it breaks down to form a fertile deep-red soil known as *terra rossa*. The natural vegetation is evergreen forest and scrub, which together with the broken lie of the land constitutes a formidable obstacle to progress. Where the forest is cleared, however, the land is productive and could have supported crops such as vines and olives, as it has done in modern times. Many presses for wine or oil are cut into the rock in this area, and others were found in the excavations at Taanach and Megiddo. There is evidence of sporadic settlement here in some periods of antiquity. Iron ore is found near Umm el-Faḥm. The more northerly hills are lower and composed of the Lower Eocene limestone, which has the same chalky character as is found in the Judaean Shephelah. This produces a fine, greyish soil (rendzina), which is less fertile than the *terra rossa* but easier to cultivate with primitive implements and consequently attractive to ancient farmers. The natural vegetation is less dense than in the hills farther south. The area is blessed with high rainfall and many springs, though water supply is a problem in the summer. Ancient settlements were mainly in the western part of this region away from the plain of Jezreel. The hills above Megiddo may perhaps have served for grazing. Because of the characteristics which this region shares with the Judaean Shephelah, some scholars have suggested that it is referred to as 'the Shephelah (low hills) of Israel' in Joshua 11:16 (compare v.2).

Wadi Ara itself, which separates these two areas of higher ground, is one of two valleys (the other emerges into the plain 12 km to the north by Tell Keimun (Jokneam)) which were created when the soft Senonian chalk was exposed at the edge of the syncline, or downfold, which forms the central part of the Carmel ridge above Megiddo. In many parts of Palestine such valleys form important lines of communication, and we have already seen that this is the case here: the chalk has eroded into a relatively easy and straight route through the hills. Nevertheless it was not without its dangers, and an Egyptian scribe of the thirteenth-century BC wrote of the fear which a journey through it could engender:

> The narrow valley is dangerous with Bedouin, hidden under the bushes. Some of them are of four or five cubits . . . and fierce of face. Their hearts are not mild, and they do not listen to wheedling. . . . Thy path is filled with boulders and pebbles, without a *toe hold* for passing by, overgrown with reeds, thorns, *brambles* and 'wolf's paw'. The ravine is on one side of thee, and the mountain rises on the other. (*ANET*, pp. 477–8. See also below, p. 52.)

The city of Megiddo therefore stood in a position where it was possible to exploit rich natural resources of several different kinds but also, as indicated at the beginning, near an important cross-country route. It lay in fact at a junction of several routes: the route along the edge of the plain of Esdraelon from Haifa, Acco and Phoenicia to Beth-shean and the Jordan; the route from the coastal plain across the Carmel ridge via Wadi Ara; and a safe route north across the plain to Galilee and Syria. As a consequence it was easily accessible to traders and migrants from all directions; but at the same time it could, if powerful enough, control access by means of these routes and so direct the course of both trade and war. It is not surprising therefore that it was at most periods of antiquity one of the wealthiest cities of Palestine, or that it was a prize often fought over and when secured strongly defended. Even so, in the great battles in its vicinity of which we know, it several times failed to be an effective barrier against armies invading from the south. Tuthmosis III, Neco and Allenby all managed to defeat those who held the north end of the Wadi Ara pass by superior numbers and generalship. Perhaps after all it was rather trade which ensured that through the centuries there was usually a major centre here. Even down to modern times the khan at Lejjun continued to be a staging-point on the road from Syria to Egypt, and Schumacher reported that during his excavations great herds of camels from Syria would pass the foot of the tell each year in July and August before drinking and resting at the stream in Wadi el-Lejjun, on their way to the Egyptian camel-markets.

10

Further reading

For information about the geography of the region C. R. Conder and H. H. Kitchener, *The Survey of Western Palestine, Memoirs* . . ., edited with additions by E. H. Palmer and W. Besant, vol. 2 (London, 1882), pp. 36–50, 73–4, and G. Adam Smith, *Historical Geography of the Holy Land*, 25th ed. (London, 1931), ch. 19, remain invaluable. Among more recent works see D. Baly, *Geography of Palestine*, rev. ed. (Guildford and London, 1974), ch. 13; T. L. Thompson, *The Settlement of Palestine in the Bronze Age* (Wiesbaden, 1979), esp. pp. 33–45; M. Zohary, *Plants of the Bible* (Cambridge, 1982). The identification of Megiddo is treated by E. Robinson, *Biblical Researches in Palestine* (London, 1841), vol. 3, pp. 177–80, and *ibid.*, 2nd ed. (London, 1856), vol. 3, pp. 115–19; Conder and Kitchener, *Survey*, vol. 2, pp. 64–6, 70, 90–9; and Smith, *Historical Geography*, pp. 385–7, 411–12. H. H. Nelson, *The Battle of Megiddo* (Chicago, 1913), was the first thorough topographical study of the relevant part of the annals of Tuthmosis III, and is still useful (but see the corrections of R. O. Faulkner, *Journal of Egyptian Archaeology* 28 (1942), 2–15; L. Christophe, *Revue d'Egyptologie* 6 (1950), 89–114, is ingenious but not ultimately convincing).

The heights above sea-level given by Schumacher are uniformly about 18 metres too high, as comparison with the American measurements shows, and I have corrected them accordingly.

2

The Excavations at
Tell el-Mutesellim (Megiddo)

It is not surprising to find that a tell of the size and importance described in the previous chapter was one of the earliest to attract the excavator's spade and one of those where a succession of archaeologists have tried to add further precision to our knowledge about its history. As will appear later in this book, the task is by no means completed and there are still some deep-seated problems of interpretation which are unlikely to be solved without yet further excavation. Up to the present the tell has been excavated by a German expedition under the direction of Gottlieb Schumacher between April 1903 and November 1905; by an American expedition from the Oriental Institute at the University of Chicago, directed in turn by Clarence S. Fisher (1925–7), P. L. O. Guy (1927–34), R. S. Lamon (1934–5) and Gordon Loud (1935–9); and by Israeli teams from the Hebrew University of Jerusalem under Yigael Yadin (1960, 1966–7, 1971–2), I. Dunayevsky (1965) and A. Eitan (1974).

The German Excavations (1903–5)

The German Society for the Study of Palestine (Deutsche Verein zur Erforschung Palästinas, or Deutsche Palästina-Verein (DPV)) was founded in 1877 and had by 1900 established its reputation by sponsoring numerous studies of Palestine, including Hermann Guthe's excavations in Jerusalem and Schumacher's attempt (unfortunately never completed) to complement the Palestine Exploration Fund's Survey of Western Palestine with a similar survey of Transjordan. But it had not so far undertaken the excavation of a tell, such as those which had occupied the Palestine Exploration Fund during the 1890s, and there seems to have been a sense among the Committee of the Society that it was falling behind in the quest for new knowledge. Perhaps a greater spur to activity, because nearer to home, was the fact that in 1902 Professor Ernst Sellin of the University of Vienna had independently begun excavation at the site of ancient Taanach. But broader intellectual currents added their force to the growing sense that a beginning must be made, for discoveries in Egypt and Mesopotamia had already begun to open up new vistas in the

12

history and religion of the ancient Near East. In Germany particularly the 'Babel-Bibel' controversy had been sparked off by the suggestion that a large part of the Old Testament had been borrowed from Egyptian or Babylonian sources, and both sides were anxious for further light on this question from excavations conducted in Palestine itself.

It appears that this latter consideration influenced the choice of a site for excavation, since the cities on the edge of the plain of Esdraelon were known from written sources (such as the Amarna letters) to have been important centres already in Canaanite times. Since Taanach was already 'reserved', Tell el-Mutesellim (Megiddo) was an obvious choice, the more so as it was readily accessible from Haifa, which as well as being a port was one of the major cities of the country. A large part of the cost was defrayed by the Kaiser himself, who had already shown his interest in the Society and in Palestine generally in a number of ways. As director of the excavations Schumacher was an obvious choice since, in addition to experience of excavation which he had gained while working with Sellin at Taanach, he was a trained surveyor. He had also lived in Palestine for many years and was therefore excellently placed to deal with the local people in whatever ways were needed. As was customary at the time, the expedition had a very small core staff but employed large numbers of villagers, men, women and children, under the direction of local foremen, for the digging and the removal of the debris. Dr I. Benzinger (who had published a volume on *Hebräische Archäologie* in 1894) acted as Deputy Director in the autumn of 1903 when Schumacher was absent from the site, and the reports refer to occasional periods spent there by distinguished visitors such as the Hebraist Professor E. Kautzsch.

The work itself began with the drawing of accurate survey maps of the tell (at a scale of 1:1000) and of its wider surroundings, including Lejjun (at 1:5000). The first area to be excavated was the highest point of the tell, which lay near its eastern edge, and here Schumacher identified what he thought were two successive building stages of a 'Temple-fortress' (*Tempelburg*). In the south a fortified gate was uncovered, and Schumacher then began the excavation, from the northern edge of the tell, of a trench twenty metres broad running due south across the summit. This work continued through the autumn of 1903, when caves in the vicinity of the tell were also explored for ancient remains, and on into the excavation seasons of 1904. By broadening his main trench to thirty metres Schumacher was able to expose two buildings which he called the North Fortress (*Nordburg*) and the Central Fortress (*Mittelburg*). The exploration of the summit was extended by the excavation of shallow test-trenches in different directions and attention was also given, by the excavation of further trenches, to the fortifications on the slopes. These Schumacher seems to have regarded as a single system of defence constructed at one and the same time. The Roman theatre and some ruins at Lejjun were also cleared in 1904.

By the following year it was clear that the Turkish authorities, who had granted a permit for the excavations to take place, would not allow them to continue beyond the autumn of 1905 and so, instead of having a pause in the hot summer months (when labour was difficult to come by anyway owing to the harvest), as had been done in the first two years, it was decided to excavate as far as possible all through the summer, in the hope of bringing the work to a satisfactory conclusion. Urgent calls for additional funds were made to the Society's subscribers in order to finance the extra weeks of work. The achievements were considerable, as the two 'fortresses' were extensively investigated and beneath the Central Fortress a series of large subterranean vaulted chambers were found, evidently tombs, some of them still containing skeletons and grave-goods. In a small area in the North Fortress the excavation was continued to the virgin rock, the only place on the tell where bedrock was reached by Schumacher, and deposits that were clearly of great antiquity were found. In addition a very finely constructed corner of walling which jutted into the north-south trench near its southern end became the starting-point for an investigation which brought to light a large enclosed courtyard with what Schumacher called a 'Palace' on its northern side. (It later emerged during the American excavations that this 'Palace' was only a gatehouse to the courtyard, and the real palace lay some distance to the south in an area not touched by Schumacher's work.) Further work was also done on the caves around the tell and other constructions in the vicinity: to the east a group of milestones was found which confirmed that the Roman road to Ptolemais, present-day Acco, had passed close by the tell.

In the report on his work, which was published in 1908, Schumacher attempted to put the various structures which he had found into chronological order. He did not attempt to correlate them precisely with particular periods of history or dates in years BC or AD – this was left for consideration in a second volume – but he sought to establish a relative chronology of his finds, and the report is set out in accordance with his conclusions. He distinguished eight strata, calling the earliest 'I' and the latest 'VIII' (the opposite procedure to that normally used today). He had intended to describe nothing but the buildings in his first volume, and he kept to this plan for his treatment of the two earliest strata. But he found it impossible to maintain a total separation between the buildings and the objects found in them and the later chapters of the report include details of many objects of pottery, stone, metal and other materials. This was extremely fortunate for subsequent research, as almost all Schumacher's unpublished notes and drawings were unaccountably lost before work on the second volume could begin. Without the photographs and descriptions which he included in the later chapters of *Tell el-Mutesellim I* the task of relating his findings to their historical setting, which was bound to be difficult in any case, could never have been attempted.

This task was not attempted until the 1920s and it was then not Schumacher who took it up but Carl Watzinger, a Professor at the University of Tübingen who had had no direct connection with the excavations at Megiddo, but had taken part in other archaeological field-work in Palestine: he had, for example, excavated with Sellin at Jericho. As we have seen, he had practically no information about Schumacher's excavations apart from what the latter had already published. On the other hand the delay did give him some advantages, for in the meantime a number of other sites in Palestine had been excavated and the results published, so that he was able to draw far more comparisons with findings from elsewhere and as a result to arrive at a much more precise chronology than would have been possible at an earlier date. Watzinger's analysis, *Tell el-Mutesellim II*, is a masterpiece of archaeological scholarship for its time and an indispensable companion to the original report. As an experienced archaeologist himself he was able to use Schumacher's often very precise information to correct errors in the latter's grander reconstructions, and his sharp eye perceived from the photographs which had been published that Schumacher's workmen had often continued digging below the floors of buildings, so that finds from a deeper and therefore earlier level were mixed in with those which were in use when a building was destroyed or abandoned. Although these 'intrusive' objects could not be identified conclusively from the limited information about find-spots given in the report, the likelihood that such were present allowed Watzinger to discount objects which would otherwise have required much too long a period of occupation for a particular building.

The first structures which Watzinger discussed were the earliest parts of the North and Central Fortresses (including two underground burial-chambers), which he dated from their architecture and finds to the end of what is now known as the Middle Bronze Age, *c*.1600 BC. The later stages of the 'fortresses' (Watzinger was sceptical about this designation, as they appeared to have little defensive strength) he assigned to the Late Bronze Age, believing that the Central Fortress was destroyed *c*.1400 BC, while the North Fortress, which included some Mycenaean sherds, lasted for approximately a century longer. Little remained in his view of the Megiddo of the next three centuries, at least in the areas excavated. But there were signs of an eventual rebuilding of the city in fine ashlar masonry and since this masonry was thought to be characteristic at other sites of Solomon's time, Watzinger concluded that this stratum (IV) was from the tenth century. The revival was short-lived and a great 'burnt layer' (*Brandschicht*) lay over the ruins of this phase: Watzinger attributed its destruction to the Egyptian king Sheshonq I (945–924), whose campaign in Palestine is commemorated in one of his own inscriptions, in which Megiddo is named (*ANET*, pp. 242–3; see also p. 96 below), and dated by 1 Kings 14:25–6 to the fifth year of Rehoboam, Solomon's son and successor. The 'Palace' found by Schumacher belonged to the next stratum (V) and represented, he thought, a ninth-century reconstruction of the city, along with some smaller structures, all of which were destroyed by the Assyrians in 733 BC. In the *Tempelburg* Watzinger retained the distinction into two phases, but denied that either of them had any religious significance: he attributed the earlier of them, which he thought was a house or part of a residential complex, to the end of Stratum V and the later phase, with its thick walls, he took to be the fortress of the Assyrian governor in Megiddo, whose existence was proved by a cuneiform contract from Assur. In several areas there were modest buildings from the period of Persian rule (sixth to fourth centuries BC), but the only structures on the tell from a later period than this were a medieval Arab watch-tower above the *Tempelburg* and two water-tanks apparently of the same date.

The later excavations at Megiddo (and elsewhere) have shown that Watzinger made a serious mistake in ascribing the construction of the Stratum IV buildings to Solomon and their destruction to Sheshonq I. Both belong at least a century earlier. The reliance on what was thought to be distinctively 'Solomonic' masonry led him astray, even against the evidence of some of the pottery associated with the destruction which he knew was from the beginning of the Iron Age. The quest for Solomonic features at Megiddo, be they masonry, stables or gates, has however been a long and tortuous one and Watzinger was only the first to embark upon it. It should also be noted that the long 'gap' in occupation between *c.*1300 and 900 BC which he observed is, with regard to the earlier part of that period, a substantially correct representation of the remains in the area about which he had the most information, namely that of the two 'fortresses'. Subsequent excavation has shown that in this part of the tell the remains from the Late Bronze Age were largely removed when the site was being prepared for reconstruction in the tenth or the ninth century. Consequently one would naturally gain the impression from excavation in this area alone that the site was unoccupied for a long period in the Late Bronze and early Iron Ages, although it is now clear that there was almost continuous occupation at the site throughout this time.

By 1929, when Watzinger's volume was published, a new expedition to Megiddo had taken the field, but the first adequate account of this work only appeared a few months before *Tell el-Mutesellim II* and Watzinger made very little reference to the new excavations. There is discernible in Professor Albrecht Alt's foreword to his volume a slight sense of grievance that the

Americans had gone ahead with the excavation without seeking the agreement of the German Society: it is regarded as 'bad form' to conduct excavations on a site without first checking whether archaeologists who have dug there before intend to return for further work.

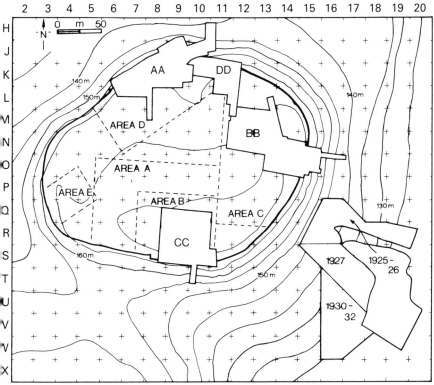

Figure 3 Plan of American excavation areas. The dates at bottom right indicate the parts of the cemetery which were cleared in different seasons. (Andrew Brown; based on G. Loud, *Megiddo II*, figure 377, and P. L. O. Guy and R. M. Engberg, *Megiddo Tombs*, figure 2)

The American excavations (1925–39) (fig. 3)

The Chicago expedition was the brainchild of the famous Egyptologist James Henry Breasted who, as Director of the Oriental Institute, secured the backing of Mr John D. Rockefeller, Jr, for this part of the Institute's 'grand plan' to advance historical study of the culture of the ancient Near East by excavations at carefully chosen sites in Egypt, Mesopotamia, Asia Minor and the

17

intervening lands. Dr Clarence Fisher, who had shared in the direction of excavations at Samaria before the First World War and at Beth-shean in 1921–3, was appointed Field Director for an operation that was initially envisaged to last for five years. He was in fact to retain this role for less than two years, becoming a victim of the outbreaks of malaria which were unpleasantly frequent in the first seasons of this excavation.

Fisher was an unashamed advocate of the clearance of large areas of a mound layer-by-layer and he clearly regarded Schumacher's 'great trench' as more of a hindrance than a help:

> In the previous section we have seen how the hill was built up layer by layer. It should be obvious that the logical method of determining the extent of the respective remains of each separate town level and securing as complete a record as possible of its character, is to reverse the process and strip off layer after layer, beginning with the topmost or latest in date. (*The Excavation of Armageddon*, p. 26)

Because Fisher and his successors have sometimes been accused of having a very naive idea of the nature of these layers or strata, the following statement of principle should be noted:

> The task is complicated by the fact that, instead of being nicely and evenly differentiated like the layers of a cake, the strata are rarely horizontal throughout and never parallel ... Successive towns expanded over the edges, either following the natural slopes or built on artificial terraces. (*The Excavation of Armageddon*, p. 27)

Ideally according to this view the whole of a particular stratum should be removed before the next is disturbed, but Fisher believed that this was impracticable in the case of a mound the size of Megiddo and his original intention was to excavate only the portion of the mound east of Schumacher's main trench, where (he supposed) the major buildings of the ancient city lay. Before this could be done, however, he had to organise the building of an excavation headquarters (part of which now comprises the museum beside the tell) and, more significant from an archaeological point of view, to make a fresh survey of the tell and a special examination of the area below its south-eastern slopes, where it was intended to deposit the debris that would be excavated on the summit. This area proved to have been used as a cemetery between the third millennium BC and the Roman period, and by the end of 1926 sixty tombs had been excavated, many of them intact and with impressive collections of grave-goods. Early reports spoke of the discovery of a Neolithic tomb, but this seems to have been due to a misunderstanding of some stone implements, which were later realised to be of no earlier than Bronze Age date.

On the summit Fisher's work was confined to the south-eastern portion of the tell (subsequently known as Area C – see fig. 3), where he investigated further what Schumacher had described as the 'Temple-fortress'. His conclusion (apparently reached independently of Watzinger) was that the two building stages were quite separate, the later being a fortress and the earlier a temple, dedicated to the goddess Astarte. In this interpretation he relied on his own discovery of a number of limestone altars and other objects of an apparently religious nature in an area a little to the south of the 'temple'. As the excavation progressed under the direction of Fisher's successors it became clear that these objects were of a much earlier date and could shed no light on the function of the 'temple' or of the very finely constructed building (later numbered 'Building 338') which Fisher began to uncover underneath it. Unfortunately this was not clear to H. G. May, who perpetuated the myth of the 'Astarte temple' in a supplementary volume to the excavation reports, in which the objects referred to were published. Fisher also identified a number of other buildings and streets, mainly from the latest periods of the city's history.

Guy, who replaced Fisher as Director in the spring of 1927, began by clearing a further area to the south-east of the mound for dumping debris, and discovered another forty-one tombs, as well as a lower circuit of walls which he tentatively dated to the period of David and Solomon. This done he resumed the excavation of the summit and concentrated his efforts in an area north of where Fisher had worked, though still to the east of Schumacher's deep trench. By the end of 1928 he had completed the clearance of the fine building (338) beneath the so-called 'temple' and also exposed, in his new area, parts of a city wall and a complex of what he believed to be the royal stables of Solomon. At the same time larger schemes were in his mind and he was able to persuade Professor Breasted and the Mandatory authorities in Palestine, with further financial help from John D. Rockefeller, Jr, to arrange the compulsory purchase of the whole mound for the Government of Palestine. The aim was to extend the excavation west of Schumacher's trench and so bring to execution Fisher's vision of a whole mound being excavated stratum by stratum to the bottom.

During 1929 the surface debris was cleared from the remainder of the mound, exposing the uppermost layer of ruins (which did not date from the same period in all areas). In the north (Area D) a city gate was excavated, linked to what appeared to be the same solid city wall that had been found in the eastern area: it too was at this stage ascribed to Solomon. Work continued intermittently in this area in the following seasons, but the major efforts of the excavators were increasingly concentrated in Areas A–B and E in the south of the tell (exclusively so from the spring of 1933), where they were rewarded by the discovery in succession of a concealed passage through the city wall leading to a spring, a rock-cut shaft and tunnel giving even more secure access to the same spring, a further set of 'Solomonic stables' and the foundations of the palace whose courtyard and gatehouse Schumacher had earlier found. Between 1931 and 1933 further work was done on the eastern slopes, adding more tombs to the inventory and also some domestic occupation levels from the very earliest periods of the tell's history. By the summer of 1934 the work in the south had reached Stratum VII, a transitional level bridging the end of the Late Bronze Age and the beginning of the Iron Age. At this point Guy resigned from the Directorship: a year later he became Director of the British School of Archaeology in Jerusalem, in succession to J. W. Crowfoot, the excavator of Samaria. It seems likely that, for all his successes, Guy's progress was too slow for his masters at the Oriental Institute and they may have been anxious to relieve him of the Directorship. He deserves, nevertheless, to be remembered for two technical innovations which he pioneered at Megiddo: the use of 'locus numbers' to designate rooms or other small areas in a stratum, which is now a universal practice, and the taking of aerial photographs of major structures by means of a camera attached to a captive balloon.

For over a year, until October 1935, digging on the tell was at a standstill, but the assistant staff used the opportunity to prepare final reports on work done during the previous ten years. The major volumes did not appear until 1938 and 1939, but three specialised studies were published during the interval. As the new Director the Oriental Institute appointed Gordon Loud, who had had recent field experience in the direction of the Institute's excavation at the Assyrian site of Khorsabad (Dur Sharrukin). It would be possible to give a much more precise account of the years of his Directorship, since his excavation diary, preserved in the archives of the Oriental Institute Museum in Chicago, records how work progressed in each area from day to day as well as the interpretation that was put on the finds at the time. This diary thus constitutes an invaluable supplement to the abbreviated account of these years in the text of *Megiddo II*. But in keeping with the character of the remainder of this chapter only the broad outlines of Loud's work will be sketched here. His strategy differed from Guy's both in aim and in technique. He abandoned as impractical the plan of excavating the whole mound, aiming instead to reach bedrock in at least a restricted area (an aim that was only to be fulfilled in the third season of his Directorship). In order to identify the areas where digging would be most productive he laid out three long, narrow test-trenches in the north, north-east and south of the mound. The first two of these cut through respectively a palace and a temple of the Late Bronze Age and became the starting-points for extensive areas of work which were designated as Areas AA and BB to distinguish them from the quite separate areas referred to as A and B in the earlier years of the expedition's work. The third trench (CC), which exposed an early city wall but otherwise only domestic buildings, was abandoned after Loud's first season.

In both the remaining areas evidence of the city's fortifications was found, from the Early Bronze Age onwards in Area BB. Area AA proved to contain a succession of city gates of the Middle Bronze, Late Bronze and Iron Ages, some directly underneath, others a little to the west of, the gate discovered by Guy and attributed to Solomon. Owing to the appearance of a much more massive Iron Age structure immediately below this gate, the latter was now assigned to the later Israelite monarchy and the earlier gate was ascribed to Solomon. The palace which had been touched in the original test-trench proved to have a long history and in rooms of two of its phases collections of ivories and other precious objects were found which gave a vivid demonstration of the wealth and international contacts of Late Bronze Age (Canaanite) Megiddo. In Area BB the temple which was the first to come to light was rich in finds of a cultic character and in later seasons three much earlier phases of sacred architecture were traced, beginning in Stratum XIX, of the Chalcolithic period. This superposition of temples indicated that the area had retained its sanctity over a very long period, probably even when there was no building standing there. To the east and west of the 'temple area' were mainly private houses, though larger (perhaps public) buildings appear from time to time and at one point Loud was able to relate them directly to the 'North Fortress' found by Schumacher. In 1938–9 an additional area, DD, was opened up to try to make a physical connection between the excavations in Areas AA and BB and so correlate the structures in the two areas with each other more definitely than had so far been possible. The excavations reached a further palatial building of the Late Bronze Age (Stratum VIII), but the outbreak of war brought a premature end to the work before the intended final season could establish any link between the two areas.

The report on the first ten years of excavation (*Megiddo I*) was finally published just after the digging finished, in July 1939, the *Tombs* volume having appeared in the preceding year. The report on the remaining seasons was ready for the printer in 1942, though it was not actually published until 1948. The outbreak of the Second World War and especially a shortage of paper placed limits on the extent of this publication, and this must be taken into account when its adequacy is assessed. It lacks the detailed description of the process of excavation and the considered interpretation of the whole site which would ideally be expected in such a report, and Loud's own reference to the work as little more than 'a catalogue of the architecture and artefacts recovered' only anticipates the description that has seemed appropriate to others. Nor is it in every respect a complete catalogue, and several important pieces of unpublished pottery have from time to time been identified by researchers working in the storerooms of the Oriental Institute. There are also gaps in our knowledge which derive not so much from the curtailment of the

21

publication as from the methods of recording (and indeed of excavating) that were employed on the site. Kathleen Kenyon and others pointed out that the 'strata' into which the mound was analysed were sometimes crudely defined, so that tombs on the summit, for example, were associated with the debris layers in which they were constructed rather than with the higher and later living surfaces from which they were excavated by the ancient inhabitants of the site. As a consequence the pottery attributed to a particular stratum is often a mixture of what genuinely derives from that level and period with later pottery found in tombs that were dug into it a century and more afterwards. Great care needs to be exercised in using the lists of pottery types and note must be taken of whether a particular piece was found in a tomb or in a deposit that is directly associated with a building or occupation level.

Nevertheless the achievements of the Megiddo staff should not be under-estimated, and they have enabled other scholars to circumvent to some extent the weaknesses which have been mentioned. The publication of a complete set of plans, stratum by stratum, area by area, with heights of walls and floors marked on them, is a substantial advance on *Megiddo I*, and the preservation of Loud's excavation diary in the archives of the Oriental Institute, together with the photographic records there, provides the possibility of compiling a much more complete account of what was found on the tell – some use of this diary will be made at a later point in this book. As for the objects, a study of the pottery sequence was published by G. M. Shipton in 1939 and it contains many comparisons with the pottery of other sites. The prompt and careful publication of other categories of objects has made it possible for others to incorporate them into more general studies of artefacts and so to establish their context in the history of Palestinian and Near Eastern culture. The Megiddo volumes are, because of the sheer numbers of objects and the geographical factors alluded to in the previous chapter, a veritable gold-mine for such studies, and the time has now come for the process to be reversed and for this more general knowledge to be put to use in new detailed work on the history of Megiddo itself. Some studies of this kind have already appeared and have provided invaluable help in the preparation of the present, necessarily brief, account of the site. Much more remains to be done, as we shall observe at appropriate places, and advances in understanding can certainly be ex-pected, in particular, from the recent excavations at the neighbouring sites of Taanach and Tell Keimun (Jokneam).

Recent Israeli excavations

In the meantime some further excavation on a small scale has been done under the auspices of the Institute of Archaeology at the Hebrew University of Jerusalem. This was initiated by Professor Yigael Yadin, who in 1960 had recently come to the end of four seasons of very extensive excavations at Hazor (Tell el-Qedaḥ) in the upper Jordan Valley. Yadin had already, in an article published in 1958, drawn attention to the similarity between the early Iron Age gates at Hazor and Megiddo and he had found in the plans of R. A. S. Macalister's early excavations at Gezer (1902–5, 1907–9) a structure which, by a brilliant conjecture, subsequently confirmed by excavation, he identified as one half of a third gate of the same period, with an almost identical plan to the other two. Thinking it strange that the gates at Hazor and Gezer were set in casemate walls while the gate at Megiddo was associated with a massive solid wall, Yadin undertook a brief investigation at Megiddo to test his theory that there too the gate in question (the so-called 'Solomonic' gate) was part of a casemate fortification system and at the same time to try to clarify other aspects of the history of Israelite Megiddo. It was an excellent example of what is called a 'problem-centred' excavation. Already after only a few days' work Yadin was able to report some startling discoveries. Beneath a stretch of the solid wall in the north-east of the tell, which the earlier excavators had left untouched, there was visible a line of fine masonry almost 30 metres long, which proved to be the outer north wall of a rectangular 'fort' of an earlier period. To the east and west of this building, but still under the solid wall, were a series of rooms which Yadin identified as casemates, and he quickly drew the conclusion that these were the fortifications that were to be associated with the Solomonic gate, so that the pattern of defence at Hazor, Gezer and Megiddo was essentially identical. The pottery found in his new excavations seemed to confirm this view and to show that the solid wall (with a later gate) represented the fortifications of the following century, probably constructed under King Ahab of Israel. Other structures found by the American expedition could be allocated to one of these two phases of Megiddo's history. Yadin's theory and alternatives to it are discussed more fully below, in Chapter 6 (see pp. 85–92). Later excavations (in 1966–7 and 1971–2) brought to light further details of the 'fort' and provided the opportunity to examine other features of the Israelite city, including the different protected approaches to the water sources. Trial excavations on the slopes of the terrace to the north of the tell showed that it was largely artificial and that it was used for burials in the early part of the Middle Bronze Age.

Some of Yadin's colleagues at the Hebrew University also made small probes in other parts of the site: in 1965 I. Dunayevsky investigated the

Bronze Age sacred area on the summit and as a result proposed new conclusions about the order and dates of the temples there, while in 1974 A. Eitan uncovered further remains of an Iron Age public building on the eastern slopes, which had been touched by one of Loud's trenches. This he associated with other Iron Age structures on the slopes further to the south which had been found by Fisher and Guy.

Further reading

On the general development of archaeological technique in Palestine see the companion volume to this one by P. R. S. Moorey, *Excavation in Palestine* (Guildford, 1982), ch.4.

The results of the major excavations at Megiddo have been published in a series of large volumes: G. Schumacher, *Tell el-Mutesellim I*, in two parts, text and plates (Leipzig, 1908); C. Watzinger, *Tell el-Mutesellim II* (Leipzig, 1929); R. S. Lamon, *The Megiddo Water System*, OIP XXXII (Chicago, 1935); H. G. May and R. M. Engberg, *Material Remains of the Megiddo Cult*, OIP XXVI (Chicago, 1935); P. L. O. Guy and R. M. Engberg, *Megiddo Tombs*, OIP XXXIII (Chicago, 1938) (the tombs found on the eastern slopes); R. S. Lamon and G. M. Shipton, *Megiddo I. The Seasons of 1925–34, Strata I–V*, OIP XLII (Chicago, 1939); G. Loud, *The Megiddo Ivories*, OIP LII (Chicago, 1939); G. Loud, *Megiddo II, Seasons of 1935–39*, OIP LXII, two parts, text and plates (Chicago, 1948). The Chicago reports are now available in microfiche from the University of Chicago Press.

Preliminary notices of Schumacher's work appeared in the *Mitteilungen und Nachrichten des DPV* between 1904 and 1906 and these provide some additional information. The preliminary reports of Fisher, *The Excavation of Armageddon* (Chicago, 1929), and Guy, *New Light from Armageddon* (Chicago, 1931), help with the background and policy of the excavation. Analyses of the pottery of the earlier strata from the Chicago excavations may be found in R. M. Engberg and G. M. Shipton, *Notes on the Chalcolithic and Early Bronze Age Pottery of Megiddo*, SAOC, 10 (Chicago, 1934) – this volume deals with the domestic occupation on the south-eastern slopes – and G. M. Shipton, *Notes on the Megiddo pottery of Strata VI–XX*, SAOC, 17 (Chicago, 1939).

For the Israeli excavations see Yadin's articles, 'New Light on Solomon's Megiddo', *BA* 23(1960), 62–8; 'Megiddo of the Kings of Israel', *BA* 33(1970), 66–96, 'Notes and News: Megiddo', *IEJ* 22(1972), 161–4; and ch.13 of his Schweich lectures for 1970, *Hazor: the Head of all those Kingdoms (Joshua 11:10)*, (London, 1972); I. Dunayevsky and A. Kempinski, 'The Megiddo Temples', *ZDPV* 89(1973), 161–87; A. Eitan, 'Notes and News: Megiddo', *IEJ* 24(1974), 275–6.

An excellent summary of the discoveries at the site can be found in M. Avi-Yonah and E. Stern (ed), *Encyclopaedia of Archaeological Excavations in the Holy Land* (Jerusalem, London and Englewood Cliffs, 1975–8), vol.3, pp. 830–56 (with bibliography). Additional bibliography is given in E. K. Vogel, *Bibliography of Holy Land Sites* (Cincinnati, 1971), and E. K. Vogel and B. Holtzclaw, *Bibliography of Holy Land Sites, Part II* (Cincinnati, 1982), both offprints from *Hebrew Union College Annual* (vols 42 and 52); and at the end of the remaining chapters of this book.

3

The Earliest Settlements at Megiddo

From Village to City

Megiddo was not, according to the evidence at present available, one of the first places in Palestine to see settled human occupation. The earliest identifiable remains come from Area BB of the American excavations and indicate a beginning of settlement in the later part of the Neolithic period, *c*.5000 BC. Some toothed sickle blades found in a cave in the bedrock (designated by the Americans as 'Stratum –XX') and potsherds with either an incised herringbone design or a painted decoration from the deposits that lay on the bedrock (Stratum XX, 1st phase) are characteristic of the Yarmukian culture of this period, as represented by the ancient site of Shaar haGolan, near the southern end of the Sea of Galilee. Our knowledge of these early levels is limited by the fact that only in two small areas, comprising together about 700 square metres, was bedrock reached on the tell, and similar if less severe limitations apply to the history of occupation in the following three millennia (5000–2000 BC), in other words to half the period during which the tell was inhabited. The American excavators reached these prehistoric levels in only one of their areas on the tell (BB) and in a small area on the south-eastern slopes below the tell, which the ancient settlers mainly used as a cemetery. Schumacher's main trench cut through the early deposits at one point, but his report provides little information about them. For this reason alone any account of the first stages of the history of Megiddo must be a tentative one. There is in addition intense discussion and controversy among archaeologists at present about the processes at work in Palestine as a whole during this period, so that no one theory can be regarded as a secure framework into which the fragmentary evidence from Megiddo might be fitted. In the following pages we shall therefore concentrate on a description of the main finds: those readers who wish to pursue the scholarly discussion may consult the works mentioned at the end of the chapter.

The Neolithic settlement was followed by a village of the Chalcolithic period whose remains have been found in Strata XX (2nd phase) and XIX on the tell and in 'Stages VII–IV' on the lower slopes. The area exposed on the

Plate 3   The Chalcolithic shrine seen from the north (G. I. Davies)

tell was at first occupied by small houses built of stone or mudbrick, with either a rounded or a rectangular plan, but in the later part of the period these were replaced by a temple with a paved courtyard and an enclosure wall extending to the east. The walls of the temple are still visible today (plate 3): the main room was four metres from front to rear and a little over twelve metres broad. A circular structure *c*.2.25 metres in diameter, perhaps an altar, was assigned by the excavators to the next higher stratum (XVIII), but it may have belonged to this shrine, as it is situated directly opposite its entrance. Some of the paving stones of the courtyard bore incised drawings of humans and animals (figure 4), as did some potsherds of this period. The pottery itself is of several different styles which are paralleled at other sites in different parts of Palestine. Some of it is characteristic of the Megiddo area, such as the grey-burnished 'Esdraelon Ware' and vessels with a striped or network pattern of decoration in brown, red or yellow ('grain wash'). Another type, with red burnish, occurs all over Palestine, including the important settlement at Jericho, while a further group belongs to the so-called 'Ghassulian' culture, which was for a time dominant in southern Palestine, including En-Gedi, where there was a shrine very similar to that described above. To deduce tribal movements from these varied contacts would be hazardous, but they suggest that Megiddo was at this time a place where a variety of cultural traditions were

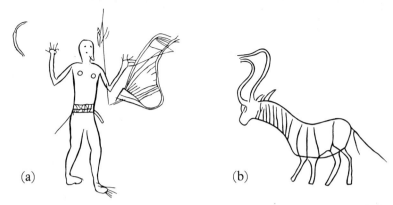

(a)   (b)

Figure 4 Drawings of (a) harpist and (b) horned animal incised on stones from the
courtyard of the Chalcolithic shrine (Stratum XIX). (*Megiddo II*, plate 273.5
and 276.12)

known, whether that came about through mixing of populations, trade or a
combination of the two. In one respect Megiddo so far stands somewhat apart
from the other Chalcolithic settlements: there is very little evidence of the use
of metal.

The Chalcolithic village may be dated approximately to the second half of
the fourth millennium BC: radiocarbon dates for Tomb A94 at Jericho, where
the red-burnished pottery was found, support this dating. There are signs,
both at Megiddo and elsewhere, that the Chalcolithic material culture continued to exist side-by-side with the new technical developments which mark
the beginning of the Early Bronze Age. Indeed, according to Kathleen
Kenyon's re-evaluation of the American excavation report, the village character of the settlement also remained unaltered in the first centuries of the third
millennium. The massive circuit wall at the edge of the mound, which the
excavators regarded as a city wall of Stratum XVIII (EB I), was interpreted by
her as a retaining wall to support the terrace on which the large buildings of
Strata XVII–XVI (EB II–III) were constructed, perhaps *c*.2700 BC. Two
other large walls which join this wall are probably also part of this system of
terracing. On this view the first Early Bronze Age settlement is represented in
the excavated areas only by a few small buildings shown on the plan of Stratum XVIII and some contemporary remains on the lower slopes.

Even in the small area excavated the change from this modest settlement to
the grand scale of the structures of Strata XVII-XVI is very apparent, and we
may legitimately speak of it as a process of urbanisation. The terracing operations already referred to presuppose the availability of a large labour force
and a substantial economic surplus, and this surely points to the rise of a complex and hierarchical structure within the population. On the new terrace a
large building was constructed (3177), with a complicated layout of rooms and

Plate 4   Round altar of Early Bronze Age II (G. I. Davies)

courts and a stone-built drainage system of which a part has survived. The
building is precisely aligned on the edges of what we have taken to be the
retaining walls beneath. Between this building and some smaller buildings to
the west there is a sharp rise in the floor level of about two metres, which probably indicates that a terrace wall also originally stood between them, although
the excavators found only the remains of later walls here.

On the presumed higher terrace, behind the small buildings, stood a circular structure, which is still visible today, some eight metres in diameter and
one and a half metres high, with a flight of steps leading up to the top on the
south-east side (4017 – see plate 4). An enclosure wall was built around it, with
an entrance apparently on the south-east. Within this wall there were large
quantities of animal bones and broken pottery. This, together with the enclosure wall and the steps, identifies the structure as an open-air altar on
which sacrifices were offered. There were very likely other cultic buildings in
the vicinity at this time, just as there were later (see pp. 30–33), but the excavation was too restricted at this depth to expose them. Possibly the small
rooms near the presumed upper terrace-wall were part of a temple precinct; at
any rate the entrance to the altar enclosure was from this side. On the south
side of the altar a street about one and a half metres wide led towards the
centre of the city and some rectangular rooms were uncovered on each side of

28

Plate 5   Copper 'ceremonial sword' of Stratum XVIII (*Megiddo II*, plate 283.1)

it, though not enough to determine the plan and character of the buildings to which they belonged. Occupation also continued on the lower slopes till the end of the EB III period and remains of buildings were found here, as well as burials in caves and rock-cut chambers. From the later part of this period burials also began to be made within the city itself, but the total number of burials so far discovered from the Early Bronze Age is small, given the length of the period and the size of the town.

The pottery associated with Strata XVIII–XVI includes typical Early Bronze Age forms such as hole-mouth jars, stump-based jars and flat platters with low rims, and it reflects marked improvements in the technique of manufacture as compared with the pottery of the Chalcolithic period. The clay was better prepared, a primitive wheel began to be used and the use of a closed kiln made for higher temperatures and more even firing. The other small finds indicate that alongside artefacts of bone, flint and basalt, the Early Bronze Age inhabitants of Megiddo used copper tools and weapons. They included a chisel, a spatula, two pins, a socketed spearhead and what the excavators described as 'a ceremonial sword(?)' (plate 5). Although no axeheads were found, there were two moulds for their manufacture, one made of baked clay and the other of limestone. Also worthy of note are over a dozen crudely made animal figurines of clay, apparently representing cattle. Surprisingly little of a distinctive type of burnished pottery of northern origin ('Khirbet Kerak ware') has been found at Megiddo, compared with the quantities known from EB III levels at neighbouring sites such as Afula, Beth-shean and Khirbet Kerak itself. This has led some archaeologists to suppose that Megiddo was abandoned early in the EB III period or, alternatively, that it was for a time a centre of Egyptian influence in Canaan, opposed to the ambitions of those who used the 'Khirbet Kerak' pottery. Neither of these theories is likely to be correct. The pottery evidence as a whole suggests that Megiddo continued to be occupied to the end of EB III, but there is no evidence at present of Egyptian contacts there at this time. At most it may be justified to see Megiddo as having remained largely aloof from the cultural and perhaps mercantile developments represented by the new pottery.

Megiddo in a time of Economic and Political Decline

The period between the end of EB III and the beginning of the Middle Bronze Age (c.2300–2000) has been, as far as the whole of Palestine is concerned, a source of particularly severe disagreement among scholars for over a generation. This is reflected in the fact that it is currently referred to by no less than three different names – 'Middle Bronze Age I', 'Intermediate Early Bronze-Middle Bronze Period' and, with growing acceptance, 'Early Bronze Age IV' – which express different views about its connections (or lack of them) with the periods which precede and follow it. But scholars also disagree over whether its beginning and end were due to the arrival of a new population group or groups or, for example, to climatic changes; and over how (if at all) it is to be sub-divided chronologically. Here again I shall refrain from any account of the more general issues and concentrate on the evidence from Megiddo itself, which in certain respects contrasts with that from other sites. Whereas this period is elsewhere represented chiefly by tombs which contain pottery of much poorer quality than that of Early Bronze Age I–III (suggesting to some a nomadic population at this time), at Megiddo some impressive buildings, including temples, are found on the tell and the pottery includes some very fine decorated wares alongside the coarser types. This would seem to imply that Megiddo was less seriously affected than other places by the factors, whatever they were, which brought about this period of widespread political and economic decline.

In the western part of Area BB the buildings of Early Bronze Age II–III were replaced in Stratum XV by three more or less identical buildings, still visible on the site, which consisted of a rectangular room with an open area in front flanked by side walls which probably formed a porch (figure 5). There is some evidence that each also had a side room, perhaps for storage. They adjoin in the north and west the round stone altar built in Stratum XVII (above, p. 28), which already suggests a religious function for them, and this is confirmed by the rectangular platforms against the rear walls, opposite the entrance, of two of them (plate 6). These temples seem to represent a new development of the sacred area, but the ground beneath them has not yet been fully excavated, so that it must remain uncertain whether they were preceded by earlier temples. A few objects which could have been connected with the cult were found, but none which defines its character at all clearly.

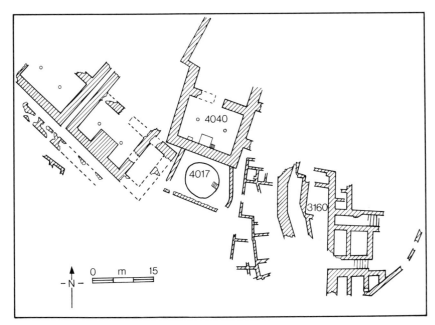

Figure 5 The Early Bronze IV temples and the 'staircase-building' (3160) to the east. The 'twin temples' are to the west of Temple 4040. (Andrew Brown; based on *Megiddo II*, figures 393–5)

The two westerly temples stand side-by-side, with parallel walls, and were undoubtedly built at the same time, perhaps for a god and his consort. Behind them is a thick wall, which may have surrounded the sacred precinct. The excavators' report gives no indication that the third temple (4040) was of a different date and the similar floor-levels of all three would support the view that they were all built at the same time. However, the third temple is oriented more to the north than the other two and actually obstructs the approach to the central temple. Kenyon therefore suggested that the two 'twin' temples were built first and were then replaced by the third temple. Her view has not gone unchallenged, and more evidence will be needed to resolve the issue conclusively. On the other hand the attribution of all three temples to Early Bronze IV (as I shall call this period) still seems the most likely view. It has been argued that they were built in EB III, but on very flimsy evidence. The pottery found in and around the temples is a mixture of EB II–III, EB IV and Middle Bronze I. The MB I pottery is almost entirely from tombs dug down from a later floor-level and can be disregarded. It is clear that the temples were in use in EB IV (for further evidence of this in relation to Temple 4040, see below) and the few EB II–III pieces could easily be intrusive.

The temples (and altar 4017, which remained in use) were not the only structures ascribed to Stratum XV. To the south-east a terrace-wall was found and beyond it, built over Building 3177 of Strata XVII–XVI, was a structure incorporating two staircases ascending the mound from the direction of the city wall. By means of these, it has been conjectured, a splendid access was provided to the temple area above. It remains something of a problem that they appear to lead to the back of the temples – though there could perhaps have been a processional way that led round to the north side – and it may be that this staircase-building (to which some walls marked on the plans of Strata XVI and XIV seem to belong) is from a secondary phase of Strata XVII–XVI. Unfortunately no pottery was reported from it, so its date cannot be definitely fixed.

In the later stages of EB IV only Temple 4040 remained in use, and its character was greatly changed. The large round altar to the south of it was abolished and a pavement was built over it. On this pavement (which was mistakenly ascribed to Stratum XIIIB in the report) was found a small deposit of clearly EB IV pottery, including a curious lamp with seven interconnecting cups. This pavement formed a raised open area behind Temple 4040, which may have been used for outdoor rites connected with the worship there. Inside the greater part of the main cult room was filled with rubble, leaving only a small walled *cella* in the centre between the entrance and the platform at the

Plate 6   Temple 4040 of Early Bronze IV from the north-east (G. I. Davies)

rear. These two changes seem to point to a move from a cult with a strongly public character and a long tradition (the round altar) to a much more enclosed style of worship, in which perhaps only a few priests participated. The date of this rebuilding of the temple is indicated by the fact that in the north wall there was found a fenestrated axehead of a kind which is typical of EB IV. Outside the temple there are also signs of rebuilding of this quarter of the city. The ceremonial gateway to the east went out of use and was replaced by a complex of small rooms.

The EB IV pottery from the temple area on the tell is of a kind which has chiefly been found in contemporary deposits in southern Palestine, for example at Lachish and Tell Beit Mirsim. The pottery from the tombs on the south-eastern slopes, however, is quite different. There is general agreement that the pottery of one of these tombs, T. 1101B–1102 Lower, stands apart from the other tombs of this period by its proximity to the styles of earlier centuries. In addition this tomb is not of the same very finely-hewn type as the others. It must be from the very beginning of EB IV, before the new features began to appear. The main group of tombs are of the 'shaft grave' type, of which about twenty-five were excavated by the American expedition. Others exhibiting the same method of construction and precisely similar types of pottery had been found by Schumacher in an area 250–350 metres south-west of the area cleared by the Americans, which shows that the cemetery was much more extensive than is usually supposed.

The common characteristic of all these tombs is the vertical shaft, square or circular in cross-section, by which access was gained to the burial chamber or chambers (figure 6). The shaft was normally about two metres deep and in some cases footholds are preserved in the sides. About a third of the tombs have a horizontal passage leading from the foot of the shaft to one side of a rectangular chamber, which has entrances to smaller chambers at a slightly higher level on its other three sides. Others have a smaller number of chambers or a different layout. The continuation of the practice of multiple burial at Megiddo and (to a lesser extent) in the similar tombs at Beth-shean marks an interesting difference from the almost contemporary graves at Jericho, which generally contained only a single burial. From the finds it appears that the people buried in these tombs used two different styles of pottery (figure 7). One is generally hand-made and characterised by a red slip or paint decoration and large ledge-handles. Jugs with wide, deep mouths, lug-handled jars and small, squat cups are common types. This kind of pottery has been found at such sites as Beth-shean and Tiberias and also east of the Jordan at el-Husn, and it can be related in various ways to Early Bronze I–III pottery. Alongside this there is another style of much finer, decorated pottery whose origin appears to lie in Syria. This is wheel-made and of a grey ware which is dec-

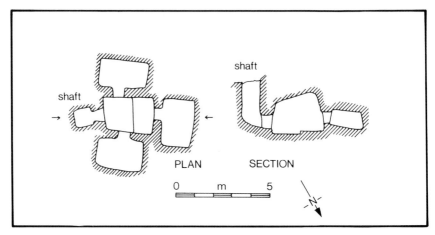

Figure 6 Plan of a four-chambered shaft tomb (T.878). (Andrew Brown; based on *Megiddo Tombs*, figure 42)

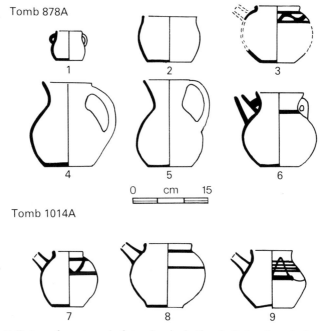

Figure 7 Pottery from two shaft tombs, including both hand-made (nos. 1 –2, 4–6) and 'grey ware' types (nos. 3, 7–9). (Andrew Brown; based on *Megiddo Tombs*, plates 20 and 22)

orated with yellowish bands, sometimes wavy, on the upper part of the vessel. Rounded cups and spouted jars ('teapots') are the most common types. While exact parallels to the decoration are few, two 'teapots' of the same shape and decoration were found at Yabrud, 60 km north-east of Damascus, and in general the shapes are so close to Syrian styles and so alien to Palestine that the Megiddo examples must be presumed to have come from Syria. Megiddo is by some way the most southerly of the sites at which this type of pottery has been found – a further pointer to its many contacts with the wider world. So far these types of pottery have not been found on the tell. At Hazor the decorated pottery was found in an area of dwellings, which suggests that evidence of related buildings may also be brought to light at Megiddo by further excavation on or around the tell. It is certainly hard to imagine that those who constructed such fine tombs for the dead did not also build houses for the living.

The mixture of locally-developed pottery styles with others of foreign origin may indicate that the group which buried its dead at Megiddo at this time was an indigenous group with trade links with inland Syria. It is possible, however, that they included families who were themselves immigrants from Syria and this seems to be confirmed by the burial customs. The regularity and excellence of the rock-cut chambers is unparalleled in the preceding period at Megiddo and the most telling comparisons are again with sites in central Syria such as Qatna. Burial practices are likely to have been conservative and it is reasonable to attribute the change to the arrival of new settlers. It is understandable that such newcomers should also employ the local pottery for everyday purposes.

In her widely-used textbook *Archaeology in the Holy Land* Kathleen Kenyon entitled the chapter which dealt with this period 'The Arrival of the Amorites'. 'Amorites' is a name used in the Old Testament to designate a people who lived in Canaan before the Israelites. Sometimes it appears to stand for the pre-Israelite population as a whole (e.g. Genesis 15:16), as an equivalent term to 'Canaanites', but elsewhere the Amorites are only one among several tribal groups who occupied the land in early times (e.g. Genesis 15:21). It was Kenyon's view that these Amorites were the direct descendants of newcomers who brought with them the material culture here under discussion. Emphasising its discontinuity from Early Bronze I–III, with its distinctive pottery and generally non-sedentary pattern of life, and its close links with Syria, she saw it as the more or less contemporary counterpart of the movement into Mesopotamia from the north-west of people who are variously called MAR.TU or Amurru in Babylonian texts. In these texts Amurru is sometimes an area in Syria, and so it seemed natural to suppose that it was from here that the biblical Amorites also came. Other archaeologists such as Nelson Glueck saw in this movement of people the historical context for the migration of Abraham and his family from Mesopotamia to Canaan (Genesis 12), and as a result it became commonplace to refer to this period as 'The Patriarchal Age'.

Recent research has cast doubt on these correlations between the Bible and archaeology in a number of ways. On the archaeological side, scholars are today much less ready than Kenyon was to attribute the EB IV material culture as a whole to invaders from the north and east. The very preference for the term 'EB IV' betokens a growing consensus that the inhabitants of Palestine at this time were, in the main, the descendants of those who had lived there for centuries past. Only a relatively small influx of newcomers is necessary to explain developments such as those which have been described above. On the other hand, both critical examination of the biblical text and more refined comparative studies have cast doubt on the view that the Hebrew patriarchs are to be seen as part of a great 'Amorite' migration. The parallels in customs cited by W. F. Albright and John Bright, for example, have proved in many cases not to be as close or as unique as was previously thought. It is now more generally accepted that the stories of the patriarchs are traditional literature to which many generations contributed, and as a result to associate these stories with one particular 'age' is less important than was once supposed.

Further reading

The primary evidence on which this chapter is based can be found in Loud, *Megiddo II* (Area BB), Engberg and Shipton, *Notes...*, Guy and Engberg, *Megiddo Tombs*, and Schumacher, *Tell el-Mutesellim I*, pp. 165–73 (tombs groups F and I): see p. 24 for publication details. On the archaeology and history of Palestine generally in this period see K. M. Kenyon, *Archaeology in the Holy Land*, 4th ed. (London and New York, 1979), pp. 43–147, and *The Cambridge Ancient History*, 3rd ed., I/1 (Cambridge, 1970), pp. 510–37, I/2 (Cambridge, 1971), pp. 208–37 and 567–94. Particular topics are dealt with by D. Ussishkin, 'The Ghassulian Shrine at En-Gedi', *Tel Aviv* 7(1980), 1–44; A. Ben-Tor, *Cylinder Seals of Third Millennium Palestine*, BASOR Supplement Series, 22 (Cambridge, Mass., 1978), pp. 101–9; I. Dunayevsky and A. Kempinski, *ZDPV* 89(1973), 161–87 (shrines); K. Kenyon, 'Some Notes on the Early and Middle Bronze Age Strata at Megiddo', *Eretz-Israel* 5(1958), 51*–60*; J. A. Callaway, 'New Perspectives on Early Bronze III in Canaan', in P. R. S. Moorey and P. J. Parr (eds), *Archaeology in the Levant. Essays for Kathleen Kenyon* (Warminster, 1978), pp. 46–58 (Egyptian involvement in Canaan); Kenyon, *Amorites and Canaanites*, Schweich Lectures for 1963 (London, 1966); E. Oren, *The Northern Cemetery of Beth-Shan* (Leiden, 1973); K. Prag, 'The Intermediate Early Bronze–Middle Bronze Age: An Interpretation of the Evidence from Transjordan, Syria and Lebanon', *Levant* 6(1974), 69–116 (also in *PEQ* 116(1984), 58–68); W. G. Dever, 'New Vistas on the EB IV ('MB I') Horizon in Syria-Palestine', *BASOR* 237(1980), 35–64 (includes surveys of the evidence and the scholarly discussion). On the 'Amorite' theory and the placing of the Hebrew patriarchs in this period see the chapters by W. G. Dever and W. M. Clark in J. H. Hayes and J. M. Miller (eds), *Israelite and Judaean History* (London, 1977).

4

Canaanite Megiddo

According to the biblical book of Judges Megiddo was one of the last Canaanite cities to fall into Israelite hands (1:27–8). In all probability, along with Jerusalem to the south and the other great cities of the plain and valley of Jezreel, it remained essentially Canaanite until the reign of David (c.1000 BC). Here Canaanite civilisation survived as both an inspiration and an enticement to the Israelite tribes and, while the pre-eminent position of Jerusalem as a transmitter of Canaanite culture is not to be denied, it is likely that the contribution of Megiddo and its neighbours to the development of the northern tribes was no less important. For this reason alone a thorough examination of the archaeological evidence from Megiddo in the second millennium BC is of particular interest and long overdue. But in addition the evidence which is available, while by no means complete or without problems of interpretation, is so impressive in both its quantity and its richness that even after nearly fifty years it is still virtually without an equal in the contribution which it has to make to our knowledge and understanding of the Canaanite civilisation in Palestine. Besides the architectural remains and the wide range of artefacts found especially in the tombs, there is a substantial corpus of written texts which help to illuminate the history of the city. These include a number of Egyptian inscriptions found at the site itself, some letters sent by the king of Megiddo to the Egyptian court and, most vivid of all, the account in the annals of Tuthmosis III of his siege of Megiddo c.1468 BC, which is sometimes referred to as 'the first recorded battle in history'.

In archaeological terms this chapter will be concerned with Megiddo in the Middle and Late Bronze Ages and the first part of the Iron Age. The transitions between these periods do not correspond to sharp cultural or political changes at Megiddo: they are not marked by evidence of violent destruction or abandonment and there is a strong element of continuity both in the architecture and in the artefacts, such as pottery. There are changes, for example in burial practice, which may represent the arrival of new elements in the population and altered political circumstances, but the general impression is of a stable society enjoying considerable prosperity and able to absorb a variety of new ideas without fundamental change. We may refer to it as 'Canaanite' on the basis of the biblical term used for its final stages, even though this name does not seem to have been generally used before the fifteenth century BC.

The evidence to be considered comes mainly from Strata XIII–VI of the American excavations, but also from some tombs on the slopes and certain of Schumacher's discoveries. In addition to Area BB in the east of the mound, the excavations in Area AA in the north now have much to contribute to our account, and to a lesser extent this is also true of Area CC in the south and Area DD in the north-east. The unsatisfactory analysis and recording of the stratification continue to pose problems, which are increased by the large numbers of burials within the city walls at this time and by disturbances due to building operations of both this and later periods, particularly in the eastern part of the mound. Kenyon, in an article published in 1969, endeavoured, by a classification of the pottery found in the tombs within the city, to establish a firmer basis for the understanding of its architectural development. But, strange as it may seem in view of her general emphasis on stratigraphy, her ideas about the sequence of pottery types (which she related to the tombs, but not the tell, at Jericho) were based on *a priori* assumptions about the relationship between different groups and come into conflict at various points with the actual structural sequence on the tell. Some of her conclusions still seem valid, but the material is in need of a fresh evaluation which would combine Kenyon's skill in salvaging useful information from old excavation reports with the growing data from more recent excavations of stratified deposits from the second millennium, such as those at Aphek (Ras el-Ain), Gezer and Lachish.

The renewal of city life (Middle Bronze I)

In Middle Bronze Age I Temple 4040 in the eastern area of excavation, with some rooms adjoining it on the south, continued in use, thus providing an indication of some continuity, in religion at least, with the preceding era. It was surrounded on all sides by burials of the period, which had been dug into the ruins of earlier houses. Kenyon was inclined to think that this was the full extent of the remains from Middle Bronze I (her phase J), but it is also necessary to attribute to this period some structures in the vicinity of the temple (shown on the plans of Strata XIIIB and XIIIA), which she dated to the beginning of Middle Bronze II. Even more impressive evidence comes from Area AA. Here the plan of Stratum XIII (figure 8) shows a brick-built city gate with a stepped approach from outside the city ascending parallel to the wall and then turning at right angles to pass through a gatehouse. The city wall itself is 1.80 metres thick, with buttresses on its outer side and a limestone glacis on

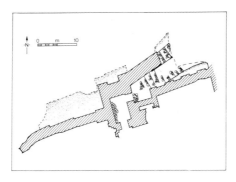

Figure 8 City wall and gate in Area AA (Stratum XIII), probably built *c.* 1850 BC. The dotted areas outside the wall mark the glacis. (Andrew Brown; based on *Megiddo II*, figure 378)

the slope of the mound beneath. Built against the inside of the wall is a Middle Bronze I tomb (T.4112), which indicates a lower chronological limit for the fortifications here. Theoretically they could belong to an earlier period (even the Early Bronze Age has been suggested), but this is unlikely in view of the fact that they were certainly enlarged and reused in Middle Bronze II. There is a close resemblance between the buttresses here and those of the wall shown on the Stratum XIIIA plan of Area BB, and it seems likely that both are part of one and the same fortification system, belonging to a late phase of Middle Bronze I. The earlier phase(s), so far as we can tell (the excavations did not reach it in Area AA), was unfortified.

In several ways the beginning of the Middle Bronze Age represents a new departure in the material culture of Megiddo. As already indicated, burials become normal on the summit of the tell. The cemetery on the slopes contains only a few tombs from this period, but some more were found by Yadin in his excavations on the 'northern terrace'. The pottery is wholly wheel-made and characterised by a burnished dark red slip: both the decoration and some of the new forms which appear may be intended to recall metal prototypes. Perhaps most significant of all, it is at this time that bronze begins to replace copper as the material of tools and weapons, a change which presupposes both a technological step forward and wider trading connections giving access to tin, whose ultimate source, east of Mesopotamia, remains unknown. (In the early eighteenth century BC we have evidence in the Mari texts for the transfer of tin to Hazor and Laish (later Dan) in northern Palestine.) New forms of dagger (with a grooved blade) and axehead (with a notch, probably to aid binding to the haft) made from casts appear at this time. The evidence of Egyptian tomb-paintings, according to G. Posener, also suggests changes in the style of clothes and hair-dressing in Palestine about now. In general there is throughout the land a gradual reversion to the urban settlements typical of Early Bronze I–III, in contrast to most of what we know of EB IV. There is ample justification in these innovations for the terminology used by Kenyon, Dever and in the present book, which makes the Middle Bronze Age begin at this point. They are not short-lived changes, but affect the local life-style for centuries to come.

But are they to be attributed to a new population becoming dominant at Megiddo and elsewhere? Or can they be explained by reference to factors like climatic change, the development of trade and consequent greater prosperity? The former explanation has enjoyed considerable popularity, and the change in burial practice may be particularly significant. If it is accepted, the origin of the new population becomes a subject for investigation and there has been wide agreement that a source in Syria, whether on the coast (Kenyon) or inland (Dever) should be envisaged. More recently, as for other cultural changes, it has become fashionable to point out how the new forms could have evolved from corresponding features in the local culture in the preceding period, with or without the stimulus of new trading links (J. N. Tubb). Megiddo at first sight looks like a prime candidate for local development since, unlike many other sites, it was more or less continuously occupied through Early Bronze IV. Yet on further examination the contrast with what immediately preceded is no less here than it is at other sites, so that continuity of development is not at all obvious. One discipline that might have something to contribute to this discussion is physical anthropology, which is able in some cases to distinguish different racial types by their skeletal characteristics, especially skull shape. According to Aleš Hrdlicka, who examined the skulls found in the tombs on the south-eastern slopes at Megiddo, there was a clear distinction between those of the Early Bronze Age, which were of a 'Mediterranean' type, and those of the Middle and Late Bronze Ages, which were shorter and broader, approximating to the 'Alpine' type. Only two skulls, both fragmentary, were available for the Middle Bronze Age, but both came from a tomb of MB I date, so they cannot be attributed to the effect of some later migration.

However the new urban phase in Palestine came about, it quickly came into contact with the revived power of Middle Kingdom Egypt, to judge from the 'Execration Texts', which probably date from the latter part of the nineteenth century BC. Two collections have been found, one earlier than the other, which are inscribed respectively on bowls and small statuettes. In each case the objects were intended for ritual smashing as a way of invoking disaster on Egypt's enemies. The names in the two collections include many localities in Palestine and their rulers and appear to indicate that between the writing of

40

Plate 7   Part of an inscribed statuette of the Egyptian official Thuthotep, found in the
Late Bronze Age temple but to be dated *c.* 1900 BC (*Megiddo II*, plate 265)

the earlier and the later texts Palestine was being quite rapidly urbanised, with
individual city-states increasingly being governed by a single ruler. This corresponds well to the transition at Megiddo during Middle Bronze I from the
loose-knit first phase(s) to the well-fortified city of the later phase. In addition
the autobiography of one Khu-sebek reports a campaign of Sesostris III of
Egypt (*c.*1878–43) against the 'Asiatics', which reached 'a foreign country
whose name was Sekmem' (*ANET*, p. 230): this is probably Shechem in central Palestine. Megiddo itself seems not to be named in any of these texts, but
this could be due to the friendly relations which existed between it and the
Egyptian court. Evidence of such contacts exists in parts of three black stone
statuettes of a clearly Egyptian style (plate 7), which derive from this period
and later suffered the indignity of being built into the altar-platform of the
temple of Stratum VIIA at Megiddo (see below, p. 61). One of them bore a
hieroglyphic inscription which begins:

> An offering which the king gives (to) Khnum, Lord of the-Foreign-Country-of-the-
> God, that he may give an invocation-offering (consisting of) bread, beer, [cattle],
> fowl etc. to the *ka* of the [revered one], the Count, Controller of the Two Thrones,
> Overseer of Priests, Chief of Five, Royal Intimate, he who sees the mysteries of [the
> house of] the king and exalts the courtiers, the Great Overlord of [the Hare Nome]
> . . . [Thut]hotep, born to Si[t-Kheper-ke].

The titles are those of a high priest of the god Thoth and nomarch of a district
in central Egypt, who is known from his tomb-inscription at el-Bersheh to
have been a prominent official during the nineteenth century BC. The discovery of this inscription may imply that Thuthotep was stationed for a time

41

Plate 8   Middle Bronze Age II bone inlays (*Megiddo II*, plate 193.9)

at Megiddo, perhaps in some kind of ambassadorial role. A less specific indication (in terms of date) of Egyptian interest in Megiddo during Middle Bronze I may be provided by a scarab seal which is inscribed: 'Head of the bureau of the cattle census, Yufseneb'. This was found in a tomb of Middle Bronze II, but according to the Egyptologist J. A. Wilson both the name and the title are attested elsewhere only in the Egyptian Middle Kingdom, which corresponds closely in time to the Middle Bronze I period in Palestine. It may have been an heirloom, deriving ultimately from an Egyptian resident in Megiddo. On a less official level the Tale of Sinuhe (*ANET*, pp. 18–20) and the Satire on the Trades (*ANET*, p. 433) provide further evidence that Egyptian travellers were a not uncommon sight in Palestine at this time.

A City of Palaces and Kings (Middle Bronze II)

The transition from MB I to MB II is now thought to fall around the middle of the eighteenth century BC. It corresponds to a time when Egypt was entering the 'Second Intermediate Period', a period extending to the middle of the sixteenth century during which the power of the native Egyptian rulers was first divided among rival dynasties and then (*c.*1650) largely taken over by rulers of foreign origin who formed the Fifteenth Dynasty. These came to be known as the 'Hyksos' (Egyptian *ḥk³ ḫswt*), 'Rulers of foreign countries' (the term does not mean, as Josephus (following Manetho) thought, 'Shepherd Kings'). During this time of Egyptian weakness, from which no Egyptian texts referring to Palestine survive, the city-states of Palestine, and Megiddo among them, flourished as never before. It is common to refer to this as 'the Hyksos period' in Palestine, but this expression is best avoided, both because the

42

period only partly overlaps with the period of Hyksos rule in Egypt in the strict sense and because it implies that we know more than in fact we do about the political relationship between Egypt and Palestine at this time. According to the interpretation of the evidence given above, Megiddo had already been fortified in the later part of Middle Bronze Age I. Its defences were maintained and indeed strengthened in the following two centuries. In Area AA (Stratum XII) the gate described earlier now went out of use and a new city-wall was built over it. Soon afterwards there is evidence of a strengthening of the city-wall both here and in Area BB (where there was also a tower) by the construction against its outer face of an additional wall which doubled its thickness. Within the city too there are new buildings. Three adjoining houses were built against the city wall in Area AA, probably with a street in front of them running parallel to the wall (such a street was certainly in existence in Stratum X). Similar houses appear near the wall in Area BB (Stratum XII, Kenyon's phases M and N), with clear evidence of a street parallel to the wall.

Further to the west, beyond the site previously occupied by Temple 4040, the American expedition found part of a much more substantial building with walls 1.50–2.00 metres thick. This lay at the very edge of Schumacher's deep north–south trench and a fresh study of the plans drawn by Schumacher made it possible to recognise that it was the eastern wing of what Schumacher had termed the *Nordburg* or 'North Fortress'. This was an approximately rectangular building at least 35 metres long from north to south with rooms apparently arranged around a central court. Beneath it Schumacher had detected walls whose haphazard layout is reminiscent of the Middle Bronze I houses found nearby by the Americans. Very little work has been done on Schumacher's reports since the American excavations, but this correlation does provide an important clue for the interpretation of Schumacher's considerable finds in this area. Immediately to the south of the *Nordburg* and at virtually the same level lay a somewhat smaller complex of rooms which he called the *Mittelburg* ('Central Fortress'). Though less impressive in scale it is in some ways more interesting than the *Nordburg* because of some tombs underneath it which had survived intact and unopened, no doubt because of their subterranean location. Schumacher tells how the existence of one of the chambers was suspected from the hollow ring of a pick striking the stones, but was confirmed only when a stone was removed and a worker fell through the hole! Burial within the city walls and indeed below the floors of houses was common at Megiddo throughout the Middle Bronze Age, as it was at the neighbouring cities of Taanach and Afula, but tombs of the size and splendour of the largest of these were found nowhere else on the site, and there is therefore a strong presumption that, as Watzinger suggested in 1929, this was a

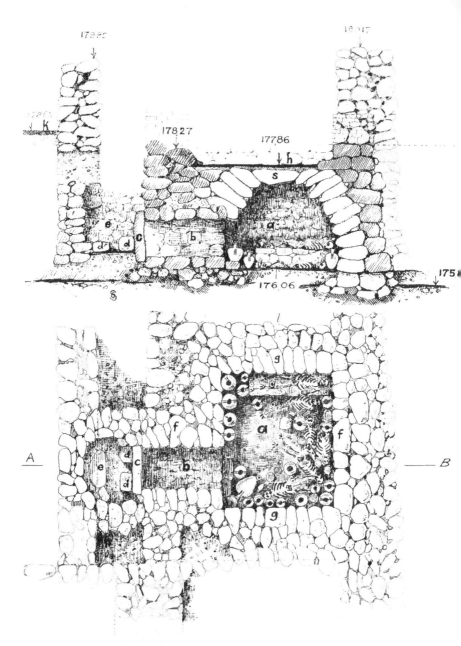

Figure 9 Plan and section of 'Burial Chamber I'. Note in the section (*above*) the crude vaulting of the roof of the underground chamber, and the skeletons and accompanying pottery marked on the plan (*below*). (G. Schumacher, *Tell el-Mutesellim I*, Tafel V)

mausoleum for a prince or king of Megiddo who had the *Nordburg* built as his palace.

One chamber ('Burial Chamber I') had internal dimensions of *c.* 2.60 metres by 2.15 metres and was covered by a vaulted stone roof showing a remarkably advanced technique for this early period (figure 9). According to Schumacher's calculations it was carrying a weight of 135 tons of overlying debris prior to his excavations without showing any signs of collapse. Entrance to the tomb was by a shaft descending from above on the east and a horizontal passage, which was closed at its outer end by a flat slab of limestone. Inside lay six undisturbed skeletons, five on the floor and one, a man, on a bench *c.* 40 cm high which extended along most of the north side of the chamber. With the latter were a variety of adornments, including several scarabs mounted in gold, dating from the Egyptian Middle Kingdom and therefore to be seen as heirlooms. Presumably this was the king or prince, while the other skeletons, two adult females, two adult males and one young male, belonged to members of his family or entourage. One of the women was laid beside the bench and may have been his wife. They were well supplied with provision for their journey into the afterlife, for no less than forty-two storage jars, large and small, were buried with them and in several of these were the remains of food, including cow and sheep bones and 'yellow remains of a milky liquid which had thickened into a hard mass', perhaps honey. In addition there were many bowls, platters and jugs, most of whose shapes point to a Middle Bronze II date for the burials. This is confirmed by the appearance of bone inlays, probably used to decorate small boxes, which were fashionable at Megiddo at just this time, as other burials on the tell and the slopes show (plate 8).

The other tomb beneath the *Mittelburg* ('Burial Chamber II') is much smaller (maximum internal dimensions 1.20 metres by 1.15 metres). The stonework is cruder but again the roof is vaulted, with a single very large stone acting as a keystone. It has a hole in the middle which could, if accessible from above, have been used to inspect the corpses and make further provisions of food for the deceased. The tomb contained the remains of twelve skeletons, piled on the southern part of the floor. Some wore bronze anklets, and a large storage jar and other vessels lay by each skull. Again there are some clear Middle Bronze II pottery types, which indicate when the burials began to be made, but the presence of some later forms shows that these tombs remained accessible down into Late Bronze Age I. Possibly gifts of food continued to be made for generations to the deceased. This grave is typical of many on the tell in the Middle Bronze Age, but none of the others seems to have contained as many as twelve skeletons. Perhaps it was the continuing existence of the palace, while the smaller surrounding houses were often being rebuilt, which led to such large numbers of burials being made in the same tomb.

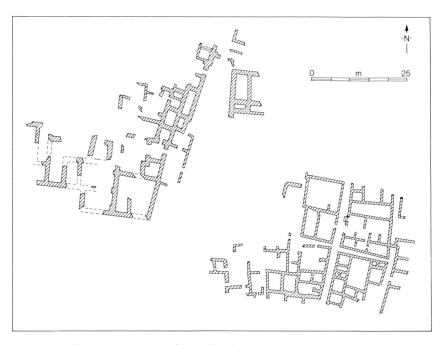

Figure 10   The eastern quarter of Megiddo (Stratum X) towards the end of the Middle
Bronze Age showing the extension to the palace on the left and the new
outer block of houses on the far right. (Andrew Brown; based on *Megiddo
II*, figure 400)

Returning to the discoveries made by the American expedition, where the
sequence of the structures is clearer, we can detect later in Middle Bronze Age
II a two-stage enlargement of the palatial building (Kenyon's phases O and P,
Strata XI–X). These alterations must reflect a growth in the power of the king
and, as a direct consequence, an expansion of his entourage. In the east of
Area BB the private houses continue, though the rooms are in several cases
larger, perhaps forming open courtyards, and the line of the city wall must
have been moved outwards, as a new block of houses was built over the wall
described earlier (figure 10). The outermost rooms of this block and the city
wall itself no longer survive in this area, having presumably collapsed through
erosion down the slope. The fortifications of this period are, however, preserved in Area AA and are particularly interesting (Stratum XI, Kenyon
phase AD). Here too the line of the wall was pushed out (by about eight
metres), though in this case the purpose seems not to have been to accommodate a larger population, as the newly incorporated area was not used to build
new houses: it may for a time have been an open space. What is more import-

ant about this new wall is the fact that it stands on a man-made earthen bank, which raised it some five metres above the existing slope of the mound. At Megiddo nothing similar had been undertaken since the Early Bronze Age (Stratum XVII–p. 27), but similar earthworks were constructed at many sites, such as Jericho, Shechem and Lachish, during Middle Bronze Age II and at Hazor the ramparts are particularly impressive, because they were built not on an already existing slope but on a flat surface. As elsewhere the artificial slope at Megiddo was protected by a glacis. Only the foundations of the wall itself survive, and they are peculiar in two respects. The wall is unusually narrow for a city wall (approximately 1.50 metres across), and every two metres or so there is a buttress on the inner side which projects about 1.50 metres. Undoubtedly these were intended to strengthen the otherwise very weak defences, and it is even possible that above ground level the space between the buttresses was filled with mud-bricks so as to make a wall of more regular thickness. Another possibility that merits consideration is that by this time Megiddo's strength was such or the danger of hostile attack so slight that its ruler thought that a token defensive wall was sufficient. At the eastern extremity of Area AA the wall abuts against a massive structure which appears to be the western half of a city gate.

The houses in Area AA at first show little change after the construction of the new wall, except that a structure connected with the presumed city gate encroaches on the easternmost house. But in the later part of Middle Bronze Age II first this house and its neighbour and then part of a third house are superseded by a large building of a quite new plan with a court at the centre (Strata X–IX, Kenyon's phases AF and AG). Its construction must be connected with a wholesale re-planning of this part of the city, as it is built over part of the city gate mentioned above. There continued to be important buildings on this site for some five hundred years (until Stratum VIIA). It is scarcely at this stage a royal palace, since that function seems more likely to have belonged to the *Nordburg* complex in the centre of the mound. Possibly its position in the area which was, because of the easy descent to the terrace below, usually the location of the main city gate can help to establish its significance, for it is likely that the city's military commander would have his headquarters near the city gate. The only difficulty with this is that it is not absolutely certain that there was a gate in this area at the time corresponding to Strata X–IX. As was noted above, the new plan abolished part of the city gate of the preceding period. It was the view of Loud that the strongly built gate a little to the east belonging to Sratum VIII may have already existed in Strata X–IX. But the alignment of this gate is different from that of the palace and the connection between them does not give the impression that they are parts of a defence system designed at one and the same time. Possibly, as Kenyon thought, the gateway at this stage lay a little higher up the mound beyond the area excavated and the approach to it passed along the east wall of the palace, which is of city-wall thickness, at least in Stratum IX. If this palace was actually in a more forward position than the city gate, this would of course add weight to the theory that it was connected with military activities.

The pottery from these levels (discounting intrusive pieces from later tombs) is of the types characteristic of the later part of the Middle Bronze Age in Palestine. The burnished red slip typical of MB I becomes less frequent. Special mention should be made of the hand-made but finely decorated pottery imported from Cyprus and Syria, which indicates the growing international trade links at this time. As is often the case, it is the tombs which have preserved some of the most precious items (plate 9). Gold jewellery was found still in place on some of the skeletons – headbands, ornate earrings, bracelets – as well as beads and small jars of alabaster and faience, which point to some commercial contact with Egypt. The Megiddo tombs bear witness to considerably greater wealth than the comtemporary tombs from inland Jericho: Megiddo's position ensured that it reaped an abundant harvest from trade as well as agriculture. Items of bronze are also numerous and include arrowheads, socketed spearheads, daggers, knife-blades, chisels, toggle-pins (now with ribbed or spiral decoration), needles and some crudely made figurines in human form. Further light is shed on everyday life at this time by a number of (unmarked) stone balance weights and a large set of twenty-six pierced clay loom weights found in the domestic quarter of Area BB. Some similar weights are stamped with impressions from a scarab seal: this is surprising, as they cannot have been worth much.

One subject on which there is comparatively little information available at present is the religion of Megiddo in the later part of the Middle Bronze Age. Given the tendency for sacred sites to persist through long periods, it would be expected that Temple 4040, which survived into Middle Bronze I, would have been immediately followed by a new temple. According to a number of scholars this did indeed happen, for they believe that Temple 2048 (which will be described later in the chapter: see pp. 60–3) or a predecessor of almost identical plan to it was built in the Middle Bronze Age, like a very similar temple at Shechem. The comparison between the two structures was already being made in the 1930s and in the Oriental Institute in Chicago there is an interesting letter written in 1939 by Ernst Sellin, the Austrian excavator of Shechem, in which he gave his view of the Shechem structure for the benefit of the American expedition. Despite the similarity of the plan, Loud felt compelled to ascribe Temple 2048 to the Late Bronze Age and Kenyon presented additional stratigraphical arguments in 1969 which strongly support this view. The foundations of Temple 2048 are separated from the ruins of Temple 4040 by

Plate 9   Gold and faience jewellery from tombs of the end of the Middle Bronze Age
and the beginning of the Late Bronze Age (*Megiddo II*, plate 225.2, 3, 6
and 7)

deposits between 1.5 and 2 metres thick. No evidence remains of any building
in this area from the intervening period. On the plan of Stratum XII a number
of upright stone slabs occupied the area south of the site of Temple 4040.
Another group of similar slabs at a higher level is shown on the Stratum IX
plan at the centre of the 'rubble pavements' which lie beneath the foundations
of the Late Bronze Age temple. There may have been an enclosed shrine here
of which all evidence has disappeared, but it is possible that the whole area
was occupied by an open-air sanctuary in which the worship centred on standing stones like those which the excavators recorded. It is worth recalling that
the line of much larger standing stones at Gezer has now been firmly dated to
the end of the Middle Bronze Age, and the Megiddo stones may represent a
similar kind of cult on a smaller scale. In a locus of Stratum X (2032), a short
distance to the east of the sacred area, a number of peculiar decorated vessels
were found which are probably of a cultic character, as well as what may be a
small bronze snake. This, together with deposits of animal bones mixed with
pottery typical of Strata X–IX, strongly suggests that a sacrificial cult was
practised here.

The 'Bichrome Ware' of Late Bronze Age I

The end of the Middle Bronze Age is conventionally placed *c*.1550 BC, close to
the time of the 'expulsion of the Hyksos' from Egypt. Culturally and architec-
turally the transition to the Late Bronze Age is barely discernible at Megiddo,
as there is considerable continuity with the preceding phase. Nor is there any
indication of disruption on the political level at this time. Nevertheless the
events of the mid-sixteenth century BC were in due course to be of great significance for the history of Palestine, and for Megiddo in particular, and it is
possible with hindsight to see that the first hundred years of the Late Bronze Age
were a period in which considerable upheavals were under way. Sharuhen in

49

the far south of Palestine was captured by Amosis, the founder of the Eighteenth Dynasty (*c*.1552–27 BC: see *ANET*, pp. 233–4) and several of his successors probably passed through Palestine, so that the destructions attested by archaeological evidence about this time at Hazor, Jericho, Lachish, Tell Beit Mirsim and Shechem could, in some cases at least, have been the result of Egyptian attacks. Literary evidence of such activity is however lacking. At Megiddo, the picture is one of continuing prosperity. The *Nordburg* and *Mittelburg* remained in existence. The blocks of houses in the south-east of Area BB were slightly modified (we follow here Kenyon's view that the very similar plans of this area in Strata IX, VIII and VIIB – apart from Temple 2048 – all relate to the late sixteenth and early fifteenth centuries). The situation in Area AA is very unclear and Kenyon's suggestion that the remains from this period were removed in an extensive rebuilding of this part of the city in the fourteenth century may well be correct. An alternative possibility is that the buildings of Stratum IX remained in existence through the first century of the Late Bronze Age.

The most distinctive feature of this rather obscure period is a very fine type of decorated pottery which has come to be known as 'Bichrome Ware'. This comprises mainly jugs, kraters and jars of a rather squat profile, finely made on the wheel from well-prepared clay (cf. figure 11). The decoration, which normally occupies the upper part of the vessel only, consists of a frieze bounded above and below by alternate bands of red and black paint. The frieze is generally divided into sections by vertical bands (often incorporating a geometrical design) and in each section there is a painting of a bird, a fish or some other kind of animal. In some cases the decoration is purely geometrical. At Megiddo this style of pottery has been found in Strata X, IX and VIII as well as in some tombs on the slopes, but the examples from Stratum X are all from tombs which (as is often the case) were dug into that level from above by the people of Stratum IX or later. Significant quantities of it also occur at Hazor and at Tell el-Ajjul south of Gaza, and some examples of it have been noted at many other sites, especially on the coast. Outside Palestine it has been found, for instance, at Ras Shamra (Ugarit), in Cyprus and in Egypt.

Not surprisingly, the origin of this fine pottery has been much discussed. Already in the 1930s it was being suggested that the close correspondence between its decorative motifs and those on some pottery found at Tell Billah in Mesopotamia justified its attribution to a Hurrian element in the population of Palestine, of whose presence there are clear indications in texts from the fifteenth and fourteenth centuries. This theory was given its fullest and most cogent expression by C. Epstein in 1966. Another view that was put forward before the Second World War was that the remarkable uniformity of the decoration pointed to its being the product of a single vase-painter working, it was suggested, at Tell el-Ajjul, from where it was exported widely in the Near East. In a modified form this view was also maintained by Ruth Amiran, who thought in terms of a school of painters (and potters) rather than a single individual and envisaged its location at 'one of the centres on the coast of Greater Canaan'. In the past ten years study of this question has been turned in an entirely new direction by the use of neutron activation analysis to determine the chemical composition of the clays out of which the bichrome ware is made. The result was to show that the great majority of the vessels from sites other than Megiddo were made of Cypriote clay and were presumably therefore produced in Cyprus itself, probably at Milia. Analysis of the pieces from

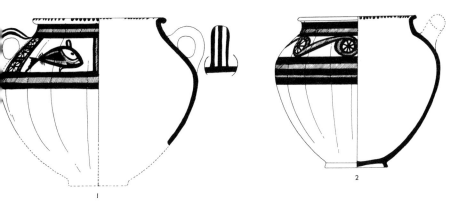

Figure 11 Bichrome pottery from Megiddo (*Megiddo II*, plate 53.1–2)

Megiddo showed, however, that while nine pieces were of Cypriote origin fourteen others were not, but had a chemical composition close to that of the local undecorated pottery from the site. Stylistic and material differences between the two groups could also be observed. It thus appears that the bichrome pottery was being made at or near to Megiddo, apparently to imitate the Cypriote originals and ensure that local potters benefited from the popularity of this presumably quite expensive ware.

'The capturing of Megiddo is the capturing of a thousand towns': the attack of Tuthmosis III

For the history of Megiddo in the fifteenth and fourteenth centuries BC we are in the unusual position of possessing written evidence in some quantity. By far the most extensive of these texts and from a historical point of view certainly the most important are a group of Egyptian inscriptions of Tuthmosis III (1490–1436) which recount the events of his first Asiatic campaign (c.1468 BC). The longest and most detailed of these inscriptions, the Annals inscribed on the walls of the temple of Amun at Karnak, declares that all Palestine north of the Egyptian garrison in Sharuhen, 'from Iursa(Tell Jemmeh?) to the outer ends of the earth' was in revolt (*ANET*, p. 235). The initiative for this 'revolt' apparently came from further north, for the force which confronted Tuthmosis was led by 'that wretched enemy of Kadesh', the king of Kadesh (Tell Nebi Mend) on the Orontes, and included not only rulers from Palestine who had previously been 'loyal' to Egypt (i.e. on good terms with her) but contingents from far-off kingdoms like Naharin, Kode and possibly Mitanni. Tuthmosis had succeeded to the throne as a boy, but for over twenty years he had been overshadowed by his step-mother Hatshepsut, who apparently died or fell from power shortly before this campaign. It is possible that the energetic young king seized control from her precisely so as to deal with a situation in Palestine which must have seemed increasingly threatening to Egyptian interests. There is little doubt that the organised hostility to Egypt was due to the movement into Palestine of Hurrian groups from the north with a chariot-owning aristocracy, who were established in a leading role in many cities in the fifteenth century.

The Annals briefly report Tuthmosis' progress to the frontier post of Tjaru (Sile), near modern El Kantara, on to Gaza and then up the coastal plain to Yehem, which must have been near Tell el-Asawir on the southern slopes of the Carmel ridge. A stele found at Armant suggests that Tuthmosis may have met with some opposition on his journey through the plain (*ANET*, p. 234; cf. pp. 22–3 and 242–3). At Yehem there took place the famous council of war. It was known by this time that the enemy had congregated at Megiddo, and Tuthmosis evidently intended to march through the Carmel hills by way of Wadi Ara, which was the normal and most direct route. His senior officers were, however, reluctant to go by 'this road which becomes so narrow' and urged instead that the army should follow one of two alternative routes, which came out at Taanach and somewhere north of Megiddo. The description of the 'narrow' road which they gave matches exactly the conditions in the northern part of the Wadi Ara pass, as was shown in detail by H. H. Nelson. The two alternative routes proposed by Tuthmosis' officers can also be identified with some certainty on the assumption that they offered a safer approach to Megiddo. The route which comes out at Taanach is probably one which passes round the south of the Carmel hills by way of the plain of Arrabeh and Jenin. This is a much more open route which was a popular alternative to Wadi Ara in the nineteenth century. The route 'to the north side of Djefti', which came out north of Megiddo, is likely to be the pass (like Wadi Ara a chalk valley)

52

which reached the plain of Esdraelon at Tell Keimun, some 14 km north of Megiddo. Militarily the advantage of both these routes was that they would allow the Egyptians to reach the open spaces of the plain at some distance from Megiddo and deploy their army in full strength before engaging the enemy. The only advantage of the more direct route would be surprise, but this could scarcely be relied upon. Nevertheless Tuthmosis stuck to his original choice, fearing (we are told by the court annalist) above all things that he might be thought a coward by his enemies, and announced that he would lead the army through the pass himself.

After a day spent making preparations the army set out on the march of some 20 km to Megiddo. It took two days to get the army through the pass and the annalist records, if the restoration of the text is correct, that they did not meet a single enemy soldier on their way. The alliance had drawn up its forces in the plain: '[their] southern wing was in Taanach, [while their] northern wing was on the south side . . .' (*ANET*, p. 236). Since the Armant stele says that the enemy were gathered at the mouth of the pass, the missing words at the end must have referred either to this (elsewhere it is called the Qina Valley) or, as seems more likely, to Megiddo itself. The king of Kadesh evidently did not know by what route the Egyptians were approaching and was guarding both the approach from the south-east and the exit from the pass. Tuthmosis was tempted to make an immediate attack, once the vanguard of his army was clear of the pass, but on this occasion he was persuaded to take the more cautious course and await the arrival of his whole army. As a result the battle was delayed until the next day (or even, if we take the date given in the Annals at face value, until the day after):

Year 23, 1st month of the third season, say 21, the day of the feast of the *true* new moon. Appearance of the king at dawn. Now a charge was laid upon the entire army to *pass by* . . . His majesty set forth in a chariot of fine gold, adorned with his accoutrements of combat, like Horus the Mighty of Arm, a lord of action like Montu, the Theban, while his father Amon made strong his arms. The southern wing of his majesty's army was at a hill south of [the] Qina [*brook*], and the northern wing was to the northwest of Megiddo, while his majesty was in their center, Amon being the protection of his person (in) the melee and the strength of [*Seth pervading*] his members. (*ANET*, p. 236)

The Egyptian army was spread out to the west and south of Megiddo, its left wing having apparently moved north into the hollow that separates the tell and the ridge to its south from the hills behind (see figure 12). It must be presumed that the enemy, seeing the danger of being cut off from Megiddo and anxious to prevent the city from falling into Egyptian hands, had fallen back on the slopes north of the Qina brook (Wadi el-Lejjun). This would have been an excellent defensive position, had it not been for the move north by the

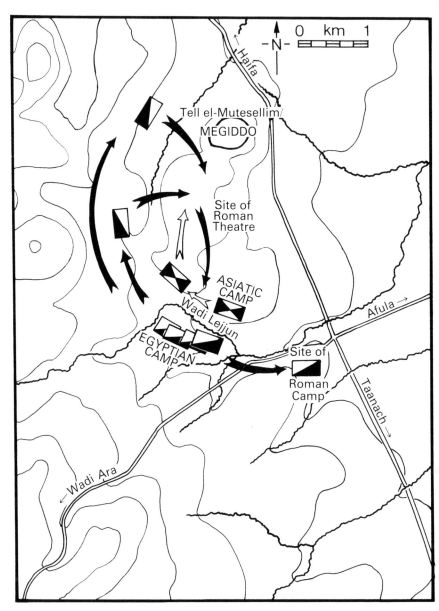

Figure 12 Map illustrating Tuthmosis III's battle at Megiddo. The dark arrows mark
Egyptian movements before and during the battle, the white arrows those
of the 'Asiatics'. (Andrew Brown; based on the Ordnance Survey 1:20 000
map of Palestine (1942), with permission, Crown copyright reserved)

Egyptian left wing, which threatened both encirclement and a direct assault on the city. The position of the enemy army is described in another inscription of Tuthmosis III, the Jebel Barkal stele, as 'in the Qina Valley *and away from it, in a tight spot*' (*ANET*, p. 238), which probably includes a reference to an attempt to extend the defensive line northwards as a counter to the Egyptian manoeuvre.

The Egyptian attack was probably directed against the enemy's right flank, where the approach was easier though still disadvantageous to the Egyptians. Few details of the attack were recorded:

> Thereupon his majesty prevailed over them at the head of his army. Then they saw his majesty prevailing over them, and they fled headlong [to] Megiddo with faces of fear. They abandoned their horses and their chariots of gold and silver, so that someone might draw them (up) into this town by *hoisting* on their garments. Now the people had shut this town against them, (but) they [let down] garments to *hoist* them up into this town. (*ANET*, p. 236)

The annalist is critical of the sequel: the Egyptians missed the opportunity to follow up their success with an immediate assault on Megiddo itself, because they were distracted by the booty and prisoners which awaited them in the enemy camp. As a result Tuthmosis had to make preparations for a siege. A moat was dug around the city, a wooden stockade was built, sentries were posted, and the Egyptians waited. It is evidence of the strength of Megiddo's fortifications and its supplies of food and water that it was able to hold out for seven months (as the Jebel Barkal stele tells us) before surrendering. The only archaeological evidence of the defences so far identified with any probability is the 2–3 metre wall of Stratum IX in Area AA, which may still have been in use, but further study of the numerous cuts which Schumacher made through the slopes of the tell, where he found a succession of city walls, may add to this. It is also still unclear how the population secured access to water during the siege, as the protected approaches to water supplies so far excavated are all of a much later date. It is possible that the approach to a water source whose existence is conjectured below (pp. 71–2) for the eleventh-century city was already in use in the fifteenth century.

There are some difficulties in reconciling the accounts of the surrender and subsequent events in the different accounts which have survived, and it seems likely that the Annals refer in part to later measures designed to establish Egyptian control over Palestine. The list of booty, however, must relate to the original battle:

> [List of the booty which his majesty's army carried off from the town of] Megiddo: 340 living prisoners and 83 hands; 2,041 horses, 191 foals, 6 stallions, and . . . colts; 1 chariot worked with gold, with a *body* of gold, belonging to that enemy, [*1*]

fine chariot worked with gold belonging to the Prince of [*Megiddo*] . . ., and 892
chariots of his wretched army – total: 924; 1 fine bronze coat of mail belonging to
that enemy, [*1*] fine bronze coat of mail belonging to the Prince of Meg[iddo, and]
200 [*leather*] coats of mail belonging to his wretched army; 502 bows; and 7 poles
of *meru*-wood, worked with silver, of the tent of that enemy. (*ANET*, p. 237)

Other figures most probably refer to provisions gathered from the surrounding country during the siege:

Now the army [of his majesty] carried off [*cattle*] . . .: 387 . . ., 1,929 cows, 2,000
goats, and 20,500 sheep. . . . Now the fields were made into arable plots and assigned to inspectors of the palace – life, prosperity, health! – in order to reap their
harvest. List of the harvest which his majesty carried off from the Megiddo acres:
207,300 [+x] sacks of wheat, apart from what was cut as forage by his majesty's
army, . . . (*ANET*, pp. 237–8)

These figures give some indication of the vast agricultural resources of
Megiddo, based on successful exploitation of both the plain to the east and the
hills behind, and presumably on effective political control over much of the
surrounding region, of which we shall gain further glimpses from the Amarna
correspondence (below, pp. 59–60).

It is surprising, on first consideration, that there is little archaeological evidence of the successful siege of Megiddo by the Egyptians. In most of the
areas excavated there is no evidence of a destruction that can be dated to the
early fifteenth century BC. A possible exception is the area of the *Nordburg* and
Mittelburg excavated by Schumacher, which we have suggested were parts of the
royal palace complex. Here there was evidence of destruction in the *Mittelburg*
above the burial-chambers described earlier, probably dating to the fifteenth century, and it would be possible to connect this with the events of the
siege. Tuthmosis III's inscriptions make no reference to any general burning
of Megiddo after its capture – it was, as we shall see, to serve as a faithful ally
of Egypt – but it would not be surprising if the king's palace had been singled
out for burning as a penalty for his leading role in the opposition to Egypt,
which is also evident in the placing of Megiddo second (after Kadesh) in the
list of the cities conquered by Tuthmosis (*ANET*, p. 243).

It was the view of Olga Tufnell and Kathleen Kenyon that after the siege
Megiddo remained unoccupied for nearly a century. That this conclusion,
which they drew from their study of the archaeological evidence, and
especially from the pottery, is incorrect is indicated by two texts from the
fifteenth century which also attest Megiddo's role at that time as an important
vassal of Egypt. One is an Egyptian papyrus, P. Hermitage 1116A, which
gives two almost identical lists of emissaries, mostly from northern Palestine,
who were supplied with provisions. In each case the representative from

Megiddo heads the list, which suggests that he had a position of leadership in these delegations. The emissaries are designated as *maryannu*, a word of Indo-Aryan origin which refers to the Hurrian aristocracy who fought in chariots. Occurrences of this word and Hurrian and Indo-Aryan personal names indicate that in the fifteenth and fourteenth centuries BC an alien ruling class had gained power in many of the cities of southern Syria and Palestine. The other text is a cuneiform letter found at the neighbouring site of Taanach (which is also mentioned in P. Hermitage 1116A) in excavations at the beginning of this century. This letter (Taanach no. 5) was written by an Egyptian official (or king?) called Amenophis to Rewašša, who was probably the king of Taanach, and it instructs him to send a party of charioteers (presumably *maryannu*), some horses, an additional gift and some prisoners to Amenophis at Megiddo by the next day. This must mean that Amenophis himself was already at Megiddo and probably implies that Megiddo was at this time the centre of Egyptian administration in northern Palestine.

The next strata on the tell, Stratum VIII in Areas AA and DD and Stratum VIIA in Area BB, must therefore belong to the fifteenth century, and not the fourteenth century, as Kenyon thought. In these levels the practice of burial within the city, which had been prevalent since the beginning of the Middle Bronze Age, suddenly ceases, and in all the areas there is evidence of new structures on a grander scale than before. The palace in Area AA, first built in the Middle Bronze Age, was enlarged still further and was surrounded by walls two metres thick on all sides (figure 13). In the south it apparently extended beyond the limits of the excavation area. A new large court, 20 metres by 11 metres, lay at its centre, with another smaller court to the south-west. Between the two courts was a small room that was probably used for bathing. The floor was covered with sea-shells set in lime-plaster and at the centre was a shallow basin of basalt, which was connected to a drain. Two similar but smaller shell pavements, one of them built over a drain, were found by Flinders Petrie at the entrances of buildings at Tell el-Ajjul. Something of the wealth of Megiddo at this time can be seen from a hoard of ivory and gold which was found under the floor of one room of this palace. To its east and a little lower down the slope was a large city-gate, the lower courses of which are still visible to the right of the main approach to the summit of the mound. The walls were faced with fine ashlar masonry, which appears at Megiddo for the first time in this period, but behind the facing was a core of rubble and earth. Some of the lower approach, paved with stones and supported by retaining walls was also found. Inside the gate was an open area paved with lime plaster and from it a flight of basalt steps (of which parts of six were found) led up to the level of the palace above. On the other side of these steps was another large building, but most of it was destroyed by the foundations of later structures. Beneath

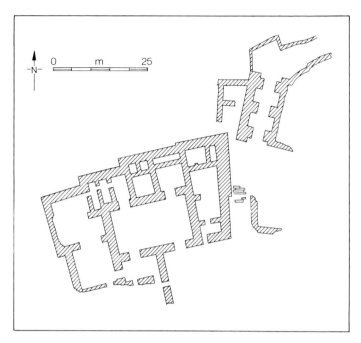

Figure 13 Fortress and city gate of the fifteenth century BC (Stratum VIII). The outer
approach to the city is at upper right. (Andrew Brown; based on *Megiddo
II*, figure 382)

ground level a drainage system carried excess water from the street and the
roofs of the adjacent buildings to the outside of the city.

The excavations in Area DD exposed part of yet another large building of
Stratum VIII about 50 metres to the east of the gate. Again there was a large
court at the centre, 15 metres by 11 metres in this case, with some features
including a small mud-brick platform coated with lime-plaster (an altar?),
which suggest that it may have been part of a shrine. In Area BB the houses to
the south-east of the sacred area continued, with a generally similar plan to
before, but a building with a new, more regular plan and thicker walls (2090)
takes the place of one of the more easterly houses. Temple 2048 belongs, it
seems, to a later stage of Stratum VIIA and will be dealt with in connection
with the Amarna age. Little that is coherent remains to the west of the sacred
area, as here too the foundations of later buildings have disturbed the deposits, but it seems that both the *Nordburg* and the *Mittelburg* were rebuilt after
Tuthmosis III's attack and they may have continued for a time to serve as the
royal palace.

Megiddo in the Amarna period

For developments in the following centuries Area BB offers little clear evidence, and it is chiefly to Areas AA and DD in the north that we must look for clues to the history and character of Megiddo down to its conquest by the Israelites around 1000 BC. In both areas the large buildings described above continue to exist with a slight raising of the floor level, but the palace west of the city gate is more compact and its walls are thinner in Strata VIIB and VIIA. This change appears to correspond approximately to the Amarna period in Egypt, when the rising power of the Hittites and subsequently the religious reforms of Amenophis IV or Akhenaten (1364–47) had led to a weakening of Egyptian power and a consequent loss of influence over affairs in the Levant. We are particularly well informed about Palestinian history at this time through the discovery, from 1887 onwards, of a diplomatic archive at Akhenaten's new capital city of Akhetaten, now (Tell) el-Amarna. The archive comprises over 350 texts written in cuneiform, of which the great majority are letters to the Pharaoh (in certain cases not Akhenaten but his father Amenophis III) from rulers of cities in Palestine and Syria. Some similar texts have been found at Palestinian sites, and at Megiddo a chance find by a shepherd in the 1950s brought to light part of a tablet on which was written a section of the Epic of Gilgamesh in cuneiform. This most likely derives from a scribal school at Megiddo, where apprentices practised the art of writing by copying out standard works of literature. Though brief, the fragment (which corresponds to part of Tablet VII of the late version) shows that the text of the Epic had not yet been fixed in its 'canonical' form. The use of cuneiform in correspondence between Canaanites and Egyptians is a valuable if surprising indication of the way in which Mesopotamian culture, for a time, extended its influence over Canaan, just as we know that it did further north at Ugarit and other Syrian cities.

Eight of the main archive of letters from el-Amarna were sent from Megiddo, most of them by Biridiya, who was apparently the king, or governor, of the city at the time (nos. 242–8, 365: nos. 244–5 are translated in *ANET*, p. 485). His name appears not to be Semitic and he was probably a member of that alien ruling class whose existence is already attested a century earlier, just like many of the other rulers in Palestine during the Amarna period. His letters are full of declarations of loyalty to Egypt: 'To the king my lord and my Sun say: Thus (says) Biridiya, the loyal servant of the king. At the two feet of the king my lord and my Sun seven times and seven times I fall down'. (no. 244.1–8) Megiddo was a place where Yašdata, the pro-Egyptian king of another city could find refuge when he was driven out by an uprising; and when the city of Shunem on the other side of the plain of Esdraelon had been abandoned, it was Biridiya (alone, he claims) who organised a labour-force to cultivate its fields, probably to send the produce to Egypt (nos. 248 and 365).

From several of the letters it is clear that Biridiya had had to contend with hostile forces himself after the withdrawal of an Egyptian force:

> Let the king know that, since the regular troops were withdrawn, Labaya has begun hostilities against me and we cannot shear the sheep(?) or (even) go out of the gate because of Labaya, since he learned about it. And you have (still) not given (us) regular troops. Behold, surely he is determined to capture Megiddo. But may the king hold his city and not let Labaya capture it, after it has been overcome by death and plague and dust . . . (no. 244.8–33).

The letter concludes with a renewed appeal for a garrison of a hundred Egyptian troops, to prevent the city from falling into Labaya's hands. Labaya is often mentioned in other letters from el-Amarna as a king or chief from Shechem (40 km south of Megiddo, near the modern town of Nablus), who is for ever intriguing against the rulers of other cities. He appears as the leader of people referred to as SA.GAZ or _ḫapiru_, a group about whose identity there has been much discussion since the Amarna letters were found, because many of their activities resemble closely those of the 'Hebrews' of the Old Testament. It has even been thought that the words _ḫapiru_ and 'Hebrew' ('_ibri_) might be related in origin, but this is not at all certain. In the Amarna letters the _ḫapiru_ appear as raiders whose forays threatened many cities in Palestine, but they are mentioned in many other texts from as far apart as Egypt and Mesopotamia.

Labaya's attempt to take Megiddo apparently failed, for another letter which is probably from Biridiya (no. 245) tells how he was captured and was about to be sent to Egypt by ship when his supporters bribed the king of Acco to release him. Biridiya made a further attempt to take him alive but he was killed by others before he and Yašdata could arrive. This was not the end of Biridiya's troubles: 'Let the king my lord know, behold two sons of Labaya have paid their silver to the SA.GAZ and to men of K[asi?]-land, who have come against me. So let the king take care of [his land]!' (no. 246. vs 4–11) The activities of Labaya's sons and the SA.GAZ again spread panic throughout Palestine and we do not know what the outcome was.

A Late Bronze Age Temple

An intriguing possibility arises from the fact that a new temple seems to have been built in the sacred precinct at Megiddo about this time. This is a rectangular building (Temple 2048), three successive phases of which are shown

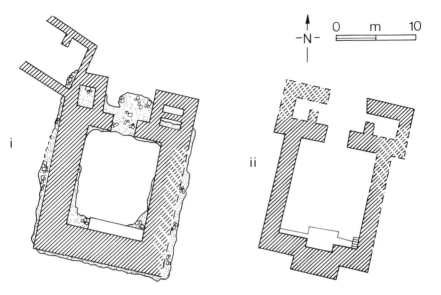

Figure 14 Plan of the two phases of Temple 2048. Broken lines indicate conjectural restorations. In the plan of phase (i) the outline of the underlying 'rubble pavements' is shown as a dotted area. (Andrew Brown; based on *Megiddo II*, figures 401, 403 and 404)

in the American report on the plans of Area BB for Strata VIII, VIIB and VIIA (figure 14). The Stratum VIII stonework is certainly (as the excavators recognised) foundational, so only two real stages of construction need to be distinguished. The single chamber, 11.5 metres by 9.6 metres, was surrounded by massive walls over three metres thick, with two wings, probably towers, flanking the entrance on the north side. Only a single floor level was identified, but rebuilding could be discerned in the raised platform at the inner end and in the main walls, which were reduced in thickness (figure 14). A flight of basalt steps led up to the later and higher platform and the drawings appear to show that it began from a higher floor level than the main one, which may have been overlooked by the excavators.

The period of construction of the temple is a matter of controversy. Two factors have been thought to favour a Middle Bronze Age date: its location and the existence of a very similar structure at Shechem (cf. pp. 48–9). The site which it occupies overlaps the eastern part of the Early Bronze IV temple (4040) which continued in use during the first part of the Middle Bronze Age. Given the general continuity of sacred sites, it is not likely (so it is argued) that a long gap would have elapsed between the abandonment of that temple and

61

the construction of Temple 2048. Moreover, the similar temple at Shechem, which was first discovered in the 1920s and is still (unlike Temple 2048 at Megiddo) visible at that site, has been shown by more recent excavations to have been built in the Middle Bronze Age. Since these two temples form such an unusual group, it is reasonable to suppose that they belong to the same period. Further support for this view is claimed to have been found in an examination of the eastern limits of the excavation area by archaeologists from the Hebrew University of Jerusalem in 1965, but some uncertainties remain in their interpretation of what they found. On the other hand – and this seems to be a decisive argument – Kenyon observed that the broken walls and floors around the site of Temple 2048 marked on the plans of Strata IX, VIII, VIIB and even VIIA indicate the demolition of parts of buildings from these periods in order to make room for its construction. Apparently a deep trench was dug into these levels and a series of 'rubble pavements' were laid in it to stabilise the ground beneath the heavy foundations of the temple. Its origin must be later than the initial phase of Stratum VIIA and perhaps therefore, on the dating followed here, falls in the fourteenth century BC. The finds reported from the temple and contemporary deposits nearby raise no difficulty for this view and could be as late as the twelfth century, when the temple went out of use, along with other major buildings in the city. Neither of the main arguments for a Middle Bronze Age date is conclusive. While, as we have already seen (p. 49), the area probably did retain its sacred character in the period between the abandonment of Temple 4040 and the building of Temple 2048, most of the evidence relating to this interval was dug out in preparation for the laying down of the 'rubble pavements'. It is only this constructional work which has made it appear as if there was a long break in the continuity of sacred buildings in this area. As for the resemblance to the temple at Shechem, it should first be noted that this temple continued to exist throughout the Late Bronze Age and was in fact rebuilt after a period of abandonment c.1450 BC. Evidently temples of this type remained in vogue. But why should such an unusual type of temple (for Palestine) suddenly have been built at Megiddo in the fourteenth century? The Amarna letters offer one possible explanation. As we have seen, it is clear from the latest letters that were sent to Akhenaten by Biridiya of Megiddo that he was under great pressure from the sons of Labaya at Shechem and had to plead with the Egyptians for support. If, as seems very likely, such support was not forthcoming or was to no avail and Megiddo came under the domination of Shechem, this would provide a setting in which the construction at Megiddo of a smaller version of the great 'fortress-temple' at Shechem would be quite understandable.

The finds from Temple 2048 clearly reflect its cultic function and make some interesting contributions to our knowledge of Canaanite religion. They

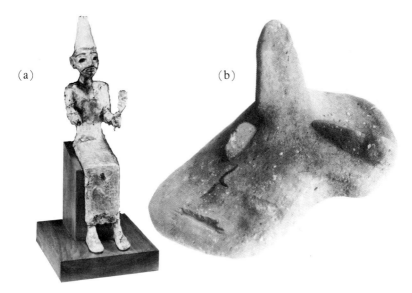

(a)

(b)

Plate 10 Cultic objects from Temple 2048: (a) bronze figurine of deity overlaid with gold (b) clay liver model for divination (*Megiddo II*, plate 238.30 and 255.1)

include, in addition to a range of jugs, bowls, flasks and lamps, several figurines of both bronze and clay. One of the bronze figurines, which was found in the destruction debris of the temple, had been coated with gold (plate 10(a)): It represents a seated figure with an oval crown, holding in its left hand a 'standard' which is embossed with a four-pointed star. There is little doubt that this figurine and the others represent the deity worshipped in the temple, but there is no clear evidence of his identity. The seated or enthroned position probably indicates that he was conceived of as a king, which would (in the light of our other knowledge of Canaanite religion) suggest an identification with either El or Baal. Another figurine, of clay, belongs to a well-known type of female figurine which is connected in some way with fertility rituals. Two clay models of animal livers found near the temple point to the practice of extispicy, the examination of the entrails of sacrificed animals, particularly the liver, to predict the future (Plate 10(b)). This is best known in the Near East from texts found in Mesopotamia, and the fact that a similar liver model from Hazor is inscribed with cuneiform omens shows that the Canaanite priests were familiar with this kind of Mesopotamian 'science'. Other objects probably used in the cult are crescent pendants in both gold and bronze and four small bronze cymbals. A collection of bronze objects buried beneath the floor may be a foundation-offering.

The ivory palace

It is Stratum VIIB which represents the Amarna period (or immediately post-Amarna) buildings in Areas AA and DD: as Kenyon pointed out, the correlation between the different areas made by the American excavators was not always accurate. The palace in Area AA was of more modest proportions now, but two features of it are of particular interest. One is a room in the north-west corner which could be approached both from the main courtyard and from some smaller rooms to the south: it has a flight of steps leading to a platform along one wall. The excavators suggested that it might be a household shrine, but in the absence of any distinctive small finds this is not certain. Another possibility is that it was an audience-chamber. The other interesting feature is a large painted 'clay shrine' (now exhibited in the Oriental Institute Museum in Chicago). It is not fully preserved, but was probably about a metre high and 40 cm square at the top. There is a frieze around its upper part, decorated with trees, wavy lines, crosses and squares, and one side shows four wild animals. Several of the designs are found on ordinary pottery of this period and it is possible that it is simply a piece of domestic furniture, without any cultic associations.

Among other small finds two seals, a cylinder seal of the Mitannian 'popular' type and a stamp seal with Hittite hieroglyphs on it, reflect the influence of the two major powers to the north of Palestine. These were found in Area CC in the south of the city, in an area from which three more cylinder seals were recorded in Stratum VIIA. A gold ring, found in a tomb on the lower slopes, bears an inscription in the proto-Canaanite script of the fourteenth or thirteenth century, which seems to read *ḥg lnštrby*, perhaps 'A ring(?) belonging to Nišitrabiya'. Finally we should note the growing popularity of amulets in this and the following strata. Small figurines of deities, animals, symbols such as the sacred eye and even parts of the human body had long been in use in Egypt as a protection against evil, but at Megiddo at least they are rare before the final century of the Late Bronze Age.

The palace of Stratum VIIB evidently suffered a catastrophe (perhaps an earthquake), as both the courtyard and the room with the shell pavement (which had continued in use) were filled with debris from fallen walls, and the floor level of Stratum VIIA seems to have been a metre and a half higher. This destruction can be dated towards the end of the thirteenth century on the basis of the pottery. The evidence from Area DD to the east of the gate is very similar, and it is possible that the raising of the floor in Temple 2048 in Area BB took place at the same time. In all three areas the large buildings were rebuilt on essentially the same plan, which suggests that there was no break in occupation. The walls of the courtyard of the palace in Area AA were painted and traces of blue, green, red, yellow, black and white paint survived, but it was not possible for the excavators to make out any design. One important change in the layout of the palace was the addition of an underground cellar block of three rooms, one behind the other, built into earlier debris on the west side. This proved to be a treasure-house, and it contained a collection of ivories (many of them now on exhibition in Chicago) which give a rare insight into the artistic and technical skills of the age, as well as casting some light on more mundane practices such as board games. Fortunately one piece, a pen-case that had belonged to an Egyptian royal official, is inscribed with the name of Pharaoh Rameses III (*c*.1184–53), which provides an upper limit both for the destruction of Stratum VIIA and for the completion of this collection: neither can be dated much before the middle of the twelfth century BC. Not that all the pieces need be as late as this, for such a collection could well be put together over a period of generations, and one of the pieces certainly seems to be at least a century older.

The ivories (382 pieces in all, though some are very small) represent several different kinds of workmanship. Some bear incised designs, while others are carved in high or low relief and yet others are in openwork in combination with one or both of these techniques. They can be divided into four main categories according to the use to which they were originally put. A large group were intended for the ancient equivalent (whatever it was) of a lady's dressing-table. There are single and double combs, several kinds of bowls, probably for cosmetics, mirror handles, flasks, fan handles or fly swatters, and a square casket beautifully carved form a single piece of ivory (plate 11). All these were decorated, some with simple geometrical designs, others with scenes drawn from nature or mythology. Another major group consisted of plaques which were probably mounted on furniture as a means of decoration. The dowel holes and tenons by which they were fixed are often clearly visible. Some of these depict scenes from battle or everyday life as well as myth and nature. Five more pieces which have hieroglyphic inscriptions are probably to be assigned to this group. One of the inscriptions reads: '(Meat offerings?) for the *ka* of the singer of Ptah-South-of-his-Wall, Lord of "Life-of-the-two-lands", Great prince of Ashkelon, Kerker'. Two others mention the same person, who must have served the Egyptian god Ptah in one of his temples, probably at Ashkelon on the coast of southern Palestine. The inscriptions incidentally provide explicit evidence of the worship of an Egyptian deity in Canaan. A third category comprises boards and pieces for some well-known ancient games, the 'Game of Twenty Squares' and the 'Game of Fifty-Eight Holes' (or 'Dogs and Jackals') (plate 12). They seem to have been 'race games' and lots or dice of some kind would have been required, though none were reported at Megiddo by the excavators (unless this is the significance of some seventy

Plate 11 Ivory casket from Stratum VIIA hoard (G. Loud, *Megiddo Ivories*, no. 1a)

sheep *astragali* found in a tomb of Middle Bronze Age date). Finally there is a unique piece, a plaque only 10 cm square which shows a meeting between two kings in Hittite style standing under winged sun-discs and supported by the Hittite pantheon and, at the bottom, four bulls. R. D. Barnett has suggested that it is a record of a political treaty, either between the Hittites and another kingdom or between a Hittite king and his successor. It was customary for the gods to be cited as the witnesses of such treaties, so their presence is readily understandable. Historians of Near Eastern art have investigated the places of origin of the ivories and have concluded that examples of Mycenaean Greek and Syrian workmanship are present as well as purely Canaanite pieces.

With the ivories were many other precious objects, including pieces of gold jewellery and necklaces. Most probably the whole hoard represented the disposable wealth of the owner of the palace rather than objects that were still in regular use. This would account not only for their presence in an underground chamber and their mixed character but also for the fact that pieces of the same ivory carving were sometimes quite widely separated in the deposit.

Much of the pottery assigned to this phase has recently been shown (by Professor Trude Dothan) to belong to the preceding period, but several new types can be discerned and decoration with groups of horizontal and vertical bands of paint begins to appear, as well as some early Philistine wares. Professor

66

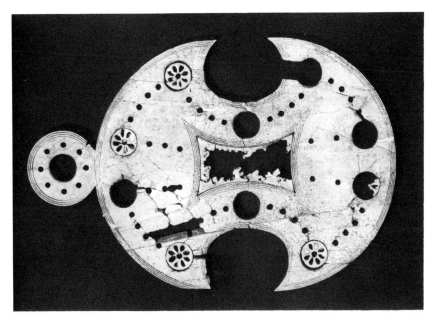

Plate 12 Ivory board for the 'Game of 58 Holes', from Stratum VIIA hoard (*Megiddo Ivories*, no. 221)

Dothan has published a number of Philistine sherds from the American excavations which were omitted from the publication. These fit well with the date suggested by the Rameses III cartouche and point to the growing influence of the Philistines at Megiddo at this time.

The Early Iron Age City: Canaanite, Philistine or Israelite?

Stratum VIIA marks the end of a long period of continuity in the town-plan of Megiddo. The palace in Area AA (where there is some evidence of burning in the northern rooms), the large building in Area DD and Temple 2048 were all abandoned and replaced by the small, poorly-built dwellings of Stratum VIB. The fact that so much treasure was left where it was in the palace vaults also implies that the previous rulers were driven out at this time. A date a little later than the time of Rameses III for this crisis may be required by an inscribed bronze statue-base found buried in debris of Stratum VIIB (plate 13). The hieroglyphic inscriptions indicate that it carried a statue of Rameses VI (*c.*1142–35). It was certainly not *in situ* where it was found, and it is most

67

Plate 13 Inscribed bronze statue base of Ramesses VI found buried in Stratum VIIB
(*Megiddo II*, figure 374)

likely that it was buried during or at the end of the period represented by Stratum VIIA. It must imply that even in the reign of Rameses VI Egyptian control was still effective at Megiddo, just as it was at the same time at
Beth-shean, but the treatment meted out to it equally points to the likelihood
of a repudiation of that control in his reign or soon afterwards.

It is not possible to say with any certainty who was responsible for the attack
soon after 1150 BC which brought about such a dramatic break in the history of
Megiddo. The neighbouring city of Taanach was apparently destroyed about
the same time and not reoccupied for over a century, so it was no isolated
occurrence. Some understanding of the possible causes of the upheaval can be
gained from a brief review of the general history of Palestine in the thirteenth
and twelfth centuries, as it may be reconstructed by a critical examination of
the textual evidence which is available. Egyptian control over Palestine was
re-established after the Amarna interlude by Sethos I (*c.*1304–1290) and
remained firm through most of the thirteenth century, although there is evidence of both Rameses II (*c.* 1290–1224) and Merneptah (*c.* 1224–04) having to
campaign against city-states who rejected their suzerainty. Rameses III still
had a 'frontier in Djahi (Syria-Palestine)' and collected 'dues of the land of
Djahi', and the Harris Papyrus lists among his benefactions to the gods the
building of a temple for Amon in 'Canaan', where non-Egyptians came to

bring their tribute (*ANET*, pp. 260, 262). After his reign, however, the texts cease to report either royal expeditions to Palestine or administrative activity there. Beth-shean apparently remained loyal to Egypt, and so did Megiddo for a short time, but these were now the exceptions rather than the rule. The idea that the fall of Megiddo VIIA may have been connected in some way with the decline of Egyptian power gains some support from this wider view.

The same texts of Merneptah and Rameses III which speak of their continuing hold on their Asiatic dependencies mention newcomers, whose growing power in the twelfth and eleventh centuries BC is also attested in the Bible. Merneptah's victory stele, dated in the fifth year of his reign (*c.*1220), makes the first (and so far only) reference to Israel in an Egyptian text (*ANET*, p. 378). It is likely that the 'Exodus group' of Israelites had arrived in Palestine shortly before this and that they gradually united with other groups of a similar character who had entered the land separately. Passages in the Old Testament such as Judges 1 (cf. Joshua 17:11–18) and 2 Samuel 2:8–9 show, contrary to the impression given by the book of Joshua, that at first the Israelite tribes were for the most part confined to the hill-country and Transjordan and that the chariot-forces of the lowland cities, which will have included Megiddo, were seen as a particular threat (Joshua 17:16). Archaeological evidence of new settlements from this period in Galilee, the central hills and the Negev can plausibly be associated with the Israelites. There is little indication in the Old Testament of open conflict between the Israelites and the Canaanite city-states from the initial period of settlement until the reign of David, but one major battle (deriving according to the text from a period of Canaanite domination of the tribes) is described in Judges 4 and 5, and it took place in the immediate vicinity of Megiddo (cf. 5:19 – 'in Taanach by the waters of Megiddo'). On the most likely reading of the text it must have taken place while Taanach was still occupied, which in the light of the archaeological evidence now seems to mean before the last quarter of the eleventh century. The biblical accounts, which consist of a victory song as well as a prose account, report the result as a crushing victory for the Israelites, so that it is certainly conceivable that it was followed up by a successful attack on the adjacent cities of Taanach and Megiddo. Nevertheless, the absence of any celebration of such an attack in the biblical accounts must make this hypothesis very unlikely. It has been argued, as we shall see in a moment, that the ensuing occupation at Megiddo (Stratum VIB) is an Israelite settlement, but even if it were it would not necessarily follow that it was the Israelites who destroyed the earlier city of Stratum VIIA: they might simply have occupied the ruined site after it had been destroyed by others who had no wish to settle there.

The other new group is referred to in the Bible as the Philistines (e.g. Joshua 13:2–3, Judges 3:3), but the Egyptian inscriptions show that the Philistines (*prst*) were only one of a number of groups which were known collectively to the Egyptians as 'Peoples of the Sea'. Some of these groups are already mentioned in the inscriptions of Merneptah, but it was in the eighth year of Rameses III's reign that they made a determined assault, by land and sea, on the Nile Delta (*ANET*, pp. 262–3). The Egyptians were able to repel this attack and carried the campaign into 'Djahi', but the Sea Peoples were eventually able to settle on the coast of Palestine. According to the Harris Papyrus this was done with the approval of the Pharaoh: 'I settled them in strongholds, bound in my name. Their military classes were as numerous as hundred-thousands. I assigned portions for them all with clothing and provisions from the treasuries and granaries every year.' (*ANET*, p. 262). Two of the cities occupied by the Philistines were long-standing centres of Egyptian influence in Canaan: Ashkelon and Gaza. Further to the north, at Dor, another group of the Sea Peoples, the Tjeker, had become dominant by the middle of the eleventh century, when they figure in the story of Wen-Amun (*ANET*, p. 26). Archaeological evidence also shows that the limits of Sea Peoples' settlements were not limited to the Pentapolis mentioned in the Bible, but extended as far north as Tell Qasileh and Aphek (Ras el-Ain) on the banks of the river Yarkon. The biblical references to the Philistines give no indication of their dependence on the Egyptians (except possibly in Genesis 10:13–14), and it was probably short-lived, in view of the Egyptians' loss of control over Palestine generally soon after the death of Rameses III. It is possible to identify a period of enlargement of Philistine domination towards the end of the twelfth century (as suggested by Professor Dothan) and the destruction of Megiddo VIIA and Taanach could easily be attributed to this, though if so the Philistines apparently did not take advantage of their success and colonise these sites, as Taanach was left unoccupied and very little Philistine pottery is reported from the following level (VIB) at Megiddo. At the present time much must remain obscure about the extent and pace of Philistine expansion in the lowland areas: the archaeological evidence is not fully clear, while the biblical sources are concerned with (generally later) conflicts between the Philistines and the Israelites but, understandably, not at all with the expansion of the former at the expense of the Canaanite city-states.

It is time to return to the description and interpretation of the archaeological evidence at Megiddo itself. The period of reoccupation (Stratum VIB) was clearly defined only in Areas AA and DD in the north of the mound and even here there are no complete building plans. The site of the earlier palace was occupied by much smaller buildings, although they are well-built for their size. There are no signs of any fortifications or a gate from this period. In several buildings rows of pillars are used instead of solid walls between some rooms: this is a characteristic found in later levels at Megiddo and at many other sites from the early Iron Age on. Stone-lined pits and ovens are also present in considerable numbers, confirming the domestic character of the buildings. In Areas BB and CC Strata VIB and VIA were not distinguished, but because of the distinctive type of mudbricks used in Stratum VIA (see below) it is sometimes possible to identify buildings belonging to a different town-plan as relics of the earlier phase. Some contemporary structures seem to have been found by Schumacher above the *Nordburg* (his 'Stratum III Upper'), including cisterns and basins linked by channels for separating out pure olive-oil. The pottery and small finds ascribed to this phase are meagre and undistinguished for the most part, even when one allows for the likelihood that some objects from the undivided Stratum VI in Areas BB and CC belong to Stratum VIB. There is an increasing tendency to decorate jugs and jars with groups of narrow horizontal bands and a few Philistine pieces occur, though not as many as in the following phase (VIA). Everything suggests that Stratum VIB represents a relatively brief period of occupation.

It was followed by a period in which a large, palatial building once again stood in Area AA, with a small city gate to the east of it and a continuous block of slighter rooms extending to the west. In Area DD too there are remains of some larger buildings once again. In both these cases the major buildings and parts of others are constructed out of an unusual kind of reddish, partially baked bricks on stone foundations. These building materials help to identify buildings of the same period in Areas BB and CC. In the south-east of the latter area it is also possible to recognise the structure excavated by Schumacher and called by him the 'Southern Gate' (squares S 10–11) and its plan can be completed from Schumacher's drawings. It was a rectangular structure 17 metres by 10 metres with walls a metre thick and openings in the south-east and north-west (the latter with an impressive stone threshold 2.50 metres wide). Another distinctive feature of the architecture of this period is the use of wooden posts to partition off sections of some houses, particularly in the south of the city. The spaces between them are very narrow, which suggests that they may have supported a screen of some kind.

There are signs that by this time, if not earlier, Megiddo had been provided with a protected access to a dependable water-supply. We are not referring here to the systems in the south-west of the mound discovered by the Chicago expedition. These were dated by the excavators to the twelfth century, but they are in fact later and they will be described in their proper place in the next chapter. We are concerned here with evidence of an earlier system which was recognised by R. S. Lamon in a depression near the city gate in the north, which can still be seen, and it can be supplemented by reference to the great depth (some eight metres) of 'sterile earth' encountered a little to the west in the southern part of Loud's test-trench. This is a filling of some kind and it could belong to a once open approach to a water channel deep under the tell. Overlying buildings of Stratum VB show that we are dealing with a hollow that was excavated not later than Stratum VIA, and it could be much older (cf. p. 55). Canaanite water-systems are already known at Gibeon and possibly at Jerusalem ('Warren's Shaft') and Gezer, and further excavations in this area could show that Megiddo also had one.

Large quantities of pottery were found in the rooms of the palace, as well as a variety of bronze objects and, just outside it on the west, three bundles of silver pieces wrapped in cloth. The silver is a mixture of earrings, pendants and such like with flat pieces, some of them bearing incised decoration, which have been cut from larger objects, perhaps cups or dishes. The excavators suggest that the silver had been prepared for melting down in a workshop; another possibility is that it represents a payment of some kind made to the ruler of Megiddo or a merchant. The most impressive metalwork came from the southern part of the city, where an unprecedented quantity of bronze jugs, bowls and strainers were found in a single locus (1739) along with the more common axeheads and spearheads. It is interesting that Schumacher also found a quantity of bronze objects in almost the same place. Evidently he penetrated the destruction debris of Stratum VI (A) – which is what he referred to as the *Brandschicht* or 'burnt layer' – and in it he reports finding a double axehead, two hoes, a javelin, four iron knifeblades and five bronze stands. The latter had a tripod support (in one case four legs) mounted on a ring base, and stood about 35 cm high. A flat bronze dish was mounted on top and in some cases this had clearly been used for burning something. The vertical part of one stand had been cast in the form of a naked female figure playing a double flute and decorative motifs are also evident elsewhere. The pottery of this period shows considerable Philistine influence, perhaps enough to establish that Megiddo had now (c.1100 BC) become a Philistine outpost. One Philistine jug is particularly noteworthy (figure 15), because the main frieze of its decoration depicts a scene of animals surrounding a lyre-player, a most unusual case of the portrayal of the human form by a Philistine painter. Similar scenes are known on seals from southeastern Turkey of a slightly earlier date, and it has been suggested that they are early representations of the Orpheus legend. Another possibility, proposed by B. Mazar, is that the animals are the subject of the musician's song. The presence of a White-Painted Cypriote bowl points to the beginnings of a recovery of wider trading relations.

In Area CC eight large storage jars (*pithoi*) of a type which is characteristic of this period ('collared-rim storage jars') were found, and Schumacher found two more a little to the east. These have often been regarded as distinctively Israelite in origin, because they are generally found at sites in the hill-country, where (as we have seen) the Israelite tribes first settled. Chiefly on the basis of

Figure 15 Frieze of Philistine jug found in Stratum VIA (*Megiddo II*, plate 76)

this evidence Y. Aharoni (following a suggestion first made, but later withdrawn, by W. F. Albright) has argued that Megiddo Stratum VI was an Israelite settlement. There are difficulties with this argument. First, the presence of these storage jars may be due to trade rather than the local population of Megiddo. Second, these jars seem rather insignificant alongside a great mass of pottery of a character quite different from what is usually found at Israelite sites. We have mentioned the Philistine influence, and note needs also to be taken of the increasing popularity of decoration with groups of horizontal bands of paint. Thirdly, it is by no means certain that this type of jar is distinctively Israelite, as examples have been found in areas well outside the limits of Israelite settlement, for example in Transjordan and in the Plains of Esdraelon and Acco. It is unfortunately not clear whether the loci in which the jars were found derive from Stratum VIB or VIA, and it is on that distinction that any reconstruction of the history of Megiddo in this period must rest.

As we have seen, the destruction of the city of Stratum VIIA was followed by a short-lived settlement of a village character, which in its turn was replaced by the flourishing city of Stratum VIA, with its palace and foreign contacts and highly developed metal industry. The settlement of Stratum VIB could conceivably be Israelite, though this cannot be proved. On the other hand, it is most improbable that this can be said of Stratum VIA, which has a much stronger claim to be regarded as Philistine. A telling argument is that Stratum VIA ends with a massive destruction, which was noted both by Schumacher and by more recent excavators. It is highly likely that this reflects campaigns of David against the Philistines, about which we are only imperfectly informed in the Bible (2 Samuel 5:17–25, 8:1). Megiddo was certainly in Israelite hands by the time of Solomon (1 Kings 4:12, 9:15). We are nowhere told how or when it was captured, but since it evidently did not form part of

73

the territory claimed by the Israelites at the time of Saul's death (2 Samuel 2:8–9: Jezreel here as elsewhere refers only to the city of that name, not the whole region), it can only have been conquered under David.

If Megiddo VIB was a short-lived Israelite settlement at the site, we may conjecture that it was a group from the tribe of Issachar that occupied it, for it was to Issachar that Megiddo and the other cities of the Jezreel plain and valley were originally assigned, according to Joshua 17:11. It appears from Genesis 49:14–15 that Issachar was forced to accept subjection to a Canaanite (or was it a Philistine?) overlord, a situation which might easily be reflected in the transition from Stratum VIB to VIA at Megiddo. The majority of the tribe seems subsequently to have been restricted to a more easterly region (Joshua 19:17–23—cf. 1 Kings 4:17), so that when the need still to conquer Megiddo is mentioned in Judges 1:27 (a document of the time of David or later) it is the powerful tribe of Manasseh which is said to be responsible for it (cf. Joshua 17:11).

Further reading

The primary evidence for these periods is found in *Megiddo II*, *Megiddo Tombs* and *Megiddo Ivories*; and in *Tell el-Mutesellim I*, pp. 11–23, 37–74, and *Tell el-Mutesellim II*, pp. 1–25 (the 'fortresses'). For fuller details of these volumes see p. 24 above. Further analysis is provided in Shipton, *Notes . . .*, and K M. Kenyon, 'The Middle and Late Bronze Age Strata at Megiddo', *Levant* 1 (1969), 25–60. For general accounts of the archaeology and history of Palestine in the second millennium see K. M. Kenyon, *Archaeology in the Holy Land*, 4th ed., pp. 148–232, and *The Cambridge Ancient History*, 3rd ed., II/1, pp. 77–116 and 526–56; and various authors in *The Cambridge Ancient History*, 3rd ed., II/2, pp. 98–116 (Amarna letters), 307–37, 359–78, 507–60.

For the MB I period there is now an excellent detailed study by P. Gerstenblith, *The Levant at the Beginning of the Middle Bronze Age*, ASOR Dissertation Series, 5 (Winona Lake, 1983), which has an extensive bibliography. She is able on pp. 23–8 to distinguish three or four MB I phases at Megiddo by a re-examination of the stratigraphy in Area BB and on p. 114 she discusses the date of the city wall ascribed here to MB I. She regards the date as not settled, but appears to incline towards a date early in MB II. Caution is certainly necessary, but I do not think that there are in fact any conclusive arguments to support a MB II date.

On particular topics see: O. Tufnell, 'The Middle Bronze Age Scarab-Seals from burials on the mound at Megiddo', *Levant* 5 (1973), 69–82; J. A. Wilson, 'The Egyptian Middle Kingdom at Megiddo', *AJSL* 58 (1941), 227–36 (the Thuthotep inscriptions); J. N. Tubb, 'The MB IIA Period in Palestine: Its Relationship with Syria and its Origin', *Levant* 15 (1983), 49–62; C. Epstein, *Palestinian Bichrome Ware* (Leiden, 1966); R. Amiran, *Ancient Pottery of the Holy Land* (Jerusalem, 1969); M. Artzy *et al.*, 'Imported and Local Bichrome Ware in Megiddo', *Levant* 10 (1978), 99–111 (on chemical analysis: cf. *Journal of the American Oriental Society* 93 (1973), 446–61); H. H. Nelson, *The Battle of Megiddo* (Chicago, 1913); W. F. Albright, 'A prince of Taanach in the Fifteenth Century BC', *BASOR* 94 (1944), 12–27; J. A. Knudtzon, *Die El-Amarna-Tafeln* (Leipzig, 1907–15); A. F. Rainey, *El-Amarna Tablets 359–379* (Neukirchen-Vluyn, 1970); Dunayevsky and Kempinski, *ZDPV* 89 (1973), 180–4 (Temple 2048); R. D. Barnett, *Ancient Ivories in the Middle East*, Qedem Monographs, 14 (Jerusalem, 1982), pp. 25–8; H. J. R. Murray, *History of Board Games other than Chess* (Oxford, 1952), pp. 12–23; T. Dothan, *The Philistines and their Material Culture* (Newhaven, London and Jerusalem, 1982), pp. 70–80; Y. Aharoni, 'New Aspects of the Israelite Occupation in the North', in J. A. Sanders (ed.), *Near Eastern Archaeology in the Twentieth Century*, Festschrift for Nelson Glueck (Garden City, 1970), pp. 254–67. I have dealt more fully with the twelfth and eleventh century remains in an article 'Megiddo in the Period of the Judges', which is to be published in a forthcoming issue of *Oudtestamentische Studien.*

Note on terminology and chronology

Disagreement over the nomenclature for the different archaeological periods continues to be a problem for the Middle Bronze Age. Those (like the Chicago expedition) who refer to the period described in the preceding chapter as 'Middle Bronze I' use the term 'Middle Bronze II' (subdivided into IIA and IIB–C) to cover what we, following Kenyon and Dever, have here called MB I and MB II. For the dates of Egyptian kings the chronology given in the revised edition of *The Cambridge Ancient History* is used up to the beginning of the New Kingdom, but for the Eighteenth and following dynasties it is about twelve years too high. We here follow the chronology worked out by E. Hornung, *Untersuchungen zur Chronologie und Geschichte des Neuen Reiches* (Wiesbaden, 1964), while recognising that a further lowering of the dates may soon be required: see M. L. Bierbrier, *The Late New Kingdom in Egypt* (Warminster, 1975).

5

Israelite Megiddo

Resettlement under David

Archaeological evidence of the reign of David has so far proved difficult to identify with any certainty, but some biblical passages suggest that in Jerusalem at least he did initiate some building, as is certainly to be expected (2 Samuel 5:9, 11; 1 Chronicles 11:8, 14:1). If our reasoning in the previous chapter is correct, Stratum VB at Megiddo will represent the reconstruction of the city under David, consequent upon its falling into Israelite hands. The remains of this stratum have been found in all the excavated areas, but they are most coherent in Area B (=CC) in the south of the mound. Even here much is unclear owing to the removal of stones by the builders of the following period and the deep foundations of their monumental buildings. Several blocks of rooms can be identified with a common orientation, but there is no clear street plan. Generally only the stone foundations of walls survive, but in a few places the mudbricks remain in place on top. The floors were of beaten earth, except for a few areas with rubble paving, which were probably open to the sky. Lime-plaster floors are notably absent in this phase. The overall impression is one of careful but unpretentious architecture. Only in Area DD was anything that might be a public building traced and the remains were both too few and too intertwined with those of the next phase for any deductions about its use to be possible. There is no evidence of any city wall, but it does seem likely that the approach road and the small gate in Area AA, which were attributed by the excavators to Stratum VA, belong here. This follows from the discussion of later structures in this area (below, pp. 90–2) and is also supported by the fact that a room (2161) contemporary with the approach road rests directly upon debris of Stratum VIA. This gate is too small to have served any defensive purpose and it may simply have marked the entrance to the city, where according to the Bible it was customary for legal and commercial transactions to be executed. Given our incomplete knowledge of the city plan at this stage, it is also possible that the houses on the perimeter of the mound formed a defensive ring, as was the case (in part) in the ensuing period at Megiddo and also at some other early Israelite settlements, for example in the Negev.

Plate 14 Bronze figurine of fighting god from the time of David (Stratum VB) (*Megiddo II*, plate 239.31)

Plate 15 'Manger' from the ninth-century 'stables' (E. P. Todd)

Only a few finds of this level were clearly identified in the reports, but they can be supplemented with those attributed indiscriminately to Stratum V in Area A, because it is now clear (cf. below, pp. 86–7) that Stratum VA is represented in this area by the higher level which the excavators called Stratum IVB (palace 1723, its courtyard and the adjacent building 1482). The structures and the finds which underlie this must belong to Stratum VB. A large quantity of domestic pottery was found here and most of it is of the typical tenth-century type, with an irregularly hand-burnished red wash overlaid on the clay. A few pieces of Cypriote 'Black-on-Red' ware are present. The other finds show that bronze was still the most widely used metal, though iron was coming to take its place where sharpness was important, as in knives and arrowheads (cf. 2 Samuel 12:31). Amulets of various kinds continue to appear, and probably to be included among them is a type of bone pendant, sometimes plain but often decorated with rows of circles with dots in the centre, which is characteristic of the Israelite monarchy period. Even more telling is a bronze figurine of a fighting god, which fully maintains the Canaan–ite tradition (plate 14). It is quite possible that the population of Mcgiddo remained mainly Canaanite in composition even after the city was incorporated into David's kingdom. The Canaanites did not simply disappear overnight.

There is no evidence at this stage of Megiddo having occupied a position of any political importance in the kingdom. Indeed it was probably the case that throughout the land the organisation of the population and the planning of their towns differed little under David from what it had been under Saul and the judges, despite the incorporation of areas which had hitherto resisted Israelite efforts at expansion. The narratives of 2 Samuel certainly point to the establishment of a court in Jerusalem (8:16–18; 20:23–6) and some preliminary attempts to organise the kingdom (2 Samuel 24), but it is clear from them that the tribal structure of the people had remained intact (15:2, 10; 19:9; 20:14; 24:2) and that, as has often been noticed, the major division between Israel in the north and Judah in the south was not overcome. 1 Chronicles 27:16–22 gives a list of the 'princes' or 'leaders' of the different tribes in the time of David (cf. 1 Chr 28:1) and this may reflect something of the constitutional arrangements of the time, even if (as seems likely) the lists in this chapter are predominantly later fictions.

Solomonic Megiddo: the American excavations

The excavation of the upper layers on the mound has made it clear that this was only a temporary eclipse of Megiddo's importance, as it was quickly built up, and then rebuilt, with strong fortifications and massive public buildings of various kinds. Unfortunately our account of this cannot be straightforward, as the relationships between the buildings of Strata VA, IVB and IV and the placing of the occasions of their construction within the history of Israel during the tenth and ninth centuries BC have been controversial questions ever since their discovery. At the present time it is no longer possible to speak, as it was ten or fifteen years ago, of a consensus on these topics. The next few pages will therefore be devoted to a review of this protracted and continuing discussion. Not only is this the clearest way to present the finds and the different points of view; it will also serve as a useful illustration of how and why archaeologists may disagree in their interpretation of the same data. At the end an attempt will be made to give an assessment of the arguments used and to present a defensible account of the architectural history of Megiddo in the early monarchy.

Our starting-point must be the buildings ascribed by the American excavators to their Strata VA, IVB and IV (figure 16). *Stratum VA* was best attested in Area AA, where in addition to the small gate and approach already mentioned there was a row of houses parallel to the edge of the tell. Their outer walls had been destroyed by the deep foundations of the city wall of Stratum IV. In a corner of the courtyard in front of one of these buildings (locus 2081) a quantity of small limestone altars was found, with offering stands, pottery of various types and other objects. Two upright stones in an entrance nearby were interpreted as *maṣṣebot* or pillars associated with Canaanite worship. Only parts of buildings from this period were identified in Areas BB and DD, but we should add to them the structures published without further qualification as Stratum V in Area C (in the east of the mound), as in several cases they overlie buildings known to belong to Stratum VB. Here too there is an almost continuous line of houses parallel to the edge of the mound, with floors paved either with rubble or with lime-plaster. One long narrow building (Building 10) seems likely to have been a storehouse: it contained a lot of pottery, and a layer of ash and the burnt grain in some of the jars are evidence of destruction at the end of this period. Close by was a building with eight upright stones, in two rows, which were thought at first to be possibly *maṣṣebot*, and the discovery of more small altars and pieces of pottery shrines nearby

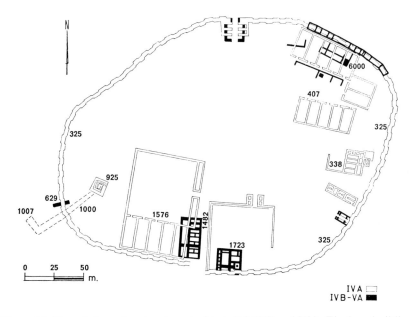

Figure 16   Plan of the major structures in Strata VA/IVB and IVA. The long building south of Building 338 (i.e. Building 10, cf. above) also belongs to Stratum VA–IVB, as Yadin recognises elsewhere. (From Y. Yadin, *Hazor* (Schweich Lectures), figure 39)

79

seemed to support a cultic interpretation of the building. In fact, as is now clear, it is one type of the ubiquitous 'four-room house'. The pottery of this stratum again included many pieces with hand-burnishing over a dark red wash, but also Cypriote pottery of both the 'Black-on-Red' and 'Bichrome II' types. Other finds included two iron axes, amulets (with four 'sacred eyes' among them), a necklace, a silver earring, a small game board and numerous female clay figurines.

The excavators found it necessary to subdivide their Stratum IV in the south of the mound, for two reasons. The city wall of this period was built over the rear of a palatial building which they also ascribed to Stratum IV; and the 'Southern Stables' overlay the northern and western rooms of another building of the same stratum. The two lower buildings, which were also linked by a lime-plaster pavement and their common orientation, were therefore referred to as *Stratum IVB*. The 'palace' (Building 1723) was a rectangular structure 23 metres by 21.5 metres, with an extension at the north-east corner which was initially thought to be a foundation for a porch. Only foundation-courses remained *in situ* but these showed that the walls were 1.25–1.50 metres thick and sufficient to carry a second storey. A study of the layout of the building by Professor D. Ussishkin has noted some similarities to palaces of the so-called *bit-ḥilani* type known in northern Syria and also to the description of Solomon's palace in Jerusalem (1 Kings 7:6–12). It is possible to identify provisionally an entrance on the north side, an open court within the building, a throne- or audience-room and two staircases leading to the upper floor. The palace stood in a large courtyard about 60 metres square, which was paved with lime-plaster and had a small gatehouse in the north-east corner of its enclosure wall (which Schumacher had already found and erroneously called a 'palace'). The adjacent building (1482) was rectangular and originally measured *c*.35 metres by 15 metres. There was nothing to indicate its function clearly, but it may have served some administrative purpose.

In its main, later, phase the city of *Stratum IV* was surrounded by a solid city wall at the top of the slope, *c*.3.60 meters thick. About half of this could still be traced during the excavation. Its plan was unusual, as it was constructed in sections about 6 metres long which were alternately set in or out by about 50 cm (plate 16). The surviving portions of the wall are entirely built of stone, some of it finely-hewn stone that must be taken from older monumental buildings.

With the possible exception of two stones, only the foundations of the city gate ascribed by the excavators to Stratum IV were found *in situ*, but even they make plain its massive plan and fine masonry technique. It was a rectangular structure 15 metres by 12 metres, with solid foundations for two towers at the

Plate 16 Section of the city wall of Stratum IV, showing 'offsets' and 'insets' (*Megiddo I*, figure 39)

outer end and three matching chambers on each side of the roadway behind them (figure 17). The roadway itself was *c*.4.25 metres wide. A door-socket was found in place by the inner end of the western tower and it was presumably matched on the east side, for the mounting of double doors. There was an outer gate some 30 metres down the roadway and the space between the two gates was strongly defended, forming a kind of bastion. A hall that opened on to the western side of this area may have been a guardroom, with its roof providing a useful defensive position. One curious feature which the excavators observed but could not explain was that the main gate and the wall of the outer court were not bonded into the city wall: Lamon describes this as 'from a structural point of view inexcusable'. Two additional features of the gate complex were a stone-built drain which passed under the city wall just west of the main gate and a (possibly subterranean) stairway that led straight down the steep slope from just outside the outer gate. The latter, which seemed to be a secondary addition, was originally thought to be a short cut for pedestrians entering or leaving the city, but Yadin has now shown that it provided access to a pool or water channel connected with the spring north of the tell.

Parts of a few buildings were identified inside the wall in Area AA, with one exception of small proportions. In the south only a few walls remained of the building which replaced Palace 1723, and the adjacent 'administrative building' (1482) continued in use at a much reduced size. The major structure in this part of the city was now the so-called 'Southern Stables' (Building 1576), which consisted of a large court about 55 metres square with two rooms on its east and a row of long, narrow rooms on its southern side. These latter rooms clearly fell into five units of three rooms each. In each unit the outer two rooms were floored with rubble while the central room was floored with lime-plaster and, while the walls dividing each unit from the next were of the normal type, each central room was divided from its flanking rooms only by a row of stone pillars, with spaces of about a metre between them. Stone 'mangers' had stood between these pillars, or at least between some of them. The horses, it was supposed, stood in the side aisles and the central room provided access to them for the stable staff. Holes in the pillars were thought to be for tethering the horses. The courtyard was floored with lime-plaster and laid on a filling of earth to level the ground surface, and great ingenuity was employed to keep this filling stable and to drain it. In the centre was a brick-built 'cistern', perhaps for watering the horses.

Similar buildings were discovered in the north-east of the city in Area C and are referred to as the 'Northern Stables' (plate 17). The later excavations in Areas BB and DD added to our knowledge of them and a missing corner in the south-west was found on Schumacher's plan of the *Nordburg*. Instead of using a filling to level the ground in this area, as in the south, the foundations were cut down into earlier levels, so that in places they are close to the floors of Stratum VIIA and no evidence of Stratum VI survives. Some of the levelling seems already to have been carried out prior to the construction of a similar building in Stratum V(A?), as walls on a slightly different line, but of the same general plan, were found just below the floor level of Stratum IV. Blocks of 'stable units' were situated around three sides of a slightly skew rectangle, five units on the north, two on the east and five again on the south. The space between the three blocks was not open but was occupied by a large building of which parts were discovered at three different points in the excavation. It is clearly of a different type from the 'stable units', yet to judge from its position it must have been connected with them. It may perhaps have been a barracks or a supply depot.

To the south-east lay another, smaller building of the same type and a small 'palace' (Building 338) which was set in its own enclosed courtyard. Part of

82

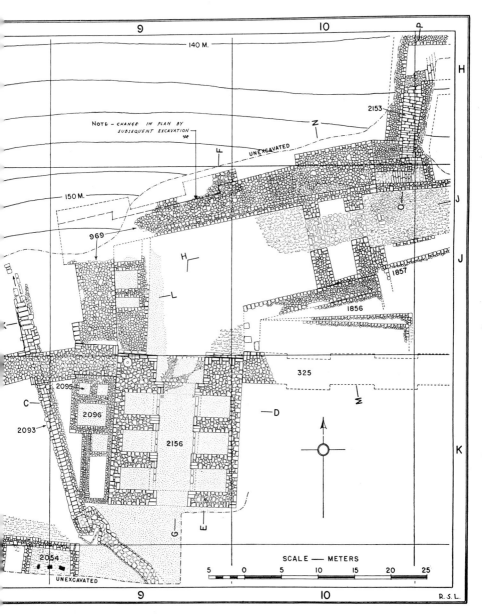

Figure 17 Plan of Gate 2156 of the Solomonic period. The adjacent city wall (325) is probably of later construction. (*Megiddo II*, figure 105)

83

Plate 17 Unit of the 'Northern Stables' of the ninth century (*Megiddo I*, figure 50)

this had been excavated by Schumacher beneath what he called 'the Astarte temple'. The three surviving courses of masonry formed a podium filled with debris from earlier levels, approached by steps along the northern side. The upper courses and the floors of the living accommodation had been destroyed, so that there can be no certainty about the location of doorways, but the plan suggests a tower in the east, from which an excellent view could be had of the plain below. Burnt remnants of the superstructure indicate that it was made of timber (as analysis showed, of cedar) and mudbrick, but it is too much to claim, as the excavators did, that they point clearly to the pattern of 'three rows of hewn stone and a row of cedar beams' known from the description of the courts of Solomon's temple (1 Kings 6:36, 7:12). The masonry was particularly fine, with ashlar piers at the corners and at intervals along the outer walls. The excavators gave special attention to the function of this building, which had been claimed as a temple by H. G. May in one of the earlier publications of the expedition. They were able to show that the arguments put forward in favour of a cultic function proved nothing and concluded that it was most likely 'a private residence of an important personage', such as the commander of the east of the city.

Given the above grouping of the buildings into three successive phases, it was thought that several factors could be used to date them. It was believed in the mid-1930s that hand-burnishing of pottery gave way to wheel-burnishing *c*.1000 BC, so the distinctive pottery of Stratum V placed it entirely before that date. An approximate date for the beginning of that stratum (i.e. of VB) *c*.1050 BC was deduced from the twelfth century date then thought likely for Stratum VI and the belief that a period of abandonment had elapsed after its destruction. This conclusion seemed to be confirmed by the ascription of the very similar Stratum II at Tell el-Ful (supposedly Gibeah) to the reign of Saul. P.L.O. Guy had already in 1931 proposed to date Stratum IV to Solomon's reign, partly because of references to the building of chariot-cities and Megiddo in particular in the biblical account of Solomon's reign, but also because of archaeological parallels to the 'stables', the pottery in them, some 'aegis of Bastet' amulets which he thought were from the time of Sheshonq I (whose reign overlapped with Solomon's) and the non-Palestinian character of the masonry of Stratum IV. He also held that Megiddo would have been an ideal centre for the trade in horses and chariots carried on by Solomon, and that the wood and stone construction of Building 338 reflected a technique used in Solomonic Jerusalem. The final report added that a fragment of a stele of Sheshonq I, found on the mound (figure 18), demanded that Megiddo be occupied *c*.930 BC and since (it was thought) Stratum V ended about 1000 BC Stratum IV must already have been in existence then. Further, the association in Stratum IV of hand-burnished pottery with wheel-burnished pottery seemed to fit the tenth century better than any later period, as the Harvard excavations at Samaria were thought to have shown that already in the ninth century hand-burnished pottery had gone out of use. It should be noted that the excavators' dating of Stratum IV was not based merely upon a desire to find 'Solomon's Stables' at Megiddo, although this correlation did play a part in it. Granted a Solomonic date for the main phase of Stratum IV, it followed that the closely similar Stratum IVB represented a small outpost on the tell built either under David or early in Solomon's reign.

Solomonic Megiddo: debate and new discoveries

When these conclusions were reviewed by other archaeologists, two major lines of criticism soon emerged. J. W. Crowfoot, who as Director of the British School of Archaeology in Jerusalem had been excavating at Samaria in the middle years of the American work at Megiddo, was strongly critical of the arguments used to associate Stratum IV with Solomon. He had himself found very similar architecture at Samaria which dated from the ninth century, and

Figure 18 Fragment of a stele of Sheshonq I found at Megiddo (R. S. Lamon and G. M. Shipton, *Megiddo I*, figure 70)

Figure 19 Seals of (a) Shema and (b) Asaph (Andrew Brown; based on C. Watzinger, *Tell el-Mutesellim II*, figures 61 and 62)

he proposed that the major buildings at Megiddo were likewise built, not by Solomon, but by the house of Omri. He pointed out that the Bible did not actually say that Megiddo was one of Solomon's chariot-cities, but distinguished it from them (cf. 1 Kings 9:15, 19), so that the 'stables' of Stratum IV were unlikely to be Solomonic. Moreover, the hand-burnished pottery of Stratum V could not be limited to a date before 1000 BC, since he had found it in ninth-century levels at Samaria. Later Kathleen Kenyon, in the final report on the pottery from Samaria, was to go further and to claim that the pottery in the constructional fill under the 'Southern Stables' and Building 338 included types known from the mid-ninth century levels at Samaria, so that these buildings could not have been constructed before that date.

Meanwhile two American archaeologists, W. F. Albright and G. E. Wright, had also been busy studying the excavators' reports, and they made the important contribution of showing that Stratum IVB in the south of the

86

city and Stratum VA('V') in the north and east were not successive phases but parts of one and the same level, dating from the time of Solomon. But in other respects they did not in the end dissent very much from the excavators' conclusions about the period under consideration; in fact they added further arguments to support the view that the gate of Stratum IV was Solomonic, including its resemblance to a gate described in Ezekiel's vision of the restored temple in Jerusalem (Ezekiel 40:5–16) which, they supposed, was modelled on a gate in the Solomonic temple.

A more drastic re-evaluation of the whole problem was, however, soon to follow. In 1957 Professor Yigael Yadin discovered in his excavations at Hazor a city gate of the Solomonic period with a plan and dimensions almost identical with those of the gate of Stratum IV at Megiddo. As if this were not enough, he went on to identify one half of a similar gate in a plan from the report of R.A.S. Macalister on his excavations at Gezer fifty years previously. Macalister had referred to this structure as part of a Maccabean palace, but Yadin's hunch proved to be correct when, in 1968 and 1969, new excavations at Gezer, by then under the direction of W. G. Dever, uncovered the other half of the gate and confirmed its tenth-century date of construction. The similarity of plan not only added weight to the arguments for a Solomonic date for the Megiddo gate: it corresponded beautifully to the conjunction of these three strategic sites in the account of Solomon's building works: 'the forced labour which King Solomon levied to build the house of the Lord and his own house and the Millo and the wall of Jerusalem and *Hazor and Megiddo and Gezer*' (1 Kings 9:15).

Yadin had, however, noticed a fly in the ointment, or what he took to be one. While the Solomonic gates at Hazor and Gezer were linked to casemate city walls the gate at Megiddo was linked (it seemed) to the solid 'offsets-and-insets' wall. Being suspicious of such irregularity – for why should the engineers who had in other respects proceeded in such remarkably similar ways depart from their pattern at Megiddo? – Yadin went to Megiddo with a small team of assistants in January 1960 to see whether a casemate wall perhaps existed there too. His task was not easy, for the whole mound had been excavated down to Stratum IV in the 1930s and in many places deeper still. But he found an area to the east of the city gate where the solid wall of Stratum IV was still standing and, even before excavations began, he was able to observe beneath the foundations of the solid wall, a straight wall which proved to be the outer wall of a rectangular fortress *c*.28 metres by 21 metres (Fortress 6000), which was built of ashlar masonry. In due course excavation showed that while this building was earlier than the solid walls (and the 'Northern Stables') it was later than both Strata VIA and VB. In other words it clearly belonged to the composite stratum VA/IVB identified by Albright and Wright, and this was confirmed by some pottery found in one of the rooms. Yadin also ascribed to this stratum a large building to the south, of which he traced the northern wall. This looks very like the outline of the central building of the 'Northern Stables' of Stratum IV (above, p. 82), and a final decision about its stratum must await the full publication of Yadin's excavations.

To the east and west of the fortress Yadin found the casemate wall that he was looking for, nicely sandwiched between the solid wall above and structures of Strata VIA and VB below. To the east the casemates were recognised to be less substantial than at Hazor, but to the west they were strongly built and the line could be traced a little further on the excavators' plan of Area DD (Stratum VB/VA). Unfortunately the earlier excavations of Schumacher and the Americans had made it impossible to follow this line to the city gate itself, but Yadin thought that there was now sufficient evidence to show that at Megiddo too the Solomonic gate had been associated with a casemate wall, as at Hazor and Gezer. More was to follow. Yadin, it seems, could not believe that Solomon dismantled the city of Stratum VA/IVB, as he must have done if he were the builder of the main part of Stratum IV; moreover, the pattern of Hazor (not to speak of Samaria) suggested that a further period of royal building was to be assumed under Omri and Ahab. His chronology of the buildings at Megiddo therefore became:

David	Stratum VB
Solomon	Stratum VA/IVB, with Fortress 6000, the casemate wall and city gate 2156
(attack of Sheshonq I)	
Jeroboam I	'Stratum IVA1': the solid wall, with reuse of city gate 2156
Omri-Ahab	'Stratum IVA2': 'Northern and Southern Stables', solid wall, city gate 500 (formerly ascribed to Stratum III)

Yadin's theory thus envisages two periods of use for Gate 2156, and he believed that they could be correlated with two different roadways, the one (normally attributed to a lower gate of Stratum VA, and here taken to belong to Stratum VB) at the foot of the surviving gate structure, which was therefore wholly above ground level in this phase and had no foundations, and the other level with its top, so that the surviving masonry then came to form the foundations for a superstructure that has completely (or almost completely) disappeared.

In essentials this is also the view accepted by Kenyon in 1971 in the light of Yadin's excavations and arguments, though the evidence from Samaria led her to insist that it was only shortly before 850 BC that the main part of Stratum IV was constructed, and no place was left for an initial rebuilding under Jeroboam. The agreement of these two eminent authorities in Palestinian archaeology – and in America the leading archaeologists also quickly indicated their support – justified one in speaking of a consensus about the architectural history of Megiddo under the early Hebrew monarchy. But it was to be a short-lived or rather, as I suspect, an interrupted consensus. The first blow was struck by Yohanan Aharoni, a former colleague of Yadin in the excavations at Hazor who in due course went his own way and founded the Institute of Archaeology at Tel Aviv University. In a sharply critical article published in 1972 he contested several of Yadin's claims. He emphasised that the solid wall was built against Gate 2156 and could not be separated from it, and that the excavators had found no evidence of a casemate wall in the vicinity of the gate. He also questioned the idea put forward by Yadin that the surviving portions of Gate 2156 had originally stood above ground, rather than being from the outset foundational, since the stones had shown no signs of weathering when they were first excavated and a gate without foundations was inconceivable. As for Yadin's excavations, Aharoni denied on the basis of his own visit to the site that a casemate wall had been found, explaining the 'western casemates' as part of a courtyard associated with Fortress 6000 and the 'eastern casemates' as the outer rooms of houses forming a ring around the mound, as had been found elsewhere in Stratum VA. There was no casemate wall, therefore, at Megiddo and no reason to depart significantly from the stratigraphy and dating proposed by the excavators. Aharoni believed that Stratum VA contained Fortress 6000 and Palace 1723 as well as its own small gate and the ciruit of private houses, and that it had been built by David. To Stratum IVB he attributed the solid wall, Gate 2156 and the 'stables', and he asserted that this had been built by Solomon, perhaps after the destruction of the Davidic city in an Egyptian invasion which he thought might have extended further to the north than Gezer (1 Kings 9:16).

The most recent assessment of the evidence is that of Ussishkin. A careful and very useful review of previous interpretations and of the archaeological evidence from all parts of the city leads him to agree with Yadin and Kenyon that Stratum VA/IVB (with Fortress 6000, Palace 1723, the circuit of private houses and fortifications 'which were probably of the casemate wall type') was built by Solomon and destroyed by Sheshonq I in the fifth year of Rehoboam of Judah (1 Kings 14:25–6), while the main part of Stratum IV ('IVA', including the solid wall and the 'stables') is later. The known facts of Solomon's building at Megiddo and Sheshonq's attack (on the latter see further p. 96) point to these conclusions, whereas Aharoni's theory has to presuppose in addition building activity by David and an earlier Egyptian attack, neither of which is historically attested in relation to Megiddo. The weakness of the Yadin–Kenyon view and the main impulse to Aharoni's chronology, Ussishkin believes, comes from the assumption that Gate 2156 is Solomonic and this, he argues, is a mistaken assumption. His argument is founded on the impression that this gate and the solid wall form an architectural unity and on the absence of any casemate wall (or room for one) adjoining the gate. From this it follows that the gate is contemporary with the solid wall and, since the latter belongs to the post-Sheshonq I reconstruction of Megiddo (Stratum IVA), the gate must do so too and cannot have been built under Solomon. There is no problem in this, since there are similar gates not only in Solomonic levels at Hazor and Gezer but also in a later level at Lachish (Stratum IV) and outside Israelite territory at Ashdod.

Evaluation of the arguments

It is time to offer some comments on this discussion which may point the way forward to a clearer picture. First, it seems that Aharoni was correct to question Yadin's idea that the 'lower roadway' was once used in conjunction with Gate 2156. The lime-plaster actually extended underneath the eastern tower of that gate, and must therefore represent a street level belonging to an earlier stage of construction, as can be seen from a comparison of the published plans. It is true, as Y. Shiloh has shown, that the excavators themselves were initially inclined to Yadin's theory, but as the work proceeded they found themselves compelled by new evidence to give it up. There is only one roadway associated with the gate, the one which is level with the top of the surviving walls, which are therefore foundational. Secondly, it is possible that Aharoni was right to question Yadin's interpretation of the rooms adjacent to Fortress 6000 as a casemate wall, particularly those in the east. Large parts of the city of Stratum VA/IVB may have been protected only by a continuous line of houses around the edge of the mound, as is known to have been the case in the western quarter at Beersheba and at several other sites.

Thirdly, on the other hand, these criticisms do not affect Yadin's main contention and in general the chronology advocated by him and by Kenyon, with Stratum VA/IVB being Solomonic and Stratum IV(A) being from the ninth century (or the end of the tenth century, after Sheshonq I's invasion), is preferable to that of Aharoni (which is close to that of the excavators and of Albright and Wright). In addition to the argument of Ussishkin to this effect, this view is the only one which is compatible with the pottery evidence from the filling under the 'Southern Stables' and Building 338. As Kenyon showed, this corresponds to Samaria Period III in the mid-ninth century. The validity of the argument is not affected by a separate controversy over the date of the pottery recorded as belonging to Samaria Periods I and II. Fourthly, the identical plan and measurements of Gate 2156 and the Solomonic gate at Hazor (Stratum X), together with the very close similarity of the Solomonic gate at Gezer, make it almost certain that the Megiddo gate is from the period of Solomon too. Were it not for its apparent connection to a ninth-century city wall, there would be no hesitation in accepting that view. So is that connection as secure as it looks? Attention has often been drawn to the fact that the wall and the gate are not bonded into one another. It may be true, as Ussishkin has pointed out, that such bonding in is not essential at the level of foundations. But the lack of it at least permits the conclusion that the two structures were not built at the same time. Furthermore, there is the fact that the solid wall was bonded into the gate ascribed to Stratum III and as a result it was built up not only against but over the abandoned foundation of Gate 2156. This can be seen from a comparison of the plans and arises inevitably from the fact that the city wall continued along the front of the gate of Stratum III. It is also evident from the way in which the discovery of Gate 2156 is described in Loud's unpublished excavation diary (in the extracts which follow 'the gate' means the gate of Stratum III and the 'earlier structure' and the 'heavy walls' are what turned out to be Gate 2156):

(Wednesday Jan. 22 [1936])
A still earlier structure – which is partly under the city wall – has been incorporated as part of the eastern outer pier of the gate. The nature of the earlier structure is not yet clear, but its heavy masonry would suggest fortifications and it seems quite likely that it is an earlier gate. It is definitely under the eastern extension of the city wall but seems vaguely connected with the western extension of what has been considered the same city wall . . .

(Saturday Jan. 25)
The floor of room 504 ['503' in the published report] of the gate was removed, and the heavy, well built walls of some very large structure were revealed. The walls all plunge under the gate – one emerges to the south (this was exposed some weeks ago), another continues east under the stone floor of the gate street, and a third extends northward under the outer western pier of the gate and appears to join (and be contemporary with) the western part of the city wall. Presumably this heavy structure is a part of the one found under the eastern part of the gate – but to the east the heavy earlier walls also underlie the only visible remains of the city wall.

One feature that might seem to conflict with the view that the city wall was built after Gate 2156 is the outer gate and its associated courtyard. It has sometimes been said that the way in which different walls abut against one another implies the following order of construction: first the main gate (2156), then the solid city wall, then the outer gate and its courtyard. If this is correct, then the whole complex, gates and wall, must have been built within a very short period, as the roadway passing through the inner gate corresponds to that which passes through the outer gate. However, on the most detailed plan a gap is shown between the city wall and the wall of the outer courtyard. The most plausible explanation of this gap is that it is due to the cutting back of the courtyard wall to make room for the foundation of the city wall; that is, the construction of the city wall was subsequent to the completion of the gate complex.

Once it is established that the solid city wall is (or can be) later than Gate 2156, there is no difficulty in following the lead of the other arguments and dating the wall to the ninth century and the gate to the Solomonic period. The problem of the fortifications which adjoined Gate 2156 still remains, of course, and it is only possible to suggest what they may have been. This is because the foundations of the solid city wall were laid so deep that in many places they rested on the ruins of Stratum VIA and so whatever existed along this line in Strata VB and VA/IVB was destroyed by the builders of this wall. Only speculation is possible. There may have been a casemate wall, against which the VA/IVB houses were built, which was dismantled by the builders of the solid wall; or these houses themselves, perhaps with a strengthened outer wall, may have formed the defensive line. We shall probably never know, because the builders of the solid wall removed all the evidence. It follows that the consensus established after Yadin's excavations was in most respects soundly based and that the studies of Aharoni and Ussishkin serve to refine it rather than, as they thought, to overthrow it. There is, however, no reason to think that Gate 2156 continued in use after Sheshonq I's attack: when Megiddo was rebuilt, probably in the second quarter of the ninth century, the new gate (500), which was originally attributed only to Stratum III, provided access to the city.

Water-systems and 'stables'

Yadin's work has one further contribution to make to our picture of the tenth- and ninth-century cities. The American expedition had discovered two protected approaches to a spring in a cave on the south-west of the tell, a stone-built 'gallery' passing beneath the solid city wall (Locus 629) and a vertical shaft linked to a horizontal tunnel dug through the solid rock (Loci 925 and 1000). The latter in particular is a most impressive piece of engineering (plate 18) and the excavators were able to reconstruct in detail how the ancient workmen must have set about their task. Their conclusion was that both systems had been constructed in the twelfth century BC (which is when they dated Stratum VI), when Canaanite Megiddo was under Egyptian control. This date was based on the discovery of pottery characteristic of Stratum VI in the cave by the spring and on the belief that the solid city wall, which passed over the gallery, was built under Solomon. Yadin's examination of the remains of Gallery 629 showed that its masonry included ashlars dressed in exactly the style of the Solomonic buildings and, more important, that it cut through structures of Strata VB and VIA. Taken together with the fact that it was clearly earlier than the city wall of Stratum IV(A), this provided excellent stratigraphical proof that the gallery approach to the spring in the cave formed part of the Solomonic city of Stratum VA/IVB. Since there would have been no point in constructing the gallery when the much more effective shaft-and-tunnel system was in existence, it is to be presumed that the latter system is later and it probably belongs to Stratum IV of the ninth century. Such a date receives some confirmation from the fact that a somewhat similar system to this was found in excavations at Hazor, where there was clear stratigraphical evidence for a ninth-century date; it would also provide a convenient explanation of the origin of the debris used for the filling under the adjacent 'Southern Stables' and their courtyard.

The function of these latter buildings and their counterparts in the north of the city constitutes one final issue which requires consideration before we are in a position to conclude with an overall account of Megiddo's role in the early Israelite monarchy. Professor J. B. Pritchard pointed out that the description of them as stables at the outset depended heavily on the belief that they were built by Solomon and on the biblical passages referring to his 'chariot-cities'. In the light of Yadin's arguments for dating these buildings with the rest of Stratum IV to the ninth century, which he accepts, Pritchard went on to ask whether the archaeological evidence is sufficient by itself to validate the description of them as stables, and he concluded that it is not. He claimed that there was no evidence for the use of stables for horses in the ancient Near East, that the similar buildings at Hazor and Tell es-Saidiyeh were probably not stables and that the so-called tethering-posts, mangers and water-tank could not have been used in the ways suggested. Moreover, the plan of the buildings was unsuited to use as stables, since a horse at the inner end could be taken out only after all those nearer to the entrance had been removed, and the excavators themselves had acknowledged that the objects (such as harness buckles) which one might expect to find in the vicinity of stables were completely absent. The few finds reported consist mainly of domestic pottery. Pritchard suggested that the buildings were possibly storehouses or barracks. Strong support for the first of these alternatives later came from the excavations at Beersheba, where very similar buildings were found near the city gate, packed

Plate 18 The horizontal tunnel cut through the rock for the ninth-century water system (G. I. Davies)

with storage jars and other kinds of pottery. Storehouses or magazines of this long narrow plan are widely attested in the cities of the ancient Near East.

Most of these points are well made and it must certainly now be acknowledged that the Iron Age pillared buildings are not all stables. On the other hand, further discussion of the matter has suggested that Pritchard overstated his case in some respects. The existence of stables has been demonstrated at Tell el-Amarna in Egypt, at Ugarit and in a relief of Ashurnasirpal II of Assyria, and references to stables occur in records of Ramesses III of Egypt and in Mesopotamian texts (Akkadian *ma"assu, qabūtu* and *urû*). The 'mangers' at any rate could well be just that. The Megiddo buildings are unique in having 'mangers' and, in the case of the southern block, the large courtyard in front is strongly reminiscent of the enclosure next to the stables in the 'police barracks' at el-Amarna and could have been used as a parade-ground. These factors perhaps justify us in continuing to refer to these complexes as 'stables'. is possible that the same type of building served different purposes at different places and times.

Summary: Megiddo as an Israelite Royal City

The remains represented by Strata VA/IVB and IV(A) thus provide evidence of Megiddo's status as a royal city with two distinct phases of existence. In the first phase, which we attribute to Solomon, that status is apparently compatible with the continued presence of a substantial population of ordinary civilians within the walls, as indicated by the houses in the north-west and east of the mound. Large areas previously occupied by domestic dwellings have, however, been taken over for the construction of public buildings, particularly in the south and north-east. It is plausible to connect the palace 1723 and the adjacent 'administrative building' (1482) in the south with the government of Solomon's fifth district (1 Kings 4:12), and Megiddo may have been its chief city. Building 10, among the houses in the south-east, seems to have been a public storehouse. If we are correct in discerning an earlier 'stable block' beneath the later 'Northern Stables' (p. 82), it may be that the public buildings in the north-east of the city, including Fortress 6000, were of a more military character. The fortification of the city is most apparent in the very strongly built gate complex and in the provision of protected access to the water-supply in the south-west (Gallery 629). The association of Megiddo with Hazor and Gezer (1 Kings 9.15) suggests a definite plan on Solomon's part to ensure the security of his kingdom and this may have been directed as much towards maintaining the loyalty of the northern tribes by force as to defence against enemies abroad. If so, the effort was counter-productive, for these very measures were a major provocation to secession after his death (1 Kings 11:27, 12:3–4).

The public buildings at Megiddo exhibit a style of masonry which represents a further refinement of the use of ashlars in the late Canaanite period (Strata VIII–VI). It has commonly been presumed that this development was due to the employment of Phoenician craftsmen by Solomon in his provincial cities as well as in Jerusalem (cf. 1 Kings 5:18), but Y. Shiloh has shown that evidence of such masonry has yet to be found this early in Phoenicia. At present it is rather to be ascribed to the workmanship of native Canaanite and Israelite masons, benefiting perhaps from the increasing availability of superior iron tools (cf. 1 Kings 6:7). The so-called 'proto–Aeolic' (or palmette) capitals also appear to be a local development of a traditional artistic motif, and they make their first appearance in this period. The references to palm-tree motifs in the description of Solomon's buildings in Jerusalem can be compared with them (1 Kings 6:29–35, 7:36). The other noteworthy feature of the remains is the large quantity of ritual vessels. These also seem for the most part to reproduce styles well known from the late Canaanite period and the likelihood that many of the old inhabitants had continued to live in the city makes this fully understandable. The small limestone incense altars, which are paralleled all over the country, particularly in this period, may be an exception and could represent an innovation connected with the opening up of the incense trade with south Arabia by Solomon.

This city was attacked by Pharaoh Sheshonq I near the end of his reign, c.925 BC. His invasion is mentioned in the Bible (1 Kings 14:25–6; 2 Chronicles 12:2–9) and dated to the fifth year after Solomon's death, but its full extent and the fact that it included a campaign against the northern kingdom only became apparent with the discovery of Sheshonq's own account of it in the temple of Amon at Karnak (*ANET*, pp. 242–3): the list of conquered cities includes Megiddo along with Taanach, Beth-shean, Mahanaim and possibly Penuel and Tirzah. There is only slight evidence of the burning of the city of Stratum VA/IVB (in Building 10) and the fact that Sheshonq erected a stele there may imply that most of it was left intact. A possible explanation for Sheshonq's campaigns against Judah and Israel might relate them to the internal strife between the two halves of Solomon's kingdom which had split apart only a few years before. Jeroboam I of Israel had been an exile at the Egyptian court (1 Kings 11:40) and he may well have sought his former protector's help in his war with Rehoboam (for which see 1 Kings 15:6). The latter, however, was perhaps able to buy Sheshonq off by handing over the temple treasures (1 Kings 15:26) and to persuade him to direct his army against Jeroboam instead.

Whether Megiddo lay in ruins for a time or briefly continued as before, its wholesale reorganisation in the form which it took in Stratum IV is best attributed to the Omride dynasty. Omri's military origin, the need to secure the new dynasty and the resurgent military power of the northern kingdom make this altogether the most plausible time. If they had not already left, it would have been necessary to displace many of the remaining civilian population, for there is very little evidence of private dwellings in the new layout of the city (and very little room for them). The episode of Naboth's vineyard at nearby Jezreel (1 Kings 21) may not have been unique. Megiddo, like the new capital at Samaria, was at this time a strongly fortified acropolis and most of the ordinary citizens presumably lived on the slopes below, where a number of Iron Age dwellings were identified but not properly published. The solid city wall dates from this period, with the so-called 'Stratum III' gate (Gate 500) in its first phase. The largest structures inside are the northern and southern 'stable complexes', and their interpretation largely determines whether we think of Megiddo at this time as a store-city or, as seems preferable, a military base with a strong chariot force. Even on the latter view other buildings (such as the 'central building' in the 'Northern Stables' and the large building south-west of the city gate) will probably have been used for the storage of provisions and military equipment. The city's ability to withstand a long siege depended not only on its strong walls but on the secure and entirely concealed access to the spring by means of the shaft-and-tunnel system. An additional means of obtaining water to the north of the city, where there was another spring, has been identified in the so-called 'pedestrian access' beyond the outer city gate and possibly it too dates from the ninth century. The obvious candidate among the excavated buildings for the governor of the city's quarters is Building 338 in the east, with its own enclosed courtyard. From here there was an excellent view across the plain below. It seems that this building took over the function previously served by Palace 1723, unless the meagre remains above the latter in fact derive from a building of comparable size and grandeur. The 'administrative building' (1482), though reduced in size, presumably continued to fulfil its earlier role. It will have been to this city that Ahaziah king of Judah fled for refuge after being wounded a few miles to the south-east during Jehu's *coup d'état* c.842 BC (2 Kings 9:27).

It is likely that this city remained in existence until the Assyrian invasions in the latter half of the eighth century brought an end, in two stages, to the independence of the northern kingdom. The completely new layout of the city in Stratum III, in which most of the city reverted to domestic occupation, and the strongly Assyrian character of such larger buildings as there were are most readily explained if they are attributed to a rebuilding after the Assyrian conquest. This conclusion seems inevitable and is now generally accepted, but the excavators' own view that Stratum IV ended c.780 BC once found considerable support, chiefly because of the argument from pottery. It does indeed appear that some of the latest developments found at Samaria are missing from the pottery of Stratum IV at Megiddo, but this need not require a date for the latter before the eighth-century Assyrian invasions. It is clear from the textual evidence (see below) that Megiddo fell into Assyrian hands some twelve years before Samaria and the latest developments in style and technique attested at Samaria could have taken place during that period. The capital may also have been somewhat more abreast of the latest fashions in pottery than the administrative and military centre of Megiddo, so that older styles would continue in use longer at Megiddo than at Samaria.

Megiddo as an Assyrian provincial capital

Evidence of destruction was provided by wood charcoal and burnt mudbrick in the debris of the 'governor's quarters' (Building 338) and the accumulation of debris in the other buildings. The city presumably fell to Tiglath-Pileser III of Assyria (745–727) in the course of his campaigns in northern Israel in 734 or

97

733 BC. These are mentioned in texts of Tiglath–Pileser himself (*ANET*, pp. 283–4) and also in the Bible:

> In the days of Pekah king of Israel Tiglath–Pileser king of Assyria came and captured Ijon, Abel-beth-maacah, Janoah, Kedesh, Hazor, Gilead and Galilee, all the land of Naphtali; and he carried the people captive to Assyria. Then Hoshea the son of Elah made a conspiracy against Pekah the son of Remaliah, and struck him down, and slew him, and reigned in his stead, in the twentieth year of Jotham the son of Uzziah. (2 Kings 15:29–30; cf. Isaiah 9:1, Hosea 5:11)

These texts make it clear that Tiglath–Pileser annexed the whole of the northern and eastern parts of Israel, leaving Hoshea as ruler only of Samaria itself and the surrounding hill-country. Many of the population were deported and probably, as happened elsewhere, they were replaced by settlers from other parts of the Assyrian empire (cf. 2 Kings 17:24). It is somewhat strange that Megiddo is not mentioned by name in any of the texts, but neither the account in Tiglath–Pileser's annals (which are in any case fragmentary) nor that of 2 Kings gives a full list of the cities that were captured. Megiddo would probably be included in the general expression 'Galilee'. The name of Megiddo does occur in some later lists of the provinces of the Assyrian Empire, and the city was probably therefore the administrative centre of this province, which is thought to have included Upper and Lower Galilee as well as the plain and valley of Jezreel. The name of one of the provincial governors, Itti-adad-a-ni-nu, has survived, because during his period of office he was the eponym official (*limmu*) for the year 679 BC. This meant that documents such as contracts written during that year were dated by his name, and at least two such documents, from Assur, are extant.

The character of the new city was quite different from that of its predecessor, in several ways, although certain features continued in use, such as the city wall, the gate complex and the shaft-and-tunnel access to the spring (the latter two in a modified form). Most of the city was occupied by houses and only in the north does there seem to have been any concentration of public buildings. The large 'stable' complexes were, with one exception (unit 404) abandoned. A large circular stone-lined pit, which can be seen in the southern part of the mound, evidently served for the storage of grain, as some chaff and grain were found in between the stones of its wall. It was at least seven metres deep and had a diameter of eleven metres at the top, giving a capacity of about 450 cubic metres (*c.*12,800 bushels). Such a quantity of grain could support population of 1,000 adults comfortably for eight or nine months. The pit had two staircases descending around the inside of the circular wall, a unique arrangement which perhaps provided separate routes for descent and ascent. The rest of the city (figure 20) was laid out according to a 'grid' street plan

98

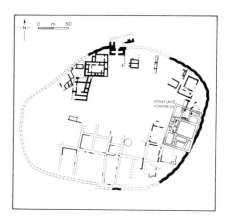

Figure 20 Plan of Strata III and II. The broken lines in the lower part of the plan indicate where the street plan has been reconstructed. (Andrew Brown; based on *Megiddo I*, figures 71, 72, 89 and 95)

except for the area directly within the city gate, where there was a group of large 'open-court' buildings. Both these features are foreign to Palestine of the Israelite period, but well attested in Mesopotamia. The streets could be distinguished by a characteristic deposit of small stones and sherds, even where house walls were not preserved. The *insulae* or 'blocks' were often divided by a 'backbone' into houses that faced respectively east and west. The buildings near the gate have a large courtyard at their centre, with a row of rooms (sometimes two) on each side and well-constructed doorways and drainage-systems. In one a pillared entrance opens on to the inner quarters. The sloping surface of the ground beneath them was levelled by artificial fillings and buttress walls were added to retain them. As a result the floor-levels of these buildings were raised well above that of the square inside the city gate. We may reasonably suppose that they were occupied by the governor of the province and his most senior officials.

One building of this period which attracted much attention in the early reports on the excavation was the so-called 'Astarte temple'. This was a rectangular room, first discovered by Schumacher and further explored by Fisher, which was built on top of what turned out to be part of the 'governor's quarters' (Building 338) of Stratum IV. The original reason for thinking that it was a shrine seems to have been two pillars built into a central dividing wall, next to one of which a flat stone formed a shelf or table: these were taken, like those found elsewhere on the tell, to be *maṣṣebot* or cultic pillars. Schumacher thought that adjacent walls were part of the same building, but some of them at least can now be seen to be parts of Building 338, which also explains the 'deep foundations' of which Schumacher wrote. The pillars are very similar to those in the 'Northern Stables' nearby and may have been taken from there. In any case there is no reason to see in them or the building any connection with worship: this was already pointed out by Watzinger. Fisher found what he took to be evidence confirming Schumacher's cultic interpretation (and a specific association of the 'temple' with Astarte) a little to the south. This material has already been described (pp. 79–80) and, since it belongs to a much earlier period, it clearly has nothing to do with this structure, which was probably part of an ordinary house.

The finds from this period can best be described after a brief account of Stratum II has been given. There is little change in the layout of the city and for Areas C and D the excavators did not construct a separate plan. In the centre and south of the mound there was more rebuilding, but the street plan remained largely intact and the character of the city was not affected. All this points to substantial continuity and in all probability gradual and piecemeal replacement of old buildings by new ones. A brick floor in square Q8 is reminiscent of an Assyrian building at Tell Jemmeh. The only major difference which the excavators envisaged between Strata III and II was the abandonment of the city wall (and presumably the gate fortifications) in Stratum II and the construction of a fortress in the east of the mound overlooking the plain. Its walls were 2–2.5 metres thick and formed, according to the American expedition's reconstruction, a rectangular enclosure c.75 metres by 50 metres, with northern, southern and western wings around a central courtyard. An eastern wing might be expected, as this was the side most open to attack, and remains of it could perhaps have collapsed down the slope of the tell. The details of the plan are otherwise unclear for lack of evidence. The same difficulty dogs attempts to date the structure securely, and it is not at all certain whether it does belong to Stratum II or to Stratum I of the Persian period. According to the excavators the city was 'subjected to a certain amount of destruction' at the end of Stratum II.

Excavations carried out by A. Eitan in 1974 have added a little to our knowledge of the seventh-century occupation at Megiddo. On the slopes beneath the fortress (squares N–O 16–17) he investigated a building with walls a metre thick and lime-plaster floors, which contained pottery of the late seventh century BC. Because of its size he considered that it was unlikely to be a private house, but its precise function remains uncertain. Its location suggests that even after the abandonment of the major public buildings of Stratum IV there was still insufficient space on the summit to accommodate both the new population and its rulers.

The finds from Strata III and II reflect the changed circumstances of the city and in some cases the arrival of a new population. Several new potter

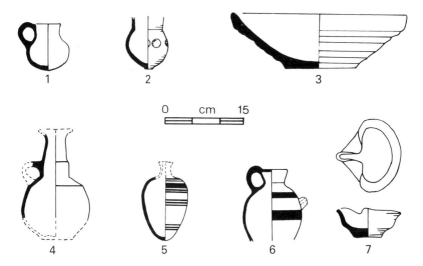

Figure 21 A selection of pottery from the Assyrian period (1, 7 standard late pre-exilic types; 2, 3, 5 Assyrian types; 4, 6 imports from Phoenicia). (Andrew Brown; drawn from *Megiddo I*, plates 1.34, 2.58, 3.78, 9.7, 12, 23.15, 37.7)

types appear, including some paralleled in the Assyrian levels at Tell Jemmeh in southern Palestine and others which appear to derive from Phoenicia to the north. Others represent late pre-exilic types known throughout Palestine (figure 21). It is surprising that hardly any Assyrian 'Palace Ware' has been found at Megiddo, in view of its administrative importance. This is in sharp contrast to other sites in Palestine administered by the Assyrians, such as Samaria, Tell el-Far'ah(N) and Tell Jemmeh, where substantial quantities of this pottery have been found. A large number of metal objects of both iron and bronze and ranging from arrowheads and sickles to jewellery and needles were present, particularly in the southern quarter. The concentration seems heavier than elsewhere in two 'blocks': these may have housed metalworkers. A possible 'smithy' (with iron ore and slag) was identified by Schumacher a little to the east: it seems likely to belong to the Assyrian period. A notable feature is the appearance in these strata of bronze fibulae or clasps of a variety of types. In several cases the pin was of iron, to give added strength and rigidity. Such clasps had been in use in the Near East (as well as the Greek world) for some centuries to fasten clothing, but they are very rare in earlier Israelite strata at Megiddo. This suggests at least a change in fashion and is perhaps also a further indication of a new element in the city population. A similar conclusion may be drawn from a group of small circular stone palettes, with a diameter of 8–10 cm, which begin to appear in Stratum III. They were possibly used for cosmetics. A cylinder seal in Assyrian style points to the new regime, and a jar found in Stratum III has a seal-impression on it which includes the prenomen of Shabako king of Egypt (*c.* 716–702). The latter provides new evidence for the current view that good relations existed between Assyria and Egypt for most of his reign. It was at first taken to point to Egyptian attempts to subvert Assyrian rule in Palestine (cf. 2 Kings 19:9), but the evidence is growing that the respective royal courts maintained trading relations with each other and the Megiddo impression fits well into such a picture.

Hebrew Seals and other inscriptions

Megiddo has so far produced disappointingly little inscribed material in Hebrew or other alphabetic scripts, compared with other major excavations in Palestine, but what has been found can conveniently be surveyed here. Apart from what may or may not be isolated letters incised on sherds, the corpus at present includes two inscriptions incised on jars, both very short and obscure, and five of the large number of scarab seals from the site. One of the inscribed jars was found by Schumacher in the 'Astarte temple': four letters of the inscription survive, *ʾbth*, but the meaning is unclear. The other jar inscription consists of the three letters *lyw* and belongs to a large group of inscriptions on jars which all begin with the Hebrew preposition *l*, 'belonging to', followed by a person's name. In this case it is probable that the inscription was not completed rather than, as was once thought, its being a dedication to Yahweh himself. The jar itself was found in a pit ascribed to Stratum II. The use of the Hebrew script in inscriptions from these levels points to the persistence of an Israelite element in the population after the Assyrian invasions, alongside the newcomers.

Seals were widely used in the ancient world to authenticate documents (1 Kings 21:8; Isaiah 29:11) or to stamp official stores or consignments of goods. Large numbers of inscribed seals are known from Palestine and neighbouring countries, but relatively few have come from controlled excavations. Pride of place among those from Megiddo must go to the splendid jasper seal inscribed *lšmʿ ʿbd yrbʿm*, 'Belonging to Shema, the servant (or minister) of Jeroboam', around a representation of a roaring lion (figure 19(a)). This was found during Schumacher's excavations in debris above the courtyard of Palace 1723 which was re-used in Stratum IVA. It passed into the private collection of the Sultan in Istanbul, because Palestine was under Turkish rule at the time of its discovery, but its present whereabouts are unknown. A bronze cast of it was made before it left Jerusalem and this can be seen in the Rockefeller Museum there. Both the find-place and the script indicate that 'Jeroboam' is the power ful king of that name who ruled the northern kingdom of Israel in the mid-eighth century BC (*c*.784/3–753/2), i.e. Jeroboam II. *'bd*, which can mean 'slave' or 'servant', is here an honorific title, so that 'minister' is a better translation (compare 2 Kings 22:12 for the title): it refers to a leading figure at the royal court. Megiddo as an important royal city would be a natural place for him to visit or even to live in. Two other seals, of serpentine and lapis lazuli respectively, are probably from about the same time. They have very similar designs, with a winged griffin wearing the double crown of Egypt occupying most of the face of the seal. This design is found on several other north Israelite seals (unlike those from Judah seals from the north nearly all bear a design of some kind) and has clear Phoenician and ultimately Egyptian affinities. One (also in the Rockefeller Museum), which is inscribed *ḥmn*, 'Haman', shows the Egyptian ankh-sign and a locust in addition, while the other, which belonged to one Asaph (*l'sp*), has a cartouche in front of the griffin containing meaningless hieroglyphs (figure 19(b)). Like the Samaria ivories these seals show how open the northern kingdom was to the cultural and no doubt religious influence of Phoenicia.

The two other seals are probably not Israelite. One, of lapis lazuli, bears the inscription *l'lmr*, 'Belonging to Elamar', and an as yet unparalleled design of two uraei and a sphinx. It comes from Stratum II, i.e. the Assyrian period, and the script has been identified as Phoenician of the first half of the seventh century, so that it reinforces the impression given by the pottery of increasing Phoenician influence at that time. The final seal, which is made of glazed faience, remains something of a mystery. It was found during the American excavations on the south-eastern slope of the mound, without an archaeological context, and both its design and its inscription have so far defied interpretation. At the centre there is what has been taken as a very stylised quadruped, while the letters (some of whose forms are Aramaic or Phoenician rather than Israelite) seem to read *zbyh/dm(??)q'*, a sequence which, taken as a whole, makes no sense at present.

The death of Josiah

The date of the transition from Stratum III to Stratum II cannot be determined precisely and it is probably pointless to try, as with the possible exception of the fortress (if that was built in the Assyrian period) the rebuilding seems to have been piecemeal. The end of Stratum II falls, on the pottery evidence, towards the end of the seventh century, a period of great political movements about which we are comparatively well informed and in which Megiddo once again comes into view in the written sources. From the middle of the seventh century Assyrian control of the empire became progressively weaker, though there is mention of an Assyrian governor in Samaria in 646 BC and a year or two later the Assyrians were able to mount a punitive campaign against Tyre and Acco. Internal struggles, the pressure of marauding tribes and the resurgence of Babylon under a Chaldaean dynasty founded by Nabopolassar hastened this process of decline after the death of Ashurbanipal in 627. The resulting power vacuum in Palestine, on the western edge of the empire, left the way open for both Egypt, under Psammetichus I (664–610) and Judah, under Josiah (640–609), to enlarge their domains. The extent of Josiah's political control can be gauged from the scope of his religious reforms, which according to the more reliable account in 2 Kings 23:19 extended to 'the high places which were in the cities of Samaria' (contrast 2 Chronicles 34:6–7). This would confine his rule to Judah itself and the former Assyrian province of Samaria. A Hebrew ostracon from this period found at Yavneh-yam (Meṣad Ḥashavyahu) has been thought to show that Josiah also controlled part of the coastal plain. The Egyptians, however, held sway over Ashdod, a few miles to the south, and the Phoenician coast. The political allegiance of Megiddo (and its province) at this time remains obscure: some scholars believe that it was in Josiah's hands, others that it must have been held by the Egyptians at least from 616, when they sent a force (presumably overland) to assist the Assyrians in their struggle for survival against the Babylonians and the Medes. The archaeological evidence is not of much help, especially as we cannot be sure that the fortress ascribed to Stratum II was actually built at this time rather than in the Persian period. If it was, it may be significant that those elements in the plan which can be reconstructed with greatest certainty have parallels in the so-called palace of Hophra/Apries (589–70) at Memphis in Egypt.

In 610 the Egyptians again lent help to the dying Assyrian cause, but apparently withdrew without achieving anything. In the following year, as we learn from the Babylonian Chronicle (*ANET*, p. 305), 'a large army from Egypt', now under Neco II (610–595), crossed the Euphrates, probably from their base at Carchemish, and succeeded in entering Haran with Ashur-uballit, the last king of Assyria, only for the latter to be killed in the city. On its way to Syria the Egyptian force passed by Megiddo where, in circumstances that are far from clear, Josiah was killed by them.

> In his days Pharaoh Neco went up to the king of Assyria to the river Euphrates; King Josiah went to meet him; and Pharaoh Neco slew him at Megiddo, when he saw him. And his servants carried him dead in a chariot from Megiddo, and brought him to Jerusalem, and buried him in his own tomb. (2 Kings 23:29–30)

Subsequent tradition (already in the books of Chronicles (2 Chr 35:20–25)) as serted that Josiah confronted Neco in battle but failed to stop his advance, and modern historians who accept the validity of this tradition have sought to explain why Josiah should have taken such a risk to prevent help reaching the beleaguered Assyrians. Was he perhaps in league with the Babylonians? In fact, if taken by itself the account in 2 Kings need not imply that there was a battle at all or any hostile intent on Josiah's part: 'went to meet him' could even mean that Josiah intended to lend support to Neco's expedition. But if so, why was Josiah killed? Perhaps not enough attention has been given to the apparently unnecessary words 'when he saw him'. If they mean anything, they suggest a hasty, perhaps unconsidered, response to Josiah's appearance. Neco may, as has been suggested, have ruthlessly decided that this was a good opportunity to gain control over the whole of Palestine by eliminating his would-be ally. The fact that on his return from Syria he removed the king who had been crowned in place of Josiah and replaced him with a man of his own choice makes such an aim quite likely (cf. 2 Kings 23:31–5). Another possibility is that Neco misinterpreted Josiah's arrival at the strategic battle-field of Megiddo, thought that he was trying to block his way and, without waiting to ask questions, made a pre-emptive strike against Josiah's camp. In any event, what promised to be a new golden age of independence for Judah was suddenly cut short by a foreign army and, even if for nothing else, the Chronicler's account is evidence that this catastrophe was commemorated in a special way (2 Chr 35:25). According to one view, the choice of 'the mountain of Megiddo', Ar-mageddon, as the site for the final battle between the people of God and the Gentile armies in the book of Revelation (16:16) goes back ulti-mately to the need to avenge the wrong done to this second David:

> Before him there was no king like him, who turned to the Lord with all his heart and with all his soul and with all his might, according to all the laws of Moses; nor did any like him arise after him. (2 Kings 23:25)

(Some have seen a reference to the battle between Josiah and Neco in Herodotus 2.159, which speaks of a battle between 'Syrians' and Neco at 'Magdolus' (Migdal), prior to Neco's capture of Kadytis (Gaza). But this is more likely to be a battle on the outskirts of Egypt itself.)

Further reading

The primary evidence for this chapter comes from *Megiddo I, Megiddo Tombs, Megiddo Water-System, Material Remains of the Megiddo Cult, Tell el-Mutesellim I* and the articles by Yadin and Eitan listed on p. 24). For general surveys of the period see K. M. Kenyon, *Archaeology in the Holy Land*, 4th ed., pp. 233–305, and *Royal Cities of the Old Testament* (London, 1971); and Y. Aharoni, *The Archaeology of the Land of Israel*

(London, 1982), pp. 192–279 (his treatment of Megiddo is on pp. 200–11, 222–5: cf. *Journal of Near Eastern Studies* 31 (1972), 302–11). On particular topics see D. Ussishkin, 'Was the "Solomonic" City Gate at Megiddo built by King Solomon?', *BASOR* 239 (1980), 1–18; Y. Yadin, 'A Rejoinder', *ibid.*, pp. 19–23; Y. Shiloh, 'Solomon's Gate at Megiddo as Recorded by its Excavator, R. Lamon, Chicago', *Levant* 12 (1980), 69–76; G. J. Wightman, 'Megiddo VIA–III: Associated Structures and Chronology', *Levant* 17 (1985), 117–29; J. B. Pritchard, 'The Megiddo Stables: A Reassessment', in J. A. Sanders (ed.), *Near Eastern Archaeology in the Twentieth Century* (Garden City, 1970), pp. 268–76; Y. Yadin, 'The Megiddo Stables', in F. M. Cross *et al.* (ed.), *Magnalia Dei*, G. E. Wright Volume (Garden City, 1976), pp. 249–52 (cf. *Eretz-Israel* 12 (1975), 57–62 (Heb.)); Y. Shiloh, *The Proto-Aeolic Capital and Israelite Ashlar Masonry*, Qedem Monographs, 11 (Jerusalem, 1979); S. Dalley, 'Foreign Chariotry and Cavalry in the Armies of Tiglath-Pileser III and Sargon II', *Iraq* 47(1985), 31–48; L. G. Herr, *The Scripts of Ancient North-West Semitic Seals*, Harvard Semitic Monographs, 18 (Missoula, 1978); R. Hestrin and M. Dayagi-Mendel, *Inscribed Seals* (Jerusalem, 1979); G. Garbini, 'I sigilli del regno di Israele', *Oriens Antiquus* 21 (1982), 163–75; A. Malamat, 'The Twilight of Judah in the Egyptian–Babylonian maelstrom', *Supplement to Vetus Testamentum* 28 (1975), 123–45; R. Nelson, 'Realpolitik in Judah (687–609 BCE)', in W. W. Hallo *et al.* (ed.), *Scripture in Context II* (Winona Lake, 1983), pp. 177–89. An extended refutation of Pritchard's article on the 'stables' was completed some years ago by Professor J. S. Holladay and is scheduled to appear in a volume in honour of S. H. Horn, *The Archaeology of Jordan and Other Studies*, which is to be published in 1986.

Note on Chronology

The dates of the kings of Israel and Judah are differently computed by scholars and are given here according to the chronology worked out by K. T. Andersen, 'Die Chronologie der Könige von Israel und Juda', *Studia Theologica* 23 (1969), 67–112, and used in S. Herrmann, *History of Israel* (London, 1975: 2nd English ed., 1981). For other systems and a brief discussion of the problems resulting from the figures given in the Old Testament see J. H. Hayes and J. M. Miller, *Israelite and Judaean History*, pp. 678–83. The dates of Egyptian kings are taken from K. A. Kitchen, *The Third Intermediate Period (1100–650 BC)* (Warminster, 1973).

6

Megiddo under the Persians and Afterwards

Some time in the late seventh century the town of Megiddo seems to have been abandoned. There was some evidence of destruction in the remains of Stratum II. In 605 BC the Babylonian army won a decisive victory over the Egyptians at Carchemish and as a result Syria and Palestine (including Judah, as 2 Kings 24:1 shows) became subject to Babylon. The inhabitants of Megiddo, which may have been an Egyptian base, were probably dispersed by the new rulers. There is at present no clear evidence of any occupation at Megiddo during the period of Babylonian rule (605–539). The American excavators did, it is true, fix the beginning of the occupation represented by Stratum I around 600 BC, because of the presence in it of pottery characteristic of the late seventh or early sixth century along with the later types. But the recent review of the evidence by E. Stern has shown that this is due to confusion in the report between structures which genuinely belong to Stratum I (and have Persian period pottery in them) and those which represent a further stage of reconstruction of the town of the Assyrian period (Strata III–II). Further study of the plans and the lists of finds may clarify the situation and the possibility should be recognised that evidence of Babylonian occupation, which is often difficult to identify at Palestinian sites because of the transitional character of the period from a cultural point of view, may emerge from such research. Much certainly remains to be gleaned from the considerable amount of information about Strata I–III provided in the American report (as well as Schumacher's work), and much more material from other excavations is available now for comparison than was the case when the report was written.

It is not certain whether Megiddo regained its political status as an administrative centre under the Persians or was simply a garrison town. In fact our knowledge of the history of northern Palestine generally during the two centuries of Persian rule (539–332 BC) is extremely slight. The Old Testament sources are interested only in Judah and, to a much lesser degree, in Samaria, while the other literary and epigraphic evidence relates, apart from some references to the northern coastal plain, exclusively to the more southerly districts. The archaeological evidence from Megiddo suggests that in the first phase of the Persian period the southern part of the tell at least was unoccupied by buildings and was used as a burial ground. The excavators found four

Plate 19 Cist grave of the Persian period with the covering slabs removed (*Megiddo I*, figure 107)

graves of the 'cist' type there, sandwiched between walls of Stratum II and Stratum I (T.1263 and T.1265 in square O8; T.1276 and T.1277 in square Q8). The dead had been placed in a supine position in rectangular cists about two metres long and 40 cm square in cross-section (plate 19), which were lined with large flat stones and covered with four or five slabs laid across the breadth of the tomb. Graves of this type have also been found at Gezer (the so-called 'Philistine graves'), Ugarit, Deve Hüyük and other sites, and they are linked with further graves of slightly different form by their grave-goods. The whole group is now dated to the Persian period, except for a few which may go back into the Babylonian period. The Megiddo tombs of this type are unusual in that they had no grave-goods in them: the only finds were tiny pieces of Roman pottery that must be intrusive. The distribution of such tombs over the whole area from Gezer in the west to Persepolis in the east and the Iranian affinities of the grave-goods where they are present strongly suggests that these are burials of Persian garrison troops stationed at Megiddo. Three similar, undated graves on the eastern slopes (T.232, T.854, T.857) could be contemporary. It may be presumed that already in this first phase of Stratum I from the late sixth century, the fortress on the east side of the mound had been reoccupied. It is possible that it was built only then, as there is nothing t

108

prove a seventh-century date for its construction and a similar fortress is now known to have been built by the Persians in an early stage of Stratum A–B at Tell Jemmeh.

In the later phase of the Persian period the south of the mound was developed as an area of domestic occupation. It is not clear whether buildings elsewhere on the tell were there from the beginning of Persian occupation or only constructed in this second phase. As noted above, not everything that is drawn on the plan of Stratum I is from the Persian period, and because of their proximity to the surface the remains are often incomplete. It is, however, possible to identify two adjacent houses of an 'open-court' plan (compare those of the Assyrian period described on p. 99) in Area A, and a building with three long parallel rooms near the earlier gate may have been barracks for the garrison troops.

The finds from this period are rather undistinguished and include few examples of the fine metalwork and imported goods which are common in contemporary levels elsewhere. The local pottery is typical of the period, showing further influence from Phoenicia. The clay itself of many of the vessels is of a type characteristic of the coastal region, which was dominated by the Phoenicians, rather than the Judaean and Samaritan sites in the hill-country. That Megiddo lay in an area that was little known to the Jews and regarded by them as alien and indeed pagan is suggested by a reference to it in a late post-exilic text: 'On that day the mourning in Jerusalem will be as great as the mourning for Hadad-rimmon in the plain of Megiddo.' (Zechariah 12.11) Hadad-rimmon (or rather, as Assyrian texts show, 'Hadad-ramman') was a form of the storm-god who was worshipped in Damascus already in the ninth century (1 Kings 15:18, 2 Kings 5:18), not, as was once thought, a place-name. The mourning referred to seems to be a fertility ritual in which the summer drought is attributed to the death of the storm-god and lamentations for his demise are thought to bring about the return of the rains in the autumn. The comparison in Zechariah 12:11 suggests that it was a 'great' festival to which people came from far and wide. There is no evidence from the excavations that it was held at Megiddo itself, although some fertility figurines, of traditional type but with some new features, were found in Stratum I.

The little evidence which there is of imported goods is sufficient to show that the occupation at Megiddo lasted throughout the Persian period, but no longer. Three sherds of Attic black-figure lekythoi are reported, dating from between the mid-sixth century and the mid-fifth century, while two Attic lamps from the middle of the fourth century indicate approximately the lower limit of the occupation. A fifth-century Athenian silver didrachma found by Schumacher and four Tyrian coins of the fourth century indicate a similar range (plate 20). Alexander the Great's march through Palestine after the capture of Tyre (322 BC) almost certainly took him past Megiddo, and either this or the troubled times which followed his death would provide a possible occasion for the abandonment of the city and the dispersal of its population.

From the following centuries there are no remains on the tell apart from a succession of coins, dropped perhaps by soldiers or others who climbed the hill for its commanding view, which mark the commercial and political relations of Palestine under Ptolemies, Seleucids, Hasmonaeans, Romans and

Plate 20 Tyrian silver didrachma, dated to the mid-fourth century BC. (*Megiddo I*, figure 124.9)

Arabs. At some time before AD 120 a Jewish village called Kefar 'Otnay (Caparcotnae) came into existence nearby. It is mentioned twice in the Mishnah (Gittin 1:5, 7:7) as a place on the border between Galilee and Samaria, where Rabban Gamaliel II (*c*.AD 100) once pronounced a bill of divorce valid although it had been witnessed by two Samaritans. Its remains probably lie at the base of the deep occupation debris at Lejjun, a kilometre and a half from the tell close by where the road from the south emerges from the Carmel hills. Evidence from milestones shows that early in the reign of Hadrian (AD 117–138) the Legio II Traiana was stationed here, perhaps already occupying the site of the Roman camp a kilometre south-east of Lejjun which was described by Schumacher. This legion's arrival doubled the strength of the Roman force in Palestine, a measure which can be seen as a response to disturbances in the Jewish communities through much of the Roman empire in AD 115–17. After the second Jewish revolt (AD 132–5), and possibly already before it, the Legio VI Ferrata took its place and was stationed at Kefar 'Otnay, as we know both from some inscriptions from Pisidian Antioch which name one of the legionaries and from a broken brick found by Schumacher which was stamped LEG VI F (figure 22). Eventually the town was renamed Legio, after the occupying force, and from this the Arab town of Lejjun in turn derived its name. Legio became the centre of an administrative district corresponding in extent to the plain formerly known as 'the plain of Megiddo' and an episcopal see, and the extensive Roman remains described by Schumacher, which include a theatre and a palace, provide further evidence of its importance which has yet to be explored thoroughly by archaeologists. About AD 300

110

was given the official title of Maximianopolis, after Diocletian's co-ruler Maximian, but the old name, Legio, persisted alongside the new one and in the

Figure 22 Stamped brick fragment of the Sixth Legion found near the Roman theatre (Andrew Brown; based on *Tell el-Mutesellim I*, figure 261)

end outlived it. The remains from the centuries of Arab rule, when Lejjun continued to be a town of note, are also considerable and await investigation. From these periods there are a few isolated structures on the tell: three tombs from the Roman or Byzantine period, and an Arab watchtower, excavated and described by Schumacher, which occupied the favoured position in the east overlooking the plain. With the latter are probably to be associated a cistern a little to the north and a pool in the south of the mound which was later rebuilt as a burial place.

Further reading

Megiddo I and Schumacher's report provide most of the material relating to these later periods. The latter (vol. I, pp. 173–90) gives the only detailed account of the ruins at Lejjun. On the Persian period generally see the comprehensive work by E. Stern, *Material Culture of the Land of the Bible in the Persian Period, 538–332 BC* (Warminster, 1982), especially pp. 5–8, 240, which deal with Megiddo. I am indebted to Dr P. R. S. Moorey for pointing out to me the parallels from elsewhere to the cist tombs of the Persian period. The identification of Kefar 'Otnay with Legio was first proposed by E. Zitterling, in *Rheinisches Museum* N.F.58 (1903), 633–5 (cf. W. M. Ramsay, *Journal of Roman Studies* 6 (1916), 129–31). For the milestone evidence see B. Isaac and I. Roll, *Zeitschrift für Papyrologie und Epigraphik* 33 (1979), 149–56, and *Latomus* 38 (1979), 54–66. The history of the whole area, with special emphasis on the Roman period, is sketched by the same authors in their *Roman Roads in Judaea I: The Legio-Scythopolis Road*, British Archaeological Reports, International Series, 141 (Oxford, 1982).

111

Plate 21 Aerial view of the tell from the west: numbers refer to main features visible

112

Appendix:

A Visit to the Site

Megiddo is easily accessible by road from Tel Aviv, Haifa, Nazareth and Tiberias. The express bus-service between Tel Aviv and Tiberias stops at Tzomet Megiddo crossroads, from which it is a walk of about one and a half kilometres to the tell.

Visitors to archaeological sites who have read a book like this one are often disappointed by the scarcity of the remains which they find or can identify. It is of course an inevitable consequence of the process of excavation that many structures, especially of the later periods, are completely removed. This has happened at Megiddo, but an impressive array of well-signposted structures remains to be seen. Some objects from the excavations are also on show in the small museum. The site is well worth a visit and the following notes are designed, with the help of an aerial photograph (plate 21) and references to earlier pages in this book, to enable visitors to place what they can see in its historical context.

The car-park, museum and reception area are situated on the north-east side of the tell and are approached by a side-road off the main road from Haifa.

Ascend by the path to the gate area (1), passing on the right the stepped approach to a water-channel (pp. 81–2) and part of the Solomonic outer gate. Ahead lies the eastern half of the foundations of the Solomonic inner gate, with a few stones of the 'Stratum III' gate visible on top (pp. 80–3, 96). Below and to the right parts of the Canaanite gate of Stratum VIII can be seen (p. 57) and a path leads further to the right to the earlier gate and city wall of Stratum XIII (Middle Bronze I; pp. 38–9)

Turning left past the Solomonic inner gate, the path has on its left walls of the public building of Stratum VIII in Area DD (p. 58) and further along is the area of Yadin's excavation in the Solomonic 'Fortress 6000' (2) (pp. 87–8). The deep, wide cut beyond is Area BB of the American excavations (3), in which can be seen the rectangular Chalcolithic shrine (p. 26), the round stone altar built in Early Bronze II (p. 28) and the three temples of EB IV–MB I (pp. 0–3). On the surface to the south of the cut are some walls of Building 338 and the city wall of the Israelite city (4), which date from the ninth century BC. From this point Schumacher's north–south trench (5) is easily discerned, with walls of the *Nordburg* and *Mittelburg* at the bottom (pp. 43–5). Beyond are houses of the Stratum III city of the Assyrian occupation (6) (pp. 98–9).

Following the path we pass the deep grain storage pit of Stratum III (7) (p. 98), which lies close by the original entrance to the courtyard of Solomon's 'southern palace' (Building 1723) (8) (p. 80) and the abandoned trial trench CC (p. 20), and come to the 'Southern Stables' (9) of the ninth century BC (p. 82). A little to the west is the open shaft (10) giving access to the water supply, of the same date, and it is possible to descend and walk through the well-lit rock-cut tunnel (pp. 92–3). From the exit, outside the city walls, there is a path to return to the gate area. To the west of the shaft is the 'Gallery' approach to the spring (11), from the time of Solomon (pp. 92–3).

The cemetery (12) and the Roman theatre lie to the right (west) of the road on the way back to the Tzomet Megiddo crossroads.

Further reading

J. Murphy O'Connor, *The Holy Land: An Archaeological Guide from Earliest Times to 1700* (Oxford, 1980), is an excellent guide to this and all the other main archaeologica sites. See also J. M. Miller, *Introducing the Holy Land. A Guidebook for First-Time Visi tors* (London, 1983).

Indexes

General

Abraham 35–6
Aharoni, Y. 73, 89–90, 92
altars 26, 28, 30, 32, 58, 79, 96, 113
Amarna letters 13, 56, 59–60, 62
Amarna period 59–64
Amorites 35
amulets 64, 77, 80, 85
Ar-Mageddon 105
ashlar masonry 15, 57, 84, 87, 93, 95
Assyria(ns) 16, 20, 94, 97–8, 100–105, 107, 109, 113

Babylon(ians) 13, 104–5, 107–8
Bell, Gertrude 8
Bethshean 3, 5, 10, 18, 29, 33, 68–9, 96

Caparcotnae (Kefar 'Otnay) 110
Chalcolithic period 25–7
chronology viii–ix, 75, 106
city gates: Middle Bronze I 21, 38, 113; Middle Bronze II 47–8; Late Bronze I 21, 57–9, 113; Iron Age I 71; 'southern gate' (Iron Age I) 13, 71; early Israelite 76, 78; Solomonic (2156) 21, 23, 80–1, 83, 87–92, 95, 113; later Israelite (500) 19, 21, 88, 91–2, 96, 98, 113
city walls 13–14, 19–20; Early Bronze Age 21, 27; Middle Bronze I 38, 74, 113; Middle Bronze II 43, 46–7; Late Bronze Age 55; casemate 23, 87–90, 92; 'offsets-and-insets' (325) 19, 23, 79–81, 83, 87–93, 96, 98, 113
coins 109–110
Conder, C. R. 4–5
cuneiform inscriptions 13, 16, 39, 57, 59–60, 62–3, 94, 98, 104
Cyprus 48, 50–1, 72, 77, 80

David 37, 69, 73–4, 76–8, 85, 88–9
divination 63
Dunayevsky, I. 12, 23

Egypt(ians) 10, 12–13, 17, 29, 40–42, 48, 50, 52–3, 55–7, 60, 62, 64–5, 68–70, 89, 94, 96, 102–4
Egyptian texts 1, 10, 13, 37, 40–42, 50, 52–3, 55–6, 65, 67, 69–70, 85, 102
Eitan, A. 12, 24, 100
Eshtori haParchi 3–4

excavation diary 20, 22, 91
excavation methods 13, 18, 20, 22–4
excavation reports 14–15, 20–1, 24

figurines 29, 48, 63, 77, 80, 109
Fisher, C. S. 12, 18–19, 24, 99–100
fortresses 13–15, 19, 23, 58, 87–90, 95, 100, 103, 108

German excavations iv, 8, 12–17
Gezer 23, 49, 87–91, 95, 108
Guy, P. L. O. 12, 19–20, 24, 85

ḥapiru 60
Hazor 23, 35, 39, 47, 50, 63, 87–91, 93, 95
Hebrew inscriptions 102–4
Hittites 59, 64, 66
Hurrians 50, 52, 57
Hyksos 42, 49

Israel 69 etc.
ivories 21, 57, 65–7, 103

Jericho 15, 26–7, 33, 47–8, 50
Jerusalem 37, 76, 78, 80, 85, 87, 95, 109
jewellery 45, 48, 57, 63, 66, 72, 80, 101
Josiah 103–5

Kenyon, K. M. iv, 22, 27, 31, 35–6, 38, 40, 46–8, 50, 56–7, 62, 86, 88–90

Lachish (Tell ed-Duweir) 38, 47, 50, 90
Lejjun (Legio) 3–5, 7, 10, 13–14, 53, 110–11
Loud, G. 12, 20–2, 29, 47–8, 71, 91

Marino Sanuto 3
maṣṣebot 79, 99
Maximianopolis 111
Megiddo: identification 1–5; geographical surroundings 6–10; agricultural resources 8–10, 48, 56, 60
Mishnah 110
Mittelburg 13–15, 43, 45, 50, 56, 58, 113

Neolithic period 18, 25
Nordburg 13–15, 21, 43, 45, 50, 56, 58, 82, 113

Oriental Institute, Chicago iv–v, 17, 20–22, 48, 64

palaces: Middle Bronze Age 43, 45–8; Late Bronze
  Age 20–1, 47, 57–9, 64, 67; Israelite 14, 16, 20,
  77, 80, 82, 89, 95, 97, 102
Palestine Exploration Fund 4–6, 9, 12
Philistines 66–7, 69–74, 104
pottery 16, 22–3, 25–6, 28–31, 33, 35, 39, 45, 48,
  56, 62–4, 66–7, 70–3, 77, 79–80, 85–6, 88, 90–95,
  97, 100–101, 103; 'Bichrome Ware' 50–51;
  collared-rim storage jars 72–3

religion (see also temples) 33, 48, 58, 77, 109
Robinson, E. 4
Romans 14, 54, 110–11, 114
routes 1, 10, 14, 52

Samaria 18, 20, 85–6, 88, 96–8, 103, 105, 107
Schumacher, G. 6–7, 10–16, 18–19, 21, 25, 33, 38,
  43, 45, 56, 71–2, 80, 82, 84, 88, 99–100, 102, 107,
  109–11, 113
seals 45, 48, 64, 72, 86, 102–3
Shechem 41, 47–8, 50, 60–2
Sheshonq I (Shishak) 16, 85, 88–90, 92, 96
Solomon 16, 19, 21, 23, 73, 78, 80, 84–9, 91, 93,

  95–6, 113
'stables' 19, 80, 82, 85–9, 93–6, 98, 100, 114
statues 41, 67
'storehouses' (see also 'stables') 79, 93–7

Taanach 3, 5, 9, 12–13, 22, 43, 52–3, 57, 68–9, 96
Tell el-Mutesellim see Megiddo
temples: Chalcolithic 21, 26, 113; Early Bronze IV
  (EB–MB) 30–33, 61, 113; Middle Bronze I 38,
  48, 61–2; Late Bronze Age 20–21, 48–50, 60–63,
  67; 'Temple-fortress' 13, 16, 19; 'Astarte
  temple' 19, 84, 99–100, 102
tombs 14–15, 18–20, 22–3, 29–30, 33, 35, 37–40,
  43–6, 48, 57, 64, 107–8, 111
trade 10, 21, 27, 35, 39–40, 48, 72–3, 85, 109
Tuthmosis III 5, 10–11, 37, 52–6, 58

water-systems 7, 19, 23, 55, 71–2, 82, 92–3, 95,
  97–8, 114
weapons 29, 39, 48, 72, 77, 101
weights 48

Yadin, Y. 12, 23, 39, 82, 87–90, 92–3

Biblical References

Genesis
10:13–14 70
12 36
15:16, 21 35
49:14–15 74
49:15 8

Joshua
11:2 10
11:16 10
13:2–3 69
17:11 1, 5, 74
17:11–18 69
17:16 69
19:17–23 74

Judges
1 69
1:27 5, 74
1:27–8 37
3:3 69
4–5 7–8, 69
5:19 5, 69

2 Samuel
2:8–9 69, 74

5:9 76
5:11 76
5:17–25 73
8:1 73
8:16–18 78
12:31 77
15:2, 10 78
19:9 78
20:14 78
20:23–6 78
24 78
24:2 78

1 Kings
4:12 5, 73, 95
4:17 74
5:18 95
6:7 95
6:29–35 95
6:36 84
7:6–12 80
7:12 84
7:36 95
9:15 73, 86–7, 95
9:16 89
9:19 86

11:27 95
11:40 96
12:3–4 95
14:25–6 16, 89, 96
15:6 96
15:18 109
15:26 96
21 96
21:8 102

2 Kings
5:18 109
9:27 5, 97
15:29–30 98
17:24 98
19:9 102
22:12 103
23:19 104
23:25 105
23:29–30 5, 104
23:31–5 105
24:1 107

1 Chronicles
7:29 5
11:8 76

14:1 76
27:16–22 78
28:1 78

2 Chronicles
12:2–9 96
34:6–7 104
35:20–25 104
35:22 5
35:25 105

Isaiah
9:1 98
29:11 102

Ezekiel
40:5–16 87

Hosea
5:11 98

Zechariah
12:11 109

Revelation
16:16 105